Lecture Notes in Artificial Intelligence

Subseries of Lecture Notes in Computer Science

Edited by J. G. Carbonell and J. Siekmann

Lecture Notes in Computer Science

Edited by G. Goos, J. Hartmanis and J. van Leeuwen

Annelies Braffort   Rachid Gherbi
Sylvie Gibet   James Richardson
Daniel Teil (Eds.)

Gesture-Based Communication in Human-Computer Interaction

International Gesture Workshop, GW'99
Gif-sur-Yvette, France, March 17-19, 1999
Proceedings

 Springer

Series Editors

Jaime G. Carbonell, Carnegie Mellon University, Pittsburgh, PA, USA
Jörg Siekmann, University of Saarland, Saarbrücken, Germany

Volume Editors

Annelies Braffort
Rachid Gherbi
Sylvie Gibet
Daniel Teil
LIMSI-CNRS
BP 133, 91403 Orsay cedex, France
E-mail: {braffort,gherbi,gibet,teil}@limsi.fr

James Richardson
Université Paris Sud, LPM
91405 Orsay, France
E-mail: james.richardson@lpm.u-psud.fr

Cataloging-in-Publication data applied for

Die Deutsche Bibliothek - CIP-Einheitsaufnahme

Gesture based communication in human computer interaction : proceedings /
International Gesture Workshop, GW '99, Gif-sur-Yvette, France, March 17 - 19,
1999. Annelies Braffort ... (ed.). - Berlin ; Heidelberg ; New York ; Barcelona ;
Hong Kong ; London ; Milan ; Paris ; Singapore ; Tokyo : Springer, 1999
(Lecture notes in computer science ; Vol. 1739 : Lectures notes in
artificial intelligence)
ISBN 3-540-66935-3

CR Subject Classification (1998): I.2, I.3.7, I.5, I.4, H.5.2

ISBN 3-540-66935-3 Springer-Verlag Berlin Heidelberg New York

Typesetting: Camera-ready by author
SPIN 10749949   06/3142 – 5 4 3 2 1 0   Printed on acid-free paper

Preface

The need to improve communication between humans and computers has been instrumental in defining new modalities of communication, and new ways of interacting with machines. Gestures can convey information for which other modalities are not efficient or suitable. In natural and user-friendly interaction, gestures can be used, as a single modality, or combined in multimodal interaction schemes which involve speech, or textual media. Specification methodologies can be developed to design advanced interaction processes in order to define what kind of gestures are used, which meaning they convey, and what the paradigms of interaction are. Research centred on gesture interaction has recently provided significant technological improvements, in particular: gesture capture and tracking (from video streams or other input devices), motion recognition, motion generation, and animation. In addition, active research in the fields of signal processing, pattern recognition, artificial intelligence, and linguistics is relevant to the areas covered by the multidisciplinary research on gesture as a means of communication.

Resulting from a three-day international workshop in Gif-sur-Yvette, France, with 80 participants from ten countries all over the world, this book presents contributions on gesture under the focus of human-computer communication. The workshop was run by Université Paris Sud, Orsay, on the lines of GW'96 at York University, UK, and GW'97 at Bielefeld University, Germany. Its purpose was to bring together scientists from research and industrial organisations working on all aspects of gesture modelling and interaction. The book is organised in six sections, covering human perception and production of gesture, gesture localisation and movement segmentation, vision-based recognition and sign language recognition, gesture synthesis and animation, and multimodality. It addresses a wide range of gestures, which are not restricted to the motion of hands and arms, but include facial expressions, motion of different parts of the body, and eye movements. Papers on major topics of interest for gesture recognition and synthesis are included from four invited speakers: Winand Dittrich, University of Hertfordshire, a cognitive neuroscientist known for his work on biological motion; Thomas Huang, University of Ohio, whose work on recognition systems is internationally renowned; Christian Cuxac, Université Paris VIII; a psycholinguist and a specialist of French sign language; and Ipke Wachsmuth, University of Bielefeld, whose interests lie in AI and multimedia systems. In addition, 17 full papers and 7 short papers, reviewed and selected after the workshop, have been included.

The first section on Human Perception and Production of Gesture presents a large panel of studies with three papers and two short papers: a presentation of the mechanisms underlying biological motion perception; the establishment of the link between gestural expressions and the sense of smell; the analysis of gestures produced by musicians playing wind instruments, and the way these gestures influence sound; affordances and gesture variability, the adaptation of muscle synergies in producing gestures.

The second section on Localisation and Segmentation is composed of three long papers and one short paper. The four papers present various vision-based segmentation systems used to extract human body features: extraction of 3-dimensional hand posture based on fingertip gesture recognition, finding and tracking the human teacher's grasping fingertip in order to teach a robot to imitate human gestures, identification of human body features using both low level image processing measurements and high level segmentation heuristics, and a modelling of image space discretisation based on face detection and body anthropometry.

The next section, concerned with Vision-Based Recognition, contains a paper which surveys the state of the art of visual interpretation of hand gestures in the context of human-computer interaction, followed by three papers and two short-papers, representing a variety of types of gestures, recognition techniques, and applications: person localisation and posture recognition by means of neural networks; statistical recognition of face and graphical gestures; pointing and waving gesture recognition using a time-delay neural network; pointing gesture recognition based on hidden Markov models; graphical gesture recognition for interaction with in-vehicle systems.

Four papers illustrate the fourth section on Sign Language Recognition: aproposition of the structural form of French Sign Language; two approaches for sign language recognition, based on hidden Markov models, and one relating the relationships between words.

The fifth section deals with Gesture Synthesis and Animation. It contains three papers and two short papers: two of them link a proposition of specification of sign language gestures to the generation of motion and the animation of a virtual avatar; the presentation of a motion generation system which reacts to changes in the user's position and direction of gaze; the description of a methodology to design complex movements requiring co-ordination mechanisms, such as juggling or walking, and an investigation into how inhabitants of collaborative virtual environments can communicate with each other through gaze, gesture, and body postures.

The final section, devoted to Multimodality, is composed of three papers. The first one is an analysis of the communicative rhythm in gesture and speech by the use of multimodal user interface on the basis of time agent systems. The second presents the integration of a symbolic representation of gestures by the way of a rule-based system in unimodal or multimodal user interfaces. The last paper describes the framework of a multimodal interface that incorporates 3D hand gestures and speech recognition systems for the user to interact in a virtual environment.

The workshop provided an occasion for lively discussions and the planning of future collaboration on research into the use of gestures as means of communication. The organisers would like to thank the participants, especially the contributors to this volume and the article reviewers. The meeting was sponsored by Université Paris-Sud, the National Center of Scientific Research (CNRS), and the Ministry of Defence (DGA/SREA), and we are very grateful for their generous financial support. The CNRS Gif-sur-Yvette also contributed generously to the local organisation of the workshop at the Château de Gif.

This volume, the third in the series, reports on the recent work in a dynamic field of research with considerable potential for application in future generations of man-machine interfaces. The editors hope that the readers will find the papers stimulating and an encouragement to participate in the multi-disciplinary area of gesture-based communication.

March 1999   *Annelies Braffort, Rachid Gherbi,*
                                    Sylvie Gibet, James Richardson, Daniel Teil

Notes:
Information about the previous workshops can be found on the following websites :

  – http://www.limsi.fr/GW99
  – http://www.TechFak.Uni-Bielefeld.DE/GW97
  – http://www.cs.york.ac.uk/gw96

The next International Gesture Workshop is planned for the end of 2000 and information can be found on the website of the next organisers:

  – http://www.gw2000.sdu.dk/

Reviewers

Yacine Bellik	Limsi-CNRS, France
Annelies Braffort	Limsi-CNRS, France
Justine Cassell	Medialab, MIT, Cambridge, USA
Christophe Collet	Limsi-CNRS, France
Winand Dittrich	University of Hertfordshire, England
Boris Doval	Limsi-CNRS, France
Alistair Edwards	University of York, England
Jean-Loup Florens	Imag, Grenoble, France
Martin Fröhlich	University of Bielefeld, Germany
Rachid Gherbi	Limsi-CNRS, France
Sylvie Gibet	Limsi-CNRS, France
Patrick Haggard	Institute of Cognitive Neuroscience, London, England
Hermann Hienz	Aachen University of Technology, Germany
Luc Julia	SRI, Menlo Park, USA
Thierry Lebourque	Limsi-CNRS, France
Pierre-François Marteau	Bertin, France
Franc Multon	IRISA, Rennes, France
David Roussel	Limsi-CNRS, France
David Roy	University of Southern Denmark
Jean-Marc Vannobel	Laboratoire I3D, Villeneuve d'Ascq, France
Ipke Wachsmuth	University of Bielefeld, Germany
Marcelo Wanderley	Ircam, Paris, France
Peter Wittenburg	Max-Planck-Inst., Nijmegen, The Netherlands

Sponsoring Institutions

Université Paris-Sud (Orsay)
National Center of Scientific Research (CNRS-SPI)
Ministry of Defence (DGA-SREA)
Regional center of innovation and technology transfert (CRITT-CCST)

Table of Contents

Section 1: Human Perception and Production of Gesture

Invited Paper

Long Papers

Short Papers

Section 2: Localisation and Segmentation

Long Papers

Short Paper

Section 3: Recognition

Section 4: Sign Language

Section 5: Gesture Synthesis and Animation

Long Papers

Short Papers

Section 6: Multimodality

Invited Paper

Long Papers

Round Table

Section 1: Human Perception and Production of Gesture

Seeing Biological Motion – Is There a Role for Cognitive Strategies?

Winand H. Dittrich

University of Hertfordshire, Department of Psychology, College Lane,
Hatfield AL10 9AB, England
w.dittrich@herts.ac.uk

Abstract. The aim of the paper is to suggest components of a model for
the processing of human movement information introducing the concept
of 'motion integrators'. Two approaches to the perception of biological
motion are contrasted: the low-level and the high-level processing approach. It is suggested that conceptually-driven processes play a prominent role in motion recognition. Examples from experimental psychology
and neurobiology are discussed. Our quasi-automatic perception of biological motion seems to involve resource-dependent cognitive processes
and an 'interactive-encoding' hypothesis is elaborated further. In particular, the role of attentional mechanisms and the influence of concept use
are highlighted. Finally, recent findings are interpreted in connection to
specific encoding strategies.

1 Introduction

The perception of other people's movements and actions is important for a range
of human activities. Most obviously, in social situations and communicative interactions the perception and interpretation of human movements is crucial for
the generation of adequate social patterns, e.g. facial expressions, body postures
or symbolic actions such as pointing or forms of sign language. Gestures can
be studied either as a form of expressive movements or as a specific form of
symbolic actions. In the context of human-computer interactions the latter form
seems the most interesting one, at least at this meeting. In the future, however,
it might well be that even spontaneous expressive gestures might become significant input characteristics for the machine to allow a real-time interaction of
man and machine. Such a situation would pose the Turing question not at the
linguistic but at the action level.

In this sense, human movements can form a part of symbolic actions and,
most often, movements are interpreted as meaningful actions extracted from
the stream of social communication patterns. In this sense, we do not perceive
movements as mere changes in spatio-temporal patterning of figures or parts of
figures. We seem to have direct and seemingly effortless access to the meaning of
human actions. This experience leads to the counter- intuitive hypothesis that
the immediateness of biological motion recognition [1] is achieved by strategic
cognitive processing and not, as often accepted, by predominantly low-level or

A. Braffort et al. (Eds.): GW'99, LNAI 1739, pp. 3–22, 1999.

early processing or specific 'biological motion' modules in the brain. At a simple level, human movements can be distinguished into locomotory, instrumental, expressive and social actions [2]. To understand the meaning of actions it seems useful to focus on the role of motion information in visual perception and its link to the symbolic information inherent in human actions. As indicated in the title, the emphasis of this overview will be on the relationship of cognition and perception while developing an information- processing framework to answer the title question. The fundamental question addressed will be 'How is biological motion information encoded by individual detectors integrated to represent a moving body engaged in various activities'?

1.1   The Role of Motion Information

Recently, the modular approach to visual perception has been restrictive in that individual properties of visual events such as form, colour, texture or motion have been discussed in isolation. However, it can be expected that perceptual channels are integrated not only across sense modalities, that is why it seems so important for human-computer interaction systems to incorporate multi-modality systems, but even more so across single object properties. We seem to recognise a visual event or an object as a whole entity and not as an accumulation of separate aspects which are fused at a later stage. Perceptual processing seems more closely related to linking information to the output of our motor system than to linking single complex processes of visual cognition. Here are some examples for the role of motion in the perception of dynamic visual events.

Table 1. Problem areas and respective roles of motion information and typical studies

Topic	Role	Example
Moving object	Approach/ withdrawal	Royden & Hildreth [3], McLeod & Dienes [4]
Optic flow	Ego-motion	Koenderink [5], Hengstenberg [6]
Correlation-type	Locally limited/ retina	Reichardt [7], Adelson & Bergen [8]
Correspondence	Local integration	Ullman [9], Shimojo et al. [10]
Coherence	Gobal integration	Adelson & Movshon [11], Nawrot & Sekuler [12]
Area segregation	Figure-Ground	McLeod et al. [13], Stoner et al. [14]
Kinetic depth	Structure detection	Braunstein [15], Ullman [9]
Eye movements	Object fixation	Schiller [16], Sparks [17]
Meaning	Semantic schema	Michotte [18], Dittrich [2]

In Table 1 one can find a first overview on some basic functions of motion information for visual processing and a few selected studies serving as typical examples for emphasising the different aspects of extracting motion information. The present list of research fields should not be seen as all inclusive but rather as an aide to focus on the very different roles for motion information[1]. Motion information is used in various areas of visual analysis and it seems unrealistic to assume a single motion detection mechanism ('motion detector'). Instead, here it is suggested that specific integration mechanisms ('motion integrators') at various levels of visual processing are available to extract appropriate motion information. The use of the term 'motion integrators' seems very similar to the originally used term 'selective movement filter' [2] whereas the former captures the integrative nature of the information encoding process and the latter its selective nature. However, the assumptions about cooperativity as well as filtering that appear to underlie much of motion processing are not different in both cases. The aim of the paper is to highlight selected aspects of human movement perception and to present the outline of a model in order to explain empirical findings on the perception of biological motion.

1.2   The Role of Symbolic Information

Motion information seems to be used in a variety of processes that normally are seen as higher-order visual processes. However, these high-level visual processes are not simply characterised by occurring at relatively late stages in the whole sequence of information processing. In some cases, they even occur at early stages when strong elements of symbolic or semantic processing are triggered immediately thus leading to a different type of processing route or level of processing. Examples for the use of motion information in the context of human actions are summarised in Table 2.

Table 2. The use of motion information in symbolic processing and typical studies

Topic	Role	Example
Actions	Categorisation	Dittrich [2], Hemeren [19]
Action qualities	Aesthetics	Ille & Cadopi [20]
Action dynamics	Object properties	Runeson & Fykholm [21], Bingham [22]
Emotions	Communication	Dittrich [23], Dittrich et al. [24]
Sign language	Speech	Poizner et al. [25]
Causality	Mental ordering	Michotte [18]
Intentionality	Animacy	Dittrich & Lea [26]

In this view, higher-level visual processing of biological motion may recruit either higher-order invariant stimuli or semantic information in top- down processing. In the latter case, recognition may start with a kind of quick look-up list of concept information similar to complex scene recognition (see below). It should be noted that in this view the later stages of motion processing are quite

---

[1] A full discussion on the role of motion information or on all aspects of the model seems beyond the purpose of this paper. For a more detailed discussion of the evolutionary perspective related to the use of motion information and avian perception of biological motion see [27].

unlike those required by computational models which mainly require a linear sequence of structure from motion reconstruction without any semantic content. At least, the latter models obligatory require that some final goal-states must be reached at various stages of the visual processing of object properties. Only then, the resulting state is passed on to a next stage of processing whether serial or parallel processing is involved. In contrast, here it is assumed that the perception of biological motion is directly accompanied by the processing of meaning. Semantic processing is not seen as the end-product or final process in visual recognition but cooperativity among states of processing appears to be an essential characteristic of the system. It is not a matter of having a mind or not, but visual exploration or seeing as part of the human activities is bound up with a highly complex behavioural repertoire that has developed in the rich environment we inhabit. Furthermore, the act of seeing is interwoven with a number of psychological variables affected by the same repertoire of actions. It is this predicative nature of seeing and its essential relation to the world that give it meaning. Machines might well miss something in this respect but this something might not prevent gesture-based human – computer interactions, only the rules will change. It seems to me that gestures and rules in human- machine interaction might need something very new, perhaps some 'spotlight search' functions [26].

2   Biological Motion and Levels of Processing

The ease with which the visual system can detect biological motion had already persuaded Johannson [1, 27] to argue that biological motion recognition is a low-level and consequently innate process. This speculative assumption found widespread acceptance (e.g. [29, 30]) and only recently such a one-sided low-level approach has been more generally questioned based on new findings (see below). Theoretical accounts that try to explain the perception of biological motion can typically be grouped under three headings: 1. Low- level and early processes, 2. Invariant high-order processes and 3. Concept-driven processes. Traditionally, the headings 1 and 2 referred to the distinction between low-level and high-level processing. However, high-order processes seem to include such divergent processes as invariant pattern recognition or semantic representation so that a further distinction of levels in cognitive processing seems preferable. Thus, the different nature of the underlying processes is emphasized.

2.1   Low-Level and Early Processes

The view that the perception of biological motion is essentially a low-level process quickly found its supporters often even led to claims that in studying biological motion one could "exclude influences of knowledge on perception. . . and thus study the functioning of the visual system in isolation" (p. 400, [31]).

What is the evidence for such an emphatic low-level view? Originally, in the perception of apparent motion low-level processes are seen to operate within a time-span of 50-70ms [32, 33] supporting extremely fast perceptual decisions.

Besides Johansson's own work [1, 27] in which he mainly emphasized two points: a) the rapidness of stimulus recognition (< 150ms) and b) the robustness (recognition was unimpaired by changes in the absolute motion characteristics[2]) there is surprisingly little evidence for the perception of biological motion based exclusively on low-level processes. In a later study [34] it has been argued that the speed of recognition make the 'low-level assumption' inevitable. In this respect, three important studies will be discussed which all tried to test the basic temporal constraints of low-level vision. In an attempt to characterise the visual processes underlying the perception of biological motion Mather and colleagues [30] investigated the effect of different inter-frame intervals on the rate of stimulus recognition. They argued that if stimulus recognition is negatively affected by inter-frame intervals above 50ms than one would assume that low-level processes are important. Results ([30] see Fig. 2) suggested that the coherence of frame sequences as well as inter-frame interval of below 50ms are crucial for the perception of biological motion. They also reported an interaction of inter-frame interval and frame increment to the effect that when an inter- frame interval was short, performance seemed best at shorter frame increments. However, at longer inter-frame intervals performance was lower for all levels of frame increments. Based on these results they suggested that the perceptions of biological motion heavily rely on low-level motion-detecting processes.

The use of very short exposure times (overall 10 frames of 24 ms) could have introduced a bias in Mather et al.'s [30] results in such a way that the first frames of each display captured all the attention. Consequently, the response required, namely a comparison between coherent vs. incoherent motion displays, might have been based on such biased first frame comparisons only. Other studies (e.g. [35, 36]) testing the role of local mechanisms in the perception of human movement have used much longer presentation times so that their results could not directly be compared with Mather et al.'s results. In this situation, Shiffrar and colleagues ([37] see Fig. 3) reported intriguing results when partly replicating Mather et al.'s original study [30]. They found a clear interaction of number of frames with inter-frame interval (ISI) as they called it. Using a shorter number of frames, here twenty and in the range of the Mather et al.'s study, direction discrimination started to deteriorate if the ISI was longer than 50 ms compared to presenting a much larger number of frames (80). In the latter condition the discrimination curve remained almost flat at a very high accuracy level. At first glance, the new findings seem to confirm the earlier data, i.e. low-level or local processes are heavily involved in motion recognition. However, a closer look reveals that despite a drop in accuracy observers were still able to discriminate movement direction to 75-80% with an ISI of more than 100ms; well above the originally envisaged limit for local motion detection of around 50ms. It should be

---

[2] In Johansson's perceptual model of object motion using vector analysis techniques he referred to absolute motion in case of motion trajectories of the whole object seen relative to the observer and to relative motion whenever single motion trajectories of parts of an object relative to the overall motion path of the object had to be addressed.

noted that Thornton et al. have used frame durations of 40ms instead of 20ms as in the earlier study. In addition, it has been reported that the perception of biological motion seems undisturbed by dichoptic presentation of portions of the animation tokens separately to the two eyes [38]. The effectiveness of dichoptic point-light displays seems in contradiction to one of the criteria (non-dichoptic) for short-range motion processes, originally proposed by Braddick [39]. Therefore, these latest results clearly support the existence of high-level processes and seem to diminish the specific importance of low-level processing. Of course, there can be no doubt that low-level processes are generally necessary for visual perception as it is anchored in physiological conditions.

2.2 Invariant High-Order Processing

As these recent findings could not easily be reconciled with the low-level view, further challenging evidence came from different studies linked by the idea that a common stimulus display may be grouped in quite different 'units' which then give rise to quite different percepts. How do we really structure a human body when we see it? Are the various groups of trunk, arms, legs and head really the 'natural body units' we see? The modeling of such natural body units or body structures from motion would become credible if percepts could mainly be based on the characteristics of low-level processes. Alternatively, perceptual analysis relies not on low-level stimulus analysis, on such individual features as motion speed or stimulus size, but on some higher-order invariants inherent in the stimulus array. In this case, perceptual information processing seems to rely on information processes that are not reducible to the sensory stimulus information itself but rely on invariant higher-order information extracted from human movement displays or biological motion. What is the evidence for such processes? Two different approaches will be discussed briefly: a) Runeson & Frykholm's 'KSD'-principle and b) Cutting's 'Cm'-assumption.

One of the controversial but influential ideas of Gibson's approach to perception is the idea of direct perception ([40], see also [41]). In this view, perception is not mediated by types of internal processing of information (e.g. feature integration, image reconstruction, event representation) but information is given directly from the optic array. Despite a changing environment and a changing retinal image Gibson suggested that certain types of information remain constant, and they were coined 'invariants'. Information contained in the optic array is "picked up" rather than "processed" and the search for such invariants inspired exciting research work, for example by Gunnar Johansson and his students. They asked the question whether observers can capitalise upon the 'lawfulness' of human movement.

What information is available in the optic array of people moving around objects? Normally, a biomechanical analysis of movement supposes that the kinematics of movement is causally affected by some factors such as mass, force, work and momentum (dynamic aspects). The kinematics of movement are restricted by various factors such as the laws of mechanics (e.g. gravity, center of mass) and biomechanical laws (e.g. body posture and limited range of adjustments) but also psychological variables (e.g. small intentional movements). Now, it has been argued that one can reverse this state and that observers are able to ascertain the nature of dynamic aspects from the mere presentation of kinematic patterns of human movement. This suggests that the perception of invariant motion information is predominantly in terms of the factors that cause them rather than the insubstantial, dynamic features which determine the actual movement path. In one experiment [21], it was asked whether observers would be able to visually judge the weight of a box being lifted by an actor from a biological motion display. No information about the object was available only the point-light display of a moving person was shown. Observers have been found to be able to discriminate and quantify the box-weights on the basis of kinematic information. When a person lifts a box, its weight is specified by the magnitude of postural adjustments relative to the acceleration of the box. Thus information is present about both the moving person and the object. Thus, it can be assumed that the dynamic factors such as box weight, work or momentum can be determined from the person's actual postural adjustments. Therefore, Runeson & Frykholm called this reversal of a typical biomechanical approach the 'Kinematics Specification of Dynamics' (KSD) - Principle [42]. Essentially, if dynamic factors (F) influence the kinematic shape of a movement (M) then it can be assumed that the kinematics of that movement M specify its dynamics F. Furthermore, it can be predicted that on the basis of the KSD-principle observers can not only perceive object characteristics such as weight or mass but also person-related dynamic factors such as expectations or intentions. Such a wider perspective of the KSD-principle makes it a prime target for studies of deception but this perspective opens up a completely new terrain beyond the current question. Can observers really distinguish between the real weight lifting and a deceptive intention? Would such findings challenge the KSD-principle as interpretative frame for the perception of biological motion (see [42])? Other major challenges to the KSD-Principle as a general model for movement perception can be seen in at least three points: 1. The principle as model for movement perception seems to depend heavily on large-scale movements and is strongly action-oriented. 2. Therefore, it seems that small-scale body movements such as gestures or facial movements cannot easily be incorporated. 3. Using the KSD-principle seems to demand specific filtering characteristics on the observer's side, such as focused attention, which are not always specified at present and which may interfere with the KSD-principle.

The basic idea that the surface patterns of movements suggest in some way higher-order motion information which can be used by observers is shared by Cutting & Proffitt's principle of 'center of moment' (Cm) as a crucial factor in how we perceive human movement [44]. Resulting from their examination of gait perception they proposed the 'center of moment' model as a biomechanical invariant utilised by observers in the perception of light-point displays. The 'center of moment' is regarded as the point of a human body about which all motion occurs and in the case of a human body can be different from the point of gravity. Sometimes, as in simple moving objects, both points could be seen as the same. In human movement, however, the center of gravity can fall outside the human body but the 'center of moment' is dependent on the torso line, e.g. the shoulder width (s) and hip width (h) relative to the height of the torso. The relationship has been expressed by the following equation:

$$Cm = s/(s + h)$$

And this point in the torso represents the first-order 'center of moment', being the point about which all twisting and pendular movements occur. The whole of the point-light display is seen as moving around this centre, all points having a mathematically constant relation to it. Now the rapid and robust recognition of biological motion is explained by the idea that all points inform about the locus of this first-order centre and the way in which it is translating. As the pivots of pendular motion, the shoulder and elbow, respectively hip and knees, represent second and third-order centres of moment, thus forming a hierarchical order for the description of movement. Limb movements are described as a nested set of pendulum actions. The centres of moment becomes the basis for forming a 'grammar' of events, being a higher-order structure which can be parsed from the immediate movement stimuli or the surface structure of moving light-points (see [44]). This "grammatical" approach to biological motion perception is still highly speculative, and in places less than convincing. In this view the necessary distinction in figure and ground motion seems highly problematic at times and more arbitrary than predictive from the "grammatical" model. Furthermore, the perception of biological motion seems possible even when the centre of motion cannot be perceived because of an unusual viewpoint. Nevertheless, instead of using the low-level / high-level distinction for studying the perception of biological motion Cutting & Proffitt's attempt to find regularities in structuring the visual scene may well be seen as useful approach. This is despite the fact, that their attempt exclusively concentrated on the structural analysis of gait and the components will be specified differently in a future model.

2.3   Concept-Driven Processes

As an alternative to the exclusive use of low-level information or even the use of higher-order invariants, the perceptual system might be able to use some stored information about human movement or the structure of the human body. In this case, we seem to be left with the paradox that invariant body structures seem available to the information processing system before the perceptual analysis has done its job. It can be assumed that such processes are top-down processes that use abstract feature or invariant higher-order information about human movement. Is there evidence available?

To understand the top-down influence on visual processing, a few simple examples of how cognition might influence the early processing of visual discrimination and recognition are discussed. One of the puzzling problems in visual scene analysis is the finding that static visual scenes can extremely rapidly be recognised despite a considerable degree of variability, large number of component objects and multipe sources of interfering factors in the image. Presentation times of 100-150 ms seem sufficient to make complex decisions about visual scenes [45]. In this respect the findings seem similar to the recognition times reported for biological motion (e.g. [28]). In an elegant study investigating the role of coarse and fine information in fast identification tasks of natural scenes it was suggested that there seems to be a coarse-to-fine processing sequence which might account for fast scene recognition [46]. It was found that there seems to be a decoupling of coarse and fine information in fast scene analysis (30 vs. 150ms). The first stage of scene analysis seems to rely on coarse and scene-specific information and the later stages are dominated by fine or object-centred information processing [46]. These results seem to suggest a role for early, scene-specific information in initiating cognitive recognition processes before a detailed scene analysis has taken place. Such cognitive processes also seem involved in some types of form perception and motion perception. Recent findings on static shape perception seem to implicate high- level recognition processes in this relatively simple task [47]. Similarly, if observers are presented with oppositely rotating luminance and colour gratings which are superimposed and, because of masking from the colour gratings, the bars of the luminance gratings were not visible they reported visible motion of the otherwise invisible bars in one direction. However, the otherwise visible colour bars could only be seen as moving when they were tracked with attention [48]. These findings seem to confirm that there are two independent motion processes: one that is "low- level" and based on early processing of single features and one that is mediated by more cognitive processes such as selective attention and relatively independent of single features being tracked.

Similarly, the perception of biological motion has been affected by global motion features which might indicate the underlying influence of such top-down processes as attention, schema use or intention. In a series of studies Shiffrar and colleagues investigated whether the primary level of biological motion analysis is local or global. Local analysis seems to depend on spatially and temporally restricted windows of processing. Although local analysis and low-level analysis have been used interchangeably [37] this mixing use of the terms seems to confuse rather than clarify issues, e.g. the local analysis of 'center of moment' might not be a low- level process at all [49]. Although a clear definition of global information seems problematic one might agree that a processing window of longer than 70 ms and of a larger area than half the body image are characteristic for a more global analysis. Despite using a multiple aperture display and hiding the joints of walkers observers easily recognised upright, walking stick figures in contrast to moving objects [50]. Furthermore, it was shown that longer trial durations, even under conditions of long Inter-Stimulus Intervals (ISI > 60ms) improve recognition using presentation conditions of apparent motion [51, 37]. Emotional face expressions can be recognised even when shown as biological motion films. Observers' responses were not impaired when the light-points were distributed rather randomly on the face compared to a distribution in which the prominent facial features such as eyes or mouth were marked by point-lights [23]. Taken together studies manipulating the spatial and temporal window of biological motion processing have shown that global information seems necessary to recognise human movements under these conditions. It has been suggested that the processing of global information is based on high-level processes such as categorisation and semantic coding [2]. Therefore, a few examples focusing on the organisation of high-level processes that are involved in the processing of biological motion information are given.

Despite the sparsity of work on action categorisation, direct evidence on the categorical nature of human movements and specifically biological motion displays might be drawn from Hemeren's interesting work [19, 52]. American and Swedish students were instructed to generate different lists of action verbs related to body movements. It was found that motion verbs on the basic-level (e.g. sprinting) tend to be listed first and more frequently than subordinate level verbs (e.g. running in 10k race) in relation to a superordinate description (e.g. moving) for a general category of actions depicting body movements [52]. Presenting point-light displays instead of words he could show the findings clearly demonstrated that there is a strong typicality effect[3] for action categories and that a context effect[4] occurs for functionally related as well as perceptually related action categories [19]. These findings give strong support to the notion of conceptually-driven processing of human movements as shown in biological motion displays [2]. Although typicality effects have been found for a variety of stimuli, it appears that the context effect has been largely restricted to categorical material of natural kinds and artifacts (e.g. [53]). The notion of conceptually-driven encoding gains further support from findings on the patterns of eye movements when viewing point-light walkers. It seems that observers heavily rely on the use of configurational cues and the overall organisation of the scene when scanning biological motion images [54]. In addition to the visual characteristics of the motion image or low-level mechanisms, descriptions of the saccadic eye movements give clear indications that observers' saccades are driven by strategic processes such as allocentric coding and expected body positions. Observer seem to anticipate the postsaccadic relative position of the walker's body parts (see below the role of such cognitive constraints). Furthermore, conceptually-driven processes such as scene organisation seem to promote strongly accurate saccade patterns in point-light scenes.

The relationship between visual and semantic modes of information processing has been studied most extensively in memory research (e.g. [55, 56]) but most relevant for the present theme of gesturing seems work which discusses this relationship in the area of action selection. Recently, a possible dissociation of the visual and verbal route to action has been discussed [57, 58]. It is argued that there is a direct visual route to action selection that is based on the association

---

[3] For most categories (e.g. run) it is the case that certain exemplars (sprint) are seen as more typical of that categoy than others (sideways run). For standard categories the typicality is determined by the number of features shared with a category prototype. Highly typical exemplars (sprint) tend to be identified as a member of the category more quickly and this is referred to as the typicality effect.

[4] In addition to the typicality effect for correct responses, a context effect has been found to occur among false responses. Responses to unrelated false items (a wave is a run) tend to be faster than to the related false item (a kick is a run)

of structural visual properties of objects and the learned actions. The authors assume that these structural properties are stored in visual form separately from the semantic memory that it strongly linked to verbal input. Therefore, a second route to action is proposed which is linked to the linguistic system and semantic in nature. To test this proposal participants had either to make naming or gesturing responses to object pictures under time pressure. Different types of visual or semantic errors were identified and error scores were compared. It was observed that the percentage of visual and semantic or semantic-visual errors did not differ under naming conditions but that visual errors dominated in gesturing. This pattern of error distribution remained stable under post-stimulus response cueing. The authors have interpreted their findings as direct support for the notion of two independent routes to gesturing from seen objects [59]. One route seems mediated by the visual activation of the semantic memory of objects and in this case semantic or semantic-visual errors occur when gestures are selected before processing along this route has been completed. The other route is mediated solely by visual information and visual errors arise when gestures are initiated prior to visual object recognition. Not surprisingly, they speculate along the lines of Goodale, Milner and colleagues [59, 60] that the direct visual route to action may be based on viewer-centered codes located in the dorsal stream, whereas the semantic route may be based on object-centered codes in the ventral stream. Putting aside speculations and looking for evidence, in the following paragraph, the neural basis for action recognition and the role of conceptually-driven processes will be discussed.

2.4   Evidence from Neuroscience

A topic much debated recently is the question of whether the visual perception of human movement may involve a simultaneous linkage between the perception and production of motor activity ('mirror coding') (e.g. [61]). Recent imaging data have been interpreted as if the perception of human movement involves the activation of both visual and motor processes (e.g. [62]). They reported that a subject asked to observe the actions of another person in order to imitate them seemed to show brain activation in those areas that are involved in motor planning. It was concluded that visual observation of others' movements might directly lead to brain activation of the motor system in the observer. Such a view seems to give a new impulse to the 19th century idea of a common perception – action coding. However, it seems that a simple perception – action-coding concept in terms of a simultaneous activation of visual and motor brain areas does not reflect the integrative nature of information processes involved in the control of actions. At present, the common coding view has not been confirmed by neurobiological data. For example, using imaging techniques and biological motion displays it has been found that observers seem to show different and quite complex patterns of brain activation depending on the particular instruction[5]

---

[5] In the paper mentioned the language terms "instruction" and "strategy" seem to be confused. To speak of a strategy normally demands a kind of choice situation or at

whether to imitate the action or not [63]. These latest results seem contradictory to basic assumptions of a common perception – action coding or mirror coding. Instead these findings support the concept, proposed here, that some cognitive processes such as attention, schema or intention are directly involved in the visual processing of human movement. At a neural level, thus, one would expect that brain areas are involved which are traditionally discussed in terms of such processes. For instance, patients with amygdala lesions show severe impairment in perceptual tasks in which it is required to recognise facial expressions (e.g. [64, 65]). The amygdala as part of the limbic system, a forebrain structure forming a border around the brain stem, has traditionally been associated with cognitive processes such as emotions, stimulus-reward effects or expectations. One of the first findings from an imaging study using biological motion displays demonstrated that the perception of biological motion displays leads to the activation of brain systems in a different manner depending on the nature of the human movement. The perception of goal-directed hand actions implicates the cortex (left hemisphere) in the intraparietal sulcus and the caudal part of the superior sulcus. By contrast the perception of body movements resulted in an increase of cerebral blood flow in the rostrocaudal part of the right superior temporal sulcus and adjacent temporal cortex but also most prominently with the amygdaloid system [66].

The Bonda et al. findings are important for two reasons: First, they support the view that the perception of human movement directly initiates specific high-level processes (e.g. emotional). Second, depending on the character of the movements different processing routes seem to be activated (e.g. hand vs. body movements) indicating that we should expect several generic "motion integrators" within the brain. Further evidence for the idea to find different "motion integration" centres at a neural level and not just one area comes from electrophysiological work (e.g. [67]) and neuropsychology [68, 69]. The neuropsychological work shows that individuals who have difficulty perceiving coherent motion in random-dot kinematograms or in moving bars seem to have no difficulty seeing biological motion. What initially appear to be contradictory and puzzling findings for the vision researcher, reported in two independent single-case studies, can parsimoniously be explained using the idea of "motion integration" centres. It should be noted that, in this paper, the terms 'route' or 'centre' certainly are hospitable to the possibility of distributed processing by more than one cortical area. In the next chapter the idea of "motion integrators" is developed at a functional level.

3   Sketch of a Model

How can we integrate the different and sometimes seemingly contradictory findings on biological motion? Early models of the perception of biological motion

---

least the possibility of a transitional change, whereas an instruction situation can be characterised by the deliberate abolishing of choice in an attempt to prevent the use of different strategies.

emphasised the low-level nature and/or local characteristics of perceptual analysis (e.g. [70, 71, 30]). In the field of computational vision it was postulated that for the recognition of human movements one has to interpret the limbs as sticks with two definite endpoints and apply the laws of physics to stick-like limb movements (planarity assumption [70]). This assumed algorithm was then generalised by Webb and Aggarwal [71] and the fixed-axis assumption formulated, i.e. in light-point displays the lights are interpreted as endpoints and a solid stick is interpolated as a limb. In this field models are influenced by the one-sided question how a 3-D model of human movement can be constructed from 2-D images of moving limbs assuming that a definite solution does exist. However, findings from behavioural studies clearly challenged such assumptions. It has been found that the recognition of biological motion was not significantly impaired when the light-points were attached to the midpoint of limbs instead of the endpoints [2, 72]. Also, findings suggesting some form of orientation specificity [73, 2, 74] indicate that a general view- independent solution as demanded in computational vision seems unlikely. Thus, it has been hypothesized that "the process of action coding may involve not only structural motion components based on the similarity of movements but also semantic coding which takes place at very early stages of movement information processing" (p. 21, [2]). Therefore, the perception of biological motion seems to depend on the integration of the low-level processing of structural motion components and the memory-driven processing of action categories (see Fig. 1). Interestingly, our percept or visual experience appears to be that of a human action and never a cluster of light-points if observers see human movement. Even when observers do not see human movement initially, they cannot stop themselves seeing a human action after being told that they are actually seeing humans moving, i.e. they can never bring back their initial, naïve impression. Some psychologists might even be tempted to suggest that biological motion is just the illusionary impression of human movement. However, another way of understanding the visual experience is to assume that a motion integration process is involved or, as suggested here, 'motion integrators' which are open to adaptation and seem to rely on attentional resources. Actions can be identified on the basis of at least three separate functional 'routes' connecting 'motion integration' centres. One route is strictly based on the analysis of structural components of human movement. In this route one might implicate the typical processing steps necessary to reconstruct a 3-D body from 2-D information. However, in a second route the reconstruction of the 3-D body movements from simple movement parameters seems to be linked to the memory system and consequently to learning mechanisms. Under a wide range of circumstances, for example ambiguity, poor light conditions or multiple activities, the structural synthesis of human movements seems aided by cognitive constraints relating to the human body and its motion trajectories. Such constraints might be the knowledge of physical regularities of motion paths of bodies or even motion categories and would form part of the semantic memory. A typical example for such a constraint has been seen in the notion of a 'representational momentum' [75, 76].

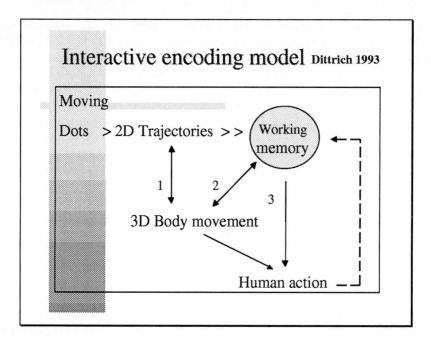

Fig. 1. Sketch of the Interactive Encoding Model suggested in [2] (arrows = conceptually-driven (but see text for differences between routes 1–3), >= input-driven, - - - = feedback)

Possibly, the 'representational momentum' effect might well be achieved by low-level processes and seems not necessarily to underlie the built-in assumptions of natural motion paths in body movements. However, alternative constraints seem equally likely (e.g. causal motion paths models, motion path concepts, implicit motion paths maps). More investigations trying to specify such constraints even for simple visual analysis (e.g. motion, shape) are needed and they might also be useful to divert the discussion that seems so fixated on the search for assumptions to allow the structure from motion reconstruction. A difference between these two routes will be that processing of motion and form information seems not necessarily to be linear or additive as assumed in 'structure-from- motion' models. Another main difference between these routes will be found in the nature and implementation modus of the built-in assumptions. A third route, however, which in the first instance seems ignorant of the structural reconstruction of human movement, instead relies strictly on visual- semantic information which is stored in respect to action categories. The role of semantic processing in the visual analysis almost disappeared when a limited view of computing emerged as the ideal model for understanding vision. Could we say something about the type of semantic-visual processing which seems necessary? The question whether this route enables processing either more similar to visual search or possibly to category discrimination must be left open at present. In both cases the perception of biological motion would heavily rely on strategic modes of processing which require additional processing resources to the mere perceptual analysis of motion structure. Applying the interactive encoding model, for example, a clear prediction would be that a canonical view or prototypical example of a point-light walker, e.g. central examples, will be recognized faster and more accurately than peripheral examples or that distractors will lead to interference.

This Interactive Encoding Model of the perception of human movement does not rely on special purpose motion detectors such as "biological motion detectors". Instead, the concept that motion signals from motion detectors can be attenuated, amplified or modified by cooperative, situation-dependent processes, as previously suggested [77], is clearly endorsed here and further developed, leading to the notion of 'motion integrators'. These integrative processes seem resource-dependent and open to learning (e.g. continuous 'up-dating' of working memory). It takes some effort to identify biological motion displays if shown under sub- optimal conditions or otherwise demanding situations. Therefore, it can be expected that visual processing of biological motion is open to distractive stimulation despite the finding that the perception of biological motion is still possible when noise dots are superimposed within the animation sequences (e.g. [49, 78]). Recent findings [78] suggest that sensitivity to biological motion seems to increase rapidly with the number of point-lights and even more rapidly than expected from a summation of simple motions has been rightly interpreted as evidence against a specialized hardware for biological motion or a 'biological motion detector'. Although their specific interpretation seems heavily biased by unspecified assumptions about local processing, certainly, their general line of argument, "Instead, the results show that biological motion may be analysed by very sensitive, but flexible, mechanisms with variable efficiency" (p. 895, [78]), seems to support some basic assumptions (e.g. sensitivity, cooperativity, adaptability) that directly derive from the notion of 'motion integration centers'. Based on the Interactive Encoding Model it can be predicted that the perception of biological motion will be impaired if an observer's efforts to identify the displays is interfered with in any way, thus suppressing either one route or level of processing. This interference would prevent adequate motion integration or interactive motion encoding. On the other hand, it can be expected that under sub-optimal conditions recognition will be enhanced because input signals are amplified by stored information. For example, the finding [78] that sensitivity to biological motion appears to be a non-linear function is not surprising when discussed independent of local or short-range mechanisms but can perfectly well be expected on the basis of the model. A prediction of the model would be that the non-linearity function in this case is a mere consequence of strategic transition from input- driven to conceptually-driven processing. The conditions for such a strategic shift seem different for either animate or inanimate things or just for different degrees of information uncertainty. Biological motion seem to have a much higher degree of uncertainty about local motion trajectories compared to most motion paths of natural objects or simple translatory body motion. Such a shift would alter the threshold levels under sub-optimal conditions as in their experiment because additional cognitive resources become available. As a direct consequence the sensitivity would be increased which may then lead to the impression of perceptual immediateness. It is argued, that the idea of 'motion integrators' operating at a cognitive level of visual processing and requiring attentional resources will be useful in explaining some findings on the perception of biological motion which otherwise seem inconclusive or even contradictory (see above). Thus, the concept of cognitive strategies as described is applied to explain otherwise inconclusive results. It seems obvious that the characteristics of the described model of visual cognition provides constraints on the one side but opportunities on the other for current attempts to design new movement-based human-machine interface systems.

Finally, a tentative answer to the question 'how is the meaning of human movement processed?' might disappoint some but might throw further light on the interactive encoding concept. Some might be disappointed by the suggestion that the possible dissociation of semantics and grammar of actions should not be taken as ground for an independent analysis of both aspects from early levels of biological motion processing. In sharp contrast to the view that there are only very abstract relations between grammar and semantics of actions at the top level of processing it is postulated that from the beginning the perception of the goals of actions and the structure of actions is processed simultaneously. It is assumed that interactive processing between different aspects of motion processing is prominent at very early levels. 'Motion integrators' form the units for these interactive encoding processes fusing visual cues of motion (e.g. direction, speed) and semantic coding (e.g. smiling). Humans seem predisposed to construe actions as being meaningful and we cannot reverse the mode of simultaneous processing. The thesis is that semantic processing seems beneficial because perception has developed in a way to represent things that are mapped in relation either to something or to our own goals of using these things. The idea that the semantic coding adds something special to the percept seems mistaken. Nothing seems to be added to the percept at the end of the perceptual analysis but the semantic aspect seems present from the beginning of motion processing. Visual processing always appears to involve some kind of intentional aspect. It is a design feature of the visual system.

4   Conclusion

To conclude, the hypothesis that the perception of biological motion and its immediateness is more the end stage of a learning process in visual perception rather than the result of low-level or early processing has been elaborated. A learning process has been implicated in the form of an integrative encoding model that relates visual input to semantic- visual but conceptually-driven information processing stages and leads to various degrees of cooperativity between motion processing modules. The level of encoding seems to be variable depending on the amount and type of information available. Perceiving biological motion appears to be a resource-dependent process of inductive inference suggesting learning units to be involved here coined 'motion integrators'. In this sense, the title question has clearly to be answered in the affirmative.

The topic of biological motion represents a model case for explaining the relationships among neural coding, cognitive processing and behavioural responding. In posing questions and proposing features of an initial model it has been attempted to cast the issues related to biological motion in a broad functional context. It should be apparent, however, that many questions remain unanswered at present. Still unresolved are fundamental issues pertaining to the specifics of complex motion detection, information selection and levels of cooperativity or integration. Furthermore, the exact 'routes' by which visual or semantic – visual information reach the motion integration centres are not known yet. Even the mechanisms of such 'motion integrators' have to be specified under a much wider variety of conditions. Also, more findings about the characteristics of the amount and type of information available to the observer for the perception of biological motion would be essential to specify a more detailed model. Despite these open questions, one might conclude that progress has been made in superseding the simplistic impression of "common fate" or "innateness" as the key issues in the perception of biological motion.

References

1. Johansson, G.: Visual perception of biological motion and a model for its analysis. Percept. Psychophys. 14, 1973, 201-211
2. Dittrich, W.H.: Action categories and the perception of biological motion. Perception 22 (1993) 15-22
3. Royden, C.S., Hildreth, E.C.: Human heading judgments in the presence of moving objects. Percept. Psychophys. 58 (1996) 836-856
4. McLeod, P., Dienes, Z.: Do fielders know where to go to catch the ball or only how to get there? J. Exp. Psychol.: Human Percept. Perform. 22 (1996) 531-543
5. Koenderink, J. J.: Optic flow. Vision Res. 26 (1986) 161-180
6. Hengstenberg, R.: Visual processing: How to know where to go. Nature 392 (1998) 231-232
7. Reichardt, W.: Autocorrelation, a principle for the evaluation of sensory information by the central nervous system, In: Rosenblith, W.A. (Ed.) Sensory communication. MIT Press, Cambridge, MA (1961) 303-317
8. Adelson, E.H., Bergen, J.R.: Spatiotemporal energy models for the perception of motion. J. Opt. Soc. Amer. A2 (1985) 284-299
9. Ullman, S.: The interpretation of visual motion. MIT Press, Cambridge, MA (1979)
10. Shimojo, S., Silverman, G.H., Nakayama, K.: Occlusion and the solution to the aperture problem for motion. Vision Res. 29 (1989) 619-626
11. Adelson, E.H., Movshon, J.A.: Phenomenal coherence of moving gratings. Nature 300 (1982) 523-525
12. Nawrot, M., Sekuler, R.: Assimilation and contrast in motion perception: explorations in cooperativity. Vision Res. 30 (1990) 1439-1451
13. McLeod, P., Driver, J., Crisp, J.: Visual-search for a conjunction of movement and form is parallel. Nature 332 (1988) 154-155

14. Stoner, G.R., Albright, T.D., Ramachandran, 0V.S.: Transparency and coherence in human motion perception. Nature 344 (1990) 153-155
15. Braunstein, M.L.: Depth perception in rotating dot patterns: Effects of numerosity and perspective. J. Exp. Psychol. 64 (1962) 415-420
16. Schiller, P.H.: The central visual system. Vision Res. 26 (1986) 1351-1389
17. Sparks, D.L.: Translation of sensory signals into commands for control of saccadic eye-movements – Role of primate superior colliculus. Physiol. Rev. 66 (1986) 118-171
18. Michotte, A.: The perception of causality. Methuen, Andover (1963)
19. Hemeren, P. E.: Typicality and Context Effects in Action Categories. In: Shafto, M.G., Langley, P. (eds.): Proceedings of the 19th Annual Conference of the Cognitive Science Society. Hillsdale, NJ: Erlbaum (1997) 949
20. Ille, A., Cadopi, M.: Reproducing choreographic walks from the observation of a kinematic point-light display: Effect of skill level. J. Human Movem. Stud. 29 (1995) 101-114
21. Runeson, S., Frykholm, G.: Visual perception of lifted weight. J. Exp. Psychol.: Human Perc. Perform. 13 (1981) 733-740
22. Bingham, G.P.: Kinematic form and scaling: Further investigations on the visual perception of lifted weight. J. Exp. Psychol.: Human Perc. Perform. 13 (1987) 155-177
23. Dittrich, W.H.: Facial motion and the recognition of emotions. Psycholog. Beitr. 33 (1991) 366-377
24. Dittrich, W.H., Troscianko, T., Lea, S.E.G., Morgan, D.: Perception of emotion from dynamic point-light displays represented in dance. Perception 25 (1996) 727-738
25. Poizner, H., Bellugi, U., Lutes-Driscoll, V.: Perception of American Sign Language in dynamic point-light displays. J. Exp. Psychol.: Human Percept. Perform. 7 (1981) 430- 440
26. Dittrich, W.H., Lea, S.E.G.: Visual perception of intentional motion. Perception 23 (1994) 253-268
27. Lea, S.E.G., Dittrich, W.H.: What do birds see in moving video images? Curr. Psychol. Cognit. 18 (1999)
28. Johansson, G.: Spatio- temporal differentiation and integration in visual motion perception. Psychol. Res. 38 (1976) 379-393
29. Fox, R., McDaniel, C.: The perception of biological motion by human infants. Science 218 (1982) 486-487
30. Mather, G., Radford, K., West, S.: Low-level processing of biological motion. Proc. Roy. Soc. Ldn B249 (1992) 149-155
31. Stranger, J., Hommel, B.: The perception of action and movement. In: Prinz, W., Bridgeman, B. (eds.) Handbook of Perception and Action, Vol.1. Academic, London, San Diego (1995) 397-451
32. Anstis, S.M.: The perception of apparent motion. Phil. Trans. Roy. Soc. Ldn B290 (1980) 153-168
33. Baker, C.L., Braddick, O.J.: Temporal properties of the short-range process in apparent motion. Perception 14 (1985) 181-192
34. Johansson, G., von Hofsten, C., Jansson, G.: Event perception. Ann. Rev. Psychol. 31 (1980) 27-64
35. Shiffrar, M., Freyd, J.J.: Apparent motion of the human body. Psychol. Sci. 1 (1990) 257-264
36. Shiffrar, M., Freyd, J.J.: Timing and apparent motion path choice with human-body photographs. Psychol. Sci. 4 (1993) 379-384

37. Thornton, I.M., Pinto, J., Shiffrar, M.: The visual perception of human locomotion. Cogn. Neuropsychol. 15 (1998) 535- 552
38. Ahlström, V., Blake, R., Ahlström, U.: Perception of biological motion. Perception 26 (1997) 1539-1548
39. Braddick, O.: A short-range process in apparent motion. Vision Res. 14 (1974) 519-527
40. Gibson, J.J.: The perception of the visual world. Houghton Mifflin, New York (1950)
41. Nakayama, K.: James J. Gibson – An appreciation. Psychol. Rev. 101 (1994) 329-335
42. Runeson, S., Frykholm, G.: Kinematic specification of dynamics as an informational basis for person and action perception. J. Exp. Psychol.: General 112 (1983) 585-612
43. Cutting, J.E., Proffitt, D.R., Kozlowski, L.T.: A biomechanical invariant for gait perception. J. Exp. Psychol.: Human Perc. Perform. 4 (1978) 357-372
44. Cutting, J.E., Proffitt, D.R.: Gait perception as an example of how we may perceive events. In: Walk, R.D., Pick, H.L. (eds.) Intersensory Perception and Sensory Integration. Plenum Press, New York (1981) 249-273
45. Potter, M.: Meaning in visual search. Science 187 (1975) 965-966
46. Schyns, P.G., Oliva, A.: From blobs to boundary edges: Evidence for time- and spatial-scale-dependent scene recognition. Psychol. Sci. 5 (1994) 195-200
47. Sinha, P., Poggio, T.: Role of learning in three-dimensional form perception. Nature 384 (1996) 460-463
48. Cavanagh, P.: Attention-based motion perception. Science 257 (1992) 1563-1565
49. Cutting, J.E., Moore, C., Morrison, R.: Masking the motions of human gait. Percept. Psychophys. 44 (1988) 339-347
50. Shiffrar, M., Lichtey, L., Heptulla-Chatterjee, S.: The perception of biological motion across apertures. Percept. Psychophys. 59 (1997) 51-59
51. Heptulla-Chatterjee, S., Freyd, J., Shiffrar, M.: Configurational processing in the perception of apparent biological motion. J. Exp. Psychol.: Human Percept. Perform. 22 (1996) 916- 929
52. Hemeren, P. E.: Frequency, ordinal position and semantic distance as measures of cross-cultural stability and hierarchies for action verbs. Acta Psychol. 91 (1996) 39-66
53. Battig, W.F., Montague, W.E.: Category norms for verbal items in 56 categories: A replication and extension of the Connecticut category norms. J. Exp. Psychol. Monographs 80 (1969) 1-46
54. Verfaillie, K., Transsaccadic memory for the egocentric and allocentric position of a biological-motion walker. J.Exp. Psychol.: Learn. Memory Cogn. 23 (1997) 739-760
55. Tulving, E.: Precis of Tulving Elements of Episodic Memory. BBS 2 (1984) 223-238
56. Hillis, A.E., Caramazza, A.: Cognitive and neural mechanisms underlying visual and semantic processing – Implications from optic aphasia. J. Cogn. Neurosci. 7 (1995) 457-478
57. Riddoch, M.J., Humphreys, G.W.: Visual object processing in a case of optic aphasia: A case of semantic access agnosia. Cogn. Neuropsychol. 4 (1987) 131-185
58. Rumiati, R.I., Humphreys, G.W.: Recognition by action: Dissociating visual and semantic routes to action in normal observers. J. Exp. Psychol.: Human Percept. Perform. 24 (1998) 631-647

59. Goodale, M.A., Meanan, J.P, Bulthoff, H.H, Nicolle, D.A., Murphy, K.J., Recicot, C.I.: Separate neural pathways for the visual analysis of object shape in perception and prehension. Curr. Biol. 4 (1994) 604-610

60. Milner, A.D., Perrett, D.I., Johnston, R.S., Benson, P.J., Jorda, T.R., Heely, D.W., Bettucci, D., Mortara, F., Mutani, R., Terazzi, E., Davidson, D.L.W.: Perception and action in "visual form agnosia". Brain 114 (1991) 405-428

61. Viviani, P., Stucchi, N.: Biological movements look uniform: Evidence for motor-percpetual interactions. J. Exp. Psychol.: Human Percept. Perform. 18 (1992) 603-623

62. Decety, J., Grezes, J., Costes, N., Perani, D., Jeannerod, M., Procyk, E., Grassi, F, Fazio, F.: Brain activity during observation of actions. Influence of action content and subject's strategy. Brain 120 (1997) 1763-1777

63. Grezes, J., Costes, N., Decety, J.: Top-down effect of strategy on the perception of human biological motion: A PET investigation. Cogn. Neuropsychol. 15 (1998) 553-582

64. Adolphs, R., Tranel, D., Damasio, H, Damasio, A.: Impaired recognition of emotioin in facial expressions following bilateral damage to the human amygdala. Nature 372 (1994) 669-672

65. Young, A.W., Aggleton, J.P., Hellawell, D.J., Johnson, M., Broks, P., Hanley, J.R..: Face processing impairments after amygdalotomy. Brain 118 (1995) 15-24

66. Bonda, E., Petrides, M., Ostry, D., Evans, A.: Specific involvement of human parietal systems and the amygdala in the perception of biological motion. J. Neurosci. 16 (1996) 3737- 3744

67. Geesaman, B.J., Andersen, R.A.: The analysis of complex motion patterns by form/cue invariant MSTd neurons. J. Neurosci. 16 (1996) 4716-4732

68. Vaina, L.M., Lemay, M., Bienfang, D.C., Choi, A.Y., Nakayama, K.: Intact "biological motion" and "structure from motion" perception in a patient with impaired motion mechanisms: a case study. Vis. Neurosci. 5 (1990) 353-369

69. McLeod, P., Dittrich, W., Driver, J., Perrett, D.,& Zihl, J.: Preserved and impaired detection of structure from motion by a "motion-blind" patient. Vis. Cognit. 3 (1996) 363- 391

70. Hoffman, D.D., Flinchbaugh, B.E.: The interpretation of biological motion. Biol. Cybern. 42 (1982) 195-204

71. Webb, J.A., Aggarwal, J.K.: Structure from motion of rigid and jointed objects. Artific. Intellig. 19 (1982) 107-130

72. Bertenthal, B.I., Pinto, J.: Global processing of biological motion. Psychol. Sci. 5 (1994) 221-225

73. Sumi, S.: Upside-down presentation of the Johansson moving light-spot pattern. Perception 13 (1984) 283-286

74. Verfaillie, K.: Orientation- dependent priming effects in the perception of biological motion. J. Exp. Psychol.: Human Percept. Perform. 19 (1993) 992-1013

75. Freyd, J.J., Finke, R.A.: Representational momentum. J. Exp. Psychol: Learn. Mem. Cogn. 10 (1984) 126-132

76. Shiffrar, M., Freyd, J.J.: Timing and apparent motion path choice with human body photographs. Psychol. Sci. 4 (1993) 379-384

77. Cavanagh, P., Mather, G.: Motion: The long and short of it. Spatial Vis. 4 (1989) 103-129

78. Neri, P., Morrone, M.C., Burr, D.C.: Seeing biological motion. Nature 395 (1998) 894-896

The Expressive Power of Gestures: Capturing Scent in a Spatial Shape

Caroline Hummels and Kees Overbeeke

Department of Industrial Design
Delft University of Technology
Jaffalaan 9, NL-2628 BX Delft, The Netherlands
C.C.M.Hummels@io.tudelft.nl
C.J.Overbeeke@io.tudelft.nl

Abstract. Our engagement with consumer products diminishes gradually over the last decades, which causes considerable usability problems. To dissolve these problems, the designer's emphasis should shift from creating beautiful products in appearance to beautiful interactions with products. Consequently, the designer needs new tools like gestural sketching. To develop a gestural design tool, we tested the suitability of gestures to capture expressive ideas and the capability of outsiders to recognise this expression. Scents were used to make this expression measurable. Twenty- two creators made four dynamic sculptures expressing these scents. Half of those sculptures were made through gesturing and half through traditional sketching. Subjects were asked to match the scents and the sculptures. Results show that there is no significant difference between sketching and gesturing. Dependent on the scent, an interpreter was able to capture the expression when looking at the gestures. These findings support the potential of a gestural design tool.

1 Introduction: Evoking Engaging Experiences

Technology brought us many new possibilities and advantages, also in the field of consumer products. However, this development changed products, both in appearance and interaction, and our relation with products in a less engaging one [1]. Take for example the kitchen balance. Whereas in the old day the balance allowed someone to weigh his food by keeping the scale in balance using different weights, nowadays we simply put our food on a thin compact platter and read the result on a tiny display. The thermostat shows a similar change. The big knob that one could turn to the desired temperature is replaced by a rectangular block with many touch- sensitive keys that regulate 'everything'.

The electronics used in such products are 'intangible', i.e. they do not relate to our mechanical world. This implies that the functional parts of a product no longer impose a specific appearance or way of interaction. The 'intangible intelligence' resulted in products that place a heavy burden on the human intellect. One has to learn how to program the thermostat and woe betide you if you accidentally change the settings of the balance from kilos to English pounds.

A. Braffort et al. (Eds.): GW'99, LNAI 1739, pp. 23–36, 1999.

Technological products cause considerable usability problems making manuals indispensable.

We believe it is time to reinstate the engaging capacity of products and focus on the experience that users can have using a product. Instead of having to instruct a 'black box', the user should be seduced and supported to enjoy cooking, adjusting the temperature ... with all senses. A designer can evoke such an engaging experience by respecting all of man's skills, not only his cognitive, but also his perceptual-motor and emotional skills. A product being a 'context for experience' can enrich our life and prevent or at least diminish usability problems [2].

By designing a 'context for experience' instead of merely a product, the focus shifts from the result of interaction, e.g. the weight or the warmth, towards the involvement during interaction, e.g. weighing food, attaining the desired warmth. This means that the designer's emphasis should shift from creating a beautiful, pleasing product in appearance, to creating a beautiful, engaging interaction with a product.

As a consequence of this shift design tools should change too. Sketching on paper, the favourite tool of designers during the conceptual phase, primarily supports the exploration of the appearance. The flat and static character of paper complicates the exploration of interaction. To create a 'context for experience', the designer needs tools that allow him to explore beautiful and engaging interactions directly in 3D, while retaining the benefits of sketching, like expressivity, ambiguity and personal style.

Gestural sketching could be such a tool. The spatial, dynamic and expressive character of gestures allows a designer not only to create the product directly in 3D, but also to design the aesthetic interaction itself. The subtle expressive possibilities of gestures support the designer developing the subtleties of an engaging context for experience.

At our department of Industrial Design, we are developing such a gestural design tool. A tool that respects all of the designer's skills, especially his perceptual-motor and emotional skills. Consequently, the tool should adapt itself to the designer and not the other way around. The computer should understand the meaning of the gestures used by the individual designer and enhance his creative freedom.

This creates a bit of a problem, because computers process information in logical rules and despite extensive research on gestures, such information about gestural design is non-existent. Therefore, we conducted explorative research to find rules and patterns necessary to develop such a personal design tool.

In our presentation at the Gesture Workshop '97 in Bielefeld we showed several global patterns for conveying the geometry of products with gestures [3]. However, we should go beyond geometrical information to design a context for experience. We have to look at interaction, doing and feeling, motion and emotion. In this paper we will therefore focus on the expressive character of gestures.

The detection and formalisation of patterns in expressive gestures is extremely complex, therefore, we limited our research and started with two central questions:

1. Is gestural sketching more suited than traditional sketching on paper to develop and visualise expressive ideas?
2. Is an outsider able to recognise the intense and extensive expression of the gestures used during the design process?

The first question can confirm our premiss that gestural sketching is a useful addition to the existing design tools. The second question needs to be answered affirmatively, to be able to formulate any rule. If one cannot recognise it, one cannot formalise it.

2   Scent as a Medium to Compare Gesturing and Sketching

To answer the aforementioned questions, we needed to find a medium to make expressivity measurable and comparable, without losing the subtleties necessary for design. The answer is implied in the next excerpt from Süskind:

> *The perfume was ghastly good. ... Baldini wished it was his, this 'Eros and Psyche'. It was not the least bit vulgar. Absolutely classic, well-rounded & harmonic it was. And nevertheless fascinating new. It was fresh without straining after effect. It was mushy without being rancid. It had depth, a marvellous absorbing guzzling dark brown depth and yet it was by no means excessive or sultry.*
> (translated by the first author from 'Het Parfum' by Süskind [4], p. 63)

Süskind shows us via Baldini the synaesthetic power of scents. Synaesthesia means a more or less constant relation between perceptions from different sense organs, like seeing colours when hearing music or seeing a marvellous absorbing guzzling dark brown depth when smelling 'Eros and Psyche' [5].

Previous research from Smets & Overbeeke [6] indicated not only that design students are able to convert patterns from one sense organ to another, but also that the results between students are often related. They asked the design students to create a sculpture expressing one of nine scents used. They found that a large part of the sculptures made within one scent are part of a family of shapes and colours.

A selection of the sculptures was tested in a matching experiment, which showed that independent subjects are able to match the sculptures with the correct scents (78% correct matches). Similar to the method of Smets and Overbeeke, we have invited students to translate scents into sculptures and asked independent subjects to match these designs.

Fig. 1. These three families of sculptures made for three different scents were matched in an experiment. The objects are reddish (*left*), bluish (*middle*) and amberish (*right*)

3   The Set-up

Because we are still in an exploration phase, we chose a rather extensive set-up with six types of stimuli, to study the different aspects of the expressivity of gestures. The experiment consisted of two parts: a design part in which the six types of stimuli were created and a matching part in which the stimuli were matched by outsiders.

3.1   The Set-up of the Design Part

The two basic types of stimuli we want to compare are (see Table 1):
SkCo   Sketches and collages made by designers directly on paper
GeDe   Recordings of gestures made by designers with the colour on paper
These two types of stimuli are completed with four additional ones:
GeDa   Recordings of dances made by dancers
SkGe   Sketches made by designers of their virtual sculptures made with gestures
SkInDe   Sketches made by an interpreter based on the gestures and the colour
SkInDa   Sketches made by an interpreter based on the dances

Let us start with the two basic types of stimuli. To answer the first question, concerning the suitability of gestural sketching compared to paper sketching, we invited eighteen senior design students to design four abstract spatial dynamic sculptures that capture the expression of four given scents. To make the exercise not too complex, we asked the students to create dynamic sculptures that change over time, without imposing any functionality. Two of these sculptures had to be made in the traditional way with sketches and collages on paper (SkCo). The other two sculptures had to be designed through gestures (GeDe). Because gestures can not convey colour, the designers captured the colour of the sculptures on paper with pencils, crayons or collages during the gestural sessions.

The sketching sessions lasted half an hour per scent and the gestural sessions took maximally twenty minutes per scent. All the variables were counterbalanced, like the order of the two conditions and the four odours. Before the actual experiment started, the designers had a trail run for both conditions.

Table 1. The six types of stimuli created and matched in our experiment

Creator:	Conditions:		
Designers and dancers creating a sculpture or a dance	SkCo	GeDe	GeDa
Designers visualising their design made with gestures in a sketch		SkGe	
An interpreter visualising the gestures and dances in a sketch		SkInDe	SkInDa

During the design exercise, the scents were continually present for the students by means of a small strip that was soaked in the scent and subsequently placed in front of the subject's nose. The scents were selected from the set of nine scents used by Smets and Overbeeke [6]. This way the previously designed sculptures could serve as reference material. The scents were so-called raw materials, i.e. singular basic scents that are used to compose, for instance, a perfume. Contrary to what you might assume when reading the descriptions of the scents, they were clearly distinct.

Name scent:	Description scent
A.Ligustral	green, privet hedge
B.Iso-amylacetate	fruity, candy, strawberry
C.Iso-bornylacetate	pine woody, fruity
D.Lacton c9 gamma	fruity, coconut

Because of the absence of a real gestural sketching tool, this set-up had two disadvantages. Firstly, the design students were experts in drawing but not in gesturing. Therefore, we extended the design exercise with experts in movements, four dance students. They were asked to express every scent in a two minute dance (GeDa). Secondly, the gestural condition did not produce an image of the design. Therefore, the designers sketched their virtual design on paper after every gestural session (SkGe), including the movements of the sculpture if present.

To answer the second question concerning the recognition of the expression of the gestures by an outsider, we engaged an interpreter, an artist/designer, to visualise her impressions of the gestures and dances in a sketch (SkInDe and SkInDa). She received the recordings of the gestures and dances randomised on videotape. Per design, she watched the tape twice for interpretation, during which she made the sketch, and a third time to verify her sketch. This process took on average three quarters of an hour per design. She was unfamiliar with the set-up and the odours.

3.2   The Set-up of the Matching Part

The expressions of the designs were judged in two ways:

1. The designers indicated their satisfaction with the expression of their own creations in relation to the scent on a scale from 1-5 (very dissatisfied - very satisfied).
2. Fifty independent subjects matched the expression of all the stimuli in relation to the scents in a matching experiment.

Before the actual matching experiment could take place, all the stimuli were digitised by the first author. She also compressed the recordings of the gestures and the dances into one-minute digital movies. She edited the movies to her best ability, striving for preservation of the essence of the process and the expression. Furthermore, she made a composition of the multiple sketches and collages per design into one picture, again aiming to preserve the essence of the expression. The sketch of the final design covered at least half of this picture. Finally, she transformed the colour scheme the designers made of their virtual sculpture into a coloured background for the movie.

We used three groups of subjects to evaluate the stimuli: eighteen design students from the Delft University of Technology, twelve dance students from the Rotterdam Dance Academy and twenty persons from various backgrounds who were laymen in the field of design and dance.

The experiment consisted of four sessions plus one trail session. Every session a different scent was evaluated. At the beginning of every session the subject received a strip soaked in the scent that had to judged. Subsequently, the subjects received on a computer screen successively thirty-two randomised sketches (SkCo, SkGe, SkInDe, SkInDa), nine randomised movies from designers including a coloured background (GeDe), and four randomised movies from dancers (GeDa). The subjects had the judge every stimulus by choosing from four answers by means of the keyboard:

expresses certainly	expresses probably	expresses probably	expresses certainly
not the scent	not the scent	the scent	the scent

The drawings were shown maximally twenty seconds and the one-minute movies were shown minimally forty seconds. After every answer, the next stimulus was automatically presented on the screen. This way every subject matched all the stimuli once. A quarter of the sculptures were presented with the scent they expressed. Three-quarter of the sculptures were made for a different scent than they were judged for.

All the answers of the subjects were logged in a computer file, containing the information of the stimulus (the creator and his background, the type of stimuli and the scent expressing) together with the information collected during the experiment (the subject and his background, the scent judged, the answer and the session). In this paper we only take into consideration those answers made by the subjects when the scent during the experiment was similar to the one during creation. Furthermore, the certainty of the answers is disregarded, which means that the answer "the stimulus expresses certainly (not) the scent" is considered similar to "the stimulus expresses probably (not) the scent". Therefore, the answer is either a correct match or an incorrect match.

4   The Hypotheses

The two central questions were tested with three hypotheses. The first hypothesis answered the two questions together, the other two hypotheses tested the questions separately.

4.1   Hypothesis 1: Gestures Are Recognisable and More Suitable

If gesturing is more suited than sketching to develop expressive sculptures, then the percentage of correct matches should be higher for the sculptures made with gestures (GeDe) than those made with sketches (SkCo). Due to the motor skills of the dancers, the percentage should even be higher for the dances (GeDa) than these gestures and sketches.

Furthermore, if gestures are not only more suited to develop but also to visualise ideas, than the percentage of correct matches for the sculptures made with gestures (GeDe) should be higher than the sketches made as a result of these gestures (SkGe).

Finally, if the interpreter is able to recognise and capture the expression, than the percentage of correct matches should be higher for the interpreter's sketches of the dances than those of the gestures, due to the excellent motor skills of the dancers. Nevertheless, sketching an interpretation is a creative activity which could produce noise. Consequently, these types of stimuli are expected to have the lowest percentage of correct matches. This leads to the following hypothesis, which will be tested with a Chi-square test ($p \leq 0.05$):

Table 2. Hypothesis 1: gestures are recognisable and more suitable

	GeDa	GeDe	SkGe	SkCo	SkInDa	SkInDe
H_0:	%Correct $\leq$	%Correct $\leq$	%Correct $\leq$	%Correct $\leq$	%Correct $\leq$	%Correct
H_1:	%Correct $>$	%Correct $>$	%Correct $>$	%Correct $>$	%Correct $>$	%Correct

4.2   Hypothesis 2: Gestures Are More Suitable

To test the suitability of gestures to develop ideas compared to sketching and disregard the recognition of gestures, hypothesis 1 posed that the %Correct of the sketches made of the virtual designs (SkGe) is higher than the %Correct of the sketches made directly (SkCo). The suitability was also judged by the designers themselves. If gestural sketching is more suited than sketching on paper to capture the expressive character of scents, than the designers should be more satisfied (= higher mark) about the expression of their designs created with gestures than with sketches. This leads to the following hypothesis, which will be tested with a t-test (p=0.05):

Table 3. Hypothesis 2: gestures are more suitable

	Designs created with gestures		Designs created with sketches
H_0:	μSatisfaction	$\leq$	μ Satisfaction
H_1:	μSatisfaction	$>$	μ Satisfaction

4.3   Hypothesis 3: Gestures Are Recognisable

Hitherto, we presupposed that there exists universal expression per scent, resulting in families of shapes and colours. Design exercises and experiments like the one from Smets and Overbeeke support this assumption. Nevertheless, the experience of a scent remains partly individual, resulting in designs that do not belong to these families.

Therefore, we are not only interested in the %Correct per type of stimulus (hypothesis 1), but also in %Correct per design, especially in the relative distance between the different types of stimuli per design. Take for example a designer who creates a deviant sculpture for scent A. If both the gestures and the sketches of these gestures made by the designer and the interpreter are judged by the subjects as not expressing scent A, this might also indicate that the expressive character is related.

Therefore, we introduce a new measure: the distance between two types of stimuli of the same design (per designer, per scent). This distance (D) is defined as the difference between the %Correct per stimulus, e.g. if the sketch that designer made of his gestures expressing scent A scores 15% correct and the sketch the interpreter made of these gestures 35%, than D = 35-15 = 20%. The question is how to interpret this 20%. Where do we draw the line to consider the expression of two stimuli similar and regard the expression as being recognised? And what does this 20% mean if the scores %Correct of two stimuli had been situated around the chance-level, say 60% and 40%?

Utts [7] shows a way to evaluate these distances, using the effect size. *"Scientific evidence in the statistical realm is based on replication of the same average*

*performance or relationship over the long run. ... In the past few decades sci-
entists have realized that true replication of experimental results should focus on
the **magnitude** of the effect, or the **effect size** rather than on replication of
the p-value. This is because the latter is heavily dependent on the size of the
study. An effect size of 0 is consistent with chance, and social scientists have,
by convention, declared an effect size of 0.2 as small, 0.5 as medium and 0.8 as
large."*

We take the effectsize (ES) of |0.2| as a limit to judge the expression. When
we convert this effectsize to percentages[1], this means that we exclude the stimuli
that lie between 40% and 60% correct matches (grey area in Figure 2), because
they are too close to the change-level. This 20% area seems also visually a breaking point for similarity, so we take 20% as a limit for distance. Therefore, the
expression of the two stimuli depicted in Figure 2 (SkGe & SkInDe) are considered partly similar. We call them partly similar, because they only similar in
their deviation from the average expression of scent A. Figure 2 encapsulates
our new criteria.

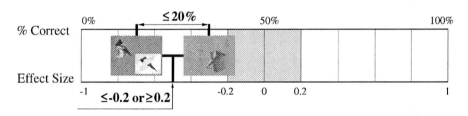

Fig. 2. Criteria to evaluate the gestures and the sketches of the gestures made by
the designers and the interpreter, divided in four categories where the expression is
considered:

similar (+2):	distance ≤ 20% & ≤ effect size ≤ 0.2 (white area on the right)
partly similar (+1):	distance ≤ 20% & ≤ effect size ≤ - 0.2 (white area on the left)
unknown (0):	distance ≤ 20% & ≤ effect size > -0.2 and < 0.2 (grey area)
different (-2):	distance > 20%

If an outsider (subject and interpreter) can recognise the expression of the
gestures and dances, the percentage of (partly) similar expressions should be
higher than the percentage of different expressions. Similar expressions are scored
as +2 points, partly similar as +1, unknown as 0 and different expressions as
-2 points. In total, three comparisons are made between the following types of
stimuli: GeDe & SkGe, GeDe/Da & SkInDe/Da, SkGe & SkInDe. This leads to
the following hypothesis:

---

[1] Effect Size = (E(R) - Average Rank)/$\sqrt{\text{Var}(R)}$, Var(R) = (N^2 - 1) / 12, E(R) = (N
+ 1) / 2 N is the number of possible choices. R = rank for one trail. In our case
R(correct) = 1 and R(wrong) = 2, N = 2, E(R) = 1.5 and Var(R) = 0.25. Effect
Size = 3 - 2Average Rank.

Table 4. Hypothesis 3: gestures are recognisable

H_0:	μ Points per comparison between two types of stimuli	$\leq$	0
H_1:	μ Points per comparison between two types of stimuli	$>$	0

Three comparisons are made: GeDe & SkGe, GeDe/Da & SkInDe/Da, SkGe & SkInDe

5   The Results

Hypothesis 1. A part of the results for hypothesis 1 are presented in Figure 3, which shows several designs that scored 50% or more correct answers. The results confirm the existence of families per scent.

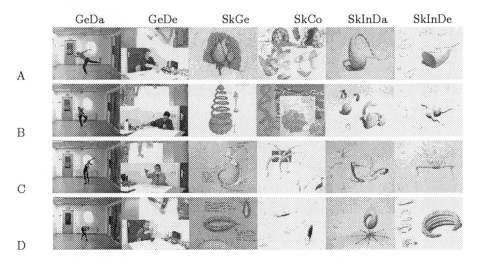

Fig. 3. Four families of sculptures made for four different scents. The families contain stimuli of all six types of stimuli. From top to bottom: A. Ligustral (yellow-greenish), B. Iso-amylacetate (reddish), C. Iso- bornylacetate (transparent - green-purple-bluish) and D. Lacton C9 gamma (amber-greyish)

Table 5 gives an overview of the percentage of correct answers made by the subjects per condition. When we look at the overall answers (%Correct all subjects) we see a slight tendency towards our H_1; the dances score the highest percentage of correct answers, the sketches made by the interpreter of the designers the lowest. Only the traditional way of sketching stands out. Except for two cases, this tendency is not significant and H_0 is accepted (Chi-square, $p \leq 0.05$). The %Correct of the sketches made by the interpreter of the designers' gestures is significantly lower than the dances and the traditional sketches.

When we take the backgrounds of the subjects into consideration, the results differ slightly. H_1 is only accepted in three cases (Chi-square, $p \leq 0.05$). The dancers are significantly better in matching the dances correct in comparison with the sketches by the designers of their own gestures and of the sketches of the interpreter of these gestures. The subjects with various background are significantly better in matching the traditional sketches correct in comparison with the sketches by the interpreter of the designers' gestures.

Table 5. The results for hypothesis 1: Percentage of correct matches

Type of stimuli:	GeDa	GeDe	SkGe	SkCo	SkInDa	SkInDe
	%Correct	%Correct	%Correct	%Correct	%Correct	%Correct
all subjects	50.8_1	48.2	46.5	50.0_2	46.7	$42.2_{1,2}$
designers	48.6	50.3	47.2	51.1	48.6	42.9
dancers	$59.6_{3,4}$	50.0	39.0_3	45.8	51.1	42.5_4
various	47.5	45.3	50.3	51.5_5	42.5	41.4_5

There are five pairs of stimuli that differ significantly (Chi-square, p=0.05), indicated by the numbers 1 to 5.

Hypothesis 2. The second hypothesis H_0 cannot be rejected, because there is no significant difference between the satisfaction of the designers of their own sculptures made through sketching or through gesturing, see Table 6.

Table 6. The results for hypothesis 2: the satisfaction of the designers about their design

	Designs created with gestures	Designs created with sketches
Mean:	3.7	3.8
Standard Deviation:	0.849	0.533

Hypothesis 3. This brings us to the results for the third hypothesis concerning the similarity between the expression of the different types of stimuli, see Table 7. The μPoints of the three comparisons are all below zero, which means that H_0 cannot be rejected. The three conditions are not significantly different (t-test, $p \leq 0.05$), except for two cases, shown in Table 7.

6   Discussion and Conclusions

The experiment shows that in general there is no significant difference in expressive quality between traditional sketching and gesturing. Although the results do not support our hypotheses, gestural sketching should not be automatically written off.

Firstly, our hypotheses were very strict. We disregarded all extenuating circumstances, like the inexperience of the designers with gesturing and the lack of feedback. Taking these circumstances into consideration, the evaluation of the sculptures by the designers themselves is hopeful.

Secondly, we focused on expressivity in general and limited our set-up due to the complexity of the problem. Therefore, we asked the design students to develop expressive dynamic sculptures without any specific functionality. It turned out that focusing on the spatial, dynamical character of sculptures is not enough to show that gestures are beneficial to sketches. This does not come as a complete surprise. When we look at our introduction, we stated that designing aesthetic interactions is one of the major advantages of gestures. Therefore, further gestural research is necessary that focuses on the aesthetic and engaging interactions.

Table 7. The results for hypothesis 3: comparing types of stimuli for individual designs

Three comparisons between types of stimuli:	1. GeDe & SkGe					2. GeDe/Da & SkInDe/Da					3. SkGe & SkInDe				
Scent:	n +2	n +1	n 0	n -2	μP	n +2	n +1	n 0	n -2	μP	n +2	n +1	n 0	n -2	μP
A	3	2	-	4	0	3	1	2	7	-0.54	4	3	-	2	0.78[1]
B	-	1	4	4	-0.78	1	2	8	2	0	-	3	4	2	-0.11
C	1	3	1	4	-0.33	2	5	3	3	0.23	-	2	2	5	-0.89[1]
D	-	1	1	7	-1.44[2]	-	3	5	5	-0.54	-	3	4	2	-0.11[2]
All scents	4	7	6	19	-0.64	6	11	18	17	-0.21	4	11	10	11	-0.08

+2 = similar expression, +1 = partly similar, 0 = unknown and -2 = different expression.
The μPoints differ significantly (t-test, p$\leq$0.05) in two cases, indicated by [1] and [2].

Thirdly, the %Correct of the six types of stimuli lies around fifty percent (= level of chance). This is mainly caused by those creations that do not fit the overall families. Nevertheless, the different types of stimuli are distributed across the entire scale from 0-100%. Despite the years of training, the designs made with sketches and collages on paper are not superior to the other designs and visualisations.

Fourthly, the results in Table 4 suggest that expertise in gesturing improves both the expression and the recognition of that expression. The availability of a gestural sketching tool could improve the skills of the designer.

Fifthly, when we look at each design separately, we see that the number of the interpreter's sketches (SkInDe) that is considered (partly) similar to the original ones made by the designer (SkGe), is higher than the number of different interpretations. We also see significant differences between the four scents. This means that we cannot determine universal rules, but only contextual ones. An outsider (subjects and interpreter) can capture and recognise the expression of a scent made through gestures, taken into consideration the influence of the creator, the scent and the outsider himself.

Finally, several of the sketches made by the interpreter support the possibility of capturing and recognising the expressive character of a scent made through gestures. Figure 4 shows the expressive strength of body movements and the relation between shape, colour and movements. Based on a black and white movie of dancer 2 for scent A, the interpreter did not only make a family member as for shape, she also established the family ties by making a sculpture of the same colour (green). Well over 80% of the subject judged all three stimuli as being created for scent A.

Fig. 4. The impression of the interpreter of dancer 2 for scent A (*left*); The sketch of designer 17 of his virtual sculpture for scent A made through gesturing (*middle*); The impression of the interpreter of the gestures designer 17 made for scent A (*right*)

In general we could say that gestural sketching is not superior to traditional sketching, but it certainly has potential in supporting the creation of a context for experience. This experiment has brought us one step closer to a gestural design tool that respects the cognitive, physical and emotional side of the designer and that allows him to create a respectful and engaging context for experience. The sooner this tool becomes reality, the sooner designers can expand their creative possibilities and focus on the aesthetics of interaction.

Acknowledgements

We would like to thank Gerda Smets, Rudolf Wormgoor, Stephan Wensveen, Tom Djajadiningrat, Rob Luxen and Onno van Nierop.

References

1. Borgmann, A. Technology and the character of contemporary life. London/Chicago: University of Chicago Press, 1984.
2. Overbeeke, C.J., Djajadiningrat, J.P., Wensveen, S.A.G. and Hummels, C.C.M., Experiential and respectful. Proceedings of the international conference Useful and critical: the position of research and design, September 9-11 1999, U.I.A.H.
3. Hummels, C., Smets, G. and Overbeeke, K. An Intuitive two-handed gestural interface for computer supported product design. in I Wachsmuth and M. Frölich (Eds). Gesture and Sign-Language in Human-Computer Interaction: Proceedings of Bielefeld Gesture Workshop 1997. Berlin: Springer-Verlag, 1998.
4. Süskind, P. Het parfum, De geschiedenis van een moordenaar. Amsterdam: Ooievaar, 1998.
5. Cytowic, R.E. Synesthesia, a union of the senses. New York: Springer Verlag, 1989.
6. Smets. G.J.F and Overbeeke, C.J. Scent and sound of vision: expressing scent or sound as visual forms. Perceptual and Motor Skills, 1989, 69, 227-233.
7. Utts, J. An assessment of the evidence for psychic functioning. Division of Statistics University of California, Davis. http://anson.ucdavis.edu/ utts/air2.html

Non-obvious Performer Gestures
in Instrumental Music

Marcelo M. Wanderley

Ircam – Centre Georges Pompidou
1, Place Igor Stravinsky
75004 - Paris - France
mwanderley@acm.org

Abstract. This paper deals with the gestural language of instrumentalists playing wind instruments. It discusses the role of non-obvious performer gestures that may nevertheless influence the final sound produced by the acoustic instrument. These gestures have not commonly been considered in sound synthesis, although they are an integral part of the instrumentalist's full gestural language. The structure of this paper will be based on an analysis of these non-obvious gestures followed by some comments on how to best classify them according to existing research on gesture reviewed in the introduction; finally, the influence of these gestures on the sound produced by the instrument will be studied and measurement and simulation results presented.

1 Introduction

Sound synthesis tools provide many different and powerful options in inexpensive general-purpose platforms. A number of synthesis paradigms are available, either signal or physical models[1], many of them in the form of public-domain software. With CD audio quality as a standard and fast synthesis algorithms, the time is right for considering in depth how best to control these environments.

A number of hardware interfaces have been proposed to perform this task, most of them resulting from composer's/player's idiosyncratic approaches to personal artistic needs. These interfaces, although often revolutionary in concept, have mostly remained specific to the needs of their inventors. One consequence is that many people still consider the piano-like MIDI[2] keyboard as the main interface for sound synthesis, something equivalent to the present role the mouse and computer keyboard play in traditional human-computer interaction (HCI).

Related to the design of alternative gestural controllers, the role of the gestures one uses to perform this control is a rich although fairly unexplored area

---

[1] Signal models intend to reproduce perceptual characteristics of a sound. Most common examples are: additive synthesis, subtractive synthesis, etc. Physical models, on the other hand, try to simulate, modify and extrapolate the functioning of an instrument by means of a computer algorithm. See [3] or [8] for an introduction.

[2] Musical Instrument Digital Interface.

A. Braffort et al. (Eds.): GW'99, LNAI 1739, pp. 37–48, 1999.

of research, i.e., the range of possible gestures meaningful in music consists of a huge set of possibilities that are still not completely understood. This paper is proposed as a contribution to this discussion, by reviewing some of the previous related work on the theory of gesture and then focusing on particular gestures of wind instrument performers.

2   On Gestures and Music

The term gesture is a rather general idea that may have many (different) meanings in music. As an example, a composer may use the term musical gestures to designate a sequence of events within a space of musical parameters; sometimes it can also have some relation to a form of thinking (a movement of thought)[3]. Whatever the definition, it is easily seen that these ideas are independent of any direct physical meaning in the sense of manipulating an instrument. A performer, on the other hand, may consider performance gesture as the technique used to play an instrument, where it encompasses not only the gestures that actually produce an excitation to/ modification of the instrument, but also the accompanying body movements and postures. Computer musicians or computer music performers using electronic means to produce/control sounds may have a concept of gestures as specific isolated movements related to specific physical variables, such as pressure, velocity, acceleration, etc. that may be captured by sensors and transformed into digital signals input to computers.

Zooming out of the musical universe, one can also identify different ideas expressed by the same term gesture. In order to consider different proposals, let us first consider gestures as divided into two groups:

- Gestures where no physical contact with a device or instrument is involved. These have been called free, semiotic or naked gestures [5].
- Gestures where some kind of physical contact takes place. These have been called ergotic [5], haptic[4] or interactive [5].

Much of the research on empty-handed gestures relate to gestural communication, such as that on co-verbal gestures, or on sign-language recognition. In a musical context, one could cite other gestures (not always empty-handed), including conductors' gestures and on broader terms, dance movements, in the case of dance-music interfaces. These gestures will not be discussed here. Moreover, research on gesture where some form of contact takes place will be reduced to the study of instrumental gesture [5].

Let's now review some specific research that may influence our discussion on performer gestures.

---

[3] I would like to thank Mikhail Malt for his comments on the subject.

[4] One may here differentiate the uses of the term *haptic*. According to Baecker et al. [1] it has its origin in the Greek language and means *having to do with contact*. It is therefore used to represent any type of computer input where contact takes place. The term haptic is nevertheless widely accepted nowadays as designing the research encompassing touch- and/or force-feedback devices.

2.1   Natural Gestures

J. Cassell uses the term gesture to address hand gestures that co-occur with spoken language. Natural gestures are, according to Cassell, types of gestures spontaneously generated by a person telling a story, speaking in public, or holding a conversation [17]. These gestures are idiosyncratic (speaker dependent) and influenced by external factors: situational, educational, and cultural. The author and collaborators have identified different types of natural gestures and also devised ways to recover their temporal structure.

2.2   Gestures in HCI

Since the gestural control of computer music is a special type of man-machine communication, it is worth considering definitions of gesture in the light of the research on Human-Computer Interaction. By doing that, one may quickly perceive that the concept of gesture may have a slightly different meaning: *a gesture is a motion of the body that contains information* [12]. Kurtenbach and Hulteen actually do not consider the act of pressing a button (or a key) as a gesture, since *motion of a finger on its way to hitting the key is neither observed nor significant. All that matters is which key was pressed.* C. Hummels and co-workers [11] have noticed the narrowness of this definition and have proposed that the word *convey* be used instead of *contain*, widening this definition to encompass human movements other than those related to empty-handed gestures.

2.3   Instrumental Gestures

Back to the musical universe (and considering only gestures where some physical contact takes place), important work relative to gestural control of music has been developed by C. Cadoz and co-workers [10] [4] [14] [5] [6]. Cadoz established guidelines for the study of a specific type of gesture that is meaningful in instrumental music, which he has defined as *instrumental gesture* [4] [5]. According to him, instrumental gestures are specific to the gestural channel[5] and are defined as the ones applied to a material object, where physical interaction with the object takes place; the physical phenomena produced during this interaction convey some form of information and can be mastered by the subject. Cadoz also proposed a three-tier functional classification of gestures as [6]: *Excitation*, either instantaneous or continuous; *Modification*, parametric or structural; and *Selection*.

3   Ensemble of Performer Gestures

What do we mean by *performer gestures*? Those that have to do with the actual way of playing an instrument, i.e. the instrumentalist's own technique, both

---

[5] Gestural channel is defined as a means of action on the physical world as well as a communication means in a double sense: emission and reception of information [5].

instrumental gestures in the sense of Cadoz's classification and those that may not be directly performed to produce a note.

One attempt in this direction has been proposed by François Delalande [7] in a study on the playing technique of Glenn Gould. He suggested the following gesture classification:

- *Effective gestures*, those that actually produce the sound;
- *Accompanist gestures*, body movements such as shoulder or head movements;
- *Figurative gestures*, gestures perceived by the audience through the produced sound, but without any direct correspondence to a movement. Examples would be changes in note articulation, melodic variations, etc.

In the light of Delalande's classification, performer gestures in the sense stated above will be related to the first two items. The first one usually represents the traditional controller outputs, such as fingering. The second item, *accompanist gestures*, is the main interest of this article, but only when it directly relates to sound production.

3.1 Example of the Clarinet

Considering Delalande's *effective gestures* or Cadoz's *instrumental gestures*, let us analyze the three most common gestures of a clarinet player: blowing, lip pressure, and fingering.

Applying the typology proposed by Cadoz, one could classify breath pressure as an *excitation* gesture, lip pressure as a *parametric modification* gesture and fingering as a *selection* gesture.

These results would clearly be a simplification of the real instrument behavior, since they do not take into account the subtle interdependencies of the above functions, such as the case of the reed's physical behavior [2] [15]. Nevertheless, they do represent the case of a MIDI wind controller, such as the Yamaha WX7, where an independent MIDI stream is output according to each of the above functions.

Although the three described gestures could account for a reasonable quality synthesis of a clarinet using a good synthesis model, one notes from the analysis of clarinet performances that instrumentalists do not only make *effective* movements but actually also express themselves by means of body movements[6]. We will use here the term *ancillary*[7] to designate only those gestures applied to the instrument, while Delalande considers *all* body movements as *accompanist*, changes in body posture and instrument movements during the performance.

---

[6] These movements will be considered as gestures, in the sense of Delalande's *accompanist gestures*.

[7] Thanks to Mark Goldstein for the suggestion.

4   Non-obvious Performer Gestures

Let us consider here *non-obvious* or *ancillary* gestures as a class of wind instrument performer gestures that are produced by means of moving the instrument during the performance - *lifting it up/putting it down, to one side or another, fast tilt-like gestures, etc.*

For the time being, two main groups of non-obvious gestures will be devised according to their amplitudes ranges: *large-amplitude* and *small-amplitude* gestures.

This paper mainly deals with gestures that present a fairly large range of movement. Although these may be produced consciously – because of composer's explicit requirements (some pieces by K. Stockhausen, for instance), as a visual effect that is immediately perceived by the audience, or as part of a communication language between players in an ensemble – the goal of this study is to analyze ancillary gestures produced by the musician while playing.

Fig. 1. Alain Damiens playing Domaines by Pierre Boulez. Two shots taken less than a second apart - *Cahier D, Original*. Note the displacement of the clarinet and also the change in posture.

In order to develop a formal analysis of these gestures, three different clarinet players were observed in different circumstances:

- A video of French clarinettist Alain Damiens rehearsing a solo clarinet piece by Pierre Boulez, *Domaines*, produced at Ircam in 1985.[8]
- A video of Marc Battier's[9] clarinet piece *Mixed Media*[10], recorded during a concert in Kobe, Japan, 1993.
- Different acoustic and electronic performances of American clarinettist/ composer Joseph Butch Rovan, during his residency at the Institute, 1996-1998.

---

[8] I would like to thank the copyright owners who kindly agreed on the usage of this video for this research.
[9] Thanks to Marc Battier for providing the film.
[10] Unfortunately, the name of the player could not be found.

Fig. 2. Three shots showing a fast upwards gesture. This sequence originally lasts one second - *Cahier C, Original.* Note (*left*) the *standard* posture, (*center*) the lowest point, and (*right*) the final point of the movement.

In order to complement the information obtained from the videos, we have further analyzed clarinet samples recorded by French clarinettist Pierre Dutrieu in the framework of the Studio-on-Line project[11]; discussed with Dutrieu and also with French alto-saxophonist Claude Delangle, and finally with German musicologist and (amateur) clarinettist Peter Hoffmann.

An analysis of the first video reveals certain gestural patterns. There are mainly three movements occurring at specific moments:

- Changes in posture at the beginning and during phrases.
- Slow continuous gestures, usually in an upward direction during long sustained notes, generally increasing in amplitude with an increase in the note's dynamics.
- Fast sweeping movements of the bell that mainly accompany short staccato notes.

Analyzing the data from the two other clarinet players, it can be seen that continuous movements may also be found in sustained notes. Nevertheless, not many fast gestures were found in the second video, but changes in posture seemed to be more frequent. Also, the amplitude range of these movements varies from player to player.

Finally, it has also been noticed that even when playing an electronic controller, the third player had the tendency to produce similar movements to the ones with an acoustic instrument.

4.1 Analysis

Due to the small quantity of analysis samples available, it cannot be stated that any of these gestural patterns will be reproduced in every circumstance, although this first analysis does suggest that these basic gesture patterns may exist, at least in the case of the same player. As an example, a phrase is repeated twice in the first film, in the introductory credits and later during the piece (Cahier D,

---

[11] A sound database with complete recordings of most orchestral instruments. For more information, see http://www.ircam.fr/

original). It is interesting to note that the player reproduced the same ancillary gestures when performing the sequence each time.

One can imagine that there may be different causes for these (different) kinds of gestures. Some of the observed gestures seem to be produced in order to express extra information than that conveyed by the sound, and we suppose that they may therefore be influenced by cultural and situational factors, such as musical style, room size and type, size of audience, etc. Others may be the result of particular technical difficulties encountered when playing the instrument, and thus have their origin in human physiological characteristics. Finally, some of the low-amplitude movements result from the simple fact that it is humanly impossible to play a wind instrument absolutely immobilized.

After discussions with clarinet and saxophone players, it seems not exact that these gestures are only produced in order to *consciously* express extra information, such as lifting the bell in order to sound brighter. Moreover, the performers reported that they are not aware of most of these movements and even were rather surprised when watching the sample movies or the sound analysis results.

Against the hypothesis of technical difficulties is the notion of *expert* performance [13]. We are here considering top performers who have long overcome most technical difficulties. Another point related to the relative role of motor control is that recent studies [9] on the roles of motor control and mental representation in children performance have shown that once a mental representation of the piece is developed, similar execution time profiles have been found between performances of the same piece in different instruments, independently from the different motor control skills required.

4.2   Further Considerations

I would also like to discuss in this paper the possible benefits gained from the research on co-verbal gestures. Although performer gestures are of a fundamentally different nature, this research may at least benefit from the techniques developed for the study of these gestures.

Considering it in more detail, one could state that some ancillary performer gestures accompany (augment or complement) the information that is conveyed by the primary channel (the sound) and give extra (visual) clues on the performer's musical intentions to the audience. Another point is that ancillary performer gestures may influence the primary information received by the audience, and this influence may also be perceptible.

It remains to be discussed whether these gestures will present universal, recognizable patterns among different players and what might be the exact influence of the environment on them.

5   Influence on the Instrument's Sound

Let's now show why it is important to study ancillary gestures by analyzing their acoustical influence on the sound. This will be done by presenting several experiments performed to understand their effects. These experiments[12] have been devised and performed in special circumstances in order to isolate specific phenomena each time.

5.1 Experiments

The main experiments performed were:

- Recording of clarinet sustained notes (7 seconds in average) in an anechoic chamber[13] under two conditions: empty anechoic chamber and anechoic chamber with the inclusion of a wooden floor. Both were performed three times:
  - Instrument kept immobilized by a mechanical apparatus;
  - Instrument played in a normal way (conventional, non-exaggerated);
  - Instrument played in an exaggerated way - i.e. large-amplitude movements.
- Room response measurements where the excitation was provided by a loudspeaker connected to a clarinet tube placed at different angles.
- Recordings with a clarinet immobilized by the same mechanical apparatus used during the anechoic chamber recordings, but in an auditorium with variable acoustics[14] in a reverberant configuration.
- Clarinet recordings from the Studio-on-Line database, where each note is available in three different dynamics (pianissimo, mezzo-forte, and fortissimo) and recorded by six different microphones - two reference (2 meters), one close (1 meter), one internal and two far microphones (around 15 meters away).

5.2 Discussion

A detailed quantitative analysis of the obtained results is beyond the scope of this article and is presented elsewhere[16]. We will here directly present some conclusions in order to show the influence of these gestures in the sound.

Movements of the instrument with respect to a close fixed microphone will mostly cause variations in the attributes of the direct sound and the first reflections captured by the microphone. Actually, both the amplitude and time of arrival of the direct sound and of the first reflection will be modified with a change in position, causing the modulations found in some of the analyzed samples.

This effect can be further explained by the analysis of the figures below. Figure 3 shows a D3 *ff* recorded in a reverberant auditorium: the left side shows a

---

[12] Performed in close cooperation with Olivier Warusfel, Philippe Depalle, René Caussé, Federico Cruz-Barney, Gérard Bertrand, Joseph Rovan and Peter Hoffmann.

[13] A special room where acoustically absorbent material is placed in order to avoid sound reflections normally produced by walls, ceiling, and floor.

[14] The Espace de Projection at Ircam. Its acoustics can be modified from dry to strongly reverberant.

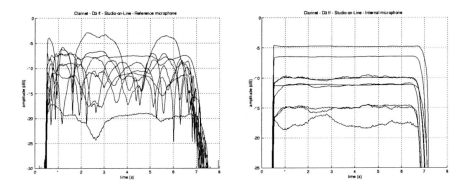

Fig. 3. Clarinet recordings in a reverberant auditorium (Espace de Projection - Ircam) - D3 recorded *ff*, standard playing - Studio-on-Line database - (P. Dutrieu): *(left)* reference microphone (2 meters in front of the instrument); *(right)* internal microphone.

sample from the Studio-on-Line database, where one can notice strong partial amplitude variations. The right side shows the same note recorded with an internal microphone. Note that the amplitudes of the sinusoidal partials are fairly constant in this case. This amounts for a certain stability of the embouchure, what could be expected since we're dealing with expert performers.

The left side of figure 4 shows the note recorded in the same auditorium with a clarinet immobilized by a mechanical apparatus. Except for minor fluctuation in one of the partials, it is clear that the same variations did not occur to the same extent. Finally, the right side of this figure shows a recording of the same note in an anechoic room. Again, the partials present a rather constant amplitude in time.

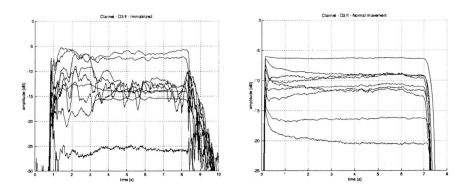

Fig. 4. Clarinet recordings - D3 recorded *ff*: *(left)* reverberant auditorium - clarinet immobilized by mechanical apparatus (Peter Hoffmann); *(right)* empty anechoic chamber - clarinet played in a standard manner (J. Rovan).

Figure 5 shows the analysis of D3 recorded in an anechoic chamber when large movements were performed. One may notice small differences in the amplitude values of the sinusoidal partials. This shows that the instrument's directivity alone does not play the major role in these variations. Furthermore, the right side of the figure shows the analysis of the same note recorded with a wooden floor placed between the instrument and the microphone, again with large movements. The floor deepens in the amplitude variations to more than 12 dB even for low frequencies, producing effects that are similar to the ones found in the original sample (figure 3).

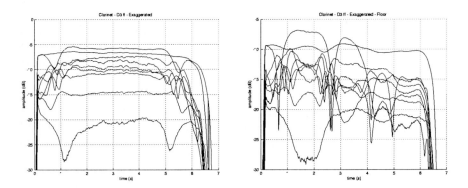

Fig. 5. Anechoic room recordings (J. Rovan) - D3 recorded *ff* and exaggerated movement: *(left)* empty anechoic room; *(right)* wooden floor placed between the instrument and microphone.

5.3   Simulation

In order to verify the previous analysis, we have made tests with a model of these variations in the FTS sound synthesis environment, where results of the room response measurements were implemented as parameters of continuous delay operations[15]. The results are shown in figure 6.

The input of the system consists of a sound file recorded in an empty anechoic chamber with the clarinet immobilized. A slider is used to simulate a one dimensional movement of the clarinet from an angle perpendicular to the floor to an horizontal position. Since the measurements presented before did not show major influences of neither the embouchure nor the instrument's directivity, the simulation model just takes into account the influence of the first reflection.

One can see that using this simplified model strong amplitude variations may be produced, depending on the clarinet movement simulated[16].

---

[15] No spectral changes due to the reflected sound have been implemented at this stage.

[16] One must not forget that the effect of early reflections is completely tied up to the microphone type and position and may even be disregarded in the case of averaging multiple recordings or using distant microphones.

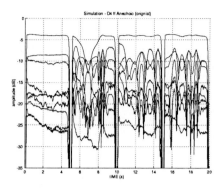

Fig. 6. Simulation of the effect of different movements by modification of direct sound and first reflection attributes according to the clarinet's angle. The first quarter of the picture displays the amplitudes of the original sound's sinusoidal partials (anechoic chamber). The remaining ones represent different movements applied to the instrument.

6   Conclusions

In this article different topics of the research on gesture applied to music have been discussed, mainly in the case of instrument performance.

I commented on the broad range of ideas the word gesture may have in a computer music context and then moved on to review some of the previous work relating gestures and music. After analyzing the existing classifications of gestures in music in the light of the behavior of acoustic wind instruments, it was pointed out that many gestures that are not usually referred to as important in sound synthesis should be considered, since they may actually affect the sound captured from the instrument.

It has been verified by measurements and simulation that the variations of the direct sound and floor reflection attributes for a specific movement may cause sinusoidal partial amplitude modulations that play an important role in the resulting sound for a particular microphone position.

7   Acknowledgements

Many thanks to Stephen McAdams, Xavier Rodet and Mark Goldstein for comments on previous versions of this manuscript, and also Philippe Depalle, Olivier Warusfel, François Delalande, Pierre Dutrieu and Federico Cruz-Barney for useful discussions and suggestions.

This work is supported in part by a scholarship from the CNPq, Brazilian National Research Council.

References

[1] Baecker, R. M., Grudin, J., Buxton, W. A. S., Greenberg, S.: *Readings in Human-Computer Interaction: Toward the Year 2000*, Morgan-Kauffmann, 2nd Edition, Part III, ch. 7 (1995) 469–482.

[2] Benade, A. H.: *Fundamentals of Musical Acoustics*, Second edition, Dover (1990).

[3] Borin, G., De Poli, G., and Sarti, A.: Musical Signal Synthesis, in *Musical Signal Processing*, C. Roads, S. T. Pope, A. Piccialli, and G. De Poli (eds), Swets & Zeitlinger B.V. ch. 1 (1997) 5–30.

[4] Cadoz, C.: Instrumental Gesture and Musical Composition, Proc. Int. Computer Music Conf., ICMC, (1988) 1–12.

[5] Cadoz, C.: Le geste canal de communication homme-machine. La communication "instrumentale" *Sciences Informatiques* - Numéro Spécial: Interface Homme-Machine (1994) 31–61.

[6] Cadoz, C.: Musique, geste technologie, in *Cultures Musicales: Les Nouveaux Gestes de la Musique*, H. Génevoix and R. De Vivo (eds), Parentheses (1999).

[7] Delalande, F.: La gestique de Glenn Gould, in *Glenn Gould Pluriel*, Louise Courteau Editrice (1988) 84–111.

[8] Depalle, P., Tassart, S., Wanderley, M.: Instruments virtuels - Les vertues du possible. Résonance, 12 (1997) 5–8.

[9] Drake, C.: Aux fondements du geste musical, *Science et Vie* - Numéro Spécial: Le Cerveau et le mouvement, A. Berthoz (ed), (1998) 114 - 121.

[10] Gibet, S.: Codage, représentation et traitement du geste instrumental, *PhD Thesis*, Institut National Polytechnique de Grenoble (1987).

[11] Hummels, C., Smets, G., and Overbeeke, K.: An Intuitive Two-Handed Gestural Interface for Computer Supported Product Design, in *Gesture and Sign Language in Human-Computer Interaction*, I. Wachsmuth and M. Frölich (eds), Springer Verlag (1998) 197–208.

[12] Kurtenbach, G. and Hulteen, E. A.: Gestures in Human-Computer Communication, in *The Art of Human-Computer Interface Design*, B. Laurel (ed), Addison Wesley, (1990).

[13] Lehmann, A. C.: Efficiency of Deliberate Practice as a Moderating Variable in Accounting for Sub-expert Performance, in *Perception and Cognition of Music*, I. Deliège and J. Sloboda (eds), Psychology Press, (1997).

[14] Ramstein, C.: Analyse, représentation et traitement du geste instrumental, *PhD Thesis*, Institut National Polytechnique de Grenoble (1991).

[15] Rovan, J., Wanderley, M., Dubnov, S., Depalle, P.: Instrumental Gestural Mapping Strategies as Expressivity Determinants in Computer Music Performance. Proceedings of the Kansei - The Technology of Emotion Workshop, A. Camurri (ed), Genoa - Italy (1997) 68–73.

[16] Wanderley, M., Depalle, P., and Warusfel, O.: Improving Instrumental Sound Synthesis by Modeling the Effects of Performer Gesture, Proc. Int. Computer Music Conf., ICMC, China (1999).

[17] Wilson, A. D., Bobick, A. F., and Cassell, J.: Recovering the Temporal Structure of Natural Gesture, Proceedings 2nd Int. Conf. on Automatic Face and Gesture Recognition (1996).

The Ecological Approach to Multimodal System Design

Antonella De Angeli[1], Fréderic Wolff[2], Laurent Romary[2], and Walter Gerbino[1]

[1] Cognitive Technology Laboratory, Department of Psychology, University of Trieste,
via dell'Università 7, 34123, Trieste, Italy
{deangeli,gerbino}@univ.trieste.it
[2] Laboratoire Loria, «Langue et Dialogue»team
BP239 54506 Vandoeuvre-Les-Nancy
{wolff,romary}@loria.fr

Abstract. Following the ecological approach to visual perception, this paper presents a framework that emphasizes the role of vision on referring actions. In particular, *affordances* are utilized to explain gestures variability in a multimodal human-computer interaction. Such a proposal is consistent with empirical findings obtained in different simulation studies showing how referring gestures are determined by the mutuality of information coming from the target and the set of movements available to the speaker. A prototype that follows anthropomorphic perceptual principles to analyze gestures has been developed and tested in preliminary computational validations.

1 Multimodal Systems

Sometimes a gesture can bebetter than a thousand words. It happens whenever we want to indicate visual objects for which a direct and unambiguous linguistic reference is not easily accessible. Gestures are efficient means for coping with the complexity of the visual world, a complexity that cannot be completely conveyed by verbal language alone [1], [4]. Gestures directly refer to the physical context of communication, so that localization is independent of the specific mental representation used by interlocutors to cognitively reconstruct space and its relations.

Multimodal systems [3] integrating speech and gesture have the potential for decreasing the difficulty of talking about space during human-computer interaction. Despite the expected usability improvement, the design is strongly hampered by the difficulty of coping with the high communication variability affecting both the verbal and the gestural part of communication. The ecological approach to multimodal systems is intended to cope with communication variability without limiting user behavior to unnatural stereotypic shapes, but anticipating spontaneous behavior.

The ecological approach had a strong impact on theories of perception, action, and cognition. Here, it is applied to multimodal system design. According to ecological psychology [2], perception and action are intrinsically linked by

A. Braffort et al. (Eds.): GW'99, LNAI 1739, pp. 49–52, 1999.

affordances. Affordances of objects and events are mediated by perceptual information that can be picked up by an active organism. They specify the actions an object can support, suggesting its functionality to the observer. For example, an hammer usually induces us to take it by the handle and not by the head, because the handle is visually more graspable. The principle of mutuality is embedded in affordances. They are not properties of an object, but relations derived by the encounter between information coming from the object and the repertoire of physical actions available to the observer. As a consequence, a stone may afford being thrown by an adult, but not by a child.

The basic assumption of our proposal states that gestures, as virtual actions, unfold in perception. Although a form of gesticulation is omnipresent during speech, referring gestures are effective only if interlocutors face each others and are exposed to the same visual scene. Factors affecting visual search influence the planning phase of motion; visual and kinesthetic feedback control execution. Understanding requires the capability of integrating explicit visual information conveyed by gestural trajectories with implicit visual information conveyed by the perceptual context. Finally, visual cues (e.g., gaze movements towards the target) allow the speaker to monitor listener's comprehension. Despite so much evidence claiming the interplay between visual perception and gesture, traditional multimodal system have usually been kept blind. The innovative aspect of our proposal relies on the importance given to visual perception as a fundamental variable in communication.

2   Empirical Evidence

Some empirical findings support the idea that gestures are determined by the mutuality of information provided by the object and the set of movements available to the speaker. The role of individual capabilities on communication behavior was demonstrated in [1]. In particular, user expertise was found to influence the occurrence of multimodal inputs. Interacting with a system based on written natural-language and mouse-mediated pointing, expert users pointed much more frequently than beginners who instead prefer pure verbal inputs. The gesture appears to be inhibited by the lack of familiarity with artificial mediators. This confirms that the repertoire of easily accessible actions influences the way referential actions are carried out. More direct evidence concerning the role of perception in non-verbal communication comes from a speech-and-pen study where users were asked to displace groups of targets into appropriate boxes [5]. Different visual scenes were tested. Results showed that form, granularity, and size of gesture were adapted to visual layout (Fig. 1). Even at the cost of producing very unusual movements, users tended to mimic the form of the target (Fig. 1a). Therefore, knowledge about the visual context is often instrumental to disambiguate the meaning of gesture.

Granularity ambiguities derive from a non 1-to-1 relation between referred area and gesture extent. As shown in Fig. 1b, when the salience of the group is very high, the gesture can be highly simplified and the entire group indicated by

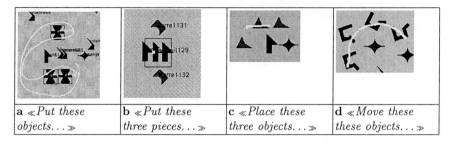

| **a** «Put these objects...» | **b** «Put these three pieces...» | **c** «Place these three objects...» | **d** «Move these these objects...» |

Fig. 1. Examples of the effect of visual perception on gesture

a small pointing. A similar phenomenon occurs in Fig. 1c, where gesture interpretation generates a strong ambiguity in choosing either the individual percept or the group. The dialogue context allow to exclude the individual reference, but only the perceptual context can disambiguate the three appropriate targets.

The gesture illustrated in Fig. 1d is an example of form ambiguity. It can be considered as a free form targeting or as an incomplete circling. According to the interpretation, the number of referential candidates is different (only the 4 U-shaped percepts or also the star shaped percept). Again, the verbal expression does not provide enough information to derive the solution, but the perceptual context induces us to favor the first interpretation. A strong effect of perceptual organization emerged also considering the number of gestures performed to identify a group. Targets could be referred by a *group access* (showing the perimeter or the area of the group) or by a number of *individual accesses* (indicating elements one by one). The occurrence of these strategies is highly influenced by visual factors. When targets were immediately perceived as a group (proximity and good continuation supported similarity), group access was the preferred strategy. On the contrary when targets were spontaneously perceived as elements of a broader heterogeneous group including also distractors (proximity and good continuation acted in opposition to similarity), users produced almost only individual accesses.

3 Computational Validation

Pattern recognition is well suited for stereotypic vocabularies, but because of trajectory variability, a contextual method is needed for natural gestures. The ecological approach attempts to explain and predict how trajectories are produced according to the visual environment. The analysis of recorded trajectories showed that users accessed referents by producing their gestures in two areas. In other words, each object affords two areas for referring: (a) the elective area, centered to each object; (b) the separative area, peripheral to the elective one. Areas extent depends on the distances between the target and the surrounding objects: close objects imply small access areas, inducing precise gesturing, whereas far objects imply larger access areas, inducing more imprecise trajectories.

Given object location in a visual scene, the ecological algorithm determines the referring affordances for each object. Trajectories can then be recognized considering in which area trajectory segments mainly appear, i.e. trajectory mainly drawn in elective (separative) areas correspond to an elective (separative) gesture. The next step consists in retrieving referents among objects on the basis of gesture type. In the case of an elective gesture, referents correspond to crossed elective areas, whereas for separative gestures referents are determined by selecting objects on the concave side of the trajectory. In this way, given a visual scene the computational model can predict which referring gestures are produced by users. In addition, elliptic gestures occurring in high salience condition are also treated by introducing simulated grouping mechanism.

The prototype has been computationally validated using real data recorded during the simulation. From a quantitative point of view, referred objects were correctly retrieved in 75% of all 852 gestures. Qualitatively, the approach has allowed to face many gestural variability, such as category, free form trajectories, partial/repetitive gesturing or gestural simplification.

4   Conclusion

Introducing gesture into the perception-action cycle help predicting gesture variability, which is very high in a human-computer interaction context too. We have presented some preliminary data demonstrating as visual field organisation affect gesturing. We need now to extend this framework identifying the relationship between visual affordances and gestures and implementing this knowledge into systems.

References

1. De Angeli, A., Gerbino, W., Petrelli, D., Cassano, G.: Visual display, pointing and natural language: The power of multimodal interaction. In: Proceedings of the Working Conference on Advanced Visual Interface AVI'98, L'Aquila, Italy, May 1998. ACM Press (1998), 164-173
2. Gibson, J.J.: The Ecological Approach to Visual Perception. Houghton Mifflin Boston (1979).
3. Maybury, M.T.: Intelligent Multimdedia Interfaces. Cambridge Mass. MIT Press (1993).
4. Oviatt, S., De Angeli. A, Kuhn, K.: Integration and sysnchronisation of input modes during multimodal human-computer interaction. In: Proceedings of the CHI'97 Conference, New York ACM Press (1997), 415-422.
5. Wolff, F., De Angeli, A. , Romary, L.: Acting on a visual world: The role of perception in multimodal HCI. In: Proceedings of the 1998 Workshop on Representations for Multi-Modal Human-Computer Interaction. AAAI Press (1998).

Analysis of Trunk and Upper Limb Synergies

Agnès Roby-Brami[12], Mounir Mokhtari[13], Isabelle Laffont[12],
Nezha Bennis[1], and Elena Biryukova[4]

[1] INSERM U483, 9 quai St Bernard, F75005, Paris, France
{Agnes.Roby-Brami, Nezha.Bennis, Mounir.Mokhtari}@snv.jussieu.fr
[2] Service de rééducation neurologique, Hôpital Raymond Poincaré,
92380, Garches, France
114037@compuserve.com
[3] Institut National des Télécommunications, rue Charles Fourier, Evry
[4] Institute of Higher Nervous Activity and Neurophysiology,
5 Butlerov street, 117865, Moscow, Russia
birds@orc.ru

Abstract. A new method of recording and reconstruction of upper-limb kinematics has been developed in order to analyze the mechanisms of motor recovery in disabled patients. It has been applied to the analysis of non constrained gestures in normal subjects and in patients with an hemiparesis following stroke. The results show evidence of new motor strategies and new co-ordinations developed to compensate for the motor impairment. In the future, this method could be applied to gesture recognition and synthesis and for the development of enhanced learning environments in rehabilitation.

1   Introduction

After a disease or an accident, inducing a motor impairment people may lose a part of their functional ability and remain handicapped. For example, after a stroke, the patients present a complete paralysis of the limbs contra-lateral to the damaged cerebral hemisphere. In half of the cases, the paralysis recovers partially within a few months but the mechanism of recovery are still disputed. The plasticity of the neural system is now well demonstrated but its relationships with the sensory- motor function, the importance of learning and the specificity of rehabilitation methods remain unclear [1].

The resulting motor function depends on the initial impairment but also on a dynamic process. The patients may adapt their residual motor function through to their environment by motor learning in order to fulfil daily living tasks. This process may include spontaneous recovery due to neural plasticity, the acquisition of some compensatory motor strategies and/or the development of new inter-joint co-ordinations thanks to the redundant properties of the motor system [2]. It is particularly important to distinguish these potential mechanisms for a better understanding of neural plasticity and for the development of functional rehabilitation methods.

A. Braffort et al. (Eds.): GW'99, LNAI 1739, pp. 53–57, 1999.

The present study was initiated following the hypothesis that the kinematic characteristics of non constrained gestures could give some indications on the underlying recovery process. We had to develop an original method since there was no other suitable or standard one. Four electromagnetic Fastrack Polhemus sensors were used in order to record the position and orientation of the upper limb segments (hand, forearm, upper-arm and scapula). Then an algorithm based on the rigid-body assumption allowed the reconstruction of the 7 inter-joint angles (degrees of freedom) of the upper-limb [3].

2   Methods

2.1   Subjects

15 patients participated in the study: 6 had a left side and 9 a right side hemiplegia after an ischemic stroke in the territory of the middle cerebral artery. 9 of them were examined at least twice at one month interval. 7 normal subjects served as controls.

2.2   Task and Procedure

The experimental set-up was planned to be as functional as possible, to allow natural reaching and grasping gestures in a context similar to everyday life, without artificial limb immobilization. The goal of the task was to grasp a hollow cardboard cone commonly used in occupational therapy. The objects were placed on an horizontal board at seven possible positions. The closer position was 15 cm in front of the subject in the midline, the others were 10 cm on the right or the left and 10 to 20 cm forward.

2.3   Recording Method and Bio-mechanical Reconstruction

Four Polhemus markers were fixed by adhesive tape on the hand, forearm, upper-arm and acromion (upper part of the scapula). They give the three co- ordinates of the origins of marker's reference frames as well as the Euler angles of marker's axes rotations relative to stationary axes. The sampling frequency is 30 Hz. In some studies in normal subjects, a 3D accelerometer was also fixed on the hand.

We used a bio-mechanical model of the human upper limb consisting of three rigid links connected by ideal joints and having 7 degrees of freedom (DoF): 3 DoF in the shoulder joint, 2 DoF both in the elbow and in the wrist joints. To reconstruct the joint angles corresponding to each DoF we have first determined the positions of the axes of rotation in the marker's reference frames. The method of calculation of position of joint centers and axes of rotation was based on the least squares method. This gave the center of the shoulder joint by reference to the scapula marker (3 variables), and the position and direction of the 2 elbow and 2 wrist axes by reference to the corresponding markers. The joint angles around the determined axes of rotation were calculated under the assumption

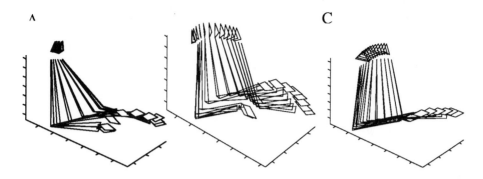

Fig. 1. Stick diagrams of a reaching to grasp movement. Left: normal subject, middle: hemiparetic patient who compensates, right: hemiparetic patients who partially recovers. The scapula is indicated by a triangle linked with the acromion sensor, the upper-arm is indicated by a triangle limited by the shoulder center of rotation and 2 points belonging to the elbow flexion- extension axis, the forearm by a quadrilateral limited by points belonging to the elbow and wrist flexion- extension axis, the hand is indicated by a polygon limited by two points belonging to the wrist abduction-adduction axis and three points linked to the hand sensor

that the shoulder joint is a ball joint with a fixed center of rotation and that the elbow and wrist joints each have two independent crossing axes of rotation. The accuracy of the proposed method was estimated by solving the direct kinematics problem on the base of the reconstructed joint angles. The calculated acceleration was compared with the data of 3D accelerometer mounted on the hand and showed that the calculated errors are rather small [3].

3   Results

3.1   Reaching and Grasping in Normal Subjects

The trajectory of the hand sensor was consistent with previous observations [4]. Briefly, the velocity profile of the hand movement showed a regular peak during the reaching movement whose amplitude was scaled to the movement distance. Grasping the cone was indicated by a sharp change in the direction of the hand trajectory and a velocity minimum. In addition, the measurement of inter joint angles showed the synergies commonly used by normal subjects during reaching toward a forward target. Reaching movement involved a slight movement of the scapula including vertical rotation and protraction and an arm synergy including a shoulder flexion and elbow extension (Fig. 1, left). A quantitative analysis showed that the amplitudes of trunk vertical rotation, shoulder flexion and elbow extension increased linearly with the distance of the object in all the normal subjects. This suggests that, despite the redundancy of the system, normal subjects regularly use and scale this scapula- shoulder-elbow synergy for reaching toward forward objects.

3.2 Hemiparetic Patients

Reaching and grasping movements in hemiparetic patients are slower and more irregular than those of normal subjects. Most of them, even those with a relatively severe disability, were able to scale the velocity peak to the movement distance. The scapula was not only rotated during reaching as in normal subjects but also translated by a trunk movement and protracted forward. The upper-limb coordination during reaching varied with the patients but two main types could be identified. In some patients, as the patient illustrated Fig. 1 (middle), the reaching movement was accompanied by a large movement of the trunk which translated and rotated the scapula. During reaching, there was no elbow extension nor shoulder flexion but a rotation involving a shoulder abduction and a rotation around a vertical axis. The abnormal trunk and upper-limb coordination resulted in an efficient transport of the hand. However, the clinical testing showed that the upper limb capacity was rather poor. Other patients, as the patient illustrated Fig. 1 (right), were able to make an elbow extension during reaching and made a smaller associated trunk movement. The longitudinal follow- up showed that during recovery, the improvement of reaching movements was due to an increase in elbow extension and shoulder flexion in parallel with a decrease of the trunk movement. The clinical outcome in these patients was generally good and they were able to use their arm in the daily life.

This analysis suggests that the recuperation of reaching movements in hemiparetic patients can be due to two associated processes: the recovery of the normal synergy (which associates for the present set- up shoulder flexion and elbow extension) and the use of an alternate compensatory movement with an increased forward movement of the trunk. The true recovery is probably due to the plasticity of the neural maps, the compensation can be interpreted as the learning of a new motor strategy [5, 6]. These results will be compared to electrophysiological analysis of the motor neural pathways and to functional cerebral imagery in order to investigate recovery mechanisms.

Prospects

The present method which merge electromagnetic recordings to a bio-mechanical model of the upper limb is the first method with allows the simultaneous measure of the upper limb inter-joint angles and scapula movement. In addition to its applications in functional rehabilitation, it could be used for gesture synthesis since it provides a concise and sufficient description of the upper-limb configuration without excessive computational load. The bio-mechanical model of the upper limb is described by a limited number of parameters and the configuration of the upper-limb at any moment can be described by only 7 intrinsic upper-limb angles computed from the position and orientation of the markers. Since the signals are available on line, the method could be used to develop some virtual or enhanced environment in order to improve sensory-motor learning during the process of rehabilitation [7].

References

1. Woods, P., Synthesis of intervention trials to improve motor recovery following stroke. Top. Stroke Rehabil. 3 (1997) 1–20.
2. Bernstein N, The coordination and regulation of movements. New York, Pergamon press, (1967).
3. Biryukova EV, Roby-Brami A, Mokhtari M, Frolov AA,.Reconstruction of 7 dof human arm kinematics from polhemus Fastrak recordings. J. Biomech, Vol 31, Suppl 1, P059 and in press.
4. Jeannerod, M. The neural and behavioral organization of goal-directed movements. Clarendon Press, Oxford (1988).
5. Roby-Brami, A., Fuchs, S., Mokhtari, M., Bussel, B., Reaching and Grasping strategies in hemiplegic patients. Motor Control, 1 (1997) 72–91.
6. Cirstea C, Levin MF, Compensatory strategies for reaching in stroke: the concept of a critical level for motor recovery. Brain, in press.
7. Mokhtari, M., Roby-Brami, A, Multimodal Environment Learning for Assisting, Manipulation by people with severe disabilities, RESNA '96 "Exploring New Horizon" Salt Lake City, June (1996), 345–347.

Section 2: Localisation and Segmentation

GREFIT: Visual Recognition of Hand Postures *

Claudia Nölker and Helge Ritter

Technische Fakultät, Neuroinformatik, Universität Bielefeld
Postfach 10 01 31, D-33501 Bielefeld
{claudia,helge}@techfak.uni-bielefeld.de

Abstract. In this paper, we present GREFIT (Gesture REcognition based on FInger Tips) which is able to extract the 3-dimensional hand posture from video images of the human hand. GREFIT uses a two-stage approach to solve this problem.

This paper is based on earlier presented results of a system to locate the 2-D positions of the fingertips in images. We now describe the second stage, where the 2-D position information is transformed by an artificial neural net into an estimate of the 3-D configuration of an articulated hand model, which is also used for visualization. This model is designed according to the dimensions and movement possibilities of a natural human hand.

The virtual hand imitates the user's hand to an astonishing accuracy and can track postures from grey scale images at a speed of 10 Hz.

1   Introduction

Our hands are perhaps our most important "interface" to the physical world. Therefore, enabling computers to visually observe our hand movements and postures opens up many important new possibilities for better and more intuitive human-computer-communication.

Instead of the numerous classification systems, where a limited number of static hand postures suffices to represent a symbol, we focus on the identification of *continuous* hand postures. This offers more extensive possibilities for human-computer communication since it makes a differentiation between infinitely many, slightly different hand postures possible. Knowledge of the exact hand pose opens application areas, where gradual information is needed, for instance CAD or navigating in virtual worlds. Lately, the motion animation of virtual characters has become very popular. Here, gesture recognition is also very advantageous.

To achieve this goal, we use a two-stage approach. The first stage is motivated by experiments with point-light displays by Poizner et al. [8]. They point out: "The movement of the fingertips, but not of any other pair of points, is

---

* This work has been supported by the Ministry of Science and Research of North Rhine-Westphalia under the grant number IV A3-107 031 96 in the framework of the project called "The Virtual Knowledge Factory".

A. Braffort et al. (Eds.): GW'99, LNAI 1739, pp. 61–72, 1999.

necessary for sign identification. [...] In general, the more distal the joint, the more information its movement carries."

This motivated much of our previous work on the detection of fingertips of unadorned hands (see [7]) using computer vision methods and neural networks. GREFIT (Gesture REcognition based on FInger Tips) uses this as its first processing stage and adds a second stage for inferring 3-D hand posture from the 2-D fingertip positions. It employs a virtual hand model together with a particular type of fast learning artificial neural net described in the present paper.

The hand model used in GREFIT is by far simpler than those used in animation, e. g. [6]. It does not include such sophisticated aspects of modeling a virtual hand as, for instance, its body tissue.

The plan of the paper is as follows: Section 2 gives an overview of related work. In Section 3, we briefly review former work on which GREFIT is based. We describe the virtual hand model in Section 4 and introduce the employed neural networks and their application in Section 5. The following section concerns the results. In Section 7, we conclude the paper with a discussion and an outlook.

2   Related Work

Previous work on reconstructing hand posture out of characteristic landmarks on the hand includes [1, 9, 4, 5]. In [1], the user wears a glove with color-coded markers on joints and fingertips in order to facilitate feature recognition. Dorner and Hagen's skeleton-like 3-D model of the hand contains joints (their location and range of possible motion) and a mathematical representation of joint-angle interdependencies that are determined by the hand's physiology. They use a 3-step iterative scheme to fit their model to the image data in order to recover the pose of the hand. In addition, a time component remembers the motion of the hand model during the previous image frames.

The hand model of DigitEyes [9] consists of 16 cylinders forming the fingers and the palm. It is modeled as a kinematic tree, which is widely used in robotics. The kinematics and geometry of the target hand must be known in advance. DigitEyes uses a set of 27 hand's degrees of freedom (DOF). Starting with the hand in a known initial configuration, a state estimation algorithm first predicts feature positions in the next frame. Afterwards the difference between measured and predicted states is minimized. A high image sampling rate is essential for this tracking algorithm.

Lee and Kunii [4] present a hand model which is based on natural movement constraints of a human hand. With the help of color-coded gloves and stereo vision, seven "characteristic points" in 3-D (all five fingertips, the wrist, and an extra point on the palm) were extracted. An iterative algorithm using external "image forces" then fits their model to the hand image. Due to the time-consuming solving of the inverse kinematics of the fingers, the algorithm is very slow.

Millar and Crawford [5] employ a geometric model of the human hand which fulfills both the physical form and the kinematic constraints of the fingers. An analysis algorithm fits this model to six 3-dimensional marker positions at the fingertips and the center of the wrist. Since the fitting of the model is done directly, the computation is fast. The algorithm requires an initial standardization of the hand data into a predefined position and orientation. It generates a skeletal model of the hand using points and lines as its output.

3   Fundamentals of GREFIT

GREFIT is based on a computer vision system for the detection of fingertips in grey scale images and is described in detail in [7]. After preprocessing, Gabor-Filters perform a low-dimensional encoding of the images. A hierarchical approach with neural networks ensures that interesting parts of the image – the fingertips – get focal attention at successive stages of increasing spatial resolution. Good results (see Fig. 1) are achieved even if the fingertips are in front of the palm where the contrast is low.

A few details have been improved in GREFIT. It now utilizes a sequence of only two neural networks for each finger. Furthermore, we were able to drastically decrease the size of the feature vector, and with it the size of the neural networks, without affecting the good results. This had also a positive effect on the computation time. The frame rate for finding the location of the fingertips was increased from 2 fps to 11 fps on a Pentium Pro (200 MHz).

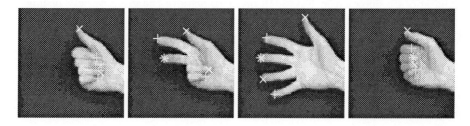

Fig. 1. Performance of the sequence of neural networks for some hand postures (upper cross = thumb; upper plus = index finger; star = middle finger; lower cross = ring finger; lower plus = small finger).

4   Structure of the Hand Model

For the visualization of the hand posture, we generated a virtual model of the hand. It emulates the shape and incorporates constraints based on the natural movement of the human hand. With the hand model *any* hand postures can be imitated which is essential for the output of GREFIT.

The basic module for the rendering of the hand model consists of two cylindrical parts joined by a third, prismatic piece, see Fig. 2. Radii, lengths and widths of the parts can be chosen freely.

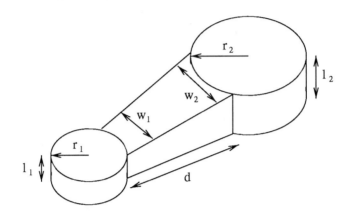

Fig. 2. Basic module for rendering

Our hand model is composed of 16 rigid elements, one for the palm and three segments for each finger and the thumb.

The sizes of the segments have been taken from a medium sized human hand and are depicted in Fig. 3. In order to achieve the great variety of finger movements, we provide four degrees of freedom (DOF) for each finger and the thumb (see Fig. 3).

The fingers and the thumb have two DOF at the anchoring joint (or the Metacarpophalangeal joint, MP) allowing flexion with an angle θ_1 as well as abduction and adduction movement expressed by θ_0. The proximal interphalangeal (PIP) and the distal interphalangeal (DIP) joint have one DOF each. The angles θ_2 and θ_3 represent their degree of flexion. Altogether, our hand model has 20 degrees of freedom.

Indeed, not all of these joint angles of a human hand are capable of independent actuation, but are correlated (see [2]). An example are the last two joints of the fingers, i. e. the PIP and DIP, which are driven by the same tendon. Approximately, their relation is

$$\theta_3 = \frac{2}{3}\theta_2.$$

Another simplification is to equate the joint angles θ_2 and θ_1 that determine the flexion of the fingers:

$$\theta_2 = \theta_1.$$

With these constraints, a 10-dimensional state vector represents the hand posture. Only these simplifying assumptions allow to reconstruct the 3-dimensional hand posture out of 2-dimensional position data.

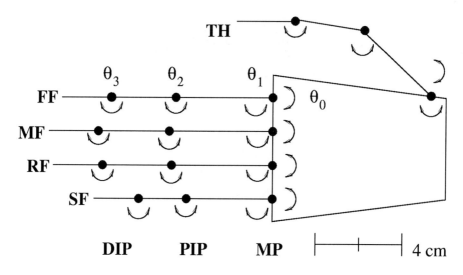

Fig. 3. Structure of the hand model, and naming of joints. See text for abbreviations.

We did also include the convergence of the fingers when the fist is clenched (see [2]): The axes of the fingers are not perpendicular to the finger segments, but are slightly oblique. As a consequence, the fingers are closely side by side at complete flexion.

Even though the allowable ranges of finger joint angles vary from person to person, general ranges as in Tab. 1 can be specified. Here, we only consider the active movements of the joints. These are activated by the tendons and muscles of the hand, whereas the passive movement is externally forced. The zero position of the thumb is defined as the state where no thumb muscles are active. The fingers are stretched when in zero position, their axes are parallel. Figure 4 depicts the shape of the virtual hand with all joints in zero position.

Table 1. Allowable ranges of joint angles of the finger and thumb. (after [2]).

	θ_0^{min}	θ_0^{max}	θ_1^{min}	θ_1^{max}
Thumb (TH)	-30	20	-20	40
Fore finger (FF)	-5	25	0	90
Middle finger (MF)	-10	10	0	90
Ring finger (RF)	-15	5	0	95
Small finger (SF)	-20	5	0	100

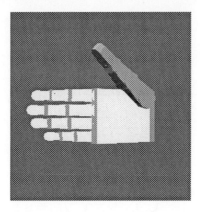

Fig. 4. Model of the hand, all joints are in zero position.

5   Recognition of the 3-D Hand Posture

5.1   PSOM

We employ a PSOM (Parametrized Self-Organizing Map) [10] to compute the appropriate finger joint angles from the 2-dimensional position of the fingertip in the image.

The PSOM is an extension of the well-known SOM by Kohonen [3]. It uses a set of nonlinear basis manifolds to construct a mapping through a number of "topologically ordered" reference vectors. The advantage of the PSOM in comparison to the SOM is that much fewer reference vectors are needed for a good result. Also, learning is very fast.

The PSOM replaces the discrete lattice of a SOM by a continuous "mapping manifold" S. Therefore, a reference vector $\mathbf{w_a}$ is assigned to each grid point $\mathbf{a} \in \mathbf{A} \subset S$ (see Fig. 5). The reference vectors have to be topologically ordered, i. e. neighbors on the lattice are neighbors in the data space, too.

A basis function $H(\mathbf{a}, \mathbf{s})$ is also associated with each grid point $\mathbf{a} \in \mathbf{A}$. The basis functions realize a smooth interpolation of intermediate positions between the grid points. The manifold M in the embedding space X can then be described as the image of S under $\mathbf{w}(\cdot)$ where

$$\mathbf{w}(\mathbf{s}) = \sum_{\mathbf{a} \in \mathbf{A}} H(\mathbf{a}, \mathbf{s})\, \mathbf{w_a}. \qquad (1)$$

The basis functions have to meet two conditions. The first *orthonormality* condition

$$H(\mathbf{a}_i, \mathbf{a}_j) = \delta_{ij} \quad \forall \mathbf{a}_i, \mathbf{a}_j \in \mathbf{A} \qquad (2)$$

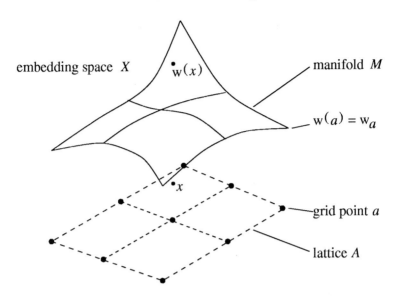

Fig. 5. Illustration of a training setup for a 3 × 3 PSOM.

ensures that the manifold M given by Eq. (1) passes through all desired support points $\mathbf{w_a}$, $\mathbf{a} \in \mathbf{A}$. Second, the sum of all contributing weights should be one:

$$\sum_{\mathbf{a} \in \mathbf{A}} H(\mathbf{a}, \mathbf{s}) = 1 \quad \forall \mathbf{s} \in \mathbf{S}. \tag{3}$$

During application, a point $\mathbf{x}$ in the data space X is mapped onto the nearest point $\mathbf{w}(\mathbf{s}^*) \in M$ with

$$\mathbf{s}^* = \min_{\mathbf{s}} \|\mathbf{x} - \mathbf{w}(\mathbf{s})\|. \tag{4}$$

This minimization is done using an iterative procedure: We start with the point $\mathbf{a}$ on the lattice $\mathbf{A}$ which has the smallest distance to $\mathbf{x}$, take the associated reference vector $\mathbf{w_a}$, and apply gradient descent along the manifold M to find the best approximation. The output $\mathbf{w}(\mathbf{s}^*)$ of the PSOM is then computed using Eq. (1). For details, see [11, 12].

The PSOM can be applied to map an input vector $\mathbf{x} \in X$ onto a map coordinate $\mathbf{s}$. Beside this mapping task, it is also able to perform an associative completion of fragmentary input. We took advantage of this ability and applied the PSOM to the inverse kinematics task.

5.2 Application of the PSOM

GREFIT employs the PSOM to complete partial data vectors. One PSOM for each finger is trained by providing the training data in topological order on a 3 × 3 grid. We split the 4-dimensional reference vector of joint angles and the resulting fingertip position into a 2-dimensional subset of input variables (the 2-D positions) and 2 remaining output variables (the joint angles). After training, the PSOM realizes the mapping from the 2-dimensional position of a fingertip in the image onto the joint angles of the respective finger.

In order to ensure the topological order of the training data, we varied the joint angles θ_0 and θ_1 on the 3×3 grid in their ranges of movement (see Tab. 1). Depicting the resulting fingertip positions yielded the shape of an "horizontal egg-timer" (see Fig. 6, left) with an intersection in the middle. This particular 2-D position can be achieved with many different joint angle combinations and represents a singular point of the kinematic transformation. Due to this ambiguity in the joint angles, the transformation between the 2-D position and the angles cannot be solved by the PSOM at this singularity.

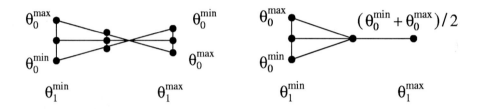

Fig. 6. Structure of the PSOM where θ_0 denotes variation in abduction/adduction, and θ_1 identifies variation in flexion. Left: Ambiguity in the joint angles at the intersection point. Right: Improved structure.

So far, our modeling of the ranges of motion was based on the assumption that the angles θ_0 and θ_1 of the fingers are *not* correlated. However, a closer look indicated that the abduction and adduction angle θ_0 decreases as the flexion angle θ_1 increases. In other words, the liberty of action in θ_0 can only be fully exploited when the fingers are roughly stretched.

Since the grid structure had to be preserved for the application of the PSOM, we merged those grid points with large values in the flexion angle. The range of movement of the fingers is now limited to a "broom"-shaped area (see Fig. 6, right). As this changed structure has no singularity, the PSOMs perform well. The internal 3×3 structure of the PSOM was maintained, but we provide only 5 different reference vectors during training instead of 9.

The thumb is the exception to this rule. Since no singularities occur for its range of movement, the training of the PSOM is based upon the original 3×3 grid. The resulting ranges of motion for all 4 fingers and the thumb are illustrated in Fig. 7.

In addition, we inactivated the ability of the PSOM to extrapolate, i. e. to infer values outside of the movement area. This ensures that the fingers do not take on "unhealthy" values for the joint angles. This constraint equips the PSOM with implicit model information, anatomically injurious postures can not occur.

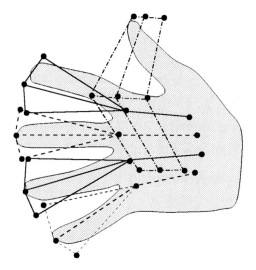

Fig. 7. Movement areas of the fingers and the thumb.

We tested the PSOMs on a set of 100 at random chosen fingertip positions for each finger. The fingertip positions for the resulting joint angles were computed and compared with the given data. The average distance between correct fingertip position and the calculated position is below 1 cm for the fingers and even less than 0.5 cm for the thumb (hand length 19 cm).

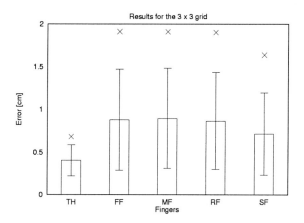

Fig. 8. Performance of the PSOMs. Depicted is the average error (box), variance (error bars) and maximum error (cross mark) in the fingertip positions.

6   Results

Figure 9 illustrates the result of GREFIT for a few sample images of the hand. The original hand posture and the reconstruction match very closely, but can only be compared visually. An exact, quantitative analysis would require a measurement with a DataGlove in order to compare the achieved values of the joint angles. This evaluation will be subject of future investigation.

7   Discussion and Outlook

The presented GREFIT system is able to compute the joint angles and to reconstruct the 3-dimensional hand posture from grey scale images of an unadorned human hand fast and reliably.

The improved structure of the PSOM (see Fig. 6, left) turned out to be also advantageous in the visualization. If the results of the neural networks were imprecise, these small errors were propagated by the PSOMs and effected a slight "trembling" of the fingers of the hand model although there was no visible movement of the natural hand in front of the camera. This was visually tiring for the user. When switching to the improved structure, these effects could be significantly reduced.

Up to now, the reconstruction of the hand posture is based only on the 2-D position of the fingertips, and we had to restrict the DOFs in order to assure an unambiguous setting of the joint angles. Therefore, GREFIT can not distinguish differences in depth, where the hand posture changes, but the 2-D position of the fingertips does not. Future research will target the extension to stereo images. We plan to take and process images with two cameras and allowing us to extract the 3-dimensional position of the fingertips. Using a PSOM with a 3-dimensional grid would then allow to obtain 3 uncorrelated angles for each finger, which will yield an even better resemblance with the human original.

In our recent hand model, every finger can be moved independently of the others. This is not possible in the natural human hand for two reasons: First, two fingers cannot be at exactly the same position at the same time, but would collide. Although collision control is not included in our current model, penetrating happens rarely. Second, we did not incorporate the constraints on flexion of adjacent fingers. A finger's extension is hindered by the flexion of neighboring fingers and vice versa. This will be included in a future hand model.

In contrast to the four fingers, the thumb has 5 DOF. The proximal interphalangeal joint (PIP) can also perform a slight sidewards movement which was neglected in our current model. We also assumed that the palm is a rigid body, but in reality, it can flex, for instance when gripping a tennis ball. The effect of this is a changing position of the anchor points of the fingers. These latter two constraints were ignored yet since they have a minor effect on the hand posture, but will probably be considered as further improvements.

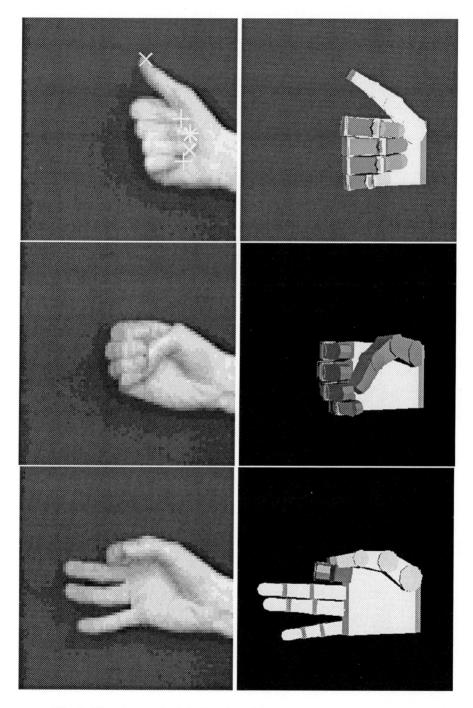

Fig. 9. Visual control of the hand model using natural hand postures.

References

1. B. Dorner and E. Hagen. Towards an American Sign Language interface. *Artificial Intelligence Review*, 8:235–253, 1994.
2. I.A. Kapandji. *Funktionelle Anatomie der Gelenke*, volume 1 of *Obere Extremität*. Enke Verlag Stuttgart, 1984.
3. T. Kohonen. The self-organizing map. In *Proc. IEEE 78*, pages 1464–1480, 1990.
4. J. Lee and T.L. Kunii. Model-based analysis of hand posture. *IEEE Computer Graphics and Applications*, 15(5):77–86, 1995.
5. R.J. Millar and G.F. Crawford. A mathematical model for hand-shape analysis. In P.A. Harling and A.D.N. Edwards, editors, *Progress in Gestural Interaction - Proceedings of Gesture Workshop'96*, pages 235–245. Springer, 1996.
6. L. Moccozet. *Hand Modeling and Animation for Virtual Humans*. PhD thesis, University of Geneva, 1996.
7. C. Nölker and H. Ritter. Detection of fingertips in human hand movement sequences. In I. Wachsmuth and M. Fröhlich, editors, *Gesture and Sign Language in Human-Computer Interaction, Proceedings of the International Gesture Workshop 1997*, pages 209–218. Springer, 1998.
8. H. Poizner, U. Bellugi, and V. Lutes-Driscoll. Perception of American Sign Language in dynamic point-light displays. *Journal of Experimental Psychology: Human Performance and Perception*, 7(2):432–440, 1981.
9. J.M. Rehg and T. Kanade. Visual tracking of high DOF articulated structures: an application to human hand tracking. In J.-O. Eklundh, editor, *Computer Vision – ECCV'94*, pages 35–46, Berlin Heidelberg, 1994. Springer Verlag. Lecture Notes in Computer Science 801.
10. H. Ritter. Parametrized self-organizing maps. *Artificial Neural Networks*, 3, 1993.
11. J. Walter. *Rapid learning in Robotics*. Cuvillier Verlag Göttingen, 1996.
12. J. Walter and H. Ritter. Rapid learning with parametrized self-organizing maps. *Neurocomputing*, 12:131–153, 1996.

Towards Imitation Learning of Grasping Movements by an Autonomous Robot

Jochen Triesch[1], Jan Wieghardt[2], Eric Maël[2], and
Christoph von der Malsburg[2,3]

[1] Department of Computer Science
University of Rochester, Rochester (NY), USA
triesch@cs.rochester.edu
[2] Institut für Neuroinformatik, Ruhr-Universität Bochum
D-44780 Bochum, Germany
{wieghardt,mael,malsburg}@neuroinformatik.ruhr-uni-bochum.de
[3] Lab. for Computational and Biological Vision
University of Southern California, Los Angeles (CA), USA

Abstract. Imitation learning holds the promise of robots which need not be programmed but instead can learn by observing a teacher. We present recent efforts being made at our laboratory towards endowing a robot with the capability of learning to imitate human hand gestures. In particular, we are interested in grasping movements. The aim is a robot that learns, e.g., to pick up a cup at its handle by imitating a human teacher grasping it like this. Our main emphasis is on the computer vision techniques for finding and tracking the human teacher's grasping fingertips. We present first experiments and discuss limitations of the approach and planned extensions.

1 Introduction

Imitation learning has received much attention recently, since researchers share the hope that it can reduce the amount of programming or teach-in required for useful robot behavior and replace it with efficient learning. BAKKER & KU-NIYOSHI define imitation as follows: "Imitation takes place when an agent learns a behavior from observing the execution of that behavior by a teacher." [1]. During classical teach-in a human operator has to teach the robot the desired arm tracectories by explicitly moving all the robot's joints in desired positions along the trajectory – a very cumbersome process. Obviously, it would be far more efficient, if the robot simply learned by following the example of a human doing the task. Imitation learning is thought to be more efficient than, e.g., reinforcement learning because the robot is provided with very rich information about the solution of the problem. While in reinforcement learning the robot typically needs hundreds of trials before behaving usefully, imitation promises one-shot learning for even difficult tasks. A problem of imitation learning is that it requires complex perceptual abilities which allow the robot to "observe" the

A. Braffort et al. (Eds.): GW'99, LNAI 1739, pp. 73–84, 1999.

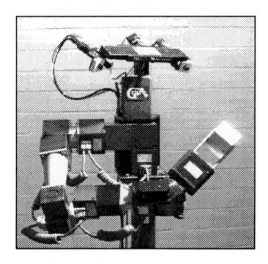

Fig. 1. The robot at the Bochum laboratory has a kinematically redundant arm and a stereo camera head with three degrees of freedom

teacher and "understand" the rich information provided to it. We see this *perceptual bottleneck* as the main reason for the negligible use of imitation in today's industrial robots.

In this paper we describe recent work towards endowing a robot with the perceptual skills necessary to imitate human grasping gestures. The robot shall learn how to pick up a particular object (e.g., grasp a cup at its handle) by imitating a human teacher. Furthermore, the learned grip shall be generalized to new situations, where the object is in a different position and orientation.

Although our motivation is the interpretation and imitation of grasping movements, the computer vision techniques described below have a wider range of applicability. The finding and tracking of hands and fingertips is a prerequisite for many applications in human computer or human robot interaction, such as gesture recognition, animation of avatars in cyber space, or teleoperation of robotic manipulators with gestures.

In the following we give an overview of our current system for imitating grasping movements (Sect. 2). We then describe in detail the computer vision techniques used for observing the grasping movement (Sect. 3) and present first experiments (Sect. 4). Section 5 gives a discussion and an outlook.

2   A Way of Imitating Grasping Movements

The robot at the Bochum laboratory [2] has a kinematically redundant arm with seven degrees of freedom, which allows it to grasp an object from various directions (Fig. 1). A stereo camera head with three degrees of freedom is mounted on top of the arm allowing for pan, tilt, and vergence motion. The cameras yield

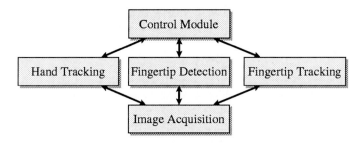

Fig. 2. Overview of the modules involved in the observation of grasping movements

images of 768×572 pixels ($\sim 35°$ horizontal field of view). We assume a proper calibration of the stereo camera system. The robot stands in front of a table with objects on it. Since the robot's gripper consists only of two jaws we consider only precision grips performed with two fingers and exclude power grips.

According to BAKKER & KUNIYOSHI any imitation task can be subdivided into three stages [1]: *Observation, Representation* and *Reproduction.* In our approach these stages are handled in the following manner:

Observation: The robot observes a teacher grasping the object in a particular manner. The observation of the grasping movement involves several *skills* orchestrated by a control module (Fig. 2). The robot searches the scene for a human hand, using the real-time *hand tracking* scheme presented in [12]. The teacher is required to hold his hand close to the object in a standard shape with thumb and index finger pointing downwards. The *hand tracking* detects the stopping of the hand and the *fingertip detection* localizes the position of thumb and index finger. The *fingertip tracking* follows the motion of the fingertips during the teacher's subsequent grasping movement. Eventually, the teacher lifts the object, indicating the end of the grasping movement, which is detected by the fingertip tracking.

Representation: The fingertip tracking yields an estimate of the 3d trajectories of the grasping fingertips. From this data we compute a linear trajectory of the robot's gripper matching the last ten centimeters of the teacher's trajectory before the object was lifted. As the fingertips' orientations are unknown, an undetermined degree of freedom results, which is specified by requiring the gripper's jaws to point into the direction of the movement.

Reproduction: For imitation of the grasping movement the robot opens its gripper, moves it along the estimated trajectory, and closes it.

In the future we inted to construct an object-centered representation of the grip, which stores the grasping position and direction relative to an object-centered coordinate system. This will allow the robot to generalize the learned grip to new situations, where the object is in a different place. The required object recognition technology is readily available at our laboratory [2]. In the following, we will focus on the techniques for observing the human teacher's grasping movements.

3 Observation of Grasping Movements

3.1 Hand Tracking

The hand tracking system has been described elsewhere [12]. It employs motion detection, skin color analysis and a stereo cue and allows for robust detection and tracking of the teacher's hand. It also shows a certain robustness with respect to other hands moving in the background of the scene which are ignored. The hand tracking serves as an attenional mechanism, selecting a region of interest for more detailed analysis.

3.2 Fingertip Detection

Following hand tracking, a 256^2 pixel image is selected around the estimate of the hand position. The image is downsampled by a factor of two in order to save computation time. In the downsampled images, fingers typically are between 12 and 18 pixels wide. For detecting fingertips in this kind of image, we try to match a fingertip template to the image and search for local maxima. The fingertip template is a composite of two different local image descriptions based on a wavelet transform. The first local image description is a GABOR *jet*, a vector of responses to convolutions of the intensity component of the images with GABOR kernels of three different sizes and eight different orientations. The complex kernels are given by [7]:

$$\psi_{\mathbf{k}}\left(\mathbf{x}\right) = \frac{\mathbf{k}^2}{\sigma^2} \exp\left(-\frac{\mathbf{k}^2\mathbf{x}^2}{2\sigma^2}\right) \left[\exp\left(i\mathbf{k}\mathbf{x}\right) - \exp\left(\frac{-\sigma^2}{2}\right)\right]. \tag{1}$$

The filters are DC-free due to the term $-\exp(-\sigma^2/2)$, and hence their responses are invariant with respect to constant offsets in the grey-level values of an image. The factor $\mathbf{k}^2$ compensates for the observed power spectrum in natural images. The responses of several such filters with different size and orientation, parameterized by the wave-vector $\mathbf{k}$, form a *jet* [7]:

$$\mathbf{k}_{\nu\mu} = k_\nu \begin{pmatrix} \cos\phi_\mu \\ \sin\phi_\mu \end{pmatrix} \quad \text{with} \quad k_\nu = k_{\max}/f^\nu, \ \phi_\mu = \frac{\mu\pi}{D}. \tag{2}$$

We use $\nu \in \{0,\ldots,L-1\}$ and $\mu \in \{0,\ldots,D-1\}$, where $L = 3$ is the number of levels and $D = 8$ is the number of orientations used. In the following we write a single index j as a shorthand for the double index $\nu\mu$. The value $f = 1/\sqrt{2}$ is the spacing factor between kernels in the frequency domain. We use $k_{\max} = \pi/8$. The width of the GAUSSIAN envelope function is given by $\sigma/|\mathbf{k}|$ with $\sigma = \pi$. A jet is a complex vector composed of the $L \times D$ complex filter responses c_j, which are represented as absolute value a_j and phase ϕ_j according to $c_j = a_j e^{i\phi_j}$.

The filters respond strongly to edge and bar-like structures, whose dimensions cover those typically produced by the teacher's grasping fingers. The similarity between two GABOR jets can be computed with two similarity functions [13].

The first uses only the absolute values a_j of the complex filter responses, thereby disregarding their phases:

$$S_{\text{abs}}(J, J') = \frac{\sum_j a_j a'_j}{\sqrt{\sum_j a_j^2 \sum_j a'_j{}^2}} \ . \tag{3}$$

The second similarity function takes the filter responses' phases into account:

$$S_{\text{pha}}(J, J') = \frac{1}{2} \left(1 + \frac{\sum_j a_j a'_j \cos(\phi_j - \phi'_j)}{\sqrt{\sum_j a_j^2 \sum_j a'_j{}^2}} \right) \ . \tag{4}$$

The difference between the similarity functions is best illustrated when a jet extracted at a location $\mathbf{x}$ in an image is compared to a jet extracted at close by position $\mathbf{x}'$. S_{abs} will slowly decrease when $\mathbf{x}'$ is moved farther away from $\mathbf{x}$. S_{pha}, however, will show oscillations, whose frequency is related to the wave vectors $\mathbf{k}$ of the used kernels.

For the GABOR jets extracted from the intensity component of the image we use S_{abs}. The advantage of disregarding the phases is that the grasping fingertips may sometimes appear against background lighter than themselves and sometimes against a darker one. An inversion of the image, however, only influences the phases of the filter responses. Discarding them in the similarity function makes it invariant with respect to this kind of inversion.

The second local image description is a *color* GABOR *jet*, which is identical to a GABOR jet but the convolutions are performed on an "image" which shows each pixel's similarity to skin color. Color is represented in the hue, saturation, intensity (HSI) color model [6]; similarity to skin color is defined by the distance to a prototypical point in the H-S plane. For the color GABOR jets similarities are computed with S_{pha}, taking the phases ϕ_j into account. The color GABOR jets respond strongly to edge and bar-like structures in the skin color segmentation. As the fingertips are assumed to be at least as close to skin-color as the background, we do not want to discard the phases of the filter responses in the similarity function.

The two local image descriptions are combined by concatenating them into a longer vector, which we call a *compound jet* [11] (Fig. 3). The similarity between two compound jets $\mathcal{J}$ and $\mathcal{J}'$ is defined as a weighted sum of the similarities between the corresponding components:

$$\hat{S}(\mathcal{J}, \mathcal{J}') = \sum_{\mathcal{F}} w_{\mathcal{F}} \, S_{\mathcal{F}}(\mathcal{J}_{\mathcal{F}}, \mathcal{J}'_{\mathcal{F}}) \ , \tag{5}$$

where $S_{\mathcal{F}}$ is the similarity between two GABOR jets or two colorGABOR jets, respectively. The weights $w_{\mathcal{F}}$ were chosen as $1/2$ in the following experiments. The advantage of using compound jets rather than relying on a single image description is an increase in robustness, which has already been demonstrated for two object recognition tasks [11].

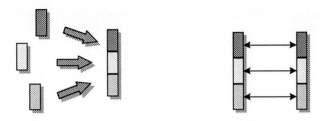

Fig. 3. Concatenation of several local image descriptions yields a *compound jet* (left). Compound jets are compared by computing a weighted sum of the corresponding components' similarities (right)

We form a template of a fingertip by averaging 18 compound jets extracted at fingertip positions in training images of three persons. For a new input image, we compute compound jets at every pixel location. Then, the fingertip template is moved across the image and compared to the compound jets in the image in order to find fingertip candidates. The positions of the two highest local maxima are interpreted as the locations of the grasping fingertips. Determination of the correspondence between the fingertips, i.e., which fingertip in the left image corresponds to which fingertip in the right image, is handeled by a simple heuristic requiring that the vector connecting the two fingertips in the left image has a similar direction to the one which connects the fingertips in the right image.

First tests have shown that the above method lacks robustness when the background contains skin-colored structures, which are sometimes erroneously recognized as fingertips. In order to alleviate the problem we introduced a scheme for palm localization and some *ad hoc* geometric constraints to the fingertip localization. We found that the palm or back of the hand can be located by looking for the biggest skin-colored blob in the image with a technique comparable to the color cue of the tracking component [12]. We now require a candidate fingertip to point away ($\pm 60°$) from the palm/back of the hand thus ruling out certain image regions. This alleviates the above-mentioned problems somewhat but does not solve them completely. An example of successful fingertip localization is given in Fig. 5.

3.3   Fingertip Tracking

Fingertip tracking is also based on the GABOR jets. Given a jet J taken at a location $\mathbf{x}$ at time t and a jet J' taken at the same or a close-by location $\mathbf{x}'$ at time $t+1$ allows for the estimation of a displacement vector $\mathbf{d}$ of the first jet. To this end, the following similarity function is applied [5, 10]:

$$S_{\mathrm{disp}}(J, J', \mathbf{d}) = \frac{\sum_j a_j a'_j \cos(\phi_j - \phi'_j - \mathbf{dk}_j)}{\sqrt{\sum_j a_j^2 \sum_j a'_j{}^2}} . \tag{6}$$

It is similar to (4) but the cosine term is "corrected" by the scalar product of the displacement vector $\mathbf{d}$ and the wave vector $\mathbf{k}_j$ of the kernel. Now the similarity is maximized with respect to $\mathbf{d}$ by expanding the cosine into a Taylor series, computing the derivative with respect to $\mathbf{d}$, and solving the resulting system of linear equations. Details on this can be found in [13]:

$$S_{\text{disp}}(J, J', \mathbf{d}) \approx \frac{\sum_j a_j a'_j \left(1 - 1/2 \left(\phi_j - \phi'_j - \mathbf{d} k_j\right)^2\right)}{\sqrt{\sum_j a_j^2 \sum_j a'^2_j}}. \tag{7}$$

This gives an estimate of $\mathbf{d}$ with subpixel accuracy. The method has already been successfully applied to tracking faces in image sequences [8]. We have extended this method for compound jets in the following manner. As a similarity function for comparing two compound jets $\mathcal{J}$ and $\mathcal{J}'$ we use:

$$\hat{S}_{\text{disp}}(\mathcal{J}, \mathcal{J}', \mathbf{d}) = \frac{\sum_{\mathcal{F}} w_{\mathcal{F}} \sum_j a_{j\mathcal{F}} a'_{j\mathcal{F}} \cos(\phi_{j\mathcal{F}} - \phi'_{j\mathcal{F}} - \mathbf{d} k_{j\mathcal{F}})}{\sqrt{\sum_{\mathcal{F}} w_{\mathcal{F}} \sum_j a_{j\mathcal{F}}^2} \sqrt{\sum_{\mathcal{F}} w_{\mathcal{F}} \sum_j a'^2_{j\mathcal{F}}}}. \tag{8}$$

This is analogous to (6), but now we also sum over the different feature types indexed by $\mathcal{F}$. Equation (8) is also expanded into a Taylor series and $\mathbf{d}$ is estimated as described above.

The fingertip tracking employs compound jets with four components. These are GABOR jets extracted from the intensity (I) component and the hue (H) component of an image, and GABOR jets extracted on the differences of the intensity (ΔI) and hue (ΔH) components of consecutive images. The parameters of the GABOR transformation are $L = 5$, $D = 8$, $f = 1/\sqrt{2}$, $k_{\max} = \pi/2$, and $\sigma = 2\pi$. The weightings are chosen as $w_I = w_H = 1/6$ and $w_{\Delta I} = w_{\Delta H} = 2/6$.

The tracking works by an iterative method of guessing a new position $\mathbf{x}$ for a fingertip from its previous movement and refining it by estimating a displacement $\mathbf{d}$ with $\hat{S}_{\text{disp}}$ (Fig. 4). The fingertips of thumb and index finger in left and right camera image are tracked independently, i.e., no geometric constraints are applied. The fingertips are required to be clearly visible until the object is actually grasped. An example of successful fingertip tracking is given in Fig. 5.

4   Experiments

Spatial Accuracy in the case of Uniform Background. In a first experiment we tested the spatial accuracy of the vision components for uniform background. An object was placed on the table and we defined a grasp point for the object, where the fingertips should be placed during grasping. We measured the grasp point's distance from the robot (x-direction) and its height above the table (z-direction) to an accuracy of 0.5 cm. Due to the stereo geometry and the robot's typical gaze direction the third direction (y-direction) is estimated with about twice the precision of the other directions. The robot observes the teacher's grasping movement and calculates the starting and end points of the linear grasping trajectory. Ideally, the calculated end point would be identical to the grasp point. The results are given in Tab. 1. Errors are of the order of 1–2 cm. The estimated distance and height are usually too small, suggesting a source of systematic error possibly related to the camera head calibration.

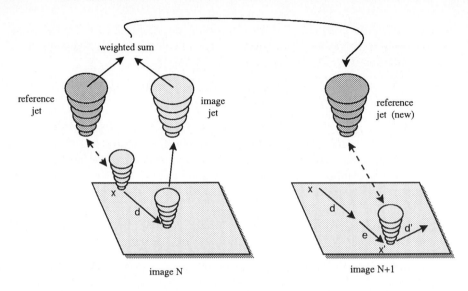

Fig. 4. Tracking of a single jet. An image jet extracted at location $\mathbf{x}$ of image N is compared to a reference jet (dashed arrow). The comparison gives a displacement estimate $\mathbf{d}$; the estimated position is given by $\mathbf{x} + \mathbf{d}$. The reference jet is updated by computing a weighted average of the old reference jet and a jet extracted at $\mathbf{x} + \mathbf{d}$. For the position in the next image $(N + 1)$, we compute a first guess for the postion according to $\mathbf{x}' = \mathbf{x} + \mathbf{d} + \mathbf{e} = \mathbf{x} + \mathbf{d} + 0.5\mathbf{d}$. The new reference jet is compared to the jet extracted at position $\mathbf{x}'$ in image $N + 1$, giving a new displacement $\mathbf{d}'$

Table 1. Precision of grip imitation

grips from right			grips from above		
distance in cm	height in cm	#trials	distance in cm	height in cm	#trials
-1 ± 1.2	-0.8 ± 1.2	10	-1.6 ± 2.0	-0.16 ± 1.5	9

Imitation of Grasping Movements. In a second experiment we also let the robot perform the grasping movement. Only uniform backgrounds were used. The results are summarized in Tab. 2. We just noted whether the gripper was satisfactorily enclosing the object in the right place. The only error occured during a mistake of the inital hand tracking, which is sometimes fooled by persons wearing short sleeves. These experiments are to be seen merely as a first test demonstrating the feasibility of the approach. More systematic experiments are required, especially for evaluating the system in the presence of complex backgrounds. During first tests (Fig. 6) we noted that the fingertip finding and tracking are less stable than for uniform background. Apparently, errors accumlate when the background shows a lot of structure, especially if there are many skin-colored parts.

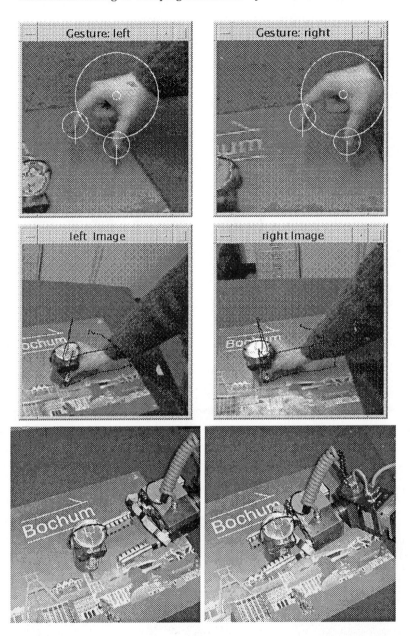

Fig. 5. Example of successful imitation. **Top:** Initial finding of fingertips in left and right camera image: The large circle marks the estimated postition of the hand. The small circles show the estimated fingertip positions. **Center:** Tracking of fingertips during the sequence: The estimated trajectories of the fingertips are shown superimposed on the last image of the sequence. The linear trajectory before the actual grasping and the lifting and placing of the object are visible. **Bottom:** Trajectory of the robot's gripper. The robot is programmed to move the tip of its gripper 5 cm farther than the computed grasp position in order to make sure the object is between the jaws

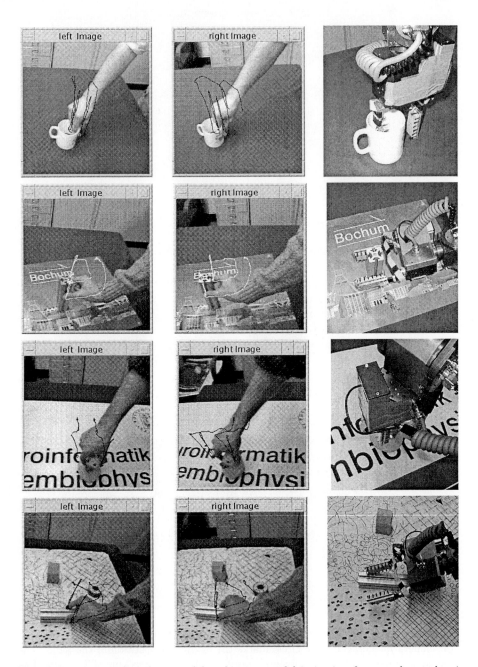

Fig. 6. Some examples of successful and unsuccessful imitation for complex and uniform background: **Left and Center column:** Result of the fingertip tracking superimposed on the last image of the sequence. **Right column:** Imitation of the grip by the robot

Table 2. Successes in grip imitation

object	grip from right	grip from above
white cup	success	success
gray box	success	initial hand tracking failed
tesa box	success	success
light bulb	success	success

5   Discussion and Outlook

We have presented first steps towards endowing a robot with the skill to imitate human grasping movements. Our emphasis was on the computer vision techniques for observing human grasping movements with high precision. This involved tracking the teacher's hand and finding and tracking the fingertips. There has been a huge number of publications on gesture recognition and a number of them are directly tackling the problem of localizing fingertips [4, 3, 9], but these authors only consider a uniform background to the hand — a restriction which clearly cannot be made for the imitation of grasping movements. In our approach we try to cope with complex backgrounds by combining several different cues. For the hand tracking, motion detection, color analysis, and a stereo cue are used. For the fingertip localization and tracking, we have employed the concept of compound jets, combinations of complementary local image descriptions based on wavelet transforms. Although our first experiments seem promising, they also demonstrate current limitations and suggest directions for future work: The initial localization and tracking of the fingertips becomes unreliable when the background shows much structure (especially if parts of the background show skin-color). To overcome these limitations, we are currently trying to use Elastic Graph Matching (EGM) for an initial analysis of the hand's posture [12], instead of relying on a sinlge compound jets as a fingertip template. With EGM we initially localize about a dozen fiducial points of the hand. For the tracking of these points we intend to apply geometric constraints, which make the tracking more robust in the presence of structured background or partial occlusion. Another line of current research is the incorporation of tactile sensors, which detect where the gripper makes contact with the object. This information shall help the robot to compensate for the visual inaccuracies. In order to compensate for errors in the robot's camera head calibration, visual servoing techniques should be considered.

In conclusion, imitation is a very promising approach to robot learning, but the perceptual requirements are very demanding. We find that gestures are an interesting testbed for studying imitation since they open a new direction for human-robot interaction.

Acknowledgments

The authors would like to express their gratitude to the members of the NEUROS project at the Institut für Neuroinformatik, Bochum, for providing the fundamentals on which this work is based: M. Becker, T. Bergener, C. Bruckhoff, P. Dahm, H. Janßen, E. Kefalea, A. Mechrouki, R. Menzner, M. Pagel, J. C. Vorbrüggen, R. P. Würtz, S. Zadel.

This work was supported by grants from the DFG (GK KOGNET) and the German Federal Ministry for Science and Technology (01 IN 504 E9).

References

1. P. Bakker and Y. Kuniyoshi. Robot see, robot do : An overview of robot imitation. In *AISB'96 Workshop on Learning in Robots and Animals*, pages 3–11, 1996.
2. M. Becker, E. Kefalea, E. Maël, C. v.d. Malsburg, M. Pagel, J. Triesch, J. C. Vorbrüggen, R. P. Würtz, and S. Zadel. GripSee: A gesture-controlled robot for object perception and manipulation. *Autonomous Robots*, 6(2):203–221, 1999.
3. R. Cipolla and N. Hollinghurst. Visually guided grasping in unstructured environments. *Robotics and Autonomous Systems*, 19:337–346, 1997.
4. J. L. Crowley. Vision for man-machine interaction. *Robotics and Autonomous Systems*, 19:347–358, 1997.
5. D. J. Fleet and A. D. Jepson. Computation of component image velocity from local phase information. *Int. Journal of Computer Vision*, 5(1), 1990.
6. R. C. Gonzales and R. E. Woods. *Digital Image Processing*. Addison-Wesley, 1992.
7. M. Lades, J. C. Vorbrüggen, J. Buhmann, J. Lange, C. von der Malsburg, R. P. Würtz, and W. Konen. Distortion invariant object recognition in the dynamic link architecture. *IEEE Transactions on Computers*, 42:300–311, 1993.
8. T. Maurer and C. v.d. Malsburg. Tracking and learning graphs and pose on image sequences of faces. In *Proceedings of the Second International Conference on Automatic Face and Gesture Recognition 1996, Killington, Vermont, USA*, 1996.
9. C. Nölker and H. Ritter. Detection of fingertips in human hand movement sequences. In Ipke Wachsmuth and Martin Fröhlich, editors, *Gesture and Sign Language in Human-Computer Interaction*, Lecture Notes in Artificial Intelligence 1371. Springer, 1997.
10. W. M. Theimer and H. A. Mallot. Phase-based binocular vergence control and depth reconstruction using active vision. *CVGIP: Image Understanding*, 60(3), 1994.
11. J. Triesch and C. Eckes. Object recognition with multiple feature types. In *ICANN'98, Proceedings of the 8th International Conference on Artificial Neural Networks*, pages 233–238. Springer, 1998.
12. J. Triesch and C. v.d. Malsburg. Robotic gesture recognition. In Ipke Wachsmuth and Martin Fröhlich, editors, *Gesture and Sign Language in Human-Computer Interaction*, Lecture Notes in Artificial Intelligence 1371. Springer, 1997.
13. L. Wiskott. *Labeled Graphs and Dynamic Link Matching for Face Recognition and Scene Analysis*, volume 53 of *Reihe Physik*. Verlag Harri Deutsch, Thun, Frankfurt a. Main, 1995. PhD thesis.

A Line-Scan Computer Vision Algorithm for Identifying Human Body Features

Damian M. Lyons and Daniel L. Pelletier

Philips Research
345 Scarborough Road
Briarcliff Manor NY 10510
{damian.lyons,daniel.pelletier}@philips.com

Abstract. A computer vision algorithm for identifying human body features algorithm, called the nine-grid algorithm, is introduced in this paper. The algorithm identifies body features via a two level hierarchy. The lower level makes a series of measurements on the image from line-scan input. The upper level uses a set of heuristics to assign the measurements to body features. A ground truth study is presented, showing the performance of the algorithm for four classes of activity that we consider typical of in-home user interface applications of computer vision. The study showed that the algorithm correctly identified features to a close degree 77% of the time. Closer investigation of the results suggested refinements for the algorithm that would improve this score.

1 Introduction

Identifying and determining the location in space of the body features of a person viewed by a video camera is a useful prerequisite for a number of applications. These include gesture-recognition, security, video-conferencing and so-called infotainment applications. We have developed a computer vision system to act as part of the user-interface for an interactive advertising application, to be deployed in a public location such as a department store or movie theatre lobby [1]. This paper introduces the approach used in that vision system to identifying key features of the human body for input to a gesture recognition system. We call this approach the *Nine-Grid* algorithm. The paper also presents a ground truth evaluation of the approach.

The remainder of the paper is laid out as follows. Section 2 reviews the existing literature in this area and shows how our approach relates to this. Section 3 overviews the equipment used in the vision system and describes the low-level vision processing. Section 4 introduces our approach to human body feature identification, the nine-grid approach, in detail. Section 5 presents the ground-truth study performed to evaluate the approach, and Section 5.4 summarizes our conclusions.

A. Braffort et al. (Eds.): GW'99, LNAI 1739, pp. 85–96, 1999.

2   Background

The most straightforward approach to identifying the parts of the human body, once the human subject has been segmented out from the image as a single body region, is to start by considering the head to be the highest point in the region. Turk [2] "drapes" a 1D sheet (along the horizontal image axis) over the body region to generate a head and shoulders silhouette. Perseus [3] uses Visual Routines to track salient parts of the image. Its *find-body-parts* visual routine locates the head by finding the highest part of the body region roughly above the centroid. Kortenkamp et al. [4] use *proximity spaces* to track salient parts of the image. Connected proximity spaces can have constraining effects on each other's location. The first proximity space attaches itself to the body region and migrates upwards as far as it can go, thus identifying the head feature. The W4 tracker [5] uses a *Cardboard Model* of the human body to identify body parts. The model is initialized by assuming the height of the body region bounding box is the height of the cardboard model. Not all approaches find the head first. For example, Pfinder [6], a seminal piece of work in this area, "walks" around the contour of the body region and classifies protrusions as body features. (This information is then integrated with a skin color-based feature classification).

Kakadiaris and Metaxas [7] describe an algorithm to determine a comprehensive geometric body model from inspecting deformations of the body region over time. However, to handle real-time issues, most approaches assume a relatively simple body model.

The Cardboard Model used by W4 identifies the arm/hand regions based on the model constraints that they be extreme regions outside the torso and connected to it. Kortenkamp et al. link their proximity spaces to a simple kinematic model of the human head, shoulder and arm. The arm proximity spaces search along the movements allowed by the kinematic model to locate the arm/hand. Perseus identifies the hands as the left and right most extreme points in the body region.

Our objective in developing the nine-grid algorithm was to build a human body feature identification algorithm that operated from line-scan input. This constraint originated in our choice of computer vision equipment, a PC equipped with the PCI-based Philips Single Board Image Processor (SBIP) [8] card. The SBIP card delivers its output in run-code in line-scan order. Thus we could not use an algorithm which assumed we had the body region contour stored without paying a time penalty. In addition, since we were unable to use SBIP in a color configuration, the classification approach should rely only upon the body region contour information and not color.

A second objective was to ensure that the algorithm provided reliable hand and foot position estimates, since these were crucial to the user interface problem for the advertising application [1]. In particular, we wanted to ensure that hand positions over the head were not mistakenly classified as head positions, as can happen if the highest point in the body region is always classified as the head.

3   Equipment and Low-Level Processing

Before we describe the nine-grid algorithm, we present a description of the equipment and low-level vision processing which we used. The background subtraction and human recognition techniques used were quite straightforward though surprisingly robust in practice.

3.1   SBIP Image Pipeline

The equipment used consists of two video cameras connected to a PCI bus image processing board resident on a PC. At any point, the board is only inspecting one of the two cameras. The image processing board is the Philips Single Board Image Processor (SBIP) [8]. A software library is provided to configure and control the board [9]. The SBIP board was configured to produce an image pipeline which:

- digitized an image from the selected camera,
- subtracted a background frame (taken earlier of the empty space) from the image, and
- fed the difference image to a dynamic thresholding module (DTC) which generates a binary image by looking at local contrast.
- Finally, the image is fed to a run-code module, which transmits all the non-zero pixels in the image in run-code format to the host PC.

3.2   Silhouette Extraction

A list of regions in the image is constructed by inspecting the run-code data and grouping all line segments that lie within (dx, dy) of each other into the same regions. Area and bounding box information is calculated for each region. The region with the largest area is considered the *target region*. A human figure is recognized if the target region has area $a > a_H$ and bounding box ratio $by/bx > 1.1$.

4   The Nine-Grid Algorithm

The nine-grid approach uses a simple body model, a grid of nine cells distributed over the bounding box for the region, to identify potential feature locations. There are a number of assumptions built into the model:

- The target is a person.
- The person is mostly upright.
- The person is mostly facing the camera.
- No body feature is occluded in the silhouette.

The assumptions are reasonable for the application domains we work in: where computer vision is being used as part of the user interface. We can reasonably assume that the user's attention and body orientation will be directed

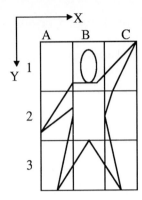

Fig. 1. The nine-grid body model

towards the camera. The assumptions are not valid for all domains, however; clearly they would not be true in a security application.

Based on these assumptions, and some coarse biometric knowledge of the human body [10], the typical human body can be divided into three zones vertically and three zones horizontally (Fig. 2). The uppermost zones can contain the head and hands. The leftmost and rightmost zones can contain the left or right hands or feet respectively. The lower zones will typically contain the feet.

Body feature identification is accomplished in two steps: In the first step, pixel extrema measurements are made within each cell in the nine-grid body model. In the second step, a set of heuristics determines which grid measurements best captures the head, hands and feet feature locations.

4.1   Two-Level Architecture

The nine-grid approach has a two-level architecture, inspired by Ullman's [11, 12] concept of visual operations and visual routines. Visual operators are bottom-up, spatially uniform, and viewer-centered. Visual routines are sequences of visual operators, and are top-down and task-oriented.

The lower level nine-grid processing consists of a set of visual operators applied bottom-up and according to a spatially uniform pattern to the image area within the bounding box identified for the target region (see Sect. 3.2). This much is identical to the Ullman concept. However, the use of these operators by the upper level of the architecture departs a little from the Ullman concept.

The upper level, or visual routines level, consists of a set of heuristics for interpreting the output of the lower-level operators in terms of features of the human body. The visual operators are each applied to a region of the bounding box, producing an output measurement for each operator. The heuristics look at all the visual operator output and determine which output corresponds to a body feature in each frame. The same set of heuristics may not be valid for interpreting all human body activities. Depending on the nature of the activity,

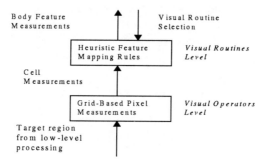

Fig. 2. Nine-grid two-level architecture

different "visual routines" consisting of different sets of heuristics, can be invoked to interpret the nine-grid data.

4.2 Visual Operators Level

Let $I(i)$ be the set of non-zero pixels (x, y) in a single image I. For simplicity, let us refer to the regions of the bounding box by their zone names as given in Fig. 2, $A1$ thru $C3$. Thus, the set of points $I(i) \cap A2$ is the set of non-zero pixels in image I which fall into zone $A2$.

We collect a set of measurements

$$D = \{d_z | z \in \{A1..3, B1, B3a, B3b, C1..3\}\} \tag{1}$$

to find salient protrusions in the silhouette. Note that we make no measurements in the center cell and we make two measurements in the $B3$ cell. In the A1 cell the measurement made is the location of the pixel with smallest x value:

$$d_{A1} = (x', y') \; s.t. \; x' = \text{MIN x for } (x, y) \in I(I) \cap A1. \tag{2}$$

The remainder of the grid measurements are detailed in Table 1.

Table 1. Grid measurements

$$
\begin{aligned}
d_{A1} &= (x', y') \; s.t. \; x' = \text{MIN x} \quad \text{for } (x, y) \in I(i) \cap A1 \\
d_{A2} &= (x', y') \; s.t. \; x' = \text{MIN x} \quad \text{for } (x, y) \in I(i) \cap A2 \\
d_{A3} &= (x', y') \; s.t. \; x' = \text{MIN x} \quad \text{for } (x, y) \in I(i) \cap A3 \\
d_{B1} &= (x', y') \; s.t. \; y' = \text{MIN y} \quad \text{for } (x, y) \in I(i) \cap B1 \\
d_{B3a} &= (x', y') \; s.t. \; x' = \text{MIN x} \quad \text{for } (x, y) \in I(i) \cap B3 \\
d_{B3b} &= (x', y') \; s.t. \; x' = \text{MAX x} \quad \text{for } (x, y) \in I(i) \cap B3 \\
d_{C1} &= (x', y') \; s.t. \; x' = \text{MAX x} \quad \text{for } (x, y) \in I(i) \cap C1 \\
d_{C2} &= (x', y') \; s.t. \; x' = \text{MAX x} \quad \text{for } (x, y) \in I(i) \cap C2 \\
d_{C3} &= (x', y') \; s.t. \; x' = \text{MAX x} \quad \text{for } (x, y) \in I(i) \cap C3
\end{aligned}
$$

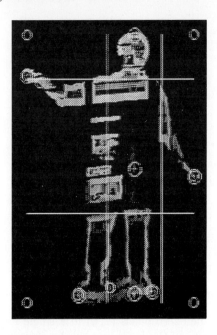

Fig. 3. Sample nine-grid measurements

The set D is constructed incrementally by updating it with (x, y) in the image as it is received in line scan format.

Some example output is shown in Fig. 3. The grid used to calculate D is shown superimposed on the silhouette generated by low-level vision processing and identified as the target region. The four circles in the corners show the bounding box limits. The smaller circles in each grid cell indicate the locations identified for each measurement. (Some of these are surrounded by larger circles with a cross in the center, and the meaning of these will be explained in the next section.)

4.3 Visual Routines Level

The data collected per cell of the 9-grid is filtered by a set of heuristic rules to generate body feature points. Generally, the two-level architecture allows for different sets of heuristics to be selected based on which kind of activity is being observed. However, in this implementation only a single set of heuristics is ever used. These heuristics are based on our assumptions about body pose. The main silhouette features we identify are the left hand, the right hand, the head, and the silhouette base. (Right and Left foot features can also be extracted, but weren't used in the evaluation in this paper.)

The heuristic that the left hand is the silhouette point with smallest x value in the upper two thirds of the bounding box can be captured by

```
if d_A1.x < d_A2.x
        then left-hand= d_A1
        else left-hand = d_A2
```

where $d.x$ refers to the x ordinate of d. The left foot can be identified as the silhouette point with smallest x in the lower third of the bounding box. This can be in A3 or B3a, and the rule is

```
if d_A3 exists
        then left-foot= d_A3
            else left-foot = d_B3a
```

In the case that the appropriate 9-Grid measurement does not exist, then the feature point is considered not to exist. The identified feature measurements are identified in Fig. 3 by the larger circles with a cross in the center.

4.4   Continuity Constraints Between Frames

The only measurements that are preserved from one frame to the next are the bounding box measurements, and the position of the head. The bounding box measurements are necessary in advance in order to determine into which grid cell a specific pixel falls. The bounding box can also be used to establish a window of interest in the next image, and hence avoid to examine the entire image each time.

In the initial version of the algorithm, no feature information was preserved between frames. However, this leads to the problem shown in Fig. 4(a). If the grid is spread evenly across the bounding box, then in some poses it is possible that the head can fall into column A or C of the grid. The solution is to have the grid centered on the head position as determined by the previous frame (Fig. 4(b)).

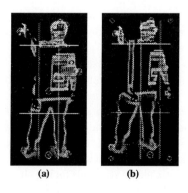

(a)   (b)

Fig. 4. Uniform (a) versus head-centered (b) grid

No attempt has been made to optimize the algorithm by preserving all measurements between frames and doing a local search around feature points instead of a global search.

4.5   Implementation

The two level architecture was implemented in C on a 200 MHz Pentium with SBIP 2.1 PC card. Low-level processing was accomplished at frame rates on the SBIP image pipeline. Silhouette extraction and low-level nine-grid processing was implemented on the TMS34020 graphics processor on the SBIP. This was necessary to minimize data transfer (the run-code) between SBIP and host PC. However, the relatively slow TMS34020 processor produced the nine-grid measurements at between 5 and 10 Hz, depending on how much diagnostics were being produced and on how many foreground pixels had been extracted. The relatively faster Pentium host implemented the high-level nine-grid processing in negligible additional time.

5   Ground-Truth Evaluation

To generate benchmarking data for our future work, we conducted a ground-truth evaluation study of the nine-grid algorithm.

5.1   Selection of Activities

Our application domain is the use of computer vision as part of the user interface. In particular, we are interested in in-home applications. We selected a small number of different kinds activities that broadly cover the kinds of activities we expect to see in in-home applications. We included activities on which we thought the algorithm would work well (1 and 2 below) and activities on which we thought the algorithm would fail (3 and 4) but which were relevant. The four activities were as follows (see Fig. 5):

1. Local motion activity: the subject was asked to carry out a task involving moving paper cards between three waist-level tables separated by about 1 meter. The subject was standing for the entire activity but wasn't always directly facing the camera.
2. Static Pointing: The subject was asked to stand in front of the camera and point to various locations with his/her right hand. The hand moved smoothly between locations.
3. Reading: The subject was asked to select a book from a waist-level table with several books stacked on it, walk to a chair (which faced the camera) and sit, flipping through the pages. The subject was asked to then get up, replace the first book and selected a second book.
4. Exercise: The subject was asked to stand facing the camera, and follow along with an exercise tape that was displayed on a screen facing him/her. The exercise actions included several very unusual body poses.

5.2   Experimental Procedure

Twelve subjects were selected to give a range of heights and weights. Each subject was asked to engage in each activity in order from 1 through 4. The computer vision system observed the live video input and generated a live diagnostic output consisting of the silhouette, superimposed nine-grid and feature measurements, as shown in the examples in Figs. 4 and 5. During the collection of the data, the nine-grid algorithm produced data at roughly 5 Hz (with intermediate frames being thrown away). The diagnostic output image was fed to a VCR. The subject was asked to continue each activity until approximately one minute of video had been collected on VHS videotape.

After the data was collected, the videotape was stepped through, collecting one frame per second in which the silhouette, grid-lines and feature points were all clearly visible. The remaining frames were discarded. This produced approximately 60 frames for each person for each activity.

The performance of the algorithm on each selected frame was scored as follows:

1. If the head, hands and base features were within 50 pixels (roughly 1.5cm) of the correct position as judged by the human evaluator, then that feature was given a *close* score.
2. If the feature was *exactly* where the human evaluator judged it should be, then the feature was given an *exact* score.
3. Otherwise the feature was given an *incorrect* score.

We interpret a close score as indicating the algorithm has made reasonable estimate of feature location, but may need additional resolution or local tuning to yield an exact score.

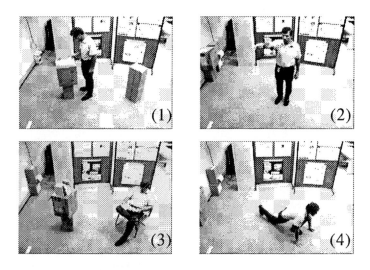

Fig. 5. Experimental activities

Two additional algorithm outputs were also scored:

1. The *grid* feature was scored if the nine-grid was centered on the head,
2. The *body* feature was scored if the center mark was placed in the center of the body.

These features give diagnostic information on the algorithm. For example, in the case of low body feature scores, a low grid score could be used to deduce that the assumption of a mostly upright body is not valid. The scoring data was used to determine the *sensitivity* per feature calculated as #correct/#total.

5.3   Results

The averaged sensitivity results per feature, per activity are shown in Table 2 and 3 below; 2 shows the close score, and 3 the exact score.

Table 2. Close score averages

Feature	Act1	Act2	Act3	Act4	All
Head	0.85	0.76	0.90	0.55	0.77
Rhand	0.74	0.79	0.83	0.53	0.72
Lhand	0.71	0.40	0.71	0.54	0.59
Grid	0.87	0.77	0.92	0.56	0.78
Body	0.87	0.95	0.95	0.87	0.91
Base	0.84	0.95	0.78	0.89	0.87
All	0.81	0.77	0.85	0.66	0.77

Table 3. Exact score averages

Feature	Act1	Act2	Act3	Act4	All
Head	0.73	0.74	0.83	0.47	0.69
RHand	0.32	0.33	0.19	0.24	0.27
LHand	0.36	0.31	0.37	0.34	0.35
Grid	0.75	0.75	0.84	0.48	0.71
Body	0.40	0.37	0.45	0.36	0.4
Base	0.31	0.27	0.31	0.40	0.32
All	0.48	0.46	0.5	0.38	0.46

Summarizing this data, the algorithm correctly identified features to a close degree 77% of the time, but to an exact degree 46% of the time. In terms of individual activities, Activity 4 (exercise) did indeed prove difficult for the algorithm. Surprisingly, Activity 3 (reading) yielded the best scores on both close and exact. Surprisingly also, Activity 2 (pointing) ranked 3rd. Figure 6 shows graphs of the averages and standard deviations estimated from the 12 subjects for the close scores.

Activity 2 revealed a flaw in the grid centering mechanism. In that activity, a hand pointing straight over the head was sometimes mistaken for the head. Since the grid becomes centered on the head position, the grid became locked on the hand, producing poor feature measurements for many subsequent frames, until the hand descended below shoulder height. The slow, smooth motion of hand from one pointing location to another invariably caused this problem. One solution to this problem is to add additional max and min X measurements to B1, so that the head width can be reported. A distinction can be made on the basis that the head feature will be typically thicker than the hand feature.

We regressed the body weight and height information against the average activity scores, to see if other biases of the algorithm emerged. We only recorded trends with a significance of 5% or better. Activity three showed a trend towards an inverse relationship between height and left hand recognition ($T = -2.91$, $p = 0.015$, $r = 0.43$) and a direct relationship between height-weight ratio and base recognition ($T = 2.23$, $p = 0.05$, $r = 0.33$). Activity one showed a trend towards an inverse relationship between height and correct base measurement ($T = 2.75$, $p = 0.02$, $r = 0.43$).

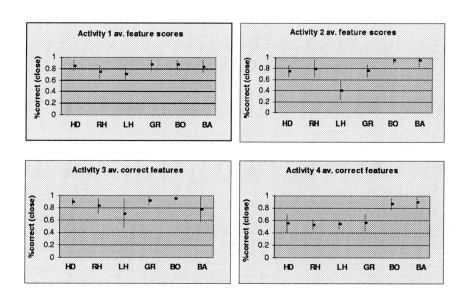

Fig. 6. Av. correct features per activity. The average feature score is indicated by the center mark and the vertical bar shows one standard deviation above and below the average. (HD=Head, RH=Right Hand, LH=Left Hand, GR=Grid, BO=Body, BA=Base)

5.4   Conclusion

This paper has introduced a line-scan algorithm for detecting human body features – the nine-grid algorithm. This algorithm has been implemented on a PC equipped with an SBIP PCI card. A ground truth study has been reported here that evaluates how well the nine-grid algorithm does on a series of four activities that are typical of our applications domain.

The ground truth study showed that the algorithm correctly identified features to a close degree 77% of the time. A surprising result was that Activity 2, which we had estimated would give good results, gave relatively bad results. This was traced to a flaw in the grid centering. Finally, the variability of results across activities reinforced the need to use different heuristics to interpret the nine-grid low-level measurements for different activities.

Acknowledgements

The authors wish to thank Korisa Stambough, who assisted in recording the activities, and scored the activity tapes (over 23,000 measurements) while a summer student at Philips Research.

References

1. Lyons, D., Pelletier, D., Knapp, D. *Multimodal Interactive Advertising.* in *Perceptual User Interfaces.* 1998. San Francisco CA.
2. Turk, M. *Visual Interaction with Lifelike Characters.* in *Face and Gesture Recognition.* 1996.
3. Kahn, R.E., and Swain, M.J. *Understanding People Pointing.* in *Int. Symp. on Computer Vision.* 1995.
4. Kortenkamp, D., Huber, E., and Bonasso, R.P. *Recognizing and Interpreting Gestures on a Mobile Robot.* in *13th Nat. Conf. on AI (AAAI-96).* 1996.
5. Haritaoglu, I., Harwood, D., and Davis, L. *W4: Who? When? Where? What? A Real-Time System for Detecting and Tracking People.* in *Face & Gesture Recognition 98.* 1998.
6. Wren, C., Azarbayejani, A., Darrell, T., and Pentland, A.,*Pfinder: Real-Time Tracking of the Human Body,* MIT Media Lab Technical Report 353, Cambridge MA.
7. Kakadiaris, I., and Metaxas, D. *3D Human Body Model Acquisition from Multiple Views.* in *5th Int. Conf. on Computer Vision.* 1995. Boston MA.
8. Philips, *SBIP User's Manual.* Document 9464-001-19201. 1996, Eindhoven, The Netherlands: Philips Center for Manufacturing Technology.
9. Philips, *Vision Library.* Document 8122-968-5645.1. 1996, Eindhoven, The Netherlands: Philips Center for Manufacturing Technology.
10. Andersson, D.B.C.a.G.B.J., *Occupational Biomechanics (2nd Edition).* 1991: Publisher: John Wiley & Sons.
11. Ullman, S.,*Visual Routines,* MIT AI Lab Memo 723, Cambridge, MA, June, 1983.
12. Chapman, D., *Vision, Instruction, and Action.* 1991, Cambridge MA: MIT Press.

Hand Posture Recognition in a Body-Face Centered Space

Sébastien Marcel and Olivier Bernier

France-Telecom CNET DTL/DLI
2 avenue Pierre Marzin, 22307 Lannion, France
{sebastien.marcel,olivier.bernier}@cnet.francetelecom.fr

Abstract. We propose a model for image space discretisation based on face location and on body anthropometry. In this body-face space, a neural network recognizes hand postures. The neural network is a constrained generative model already applied to face detection.

1 Introduction

LISTEN is a real-time computer vision system which detects and tracks a face in a video image [1]. In this system, faces are detected, within skin color blobs, by a modular neural network. This paper deals with a LISTEN based system using hand posture recognition to execute a command [2]. In order to detect the intention of the user to issue a command, "active windows" are defined in the body-face space. When a skin color blob enters an "active window", hand posture recognition , using a specific neural network for each hand posture, is triggered.

2 The Body-Face Space

The aim of this section is to introduce a technique of spatial segmentation, the body-face space, in order to assist in hand posture recognition.

Fig. 1. The body-face space in a full body user image

A. Braffort et al. (Eds.): GW'99, LNAI 1739, pp. 97–100, 1999.

We map over the user a body-face space based on a "discrete space for hand location" [3] centered on the face of the user as detected by LISTEN.

The body-face space (Fig. 1) is built using the anthropometric body model expressed as a function of the total height of the user (Fig. 2). The total height is itself calculated from the face height.

Given the body-face space, we can define "active windows" as areas of interest where hand postures are detected. An "active window" can be placed where hand gestures are usually executed, for example at the left (right) of the body-face space for deictic gesture or at the left (right) of shoulders for command gestures.

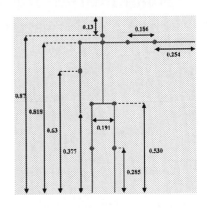

Fig. 2. Anthropometric body model

When a skin color blob enters an "active window", hand posture recognition is triggered. In order to see the whole body, our images are taken with a large field of view. Therefore, faces and hands have small sizes (15x20 pixels for faces and 18x30 pixels for hands) and hand posture recognition becomes a hard task. Nevertheless, LISTEN is able to detect such faces using neural networks. Consequently, we apply the same approach for hand posture recognition.

3   The Neural Network Model

Neural networks, such as discriminant models [4] or Kohonen features maps models [5], have previously been applied to hand posture recognition. In this work, we propose to use a neural network model already applied to face detection: the constrained generative model (CGM) [6] (Fig. 3).

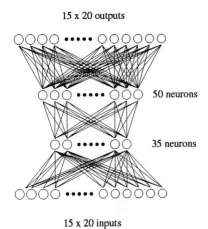

Fig. 3. Constrained generative model

The goal of the constrained generative learning is to closely fit the probability distribution of the set of hands using a non-linear compression neural network and non-hand examples. Each hand example is reconstructed as itself and each non-hand example is constrained to be reconstructed as the mean neighbourhood of the nearest hand example.

After learning, the Euclidean distance between inputs and outputs of the neural network is smaller for hand examples than for non-hands examples. Using this distance, and given a distance threshold estimated on a generalisation set, the classification of the input image is possible.

In order to frame the hand posture, images are tested by the specific CGMs at different position and scale.

4 Results on Our Database

Our goal is to recognize hand postures used in command gestures. A small set of hand postures was selected: A, B, C, Five, Point and V. A database of thousands various hand posture images with both uniform and complex backgrounds was built. The window sizes for each posture (corresponding to the number of inputs for each CGM) are: 20x20 for A, 18x20 for C and Five, and 18x30 for B, Point and V (Fig. 4). Most of the database was used for training (80 %) and the remainder was used for test ing (20 %).

Fig. 4. Examples of hand postures from our test database

Although the images with complex backgrounds are more difficult, the CGM achieves a good recognition rate and a small false alarm rate (Table 1).

Table 1. Mean results on our test database with uniform and complex backgrounds

Uniform backgrounds			
Hand Postures	Number of images	Mean detection rate	Mean false alarm rate
A,B,C,V	241	93.8%	1/11, 100
A to V	382	93.4%	1/12, 000
Complex backgrounds			
Hand Postures	Number of images	Mean detection rate	Mean false alarm rate
A,B,C,V	165	74.8%	1/18, 900
A to V	277	76.1%	1/14, 000

The false alarm rate is of prime necessity to evaluate the performance of the system, and must be small comparing to the number of tests in a image. At the present time, the false alarm rate on various images containing no hands is around 1 false alarm for 27800 tests.

5 Results on a Benchmark Database

The CGM was also tested on the Jochen hand posture gallery [7]. This database contains 128x128 grey-scale images of 10 hand signs performed by 24 persons against uniform light, uniform dark and complex backgrounds. We only tested the A, B, C and V postures (Fig. 5). The CGM applied to hand posture recognition gives satisfactory recognition results (Table 2) on this benchmark database. These results can be improved by adding more non-hand examples in order to lower the false alarm rate.

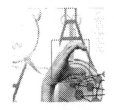

Fig. 5. Examples of hand posture from Jochen Triesch Gallery

Table 2. Mean results on Jochen Triesch gallery with uniform and complex backgrounds

Uniform backgrounds			
Hand Postures	Number of images	Mean detection rate	Mean false alarm rate
A,B,C,V	191	93.7%	1/25,600
Complex backgrounds			
Hand Postures	Number of images	Mean detection rate	Mean false alarm rate
A,B,C,V	96	84.4%	1/15,900

6   Conclusion

We have recently integrate the hand posture detection and the body-face space in a new LISTEN based system running in real-time at 12Hz. Currently, when an unknown hand posture is presented, there is no strategy to choose the neural network to use. All the neural networks are used and the best response identify the hand posture. Future work is to find a strategy for choosing the CGM to use and to supply this system with a hand gesture recognition kernel based on stroke detection and motion analysis.

References

1. Collobert, M. and Feraud, R. and Le Tourneur G. and Bernier, O. and Viallet, J.E. and Mahieux, Y. and Collobert, D.: LISTEN: A System for Locating and Tracking Individual Speakers. 2nd Int. Conf. on Automatic Face and Gesture Recognition (1996) 283–288
2. Baudel, T. and Braffort, A.: Reconnaissance de gestes de la main en environnement réel. Actes de Informatique'93 - L'interface des mondes réels et virtuel (1993) 207–216
3. McNeill, D.: Hand and Mind: What gestures reveal about thought. Chicago Press (1992)
4. Murakami, K. and Taguchi, H.: Gesture recognition using Recurrent Neural Networks. CHI'91, 237-242
5. Boehm, K. and Broll, W. and Sokolewicz, M.: Dynamic Gesture Recognition Using Neural Networks: A Fundament for Advanced Interaction Construction. SPIE, Conference Electronic Imaging Science and Technology (1994)
6. Feraud, R.: PCA, Neural Networks and Estimation for Face Detection. NATO ASI, Face Recognition: from Theory to Applications (1997), 424-432
7. Triesch, J. and Malsburg, C.: Robust Classification of Hand Postures against Complex Backgrounds. 2nd Int. Conf. on Automatic Face and Gesture (1996), 170-175

Section 3: Recognition

Vision-Based Gesture Recognition: A Review

Ying Wu and Thomas S. Huang

Beckman Institute
405 N. Mathews
University of Illinois at Urbana-Champaign
Urbana, IL 61801
{yingwu,huang}@ifp.uiuc.edu

Abstract. The use of gesture as a natural interface serves as a motivating force for research in modeling, analyzing and recognition of gestures. In particular, human computer intelligent interaction needs vision-based gesture recognition, which involves many interdisciplinary studies. A survey on recent vision-based gesture recognition approaches is given in this paper. We shall review methods of static hand posture and temporal gesture recognition. Several application systems of gesture recognition are also described in this paper. We conclude with some thoughts about future research directions.

1 Introduction

The evolution of user interface (UI) has witnessed the development from text-based UI based on the keyboard to GUI based on a mice. What will be the counterpart of the mouse when we are trying to explore 3D virtual environments (VEs) in Human Computer Intelligent Interaction (HCII) or Perceptual User Interface (PUI)? In current VE applications, keyboards, mice, wands and joysticks are still the most popular and dominant devices. However, they are inconvenient and unnatural. The use of human movements, especially hand gestures, has become an important part of HCII in recent years, which serves as a motivating force for research in modeling, analyzing and recognition of hand gestures. Many techniques developed in HCII can be extended to other areas such as surveillance, robot control and teleconferencing.

Recognizing gestures is a complex task which involves many aspects such as motion modeling, motion analysis, pattern recognition and machine learning, even psycholinguistic studies. There are already several survey papers in human motion analysis [21,54] and interpretation [35]. Since gesture recognition is receiving more and more attention in recent research, a comprehensive review on various gesture recognition techniques developed in recent years is needed.

This paper surveys recent studies on vision-based gesture recognition techniques. Section 2 discusses several human gesture representation paradigms in psycholinguistic and cognitive studies, since almost all high-level temporal gesture recognition tasks can be represented by those paradigms which serve as a cognitive model for many complicated temporal hand gestures. Some promising application systems are given in Section 3. Since any recognition method

A. Braffort et al. (Eds.): GW'99, LNAI 1739, pp. 103–115, 1999.

needs feature extraction and data collection, Section 4 discusses the gesture features used in current studies, and Section 5 provides a brief overview of tracking techniques which serve as the data collection process for vision-based gesture recognition.

Since meaningful hand gestures can be classified as static hand postures and temporal gestures, Section 6 and Section 7 discuss various techniques for hand posture recognition and temporal gesture recognition respectively. Especially, recognition by modeling dynamics (Section 7.1), recognition by modeling semantics (Section 7.2), recognition in the HMM framework (Section 7.3), (and many other techniques (Section 7.4) are given in Section 7).

Since sign language recognition is an important task, Section 8 discusses several studies related to it. Some thoughts about future work and the conclusion of this paper are given in Section 9 and Section 10 respectively.

2   Human Gesture Representation

There have been many studies on human gestures in psycholinguistic research. Stokoe [44] represents gestures as four aspects which are *hand shape*, *position*, *orientation* and *movement*. Kendon [26] describes a philology of gesture, which consists of *gesticulation*, *language-like gestures*, *pantomimes*, *emblems*, and *sign language*. *Sign languages* are characterized by a specific set of vocabulary and grammar. *Emblems* are informal gestural expressions in which the meaning depends on convention, culture and lexicon.

According to different application scenarios, hand gestures can be classified into several categories such as *conversational gestures*, *controlling gestures*, *manipulative gestures*, and *communicative gestures*[54]. Sign language is an important case of *communicative gestures*. Since sign languages are highly structural, they are very suitable for acting as a test-bed for vision algorithms. At the same time, they can also be a good way to help the disabled to interact with computers. *Controlling gestures* are the focus of current research in vision-based interfaces (VBI). Virtual objects can be located by analyzing pointing gestures. Some display- control applications demonstrate the potential of pointing gestures in HCI. Another controlling gesture is the navigating gesture. Instead of using wands, the orientation of hands can be captured as a 3D directional input to navigate within VEs. The manipulative gesture will serve as a natural way to interact with virtual objects. Tele-operation and virtual assembly are good examples of applications. Communicative gestures are subtle in human interaction, which involves psychological studies, however, vision-based motion capturing techniques can help those studies.

Communicative gestures can be decomposed into three motion phases: *preparation*, *stroke*, and *retraction* [26]. Psycholinguistic studies show that *stroke* may be distinguished from other gesture phases, since *stroke* contains the most information. This model is taken from Quek [39]. He also makes a distinction between *presentation* gestures and *repetitive* gestures.

Bobick [4] emphasizes the dynamical part of gestures. He represents gestures as *movement, activity* and *action. Movements* are typically atomic and are the most primitive form of motion that can be interpreted semantically. *Activity* is a sequence of either movements or of static configurations. Dynamic models may be used to recognize activities. *Actions* are the high-level entities that people typically use to describe what is happening. Time and context becomes fundamental, though how much one has to reason about context is unclear.

3   Application Systems

There have been many implemented application systems in domains such as virtual environments, smart surveillance, HCII, teleconferencing, sign language translation, etc..

Zeller et al. [57] present a visual environment for a very large scale biomolecular modeling application. This system permits interactive modeling of biopolymers by linking 3D molecular graphics and a molecular dynamics simulation program. Hand gestures serve as the input and controlling device of the virtual environment. Pavlovic and Berry [2] integrate controlling gestures into the virtual environment *BattleField*, in which hand gestures are used not only for navigating the VE, but also as an interactive device to select and move the virtual objects in the *BattleField*. Ju et al. [25] develop an automatic system for analyzing and annotating video sequences of technical talks. Speaker's gestures such as pointing or writing are automatically tracked and recognized to provide a rich annotation of the sequence that can be used to access a condensed version of the talk. Davis and Bobick [17] implement a prototype system for a virtual *Personal Aerobics Trainer* (PAT). Their system allows the user to create and personalize an aerobics session to meet the user's needs and desires. Six stretching and aerobic movements are recognized by the system. Quek [39] presents a *FingerMouse* application to recognize 2-D finger movements which are the input to the desktop. Crowley and Coutaz [11] also develop an application *FingerPaint* to use a finger as an input device for augmented reality. Triesch and Maslburg [47] develop a person-independent gesture interface on a real robot which allows the user to give simple commands such as how to grasp an object and where to put it. Imagawa et al. [23] implement a bi-directional translation system between Japanese Sign Language (JSL) and Japanese in order to help the hearing impaired communicate with normal speaking people through sign language.

4   Features for Gesture Recognition

Selecting good features is crucial to gesture recognition, since hand gestures are very rich in shape variation, motion and textures. For static hand posture recognition, although it is possible to recognize hand posture by extracting some geometric features such as fingertips, finger directions and hand contours, such features are not always available and reliable due to self-occlusion and lighting conditions. There are also many other non-geometric features such as color, silhouette and textures, however, they are inadequate in recognition. Since it is not easy to specify features explicitly, the whole image or transformed image is taken as the input and features are selected implicitly and automatically by the recognizer

Cui and Weng [14] investigate the difference between the *most discriminating features (MDF)* and the *most expressive features (MEF)*. MEFs are extracted by K-L projection. However, MEFs may not be the best for classification, because the features that describe some major variations in the class are typically irrelevant to how the subclasses are divided. MDFs are selected by multi-class, multivariate discriminate analysis and have a significantly higher capability to catch major differences between classes. Their experiments also showed that MDFs are superior to the MEFs in automatic feature selection for classification.

Recognizing temporal gestures not only needs spatial features, but also requires temporal features. It is possible to recognize some gestures by 2D locations of the hands, however, it is not general and view-dependent. The most fundamental feature is the 2D location of the interested blob. Wren et.al [53] use a multi-class statistical model of color and shape to obtain a 2D representation of the head of the hand in a wide range of viewing conditions in their tracking system *Pfinder*.

In order to achieve spatial invariant recognition, 3D features are necessary. Campbell et al.[9] investigated the 3D invariant features by comparing the recognition performance on ten different feature vectors derived from a single set of 18 T'ai Chi gestures which are used in the *Staying Alive* application developed by Becker and Pentland [1]. A Hidden Markov Model (HMM) is taken as the recognizer. They reported that $(dr, d\theta, dz)$ had the best overall recognition rates. At the same time, their experiments highlight the fact that choosing the right set of features can be crucial to the performance.

Features for temporally invariant gesture recognition are hard to specify since it depends on the temporal representation of gestures. However, it can be handled implicitly in some recognition approaches such as finite state machines and HMM, which will discussed later in Section 7.

5   Data Collection for Recognition

To collect data for temporal gesture recognition is not a trivial task. The hand has to be localized in the image sequences and segmented from the background. 2-D tracking supplies the localized information such as hand bounding boxes and the centroid of hand blobs. Simple 2-D motion trajectories can be extracted from the image sequences. In some cases, these 2-D features are sufficient for gesture recognition. There have been many 2-D tracking algorithms such as color tracking, motion tracking, template matching, blob tracking, and multiple cue integrating.

Although 2-D tracking gives the position information of hand, some recognition applications still need more features such as hand orientation and hand shape. 3-D tracking approaches try to locate the hand in 3-D space by giving the

3-D position and orientation of hand. However, since the hand can not be treated as a rigid object, it is very hard to estimate the hand orientation. 3-D position of the hand can be achieved by stereo cameras or model-based approaches.

Since the hand is highly articulated and shape depends on viewpoint, hand shape is hard to describe. Several studies try to recover the *state of the hand* which is represented by the set of joint angles, which is full DOF tracking. If the hand configuration can be estimated, recognizing finger spelling may be easier. However, how to estimate the configuration of articulated objects needs more study.

6   Static Hand Posture Recognition

Since hand postures can express not only some concepts, but also can act as special transition states in temporal gestures, recognizing or estimating hand postures or human postures is one of the main topics in gesture recognition.

Cui and Weng [14] use the most discriminating features to classify hand signs by partitioning the MDF space. A manifold interpolation scheme is introduced to generalize to other variations from a limited number of learned samples. Their algorithm can handle complex backgrounds.

Triesch and Malsburg [46] employ the *elastic graph matching* technique to classify hand postures against complex backgrounds. Hand postures are represented by labeled graphs with an underlying two-dimensional topology. Attached to the nodes are *jets*, which is a sort of local image description based on Gabor filters. The recognition rate against complex background is 86.2%. This approach can achieve scale-invariant and user-independent recognition, and it does not need hand segmentation. Since using one graph for one hand posture is insufficient, this approach is not view-independent.

Quek and Zhao [40] introduced an inductive learning system which is able to derive rules of disjunctive normal form formula. Each DNF describes a hand pose, and each conjunct within the DNF constitutes a single rule. Twenty-eight features such as the area of the bounding box, the compactness of the hand, the normalized moments, serve as the input feature vector for their learning algorithm. They obtained 94% recognition rate.

Nolker and Ritter [33] detected the 2D location of fingertips by the *Local Linear Mapping* (LLN) neural network, and those 2D locations are mapped to 3D position by the *Parametric Self-Organizing Map* (PSOM) neural network, since PSOM has the ability to perform an associative completion of fragmentary input. By this means, their approach can recognize hand posture under different views.

7   Temporal Gesture Modeling and Recognition

There are some similarities between temporal gestures and speech so that some techniques in speech such as HMM can be applied to gesture. However, temporal gesture is more complicated than speech. Some low-level movements can be recognized using dynamic models. Some gesture semantics can be exploited to recognize high-level activities. Example-based learning methods can also be used. There are also many other techniques developed in recent years.

7.1   Recognition by Modeling the Dynamics

Modeling the low-level dynamics of human motion is important not only for human tracking, but also for human motion recognition. It serves as a quantitative representation of simple movements so that those simple movements can be recognized in a reduced space by the trajectories of motion parameters. However, those low-level dynamics models are not sufficient to represent more complicated human motions. Some low-level motions can be represented by simple dynamic processes, in which the *Kalman filter* is often employed to estimate, interpolate and predict the motion parameters. However, this simple dynamic model is not sufficient to model most cases of human motion, and the Gaussian assumption of the Kalman filtering is usually invalid.

Black and Jepson [3] extended the *Condensation* algorithm to recognize temporal trajectories. Since a *sampling* technique is used to represent the probability density in the *Condensation* algorithm, their approach avoids some difficulties of Kalman filtering. Gesture recognition is achieved by matching input motion trajectories and model trajectories using *Dynamic Time Warping* (DTW).

Pentland and Liu [36] try to represent human behavior by a complex, multi-state model. They used several alternative models to represent human dynamics, one for each class of response. Model switching is based on the observation of the state of the dynamics. This approach produces a generalized maximum likelihood estimate of the current and future values of the state variables. Recognition is achieved by determining which model best fits the observation.

Rittscher and Blake [42] push the technique of combining the idea of model switching and *Condensation*. They use mixed discrete/continuous states to couple perception with classification, in which the continuous variable describes the motion parameters and the discrete variable labels the class of the motion. An ARMA model is used to represent the dynamics. This approach can achieve automatic temporal sequence segmentation.

There is also some work dealing with specific gestures. Cohen et.al [10] use a dynamic model to represent circle and line gestures to generate and to recognize basic oscillatory gestures such as crane control gestures.

7.2   Recognition by Modeling the Semantics

Many applications need to recognize more complex gestures which include semantic meaning in the movements. Modeling the dynamics alone is not sufficient in such tasks.

The *Finite State Machine* is a technique usually employed to handle this situation. Davis and Shah [19] use this technique to recognize simple hand gestures. Jo, Kuno and Shirai [24] take this approach to recognize manipulative hand gestures such as grasping, holding and extending. The task knowledge is represented by a state transition diagram, in which each state indicates possible gesture states at the next moment. By using a rest state, all unintentional actions can be ignored. Pavlovic and Berry [2] also take this approach.

Another approach is rule-based modeling. Quek [39] uses *extended variable-valued logic* and rule-based induction algorithm to build an inductive learning system to recognize 3-D gestures. Cutler and Turk [15] build a set of simple rules to recognize gestures such as waving, jumping, marching etc.

Pinhanez and Bobick [37] develop a new representation for temporal gestures, a 3-valued domain {past, now, fut}(PNF) network. The occurrence of an action is computed by minimizing the domain of its PNF-network, under constraints imposed by the current state of the sensors and the previous states of the network.

Another promising approach to modeling the semantics of temporal gestures is the *Bayesian Network* and the *Dynamic Bayesian Network*. Pavlovic [34] has promoted this idea recently.

7.3   Gesture Recognition in the HMM Framework

HMM is a type of statistical model. A HMM λ consists of N states and a transition matrix. Each state has assigned an output probability distribution function $b_i(O)$, which gives the probability of the state S_i generating observation O under the condition that the system is in S_i. There are three basic problems in HMMs. The first problem is evaluation $P(O|\lambda)$, which can be solved by forward-backward algorithm. The second problem is to find the most likely state sequence S, given an observation and a HMM model, i.e. $maxP(S|O, \lambda)$. The third problem is to train the HMM. The second and third problems are respectively solved by applying the Viterbi and Baum-Welch algorithms.

Pentland and Liu [36] use HMM to model the state transitions among a set of dynamic models. Bregler [8] takes the same approach. HMM has the capacity for not only modeling the low-level dynamics, but also the semantics in some gestures. Stoll and Ohya [45] employ HMM to model semantically meaningful human movements, in which one HMM is learned for each motion class. The data used for modeling the human motions is an approximate pose derived from an image sequence. Nam and Wohn [32] present a HMM-based method to recognize some controlling gestures. Their approach takes into account not only hand movement, but also hand postures and palm orientations.

There are also many variations of HMM. Yang et al. [55] model the gesture by employing a multi-dimensional HMM, which contains more than one observation symbol at each time. Their approach is able to model multi-path gestures and provides a means to integrate multiple modality to increase the recognition rate.

Since the output probability of feature vectors of each state in HMM is unique, HMM can handle only piecewise stationary processes which are not adequate in gesture modeling. Kobayashi and Haruyama [28] introduce *Partly-Hidden Markov Model* (PHMM) for temporal matching. Darrell and Pentland

[16] introduce a hidden-state reinforcement learning paradigm based on the *Partially Observable Markov Decision Process* to gesture recognition by which is guided an active camera.

When Markov condition is violated, conventional HMMs fail. HMMs are ill-suited to systems that have compositional states. Brand et.al. [7] presented an algorithm for coupling and training HMMs to model interactions between processes that may have different state structures and degrees of influence on each other. These problems often occur in vision, speech, or both–coupled HMMs are well suited to applications requiring sensor fusion across modalities.

Wilson and Bobick [52] extended the standard HMM method to include a global parametric variation in the output probabilities of the HMM to handle parameterized movements such as musical conducting and driving by EM algorithm. They presented results on two different movements – a size gesture and a point gesture – and show robustness with respect to noise in the input features.

7.4   Other Techniques

There are also many statistical learning techniques applied to gesture recognition. As we describe before, Cui and Weng [12] use the multiclass, multidimensional discriminant analysis to automatically select the most discriminating features for gesture recognition. Polana and Nelson [38] attempt to recognize motion by low-level statistical features of image motion information. A simple nearest centroid algorithm serves as the classifier. Their experiments show their approach is suitable for repetitive gesture recognition. Watanabe and Yachida [51] introduce an eigenspace which is constructed from multi input image sequences to recognize gestures. Since this eigenspace represents the approximate 3-D information for gestures, their approach can handle self-occlusion.

Bobick and Ivanov [4] model the low-level temporal behaviors by HMM techniques. The outputs of HMM serve as the input stream of a stochastic context-free grammar parsing system. The grammar and parser provide longer range temporal constraints. The uncertainty of low level movement detection is disambiguated in the high level parser which includes a priori knowledge about the structure of temporal actions.

Yang and Ahuja [56] use *Time-Delay Neural Networks* (TDNN) to classify motion patterns. TDNN is trained with a database of more than ASL signs. The input of the TDNN is the motion trajectories extracted by multi-scale motion segmentation.

8   Sign Language Recognition

Unlike general gestures, sign languages are highly structured so that it provides an appealing test bed for understanding more general principles. However, there are no clear boundaries between individual signs, recognition of sign languages are still very difficult. Speech recognition and sign language recognition are parallels. Both are time-varying processes, which show statistical variations, making

HMMs a plausible choice for modeling the processes. And both must devise ways to cope with context and co-articulation effects. HMMs provide a framework for capturing the statistical variations in both position and duration of the movement. In addition, it can segment the gesture stream implicitly.

There are two kinds of gestures to be recognized, one is isolated gesture, and the other is continuous gesture. The presence of silence makes the boundaries of isolated gestures easy to spot. Each sign can be extracted and presented to the trained HMMs individually. Continuous sign recognition, on the other hand, is much harder since there is no silence between the signs. Here HMMs offer the compelling advantage of being able to segment the streams of signs automatically with the Viterbi algorithm. Co-articulation is difficult to handle in continuous recognition, since it results in the insertion of an extra movement between the two signs.

Starner et al.[43] employ HMM to recognize American Sign Language (ASL). They assume that detailed information about hand shape is not necessary for humans to interpret sign language, so a coarse tracking system is used in their studies.

There are several possible approaches to deal with the co-articulation problem. One is to use context-dependent HMMs, and the other is modeling the co-articulation. The idea of context- dependent HMMs is to train bi-sign or even tri-sign context dependent HMMs. However, this method can not work well. Vogler and Metaxas [49, 50] study the co-articulation in sign language recognition. They propose an unsupervised clustering scheme to obtain the necessary classes of "phonemes" for modeling the movements between signs. Recently, they use phonemes instead of whole signs as the basic units so that the ASL signs can be broken into phonemes such as movements and holds, and HMMs are trained to recognize the phonemes [50]. Since the number of phonemes is limited, it is possible to use HMMs to recognize large-scale vocabularies.

Liang and Ouhyoung [30] also take the HMM approach to the recognition of continuous Taiwanese Sign Language with a vocabulary of 250 signs. The temporal segmentation is performed explicitly based on the discontinuity of the movements according to 4 gesture parameters such as posture, position, orientation and motion.

9   Future Directions

Current static hand posture recognition techniques seldom try to achieve rotation-invariant and view-independent recognition. One approach is to extract some 3-D features or to estimate the hand configuration. Another approach is based on learning. These two approaches need more investigation in hand gestures.

The representation for temporal gesture is crucial to recognition. In low-level movement recognition and tracking, automatic switching among different motion models should be considered more in future studies. Most current gesture applications only look into symbolic gesture commands. Automatic segmentation of temporal gestures plays an important role in extracting or segmenting these gesture commands in continuous movements. However, it is still an open problem and it should receive more attention. Although HMM can handle segmentation in some cases, it may fail in the presence of co-articulation. Two-handed gestures not only make the tracking more difficult, but also make the interpretation of gesture harder. These problems should be investigated in future research. Since speech and gestures are coupled, it is natural to consider combing gesture and speech to a multi-modality system.

10   Conclusion

In this paper, we report the recent development on the research of hand gesture recognition with focus on various recognition techniques. Feature selection, which can be specified explicitly or implicitly by the recognizer, is crucial to the recognition algorithms. Data collection for visual gesture learning is not a trivial task. Various algorithms on static hand posture recognition and temporal gesture recognition are surveyed in this paper. HMM and its variants can be used in sign language recognition. Due to the complexity of gesture, machine leaning techniques seems promising in this task.

Overall, gesture recognition is still in its infancy. It involves the cooperation of many disciplines. In order to understand hand gestures, not only for machines, but also for humans, substantial research efforts in computer vision, machine learning and psycholinguistics will be needed.

Acknowledgements

This work was supported in part by National Science Foundation Grants CDA-96-24396 and IRI- 96-34618.

References

1. Becker,D.: Sensei: A Real-Time Recognition, Feedback and Training System for Tai Chi Gestures, *MIT Media Lab, MS thesis* (1997)
2. Berry,G.: Small-wall: A Multimodal Human Computer Intelligent Interaction Test Bed with Applications, *Dept. of ECE, University of Illinois at Urbana-Champaign, MS thesis* (1998)
3. Black,M., Jepson,A.: Recognition Temporal Trajectories using the Condensation Algorithm, *Int'l Conf. on Automatic Face and Gesture Recognition*, Japan, pp.16-21 (1998)
4. Bobick,A., Ivanov,Y.: Action Recognition using Probabilistic Parsing, *IEEE Int'l Conf. on Computer Vision and Pattern Recognition* (1998)
5. Bobick, A., Wilson,A.: A State-Based Approach to the Representation and Recognition of Gesture, *IEEE trans. PAMI*, Vol.19, No.12, Dec., pp1325-1337 (1997)
6. Bradski,G., Yeo,B., Yeung,M.: Gesture and Speech for Video Content Navigation, *Proc. Workshop on Perceptual User Interfaces* (1998)
7. Brand,M., Oliver,N., Pentland,A.: Coupled Hidden Markov Models for Complex Action Recognition, *Proc. IEEE Int'l Conf. on Computer Vision and Pattern Recognition* (1997)

8. Bregler,C.: Learning and Recognizing Human Dynamics in Video Sequences, *Proc. IEEE Int'l Conf. on Computer Vision and Pattern Recognition* (1997)

9. Campbell,L., et al.: Invariant Features for 3-D Gesture Recognition, *Int'l Conf. on Automatic Face and Gesture Recognition*, Killington, pp.157-162. (1996)

10. Cohen,C., Conway,L., Koditschek,D.: Dynamical System Representation, Generation, and Recognition of Basic Oscillatory Motion Gestures, *Int'l Conf. on Automatic Face and Gesture Recognition* , Killington (1996)

11. Crowley,J., Berard,F., Coutaz,J.: Finger Tracking as An Input Device for Augmented Reality, *Int.Workshop on Automatic Face and Gesture Recognition*, Zurich, pp.195-200. (1995)

12. Cui,Y, Weng,J.: Hand Sign Recognition from Intensity Image Sequences with Complex Background, *Proc. IEEE Conference on Computer Vision and Pattern Recognition*, pp.88-93. (1996)

13. Cui,Y., Weng,J.: Hand Segmentation Using Learning-Based Prediction and Verification for Hand Sign Recognition, *Int'l Conf. on Automatic Face and Gesture Recognition* , Killington (1996)

14. Cui,Y., Swets,D., Weng,J.: Learning-Based Hand Sign Recognition Using SHOSLIF-M, *Int. Workshop on Automatic Face and Gesture Recognition*, Zurich, pp.201-206. (1995)

15. Cutler,R., Turk,M.: View-based Interpretation of Real-Time Optical Flow for Gesture Recognition, *IEEE Int. Conf. on Automatic Face and Gesture Recognition*, Japan. (1998)

16. Darrell,T., Pentland,A.: Active Gesture Recognition Using Partially Observable Markov Decision Processes, *IEEE Int'l Conf. on Pattern Recognition* (1996)

17. Davis,J., Bobick,A.: Virtual PAT: A Virtual Personal Aerobic Trainer, *Proc. Workshop on Perceptual User Interfaces*, pp.13-18. (1998)

18. Davis, J., Bobick, A.: The Representation and Recognition of Action Using Temporal Templates, *IEEE CVPR*, pp.928-934. (1997)

19. Davis, J., Shah, M.: Visual Gesture Recognition, *Vision, Image and Signal Processing*, 141(2), pp.101-106. (1994)

20. Fernandez, R.: Stochastic Modeling of Physiological Signals with Hidden Markov Models: A Step Toward Frustration Detection in Human-Computer Interfaces, *MIT Media Lab, MS thesis.* (1997)

21. Gavrila, D.: The Visual Analysis of Human Movement: A Survey, *Computer Vision and Image Understanding*, Vol.73, No.1, Jan, pp.82-98. (1999)

22. Goncalves, L., Bernardo, E., Perona, P.: Reach Out and Touch Space, *IEEE Int. Conf. on Automatic Face and Gesture Recognition*, Japan.(1998)

23. Imagawa, K., Lu, S., Igi, S.: Color-Based Hand Tracking System for Sign Language Recognition, *IEEE Int. Conf. on Automatic Face and Gesture Recognition*, Japan. (1998)

24. Jo, K., Kuno, Y., Shirai, Y.: Manipulative Hand Gestures Recognition Using Task Knowledge for Human Computer Interaction, *IEEE Int. Conf. on Automatic Face and Gesture Recognition*, Japan. (1998)

25. Ju, S., Black, M., Minneman, S., Kimber, D.: Analysis of Gesture and Action in Technical Talks for Video Indexing, *IEEE Conf. on Computer Vision and Pattern Recognition, CVPR97* . (1997)

26. Kendon, A.: urrent Issues in the Study of Gesture *The Biological Foundation of Gestures: Motor and Semiotic Aspects*, pp.23-47, Lawrence Erlbaum Associate, Hillsdale, NJ, (1986)

27. Kjeldsen, R., Kender, J.: Interaction with On-Screen Objects using Visual Gesture Recognition, *Proc. IEEE CVPR97*, (1997)

28. Kobayashi, T., Haruyama,S.: Partly-Hidden Markov Model and Its Application to Gesture Recognition, *IEEE Proceedings of ICASSP97*, Vol. VI, pp.3081-84. (1997)
29. Kurita, T., Hayamizu, S.: Gesture Recognition using HLAC Features of PARCOR Images and HMM based Recognizer, *IEEE Int. Conf. on Automatic Face and Gesture Recognition* , Japan. (1998)
30. Liang, R., Ouhyoung, M.: A Real-time Continuous Gesture Recognition System for Sign Language, *IEEE Int. Conf. on Automatic Face and Gesture Recognition*, Japan. (1998)
31. McNeil, D.: Hand and Mind, University of Chicago Press, Chicago. (1992)
32. Nam, Y., Wohn, K.: Recognition of Space-Time Hand-Gestures using Hidden Markov Mdel, *ACM Symposium on Virtual Reality Software and Technology*, HongKong, pp. 51-58. (1996)
33. Nolker, C., Ritter, H.: Illumination Independent Recognition of Deictic Arm Postures, *Proc. 24th Annual Conf. of the IEEE Industrial Electronics Society*, Germany, pp. 2006- 2011. (1998)
34. Pavlovic,V.: Dynamic Bayesian Networks for Information Fusion with Applications to Human–Computer Interfaces, *Dept. of ECE, University of Illinois at Urbana-Champaign, Ph.D. Dissertation*, (1999)
35. Pavlovic, V., Sharma, R., Huang, T.: Visual Interpretation of Hand Gestures for Human-Computer Interaction: A Review, *IEEE trans. PAMI*, Vol.19, No.7, July, pp677-695, (1997)
36. Pentland, A., Liu, A.: Modeling and Prediction of Human Behavior, *IEEE Intelligent Vehicles*, (1995)
37. Pinhanez, C. Bobick, A.: Human Action Detection Using PNF Propagation of Temporal Constraints, *IEEE ICCV*, (1998)
38. Polana, R. Nelson, R.: Low Level Recognition of Human Motion, *IEEE Workshop on Motion of Non-Rigid and Articulated Objects*, Austin, pp77-82. (1994)
39. Quek, F.: Unencumbered Gestural Interaction, *IEEE Multimedia*, Vol.3, No.4, pp.36-47, (1997)
40. Quek, F., Zhao, M.: Inductive Learning in Hand Pose Recognition, *IEEE Automatic Face and Gesture Recognition*, (1996)
41. Rohr, K.: Towards Model-Based Recognition of Human Movements in Image Sequences, *CVGIP:Image Understanding*, Vol.59, No.1, Jan, pp.94-115, (1994)
42. Rittscher, J., Blake, A.: Classification of Human Body Motion, *IEEE Int'l Conf. on Computer Vision*, (1999)
43. Starner, T., Weaver, J., Pentland, A.: Real-Time American Sign Language Recognition Using Desk and Wearable Computer Based Video, *IEEE trans. PAMI*, (1998)
44. Stokoe, W.: Sign Language Structure, University of Buffalo Press, (1960)
45. Stoll, P., Ohya, J.: Applications of HMM Modeling to Recognizing Human Gestures in Image Sequences for a Man-Machine Interface, *IEEE Intl Workshop on Robot and Human Communication*, (1995)
46. Triesch, J., Malsburg, C.: Robust Classification of Hand Postures Against Complex Background, *Intl Conf. On Automatic Face and Gesture Recognition*, (1996)
47. Triesch, J., Malsburg, C.: A Gesture Interface for Human-Robot-Interaction, *Intl Conf. On Automatic Face and Gesture Recognition*, (1998)
48. Utsumi, A., Miyasato, T., Kishino, F., Nakatsu, R.: Hand Gesture Recognition System Using Multiple Cameras, *IEEE ICPR*, (1996)
49. Vogler, C., Metaxas, D.: ASL Recognition Based on A Coupling Between HMMs and 3D Motion Analysis, *IEEE ICCV*, (1998)

50. Vogler, C., Metaxas, D.: Toward Scalability in ASL Recognition: Breaking Down Signs into Phonemes, *IEEE Gesture Workshop*, (1999)

51. Watanabe, T., Yachida, M.: Real Time Gesture Recognition Using Eigenspace from Multi Input Image Sequences, *Intl Conf. On Automatic Face and Gesture Recognition* , Japan.(1998)

52. Wilson, A., Bobick, A.: Recognition and Interpretation of Parametric Gesture, *IEEE Intl Conf. Computer Vision*, (1998)

53. Wren, C., Pentland, A.: Dynamic Modeling of Human Motion, *IEEE Intl Conf. Automatic Face and Gesture Recognition*, (1997)

54. Wu, Y., Huang, T.: Human Hand Modeling, Analysis and Animation in the Context of HCI, *IEEE Intl Conf. Image Processing*, (1999)

55. Yang, J., Xu, Y., Chen, C.: Gesture Interface: Modeling and Learning, *Proc. IEEE Int. Conf. on Robotics and Automation*, Vol. 2, pp.1747-1752. (1994)

56. Yang, M., Ahuja, N.: Extraction and Classification of Visual Motion Patterns for Hand Gesture Recognition, *IEEE Int'l Conf. on Computer Vision and Pattern Recognition*, (1998)

57. Zeller, M., et al.: A Visual Computing Environment for Very Large Scale Biomolecular Modeling, *Proc. IEEE Int. Conf. on Application-specific Systems, Architectures and Processors (ASAP)*, Zurich, pp. 3-12. (1997)

Person Localization and Posture Recognition for Human-Robot Interaction

Hans-Joachim Boehme, Ulf-Dietrich Braumann, and Andrea Corradini*,
and Horst-Michael Gross

Department of Neuroinformatics, Technical University of Ilmenau,
D-98684 Ilmenau, Germany
{hans,ulf,andreac,homi}@informatik.tu-ilmenau.de

Abstract. The development of a hybrid system for (mainly) gesture-based human-robot interaction is presented, thereby describing the progress in comparison to the work shown at the last gesture workshop (see [2]). The system makes use of standard image processing techniques as well as of neural information processing. The performance of our architecture includes the detection of a person as a potential user in an indoor environment, followed by the recognition of her gestural instructions. In this paper, we concentrate on two major mechanisms: (i), the contour-based person localization via a combination of steerable filters and three-dimensional dynamic neural fields, and (ii), our first experiences concerning the recognition of different instructional postures via a combination of statistical moments and neural classifiers.

Keywords: Human-Robot Interaction, Neural Networks, Dynamic Neural Fields

1 Introduction

Our group is especially interested in novel techniques for interaction with mobile service systems in indoor environments. Such service systems should be able to observe their operation area in an active manner, to localize and contact a potential user, to interact with their users immediately and continuously, and to offer their services (transport, information presentation, or simply entertainment) in the context of the actual situation. Our robot platform MILVA (Multisensoric Intelligent Learning Vehicle in a neural Architecture) serves as the testbed for natural human-robot interaction. A two-camera system with 7 degrees of freedom (for each camera pan, tilt and zoom, additional pan for both cameras) will both capture the robot's environment and all interactional details expressed by persons. An additional camera in the front of the robot provides the visual information for navigation.

Several systems for gesture-based human-machine interaction have been developed recently (e. g. see [6, 16, 17, 13, 19, 7]). A comprehensive collection of video-based gesture recognition systems can be found in [14]. Most of these approaches

---

* supported by the TMR Marie Curie Research Training Grant # ERB FMBI CT 97 2613

A. Braffort et al. (Eds.): GW'99, LNAI 1739, pp. 117–128, 1999.

require certain constraints concerning the environmental conditions (lighting, distance between camera and person, etc.). During interaction with a mobile service system operating in an unconstrained indoor ar ea one cannot assume such predefined circumstances. Therefore, the service system has to deal with highly varying environmental conditions which can neither be estimated nor influenced. Taking into account this fact, we developed a robust saliency system for person localization (Sec. 2). This saliency system integrates different visual cues into the localization process. Furthermore, acoustic information (estimation of source direction) is used to support the visual detection (Sec. 2.3).

After the detection of a person which is aligned towards the robot, a gesture recognition process must be carried out to transmit the behavioral instructions from the user to the robot (Sec. 3). Currently, we use a posture alphabet (see Fig. 1), i.e. we recognize a set of gestural symbols. In our future work we want to overcome this limitation and develop a system capable of continuously recognizing dynamic gestures.

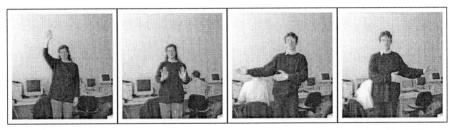

Fig. 1. Gestures (postures) to be recognized; from left to right they carry the following meanings for the robot: come to me, stop, move left, move right

2 Saliency System for Person Localization

Fig. 2 provides a coarse sketch of the saliency system for user localization. Initially, both cameras of the two-camera system operate in wide-angle mode in order to cover the greatest possible area of the environment. Multiresolution pyramids transform the images into a multiscale representation. Two cue modules sensitive to *facial structure* and *structure of a head-shoulder contour*, respectively, operate at all levels of a grayscale pyramid. The cue module for *skin color* detection uses the original color image. Its segmentation result is transformed into a pyramid representation, too, to obtain an uniform data structure for the different cues. The utility of the different parallel processing cue modules is to make the saliency system robust and independent of the presence of one certain information source in the images. Hence, we can handle varying environmental circumstances much easier, which, for instance, make the skin color detection difficult or almost impossible. Furthermore, high expense for the development of the cue modules can be avoided (see [4, 3], too).

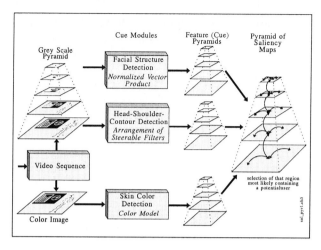

Fig. 2. Components of the saliency system for person localization

The output of the cue modules serves as the input for the saliency pyramid at each resolutional level. The maps are topographically organized neural fields containing dynamic neurons interacting among each other (see [1, 15]). In the saliency maps *all those regions* shall become prominent that most likely cover *the upper part of a person*.

2.1   Cues for Person Specific Saliency

In our previous work (see [2]) the three cues were assumed to be of equal importance. After a period of practical experiences we had to face that the shape-based approach provides much more reliable contributions to the localization process compared to the skin color and facial structure cues. The reasons are quite obvious: Skin color detection is highly influenced by illumination. Although we use an additional color adaptation method (see [18]) to yield constant color sensation, robust skin color detection cannot ensured in general. Further, solving the localization problem becomes more interesting the farther away the person is. Necessarily, relevant features should appear even on rather coarse resolutional scales so that details, as facial structures, are less prominent. Facial structure can be detected confidently only if the distance between person and camera is not too large. Otherwise, the region covered by the face becomes to small to be localized.

Against this background, the method for head-shoulder contour detection was improved significantly. The actual method is described in more detail in the following subsection. Since the other cues can only support the person localization, but cannot ensure the localization alone, their methods were reduced to rather simple, but computationally efficient algorithms.

Head-Shoulder Contour   The contour which we refer to is that of the upper body of frontally aligned persons. Our simple contour shape prototype model consists of an arrangement of oriented filters doing a piecewise approximation of the upper shape (head, shoulder) of a frontally aligned person. The arrangement itself was learned based on a set of training images. Applying such a filter arrangement in a multi-resolutional manner, this leads to a robust localization of frontally aligned persons even in depth.

Arrangements of Steerable Filters – Motivation and Related Work: The idea of this method refers just to a description of the outer shape of head and shoulders and is based both on some physiological considerations as well as on psychophysical effects.

The visual cortex consists in several parts of cells with oriented receptive fields. A lot of investigations have shown that the profile of receptive fields of simple cells in the mammalian primary visual cortex can be modeled by some two-dimensional mathematical functions. Gaborian [11] and Gaussian functions (incl. low order derivatives) [12] appear to provide the typical profiles for visual receptive fields. So, local operations decompose the visual information with respect to the frequency space.

Psychophysical aspects for the contour-shape based approach, e. g., good continuation or symmetry (both belonging to the Gestalt laws), obviously describe effects which necessitate grouping mechanisms. Against this background, we conceptualized the approach of an *arrangement* of oriented filters.

Because each section of the contour should be approximated by a special oriented filter, localizing a person would require possibly as many *differently oriented* filters as orientations belong to the arrangement. Since that would be computationally very costly we turn to steerable filters.

Determining the Course of Contour: Steerable filters have the nice property that an a-priori limited number of convolutions is sufficient to derive any orientation information within an image. Thus, their use provides an extended set of orientations, avoids the necessity of numerous additional filters, and enables a more accurate computation of the course of contour.

Our complete data set consists of images showing ten persons in front of a homogeneous background under three different viewing angles ($0°$, $+10°$ and $-10°$, where $0°$ corresponds to an exactly frontally aligned body). All these images have been recorded under identic conditions (position, illumination, distance). Additionally, in order to achieve a symmetrical contour model the whole data set was vertically mirrored extending the data set to 60 images. Subsequently, the 256×256-images (grayscale) were low-pass filtered and scaled down to 16×16. Then, we applied a Sobel operator to the images enhancing the edges of each image. Next, all of those edge-marked intermediate images were averaged, since the contour to be determined *on average* should match the real outer contour. After this we thresholded to find *that* edge representing the typical contour shape.

Now, we have the course of the contour of interest resulting in a 16×16 binary matrix where the elements along the contour are set to 1, the others remain 0.

We refer to this contour matrix, our template, as $\Lambda^\star$. The local orientation of each contour element is determined by means of the steerable filters (see below). These are applied to the binary contour shape so that for each element of $\Lambda^\star$ an angle of orientation can be determined resulting in a matrix Λ (see Fig. 3).

Fig. 3. The determined shape of contour Λ: orientation angles coded by gray values (0°: black; 90°: medium gray; 180°: white). Note that around the forehead transitions from 180° to 0° occur. The contour shape is symmetric since the original data set was mirrored.

Applying Steerable Filters: After determining the binary contour, we measure the local orientation by means of a set of filters which are oriented in every direction. We take the powerful approach of *steerable filters* (see [8]) for orientation estimation. It provides an efficient filtering output by applying a few *basis filters* corresponding to a few angles and then interpolating the basis filter responses in the desired direction. Steerable filters are computationally efficient and do not suffer from the orientation selection problem.

In general, a function $f(\cdot)$ is considered to be steerable if the following two conditions are satisfied. First, its basis filter set is made up of M rotated copies of the function $f^{\alpha_1}(\cdot) \ldots f^{\alpha_M}(\cdot)$ on any certain angles $\alpha_1 \ldots \alpha_M$. Second, a rotated copy $f^{\vartheta}(\cdot)$ of it on some angle ϑ has to be obtained by a superposition of its basis set multiplied by the interpolation functions $k_j(\vartheta)$ as in

$$f^{\vartheta}(\cdot) = \sum_{j=1}^{M} k_j(\vartheta) f^{\alpha_j}(\cdot) \qquad (1)$$

In our work we take a quadrature pair by using the second derivative of a Gaussian and an approximation of its Hilbert transform by a third-order polynomial modulating a Gaussian. From the steering theorem [8] these functions are steerable and need $M = 7$ basis functions. To measure the orientation along the contour, we use the phase independent squared sum of the output of the quadrature pair. This squared response as a function of the filter orientation ϑ at a point (x, y) represents an *oriented energy* $E^{(x,y)}(\vartheta)$. Because of the symmetry of the functions, the energy at every pixel is periodic with period π. To accurately estimate the *dominant* local orientation one could *pointwise* maximize the orientation energy by taking $\vartheta^{(x,y)}_{MAX} = \arg\max\{E^{(x,y)}(\vartheta) \mid \vartheta \in [0, \pi)\}$. However, to find this maximum value we do not search degree-wise for the maximum because there already exists an analytical solution for the maximization [8]. We further refer to the matrix of all these angular values $\vartheta^{(x,y)}_{MAX}$ corresponding to the image as Θ. Furthermore, there exists a separable basis set in Cartesian coordinates which considerably lowers the computational costs.

Computing the Neural Field Input: The previous section described the theory and use of steerable filters. By means of those filters we calculate both the matrix Λ describing a typical course of the head-shoulder-portrait and the matrix Θ

(computed from the image wherein a person is to be found) containing the dominant local orientation values.

Subsequently, we search for the presence of the *visual cue* head-shoulder-portrait, represented by the kernel Λ, within the matrix Θ. To do this, we utilize a matching technique based on a *similarity measure* $m^{(x,y)}$. Due to the π-periodicity of the outcome of the steerable filters and in order to properly describe the likeness between two elements of Λ and Θ, the similarity function requires the same periodicity.

$$
m^{(x,y)} = \frac{\displaystyle\sum_{\substack{i=0 \\ \lambda_{i,j}\neq 0}}^{I-1}\sum_{j=0}^{J-1}\frac{1}{2}\left[\cos\left(2\left|\lambda_{i,j} - \vartheta_{MAX}^{(x+i-\frac{I}{2},y+j-\frac{J}{2})}\right|\right)+1\right]}{\mathrm{card}\left(\mathrm{supp}\left(\Lambda\right)\right)}
\tag{2}
$$

Herein, $\lambda_{i,j}$ refers to the element of Λ at position (i,j) and $\vartheta_{MAX}^{(x+i-\frac{I}{2},y+j-\frac{J}{2})}$ to the one of Θ at $(x+i-\frac{I}{2},y+j-\frac{J}{2})$. $I = J = 16$ represent the dimensions of the matrix Λ. The normalization to the cardinality of the support of Λ (the support of a matrix considers only nonzero elements) ensures $m^{(x,y)} \in [0,1]$ for the further processing. Fig. 4 summarizes the processing steps.

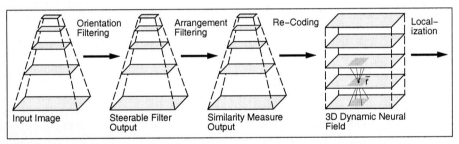

Fig. 4. Starting from a multi-resolution representation of the image, each level is treated by steerable filters. Applying the filter arrangement we determine a distance measure which is taken as input to a three-dimensional field of dynamic neurons. The resulting blob (locally delimited pattern of active neurons) is used to localize a person.

Skin Color For the generation of a skin color training data set, portrait images of different persons (of our lab) were segmented manually. The images were acquired under appropriate lighting conditions (typical for our lab environment). The skin color detection uses the original color image. In order to obtain almost constant color sensation, we first map the RGB color space into a fundamental color space and employ a color adaptation method (see [18]). Then, we return into the RGB color space, use the chromatic projection $r = \frac{R}{R+G+B}$ and $g = \frac{G}{R+G+B}$, and define a bimodal Gaussian function via calculation of the mean and the covariance of that skin color data set to roughly model the obtained skin color distribution. Furthermore, after a person (face region) could be localized, a new

Gaussian model is created, more specific for the illumination and the skin type at hand. Via this model the detection of skin colored regions, especially hands, can be improved. This is of special importance because the hand regions cannot be segmented by structural information (see [10], and Sec. 3.1). A Mahalanobis-based distance measure is employed to compute the similarity between the color value of each pixel and the color model. To achieve an appropriate input for the 3D dynamic neural field, the resulting similarity map is recoded into an activity map, where the highest activity stands for the highest similarity. A more detailed description of our skin color investigations can be found in [2].

Facial Structure   We assume that a person can considered to be a user if her face is oriented towards the robot.

In our previous work, the detection of facial structure employed eigenfaces (see [2, 4]). The disadvantage of that method is their computational complexity, resulting in time consuming calculations. Due to real-time constraints a new, similar method was implemented. First, a prototype (mean) pattern of a frontally aligned face (15 x 15 pixels) was created by means of the images contained in the ORL data set (`http://www.cam-orl.co.uk/facedatabase.html`). Then we calculate the similarity between each image region and the prototype pattern via normalized convolution. The higher the convolution result, the higher the similarity, and the convolution result can be used directly as the input for the saliency pyramid.

2.2   The Saliency Pyramid as a 3D Nonlinear Dynamic Field

To achieve a good localization, a *selection mechanism* is needed to make a definite choice among those regions within the pyramid where rather high similarity measures concerning the different cues are concentrated. Since dynamic neural fields are powerful for dynamic selection and pattern formation using simple homogeneous internal interaction rules, we adapted them to our purposes. Because we use five fine-to-coarse resolutions in our scale space (see Fig. 2), we can actually localize pe rsons even at different distances. Therefore, a neural field for selecting the most salient region should be three-dimensional. That field F can be described as a recurrent nonlinear dynamic system. Regarding the selection task, we need a dynamic behavior which leads to *one* local region of active neurons successfully competing against the others, i. e. the formation of one single blob of active neurons as an equilibrium state of the field. The following equation describes the system:

$$\tau \frac{d}{dt} z(\boldsymbol{r}, t) = -z(\boldsymbol{r}, t) - c_h h(t) + c_i x(\boldsymbol{r}, t) + c_l \int_N w(\boldsymbol{r} - \boldsymbol{r}') y(\boldsymbol{r}', t) \mathrm{d}^3 \boldsymbol{r}' \quad (3)$$

Herein $\boldsymbol{r}$ denotes the three-dimensional coordinate of a neuron position in the field, $z(\boldsymbol{r}, t)$ is the activation of a neuron $\boldsymbol{r}$ at time t, $y(\boldsymbol{r}, t)$ is the output activity of this neuron computed as a sigmoidal function of $\boldsymbol{r}$ alone, $x(\boldsymbol{r}, t)$ denotes the external inputs (corresponding to the re-coded similarity measures for the different cues, combined by a Min-Max fuzzy operator), $h(t)$ is the global inhibition at time t gathering the activity from each neuron over the entire field $F \subseteq \mathrm{R}^3$. $w(r - r')$ denotes the Mexican-hat-like function of lateral activation of neuron r from the surrounding neighborhood $N \subseteq \mathrm{R}^3$. For one r, N is symbolically marked as dark regions in Fig. 4 (right). The constants c_h, c_l and c_i represent parameters of the system.

As also illustrated in Fig. 4, to use a three-dimensional neural field, we have to consider the local correspondences between the resolution levels. Therefore, we apply a re-coding into a cuboid structure. One side effect is that the coarser a pyramid level is the less we can locate something by means of the similarity measure. However, without particularly treating this effect we just noticed that those levels z of the neural field activated from the rather coarse pyramid levels take little a few more steps to develop a blob (or a part of a blob, respectively).

Results for Person Localization The results of the saliency system are qualitatively illustrated in Fig. 5.

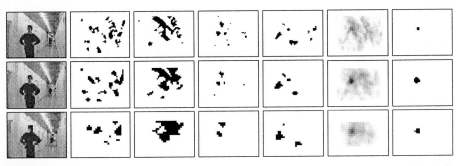

Fig. 5. Localization results in an indoor environment (middle three layers of the multiscale representation): The localization of a person occurs not sharply at one of the pyramidal planes, the originating spatial blob (rightmost column) is most strongly developed on the central of the five planes. Each row contains the results of one of the five (distance $1/\sqrt{2}$) computed resolution steps. The seven columns depict the following: input, results of the orientation filtering for selected angles $0°$, $45°$, $90°$ and $135°$, the result of the filtering with the filter arrangement and finally the result of the selection within a three-dimensional field of dynamic neurons.

The images of the rightmost column show the state of three layers of the dynamic neural field in a snapshot at that moment when the activity change of the most active neuron became less than 1%. On average, the system takes 11 iteration steps using a time-discrete Euler method. The range of the blob is not restricted to one plane. To get a more precise specification of the distance of a person one could interpolate the z-coordinate of the blob center within the field.

Our presented results are exemplary, the usage of the shape of contour and the additional cues skin color and facial structure provide a robust solution for the person localization problem, even under quite different conditions. Unfortunately, other results cannot be shown here due to space limits. The novel approach with a three-dimensional dynamic neural field can be assessed as robust method for the selection process.

2.3   Auditory Saliency

Additionally to the visually-based saliency system a model for selective auditory attention was developed in our department (see [20]). This model was already implemented on MILVA and is to support the user localization. For example, the user can attract MILVA's attention by clapping her hands, i.e. MILVA will align her active-vision system towards that direction in which an auditory signal source was recognized.

3   Posture Recognition

In this section we describe the processing steps to be carried out to recognize the postures shown in Fig. 1. The first step consists of a camera control procedure. The second camera of the active vision head is aligned towards the selected person and acquires the "posture images". An additional zoom control ensures that the person emerges in an approximately constant, predefined scale.

3.1   Posture Segmentation

The segmentation of face and hands as the gesture relevant parts is exclusively based on skin color processing. From the face region we take color values to construct a specific color model for the skin type and the illumination at hand.

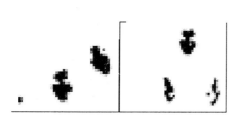

Fig. 6. Skin color segmented "posture images"

Via a simple distance measure (Mahalanobis based) each pixel is classified to be a member of the skin class or not (see Fig. 6) to obtain a binarized image.

3.2   Moment-Based Posture Description

From the skin color segmented posture image, sub-sampled to a size of 64×64 pixels, we compute a feature vector v containing 9 statistical moments (normalized central moments). For these moments the corresponding equation is given by equ. 4.

$$\mu_{pq} = \sum_{x,y} (x - \bar{x})^p \cdot (y - \bar{y})^q \cdot f(x,y) \qquad (4)$$

Herein μ_{pq} denotes the moment, x and y are the image coordinates, $\bar{x}$ and $\bar{y}$ describe the center of gravity, and $f(x, y)$ is the binary value at position (x, y).

Before classifying the feature vectors into the four posture classes, in the next step we investigated the alteration of the feature vectors when the person (the posture, respectively) is slightly shifted. The result for one posture image is shown in Fig. 7.

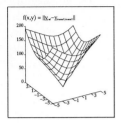

Fig. 7. Fluctuation of the feature vector v depending on the deviation of the same posture. We can see, that the Euclidean distance between the reference feature vector v_{ref}, obtained at the central position, and the feature vectors calculated under deviations up to 5 pixels, grows smoothly. The shown distance values up to 200 are small in relation to the number of 9 moments and their value intervals.

3.3   Posture Recognition with Neural Classifiers

For the training of the neural classifiers we used a data set containing 360 feature vectors. These vectors were computed from the four postures, 90 examples of each. We used 180 vectors for the training and 180 vectors for the test of the networks.

First, we used a Radial Basis Function (RBF) network containing 9 input nodes, 20 hidden (RBF) nodes, and 4 output nodes. The RBF layer was trained first with a Neural Gas algorithm to approximate the input data distribution. Then, the second weight layer was trained via the standard delta rule.

Second, a modified Counterpropagation (CP) network was employed for posture recognition. The network had the same topology as the RBF network. The hidden layer was trained first with a Neural Gas algorithm, too. Then, the second weight layer was trained by a learning rule similar to Grossberg's outstar model (see [9]).

Network	Topology	# of Trainingspatterns	# of Testpatterns	# of false classified patterns	# of unclassified patterns	Recognition Rate
RBF	9-20-4	180	180	6	10	91.2 %
CP	9-20-4	180	180	40	48	75.6 %

The table summarizes the performance achieved by the two networks. The RBF network yielded robust performance, and the number of false classified patterns was rather low, whereas the CP network suffers from a large number of misclassifications and additionally from a lower recognition rate. Concluding these results, we are currently implementing the RBF based approach on our mobile robot.

4   Overall Performance, Conclusions, and Outlook

Besides the performance concerning posture recognition, the person localization is the most crucial but absolutely necessary prerequistite for the function of the whole system. The use of multiple cues and their integration into a selection process via 3D dynamic neural fields led to a satisfying person specific saliency system. Using a CHUGAI BOYEKI CD 08 video camera with maximum wide angle mode, the multiscale representation covers a distance from 0.5 to about 2.5 meters. Within this interval, the localization is very robust against slight rotations (up to 15°), scene content, and illumination. Furthermore, the integration of auditory saliency makes it easy for the user to attract the attention of the robot and to speed up the localization process significantly.

The work for posture and gesture recognition is still ongoing. Therefore, the presented approach is just the begin of the investigations. Nevertheless, the already implemented method is appropriate to transmit several gesticulated commands to the robot, but is, of coarse, still far away from really natural human-robot interaction. Our future work will concern a dynamic approach for continuous gesture recognition. More precisely, we try to describe different space-time gestures via the observed trajectory in the moment feature space. The more crucial problem consists in the "behavioral grounding" of such dynamic gestures, whereas the correspondence between the postures used in our example and the behavioral meanings for the robot is rather simple. One possible way could be the parallel utilization of speech and gesture to find out coherences between these two information channels in order to teach the robot to use gesticulated or spoken commands alternatively. In the present state, the recognition of the po stural commands is mostly dedicated to close the perception-action cycle in an exemplary way.

For a more detailled description of the overall application scenario the presented system is embedded in we refer to [5], where aspects such as navigation behavior and behavioral organisation are pointed out, too.

References

1. Amari, S. Dynamics of pattern formation in lateral-inhibition type neural fields. *Biological Cybernetics*, 27:77–87, 1977.
2. Boehme, H.-J., Brakensiek, A., Braumann, U.-D., Krabbes, M., and Gross, H.-M. Neural Architecture for Gesture-Based Human-Machine-Interaction. In *Gesture and Sign-Language in Human-Computer Interaction*, Lecture Notes in Artificial Intelligence, pages 219–232. Springer, 1998.
3. Boehme, H.-J., Braumann, U.-D., Brakensiek, A., Krabbes, M., Corradini, A., and Gross, H.-M. Neural Networks for Gesture-based Remote Control of a Mobile Robot. In *International Joint Conference on Neural Networks*, volume 1, pages 372–377. IEEE Computer Society Press, 1998.
4. Boehme, H.-J., Braumann, U.-D., Brakensiek, A., Krabbes, M., Corradini, A., and Gross, H.-M. User Localisation for Visually-based Human-Machine-Interaction. In *International Conference on Automatic Face- and Gesture Recognition*, pages 486–491. IEEE Computer Society Press, 1998.

5. Boehme, H.-J. and Gross, H.-M. Ein Interaktives Mobiles Service=System für den Baumarkt. In *14. Fachgespräch Autonome Mobile Systeme (AMS'99), München.* Springer, 1999. in press.
6. Darrell, T., Basu, S., Wren, C., and Pentland, A. Perceptually-driven Avatars and Interfaces: active methods for direct control. In *SIGGRAPH'97*, 1997. M.I.T. Media Lab Perceptual Computation Section, TR 416.
7. Fjeld, M., Bichsel, M., and Rauterberg, M. BUILD-IT: An Intuitive Design Tool Based on Direct Object Manipulation. In *Gesture and Sign-Language in Human-Computer Interaction*, pages 297–308, 1998.
8. Freeman, W.T. and Adelson, E.H. The Design and Use of Steerable Filters. *IEEE Transactions on Pattern Analysis and Machine Intelligence (PAMI)*, 13(9):891–906, 1991.
9. Grossberg, S. Some Networks That Can Learn, Remember, and Reproduce Any Number of Complicated Space-Time Patterns. *Journal of Mathematics and Mechanics*, 19(1):53–99, 1969.
10. Hunke, M.H. Locating and Tracking of Human Faces with Neural Networks. Technical report, Carnegie Mellon University Pittsburgh, 1994. CMU-CS-94-155.
11. Jones, J.P. and Palmer, L.A. An Evaluation of the Two-Dimensional Gabor Filter Model of Simple Receptive Fields in Cat Striate Cortex. *Journal of Neurophysiology*, 56(8):1233–1258, 1987.
12. Koenderink, J.J. and van Doorn, A.J. Receptive Field Families. *Biological Cybernetics*, 63:291–297, 1990.
13. Kohler, M. Special Topics of Gesture Recognition Applied in Intelligent Home Environments. In *Gesture and Sign-Language in Human-Computer Interaction*, pages 285–296, 1998.
14. Kohler, M. Vision Based Gesture Recognition Systems, 1998. `http://ls7-www.informatik.uni-dortmund.de/html/englisch/gesture/vbgr-table.html`.
15. K. Kopecz. Neural field dynamics provide robust control for attentional resources. In *Aktives Sehen in technischen und biologischen Systemen*, pages 137–144. Infix-Verlag, 1996.
16. Kortenkamp, D., Huber, E., and Bonasso, P.R. Recognizing and interpreting gestures on a mobile robot. In *Thirteenth National Conference on Artificial Intelligence (AAAI-96)*, 1996.
17. Maggioni, C. and Kämmerer, B. GestureComputer – History, Design, and Applications. In *Proceedings of the Workshop on Computer Vision in Man-Machine Interfaces*, 1996.
18. Pomierski, T. and Gross, H.-M. Biological Neural Architectures for Chromatic Adaptation resulting in Constant Color Sensations. In *ICNN'96, IEEE International Conference on Neural Networks*, pages 734–739. IEEE Press, 1996.
19. Rigoll, G., Kosmala, A., and Eickeler, S. High Performance Real-Time Gesture Recognition Using Hidden Markov Models. In *Gesture and Sign-Language in Human-Computer Interaction*, pages 69–80, 1998.
20. Zahn, T., Izak, R., Trott, T., and Paschke, P. A paced analog silicon model of auditory attention. In *Neuromorphic Systems: Engineering Silicon from Neurobiology. 1st European Workshop on Neuromorphic Systems*, pages 99–112. World Scientific Publishing, 1997.

Statistical Gesture Recognition Through Modelling of Parameter Trajectories

J. Martin, D. Hall, and J. L. Crowley

Projet PRIMA — Lab. GRAVIR–IMAG
INRIA Rhônes–Alpes
655, avenue de l'Europe
38330 – Montbonnot Saint Martin, France
Jerome.Martin@imag.fr

Abstract. The recognition of human gestures is a challenging problem that can contribute to a natural man–machine interface. In this paper, we present a new technique for gesture recognition. Gestures are modelled as temporal trajectories of parameters. Local sub-sequences of these trajectories are extracted and used to define an orthogonal space using principal component analysis. In this space the probabilistic density function of the training trajectories is represented by a multidimensional histogram, which builds the basis for the recognition. Experiments on three different recognition problems show the general utility of the approach.

1 Introduction

The use of gestures provides an alternative to popular but slow and unnatural devices — such as mice, keyboards and joystick — for human–computer interaction. Tremendous progress in computer vision techniques and the availability of fast computing make real–time visual interpretation of gestures feasible. As a consequence the integration of vision based gesture recognition has had an increasing interest in recent years [1, 2]. This includes human body movements, movements of the arm and hand and facial expressions.

A vision–based gesture interpretation system is composed of three phases [3]: *Gesture Modelling*, *Gesture Analysis* and *Gesture Recognition*. The first task is choosing a gesture model. The model may consider spatial and temporal parameters depending on the application. Spatial parameters include pose and motion in space. The analysis phase extracts model parameters from images. This phase is followed by gesture recognition in which the parameters are classified and interpreted to infer the observed gesture.

Gesture interpretation currently provides an interesting scientific problem which challenges the state of the art in computer vision. Recent progress with

A. Braffort et al. (Eds.): GW'99, LNAI 1739, pp. 129–140, 1999.

specifically engineered techniques has shown that visual recognition of gestures is possible, and has excited interest in finding a general theoretical framework for gesture recognition. Starner [4] describes the use of Hidden Markov Models (HMM's) for the recognition of complex, structured hand gestures such as found in American Sign Language. His HMM–based system recognises a 40 word lexicon in real–time. The hand tracking stage of the system uses one colour camera to track hands wearing coloured gloves. In later work [5] the system has matured to a natural hand skin tracking. Darrell and Pentland [6] use dynamic time warping (DTW) to match gestures with stored gesture patterns learned from examples. The matching process is the normalised image correlation between the image and a set of learned view models. Davis and Bobick [7] propose a view–based approach to the representation and recognition of action. A *motion history image* (MHI) is the representation basis. The MHI is a statistic image where pixel intensity is a function of the frequency of the motion sequence. Recognition is accomplished in a feature–based statistical framework. Guttan, Imam and Wechsler [8] propose a hybrid approach using a combination of connectionnist networks — radial basis functions (RBF) — and inductive decision trees. Erenshteyn *et al* [9] developed an architecture based on two neural networks for the recognition of American Sign Language.

Many of these approaches use trajectories for data representation. A gesture is represented as a sequence of observed vectors in some measurement space. This space may be physical (position and orientation of the hand) or may be based on the configuration of the hand and arm (a configuration space). While Hidden Markov Models are a popular means for representing and recognising such trajectories, the determination of the states and transition probabilities is a difficult problem.

In this paper, we present an alternative gesture recognition technique. Gestures are modelled as temporal trajectories of parameters. Recognition of trajectories is based on joint statistics of local parameters. In our approach, local sub–sequences of a trajectory are projected into an orthogonal subspace. The vector of local parameters is determined by principal component analysis of sub–sequences of the trajectory. The first principal components are selected and used to define an orthogonal parameter space. A multidimensional histogram of values in this parameter space is used to compute the probability that a trajectory belongs to a gesture class.

In Section 2 the transformation of gestures into trajectories is explained for head movements, hand gestures and facial expressions. Section 3 describes the construction of the local parameters and reviews the theoretical background of the histogram technique. In the experimental section 4 the developed technique is applied to head movements, hand gestures and facial expressions. The main result is that such a representation provides a reliable means for representation and recognition of gestures. The success on all these domains demonstrates the general utility of the approach.

2   Representing Gestures as Trajectories in Parameters Space

Selecting the appropriate parameter vector for recognising gesture classes is a difficult problem. Head and hand position can be modelled by parameters such as position, scale, pitch, role and yaw. The first and second derivatives of these parameters can be used to model patterns of movement and change. The starting point for this investigation was the use of principal component analysis to construct optimal parameter vectors for gesture recognition.

A trajectory is an ordered sequence of measurement vectors m_{t_i} at time t_i. The trajectory of gesture G in the parameter space $\mathcal{S}$, is denoted $T_{\mathcal{S}}$:

$$T_{\mathcal{S}} = \left(m_{t_0}, \ldots, m_{t_{k-s}}, \ldots, m_{t_{k-2}}, m_{t_{k-1}}, m_{t_k}\right) \qquad (1)$$

The dimensionality and structure of the parameter vector that composes the trajectory depends upon the parameter set. A trajectory can be visualised by the plots of the values of each coordinate of the parameter vector over time as shown in Figure 1. Figure 1 shows two examples of two different gestures in a 2 dimensional space.

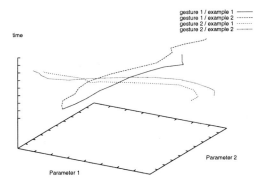

Fig. 1. Trajectories of differents gestures in a two dimensional parameter space.

The technique developed in this paper is illustrated with three classes of gestures. A first, trivial, dataset is provided by the position of a face observed during nodding and shaking of a head to indicate yes and no respectivley. The position data is provided by a previously built face tracker [10]. A second experiment concerns recognition of the Graffiti character set [11] as it is written. Data is obtained by tracking the finger tip [12]. The third experiment is recognition of facial expressions from the trajectory of projections into an eigenspace of faces. Image eigenvectors provide an easy solution to derived parameters from images, *image property parameters* [3].

3   Statistical Recognition of Trajectories

Statistical recognition has been successfully employed by Schiele [13] in demonstrating a novel method for recognition of objects from the joint statistics of local feature vectors. Feature vectors are obtained by projection onto a set of local neighborhood operators, such as Gaussian derivative or Gabor filters. Joint statistics are represented as multidimensional histograms. Histograms provide the probability density functions required for application of Bayes rule. Schiele's work shows that a histogram representation provides a reliable and accurate means for the recognition of a large number of objects from images.

The work described in this paper extends Schiele's approach to statistical recognition gestures and trajectories. Recognition is based on the probability density function of local parameters of a gesture trajectory. We employ a histogram to provide the probability density function of a gesture G_i considering a set of local parameters.

3.1   Signature of Parameters

Local measurement sequence The *local measurements sequence*, w_{t_i}, is the measurement vectors m_{t_i} at time t_i and its recent history. The sequence w_{t_i} is defined by:

$$w_{t_i} = \left(m_{t_{i-s+1}}, \ldots, m_{t_i}\right) \tag{2}$$

where m_{t_x} is the measurement vectors at time t_x and s is the size of the temporal window.

The size s defines the period of time in which a parameter vector is considered as recent enough to contribute to the parameter sequence. s has a value that is small so that the sequence can be considered as local itself. In our experiments, we use values between 5 and 20 with a frame rate of 10 images per second.

Eigen–space of local measurements From a trajectory with n vectors, $n - s$ *local parameter sequences* w_{t_i} can be extracted. These sequences are used to compute the linear eigenfeature space $\mathcal{M}$ by applying principal component analysis (PCA). $\mathcal{M}$ is spanned by the eigenvectors e_i computed by the PCA. For many problems it is not necessary to keep $\mathcal{M}$ in its full dimensionality. In this paper $\mathcal{M}$ is reduced to the m most dominant eigen vectors as axes. m varies with the complexity of the problem. Those eigenvectors represent the *local eigen-features*.

Signature of parameters The projection of a *local parameter sequence* w_{t_i} onto $\mathcal{M}$ is called a *signature of parameters* and is denoted γ_{t_i}. The projection of a trajectory composed of w_{t_i} results in a trajectory $T_{\mathcal{M}}$ in $\mathcal{M}$:

$$T_{\mathcal{M}} = \left(\gamma_{t_{s-1}}, \ldots, \gamma_{tk-1}, \gamma_{t_k}\right) \tag{3}$$

3.2   Probability Density of Signatures

This section develops local gesture recognition based on the analysis of probabilistic density functions. The output from the projection of a parameter measurement and its local history provides a *parameters signature*, γ_t. Probabilistic recognition of gesture G_n is achieved considering the local signature γ_t. The probability $p(G_n \mid \gamma_t)$ is computed using the Bayes Rule:

$$p(G_n \mid \gamma_t) = \frac{p(\gamma_t \mid G_n)p(G_n)}{p(\gamma_t)} \tag{4}$$

where $p(G_n)$ is the *a priori* probability of gesture G_n, $p(\gamma_t \mid G_i)$ is the *a priori* probability of signature γ_t given the gesture G_i, and $p(\gamma_t)$ denotes the probability of signature γ_t.

A classical approach to compute the probability $p(G_n)$ is to consider all gestures with equal probability. The probability $p(G_n)$ is the ratio of samples n_n of gestures G_n to all gestures samples N:

$$p(G_n) = \frac{n_n}{N} \tag{5}$$

A extensive analysis of the problem allows the refinement of the probability of each class. In the example of Unistroke recognition (see Section 4.2), the probabilty for letter A is higher than for letter Q. In this paper we count 1303 A (7.2%) and 48 Q (0.3%).

The probability of signature γ_t is computed for all gestures G_i by:

$$p(\gamma_t) = \sum_i \left(p(\gamma_t \mid G_i)p(G_i) \right) \tag{6}$$

Probablistic density function as multidimensional histograms. The probabilistic density function can be represented by multidimensional histograms of signature vectors. A histogram is constructed by subdividing the space $\mathcal{M}$ containing the training set of all gestures signature into equidistant cells.

The histogram resolution, the number of cells per dimension is kept relatively small to compensate for the number of dimensions (of order 2 to 5). Discriminability between vectors decreases with the number of histogram cells, as similar vectors map to the same histogram cell. Thus an important parameter for our method is the number of histogram cells.

The use of discrete samples of a gesture with a given sampling period implies that points between the parameters are not captured by the histogram. The larger the number of histogram cells, the more training data is required to fill the histogram. This is especially important when using Bayes rule, as empty histogram cells will give a zero probability. In order to reduce the number of training samples required for a given histogram resolution, we smooth the histogram by convolution with a Gaussian filter.

In the case of histograms, the probabilistic density function for a signature γ_t given gesture G_n is:

$$p(\gamma_t \mid G_n) = \frac{1}{n_n} h_n(\gamma_t) \qquad (7)$$

where n_n is the number of samples for gesture G_n and h_n the histogram.

Decomposition of (6) leads to:

$$p(\gamma_t) = \sum_i \left(\frac{1}{n_i} h_i(\gamma_t) \frac{n_i}{N} \right) = \sum_i \left(\frac{1}{N} h_i(\gamma_t) \right) \qquad (8)$$

Incorporating (5, 7, 8) in Bayes rules (4) leads to the probabilistic density function for a gesture G_n given γ_t

$$p(G_n \mid \gamma_t) = \frac{h_n(\gamma_t)}{\sum_i (h_i(\gamma_t))} = \frac{h_n(\gamma_t)}{H(\gamma_t)} \qquad (9)$$

where h_n is the histogram for the gesture G_n and h_G is the cumulated histogram of all gestures G. The probabilistic density function of a gesture G_n given γ_t can be obtained by dividing the histogram h_n by the global histogram H.

4   Experimental Results

Perception of human action is a challenging problem in computer vision. The technique is designed to solve recognition problems where the appearance is represented by a model with many dimensions. During the development process the technique was applied to three different problems, with increasing complexity. The first problem is the recognition of head gestures for yes and no.

4.1   Head Movements

As a first experiment, we look at the problem of discriminating simple head movements. The position of the face relative to its centre position is measured by a face tracker in a video sequence. The result is a two dimensional trajectory containing the coordinates x and y of the centre of the face.

Twenty repetitions of the same movement performed by one of the authors were recorded to provide a training set. A history of 20 samples is considered to extract *local measurement sequences* and to compute a 40 dimensional $\mathcal{M}$–space. Due to the low complexity of the problem it can be reduced to two dimensions. Projection of training trajectory in the reduced $\mathcal{M}$–space fill the 16 by 16 cells histogram on which the recognition is based.

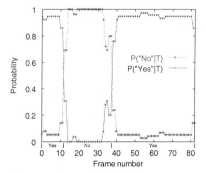

Table 1. Recognition rates for histogram with two dimensions and 16 cells per dimension.

Type	Success	Reliability
No	100%	100%
Yes	100%	97.0%

Probability change in a test sequence containing
no followed by yes.

Table 1 shows results of recognition performed on trajectories containing repetitions of the same gesture and trajectories containing two gestures shaking and nodding. The success rate gives the ratio of correct matches. The reliability is the percentage that a detection is correct.

The quality of the recognition is very good, because all movements are correctly detected and very few false detections in the confusion test give a very high reliability in the results. Figure 4.1 shows the change of the probability for the different gestures on different trajectories.

The results show that the technique can be applied for this kind of problem. With the eigen-space technique it is possible to select few dominant eigenfeatures, such that better results are achieved than by using the x and y coordinates of the parameter directly. Reasons for the very good results are the good adaptation to the problem by the selection of the eigen-features with help of PCA and the normalisation according to the Bayes rule, which decreases the number of confusions as have shown experiments with non-normalised histograms. An-

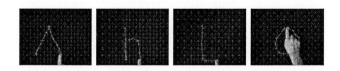

Fig. 2. Some graffiti–characters from Unistroke: letters *A*, *H*, *L* and *O*.

Fig. 3. Some images from a sequence of *A*–drawing gesture.

other reason is the trivial nature of the problem, in which the two movements to be discriminated are characterised by activity in two different parameters. The next section describes the application of the technique to the more difficult problem of recognising hand gestures from the trajectory generated by a finger tracker.

4.2   Hand–Based Writing Gestures

The following experiments concern a hand–based writing scheme. The scheme is inspired by *Unistroke* the language of the 3Com PalmPilot [11] for letter and digit recognition. Four graffiti–letters have been selected from *Unistroke* and are shown in Figure 2. Figure 3 shows some images and the trajectory extracted from a sequence drawing of the character *A*.

The experiment data consists of 25 different sequences for each gesture. The sequences have a mean length of 16 images. The database is split into a training set of 12 sequences and a testing set composed of the remaining sequences. The models are trained using different values for the size of *parameter sequences*, $\boldsymbol{w}_{t_i}$, ("sample–size"), different values for the number dimension of space $\mathcal{M}$ ("eigen–size") and different values for the number of cells in histograms ("histo–size"). Table 2 shows recognition results.

Table 2. Experimental results on *Unistroke* for different values of parameters.

"Sample–size"	Success	Reliability
5	77.2%	76.4%
10	81.5%	80.6%
15	82.9%	80.8%

"Eigen–size"	Success	Reliability
2	74.8%	71.5%
3	80.7%	80.0%
4	84.6%	85.6%

"Histo–size"	Success	Reliability
10	79.5%	77.5%
15	80.5%	79.4%
20	80.0%	79.7%

As expected, the comparison of the results shows that recognition rates increase with the size of the histogram, the number of measurements, and the number of principal components used. However recognition is impossible if the selected sample size is larger than the sequence. In our experiments, the result does not take into account sequences smaller than 15 frames. Another drawback is the limitation for both sizes of eigenspace, $\mathcal{M}$, and number of cells in the histogram for memory space reasons. As consequence the parameters need to be adjusted for each problem class in order to optimise the ratio between recognition rate and memory space.

Table 3. Experimental results on *Unistroke* for the "optimal" values of parameters: the size of the temporal window is 15, the size of the eigenspace 4 and histograms are composed of 20 cells per dimensions.

Type	Success	Reliability
A	87.5%	87.5%
H	76.6%	94.6%
L	84.6%	94.0%
O	96.2%	85.7%
Total	86.8%	89.1%

Table 3 presents recognition rates for each gesture using sets of "optimal" parameters where the size of the temporal window is 15, the size of the eigenspace 4 and histograms are composed of 20 cells per dimension. The "optimal" parameters are selected in correspondance with the previous results. Recognition rates are higher for character *O* because of the specific curve which can not be found in other characters (except for *H*, which represents 100% of the error). Character *H* has the lowest recognition rate due to a common structure with character *O* (22% of the error) and character *L* (63% of the error).

4.3 Facial Expressions

The third experimental scenario is the application of the technique to recognising facial expressions. The considered expressions are anger, raised eyebrows, disgust, happiness, surprise and neutral. Figure 4 gives an example of the considered expressions.

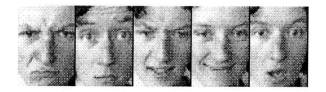

Fig. 4. Facial expressions treated in the experiment: raised eyebrows, disgust, happiness and surprise.

Eigenspaces for appearance representation The use of PCA for face recognition was introduced by Sirovitch and Kirby [14], and popularised by Turk and Pentland [15]. PCA of a population of vectors provides a new orthogonal basis for describing the population. The basis vectors are ordered on the degree of scatter of the population set. Similarity between members in the population result in a small number of basis vectors for describing the scatter within the population.

In this case, the population can be described in a much smaller linear subspace. Such a space is referred to as an *eigenspace*.

An image can be considered as a vector of pixels. The calculation of the principal components of a large set of faces (or hand postures) distribution defines an optimal set of orthogonal images in the sense for representing data. Each image of the set defines a dimension in this basis and is referred to as *eigen-image*. Similar images tend to have similar projections into the eigenspace. The eigenspace is used as the measurement space where a face expressing emotion is represented by a trajectory.

Eigenvectors with high eigenvalues code the coarse differences between the images. Detailed movements of single features like the eyebrows are captured by eigen-vectors with lower eigenvalues. Such eigenvectors are important for the distinction of facial expressions. Therefore the first 12 eigenvectors are considered as possible candidates for the histogram creation. From this group those eigen vectors that do not contribute to the distinction of the expressions are removed. From the remaining eigenvectors a histogram is created and the recognition is performed as in the experiments above set to section 4.2.

In this experiment four dimensional histograms of the 2nd, 7th, 8th and 11th eigen-vectors are built. We experimented with cell numbers of 16 and 24 cells per dimension. Table 4 shows the recognition results.

Table 4. Experimental results of facial expression recognition with four dimensional histogram.

Type	Success	Reliability
Anger	100%	61.5%
Brows	66.7%	57.1%
Disgust	100%	100%
Happy	100%	50.0%
Surprise	76.9%	83.3%

Experiment with 16 cells

Type	Success	Reliability
Anger	75.0%	100%
Brows	44.4%	44.4%
Disgust	100%	66.7%
Happy	100%	63.6%
Surprise	53.8%	70.0%

Experiment with 24 cells

The comparison of the results in table 4 show that superior recognition rates are obtained by the histogram with 16 cells. This is convenient because the memory space requirements are lower. The reason for the poorer results in the spontaneous expressions like raising eyebrows and surprise is the small number of training images available. The performance of a surprise expression has a much shorter period than an anger expression. Therefore fewer images are available for the short and spontaneous expressions. It is likely that a larger training set would improve the results.

The technique is very successful for the recognition of long expressions like anger, disgust and happiness. All test expressions are correctly detected. In the confusion test insertions are observed several times. The reason for the decreased reliability can be found in the small number of training images and the many dimensions of the histogram, that both cause many empty histogram cells.

A detection is announced when just one frame of the trajectory is projected on the detection area of a different expression. This sort of error happens because the detection areas of the different expressions are close in the histogram and the projections in the eigenspace are very sensitive to image normalisation. Such a false detection stands in contrast to a correct detection where the observed trajectory has to follow the model trajectory for a minimum number of frames.

An unstable normalisation of face position in the images was the dominant source of error in this experiment. The face tracker used for position normalisation produced a jitter of several pixels. Such translations can cause important changes in the eigenspace projection of the image, thus causing discontinuities in the trajectory which represents the face expression. Such discontinuities break up projection into the histogram. We have demonstrated this effect by stabilising the face tracker by hand. The resulting normalised image yield smooth trajectories and much higher recognition rates. Unfortunately hand stabilisation of the face tracker is much too time consuming to be applied to such a large dataset in time for production of this paper. None-the-less, as tested, the experiment demonstrates that the technique can operate in the presence of noisy trajectory data. Systematic evaluation of recognition under controlled noise conditions remains to be performed.

5   Conclusion

We have described a novel approach for recognition of parameter trajectories. The construction of an orthogonal space with principal component analysis is based on parameter sequences containing a parameter with its recent history. Joint statistics as represented by a multidimensional histogram of local parameter sequences was found to provide a simple and powerful method for recognising trajectories. Good results from the application to a variety of recognition problems confirms the general utility of the approach.

With respect to the recognition of trajectories, projection onto a local feature space provides a representation with a number of interesting properties:

1. Invariance to amplitude (by normalising the energy of the projection)
2. Invariance to position, when the first dominant eigenvector is removed,
3. Robustness to changes in the rate of execution of the gesture, provided the eigenvectors are built from datasets with different time rates.
4. Robustness to spurious data points. The projection to a local feature vector "smoothes out" spurious data points, such as those due to mis–normalisation, which would otherwise break up a trajectory. However, this method recognises short scale structure in the gesture. It can not discriminate structures whose temporal structure is much greater than the duration of the local sub-sequence.

For the recognition of facial expressions very good results are obtained under the condition of a perfect normalisation. Normalisation errors can introduce large jumps in the eigenspace, making trajectory matching unreliable. The most reliable eigen–vectors for face expression recognition are not necessarily the eigen–vectors with the largest eigen–values. Eigen–values are caused by scatter in the sample population, and this scatter can be due to sources, such as lighting and normalisation which are independent of face expressions.

References

1. T. S. Huand and V. I. Pavlović. Hand gesture modelling, analysis and synthesis. In *International Conference on Face and Gesture Recognition FG'95*, pp 73–79, Zurich, June 1995.
2. W. T. Freeman, K. Tanaka, J. Ohta, and K. Kyuma. Computer vision for computer games. In Irfan Essa, editor, *FG'96*, pp 100–105, Kilington, USA, Oct. 1996.
3. V. I. Pavlović, G. A. Berry, and T. S. Huang. Fusion of audio and visual information for use in human–computer interaction. In *Proceedings of Perceptual User Interface, PUI'97*, pp 68–70, Banff, Alberta, Canada, Oct. 1997.
4. T. Starner and A. Pentland. Real–time amercian sign language recognition form video using hidden markov model. Technical Report 375, MIT, Media Laboratory, 1995.
5. C. Wren, A. Azarbayejani, T. Darrell, and A. Pentland. Pfinder: Real–time tracking of tge human body. In *FG'96*, pp 51–56, Killington, USA, Oct. 1996.
6. T. J. Darrell and A. P. Pentland. Recognition of space–time gestures using distributed representation. Technical Report 197, MIT, Media Laboratory, 1992.
7. J. W. Davis. Appearance–based motion recognition of human actions. Technical Report 387, MIT, Media Laboratory, 1996.
8. S. Gutta, I. F. Imam, and H. Wechsler. Hand gesture recognition using ensembles of raidal basis function (rbf) networks and decision trees. *International Journal of Pattern Recognition and Artificial Intelligence*, 11(6):845–872, 1997.
9. R. Erenshteyn, P. Laskov, R. Foulds, L. Messing, and G. Stern. Recognition approach to gesture language understanding. In *ICPR'96*, pp 431–435, Vienna, Austria, 1996.
10. J. L. Crowley and F. Bérard. Multi–modal tracking of faces for video communications. In *CVPR'97*, pp 640–645, San Juan, Puerto Rico, June 1997.
11. 3Com. *PalmPilot, Users Manual*.
12. J. Martin, D. Hall, and J. L. Crowley. Statistical recognition of parameter trajectories for hand gestures and face expressions. In *ECCV Workshop on Perception of Human Actions*, Freiburg, Germany, June 1998.
13. B. Schiele. *Reconnaissance d'Objets utilisant des Histogrammes Multidimentsionnels de Champs Réceptifs*. PhD thesis, INP Grenoble, July 1997. In French.
14. I. Sirovich and M. Kirby. Low-dimensional procedure for the caracterization of human faces. *Journal of Optical Society of America A*, 4(3):519–524, March 1987.
15. M. Turk and A. Pentland. Eigenfaces for recognition. *Journal of Neuroscience*, 3(1):71–86, 1991.
16. A. Lux and B. Zoppis. An Experimental Multi-language Environment for the Development of Intelligent Robot Systems. In *5th International Symposium on Intelligent Robotic Systems, SIRS'97*, pp 169–174, 1997. Details at http://www-prima.imag.fr/Ravi/.

Experiments presented in this article were programmed using the RAVI multi–language environment [16].

Gesture Recognition for Visually Mediated Interaction

A. Jonathan Howell and Hilary Buxton

School of Cognitive and Computing Sciences
University of Sussex, Falmer, Brighton BN1 9QH, UK

Abstract. This paper reports initial research on supporting Visually Mediated Interaction (VMI) by developing person-specific and generic gesture models for the control of active cameras. We describe a time-delay variant of the Radial Basis Function (TDRBF) network and evaluate its performance on recognising simple pointing and waving hand gestures in image sequences. Experimental results are presented that show that high levels of performance can be obtained for this type of gesture recognition using such techniques, both for particular individuals and across a set of individuals. Characteristic visual evidence can be automatically selected, depending on the task demands.

1   Introduction

In general, robust tracking of non-rigid objects such as human bodies is difficult due to rapid motion, occlusion and ambiguities in segmentation and model matching. Ongoing research at the MIT Media Lab has shown progress in the modelling and interpretation of human body activity [24, 30, 31]. Computationally simple view-based approaches to action recognition have also been proposed [4] and similar attempts have been made at Microsoft Research [28, 6]. However, these systems do not attempt intentional tracking and modelling to control active cameras for Visually Mediated Interaction (VMI). Previous work on vision-based camera control has been based on off-line execution of pre-written scripts of a set of defined camera actions [25]. This system used a fixed wide angle camera with virtual windows for the control of field-of-view. Here we propose to model and exploit a set of 'interaction-relevant' gestures for reactive on-line visual control. These will be interpreted as user intentions for live control of an active camera with adaptive view direction and attentional focus. In particular, pointing (for direction) and waving (for attention) are important for deliberative control and the reactive camera movements could provide the necessary visual context for applications such as group video-conferencing as well as automated studio direction.

There is growing interest in recognising human gestures from real-time video as a nonverbal modality for human-computer interaction. The main approaches

A. Braffort et al. (Eds.): GW'99, LNAI 1739, pp. 141–151, 1999.

involve computing low-level features from motion to form temporal trajectories that can be tracked by Hidden Markov Models or Dynamic Time Warping. However, here we explore the potential of using simple image-based differences from video sequences in conjunction with a powerful connectionist learning paradigm to account for variability in the appearance of a set of predefined gestures. The adaptive learning component is based on RBF networks, which have been identified as valuable models by a wide range of researchers [21, 1, 3]. Their main advantages are computational simplicity and robust generalisation supported by a well-developed mathematical theory. Here studies using video sequences for recognition of pointing and waving gestures involve time-delay RBFs [14] to provide fast training and on-line performance for the interactive responses required by applications with active camera control.

The main purpose of this paper is to present experimental results that show that high levels of performance for this type of gesture recognition can be obtained using these techniques both for particular individuals and across a set of individuals. Characteristic visual evidence can be automatically selected and used even to recognise individuals from their gestures, depending on the task demands [15].

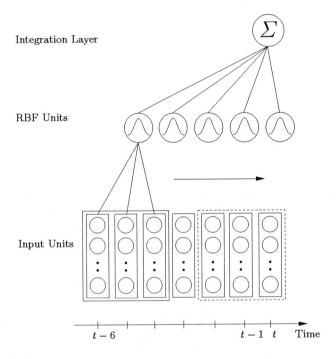

Fig. 1. Structure of a single class for a TDRBF network with time window of 3 and a integration window of 5 (after [2]).

2   The Time-Delay RBF Model

The RBF network is a two-layer, hybrid learning network [21, 22], which combines a supervised layer from the hidden to the output units with an unsupervised layer from the input to the hidden units. The network model is characterised by individual radial Gaussian functions for each hidden unit, which simulate the effect of overlapping and locally tuned receptive fields.

Dynamic neural networks can be constructed by adding recurrent connections to standard multi-layer perceptrons which then form a contextual memory for prediction over time [16, 7, 23]. These partially recurrent neural networks can be trained using back-propagation but there may be problems with stability and very long training sequences when using dynamic representations. An alternative is the Time-Delay Neural Network (TDNN) model (for an introduction, see [9]), which incorporates the concept of time-delays in order to process temporal context, combining data from a fixed time 'window' into a single vector as input, see Fig. 1. The TDNN has been successfully applied to speech and handwriting recognition tasks [29]. Its structured design allows it to specialise on spatio-temporal tasks, but, as in weight-sharing network, the reduction of trainable parameters over fully connected models can increase generalisation [17]. This simple Time-Delay mechanism can be added to an RBF network, termed a TDRBF network [2], to allow fast, robust solutions to difficult real-life problems. In its original form, the TDRBF network used a constructive RBF training stage, combining the idea of a sliding input window from the standard TDNN network with a training procedure for adding and adjusting RBF units when required. We have applied a simpler technique, successful in previous work with RBF networks [12], which uses an RBF unit for each training example, and a simple pseudo-inverse process to calculate weights.

3   Method

Simple experiments have previously been made with the TDRBF network to learn certain simple behaviours based on y-axis head rotation [14], distinguishing between left-to-right and right-to-left movements and static head pose. The network was shown to maintain a high level of performance even on test data containing individuals not seen during training. However, such tasks are simplified by their constant motion, so that arbitrary short segments (2/3 frames) of the whole sequence could be used to identify the overall direction of head turning. In this paper, we are addressing more complex gestures: pointing and waving with a hand. Due to the complex motion involved here, characteristic parts of the complete action will need to be contained in the time window presented to the network in order that it can be recognised.

3.1   The Gesture Database

Within the context of a video-conferencing active camera control scenario, we are concentrating on two specific behaviours which could be used to move the camera or adapt its field of view: *pointing*, which is interpreted as a request to pass camera attention, and is implemented by zooming out and panning in the pointing direction, and *waving*, which is interpreted as a request for camera attention, and implemented by panning towards the waver and zooming in. We have two types of each behaviour, giving four gestures in all, shown in Table 1.

Table 1. Definitions for the four gestures used.

Gesture	Body Movement	Behaviour
pntrl	point right hand to left	pointing left
pntrr	point right hand to right	pointing right
wavea	wave right hand above head	urgent wave
waveb	wave right hand below head	non-urgent wave

We have collected four examples of each gesture from three people, 48 sequences in all, so far. Each sequence contains 59 378×288 8-bit monochrome images (having been collected at 12 frames/sec for roughly 5 seconds), for a total of 2832 images. These image sequences are the result of our collaboration in the ISCANIT project with Shaogang Gong at Queen Mary and Westfield College, London and Stephen McKenna at the University of Dundee, who are researching real-time face detection and tracking [18, 20, 19, 27]. The standard RBF and TD-RBF networks have already been shown to work well with such image sequences for face recognition tasks [13, 14].

We are specifically interested in the areas of motion within each image, so each frame is differenced with the previous one: any pixel in the current frame within 5 grey-levels of the corresponding pixel from the previous frame is discarded (set to zero), see Fig. 2. A count of the number of pixels retained in each frame after this process can be used to segment the gesture in time, using a simple threshold to signal the first and last frame with significant numbers of changing pixels, see Fig. 3. Frames before and after this threshold are discarded to align the start point of the gesture. The sequences are then padded at the end with nil values to the length of the longest gesture found, to give an equal length for all sequences in the testset. An integration layer on the TDRBF network can be used to combine results from successive time windows, which will give smooth gradations between serial actions. Here we know each sequence contains only one action, and so can rely on our temporal segmentation to give the single best frame position for classification. A sparse arrangement of Gabor filters is used to preprocess the differenced images [11]: data is sampled at four non-overlapping scales and three orientations with sine and cosine components for a total of 510 coefficients per frame.

Fig. 2. Example of differencing two consecutive frames (a) and (b), result in (c), from a 'point with the right hand to the right' (*pntrr*) gesture.

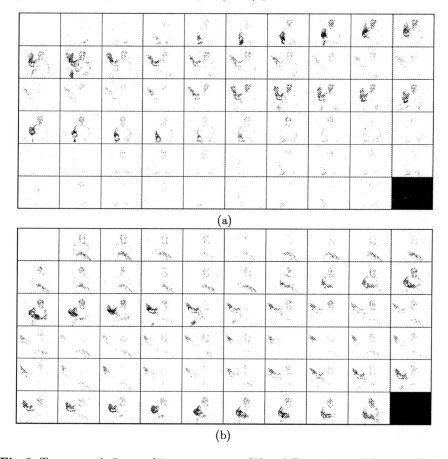

Fig. 3. Two example 5-second image sequences (after differencing each frame with the previous one) of the 'point with the right hand to the right' (*pntrr*) gesture, from two different people, demonstrating the type of variability present in a single action: (a) subject *jonh*, starting frame was automatically determined as frame 4, ending frame 32 (b) subject *step*, starting frame 18, ending frame 57.

4 Results

Table 2 summarises the results obtained. For all the experiments in this paper, the database was split into two separate parts, one for training and the other for testing. The 'Train/Test' column shows the actual number of sequences in each part for the experiment. 'Initial % Correct' shows the raw generalisation rate for the TDRBF network. This value can be adapted via a 'low-confidence' measure which has previously been shown to be a powerful method for improving generalisation [13] through the removal of ambiguous results. The '% Discarded' column indicates how many classifications were discarded in this way, and '% Correct After Discard' shows the final generalisation rate using only the resulting high-confidence output.

4.1 Person-Specific Gesture Modelling

We first looked at creating person-specific networks, trained and tested using data from one individual. For this, we used the 16 sequences of each person separately in turn. Here we are looking to distinguish the four gestures, so there are four classes to be learnt.

Table 2(a) lists the results for two training configurations, averaged over the three sets of data. These show that the task could be learnt extremely well even with only one training example of each gesture (the 4/12 test), but that providing two examples (the 8/8 test) can reduce the number of low-confidence discards, indicating a more effective separation of the gesture classes within the network.

Table 2. Average results for various TDRBF gesture networks: (a) *person-specific*, trained and tested with gesture sequences from a single person, (b) *group-based*, trained and tested with gesture sequences from three people: 'Fixed window' used the training sequences at their original length, 'Warped window' used three versions (shorter, normal, longer) of the training sequences, and (c) *generic*, trained with gesture sequences from one person, and tested on the other two.

Gesture Model	Train/Test Sequences	Initial % Correct	% Discarded	% Correct After Discard
(a) Person-specific	4/12	92	51	100
	8/8	100	16	100
(b) Group-based: Fixed	12/36	97	39	100
	24/24	96	4	100
Warped (±10%)	36/36	97	19	100
	72/24	96	4	100
(c) Generic	4/32	69	75	100
	8/32	75	53	100

4.2   Group-Based Gesture Modelling

We now combine the data from the three people in the database, using all 48 sequences, looking at generalisation in the TDRBF network within a group seen during both training and testing. Again we are looking to distinguish the four gestures, so there are four classes to be learnt. In general, the results in Table 2(b) are slightly better than before: the final result is still 100%, but at lower levels of low-confidence discard, especially where two training examples of each gesture are given (the 24/24 test).

To cope with different speeds of movement, we looked at adapting the training data to explicitly demonstrate the classes at different speeds through simple time-warping. This was applied to our training sequences by cutting out or repeating frames in the time window to shorten or lengthen the training sequences. Using one shorter and one longer version of each sequence meant that there were three times more training examples than for the previous experiment (with fixed time windows). The results for this are also shown in Table 2(b). Interestingly, varying the length by $\pm 10\%$ did not increase generalisation rates (perhaps because there was very little improvement that could be made), though it did make a useful reduction in the proportion of output that needed to be discarded through low confidence. However, it should be noted that such global methods are limited in their application, as they can only address overall gesture tempo, not within-gesture speed changes.

4.3   Generic Gesture Modelling

Having tested the TDRBF network with single and multiple-person data, we also wanted to see how it would generalise with gestures from people it had not seen during training: could gesture be effectively characterised in the absence of identity-specific information? There are still four classes to be learnt, but the network sees examples from one person during training, and the other two during testing.

The test results in Table 2(c) follow the previous pattern of using one (4/32) and two (8/32) training examples. It can be seen here that the TDRBF network was able to learn the classification task from one person and effectively generalise to data from other people. Such an ability is potentially much more useful than generalisation within specific people or known groups, because the network, once trained, can be applied to much more general data.

4.4   Combined Gesture and Identity Modelling

Our final test was to see if the individual, as well as the gesture, could be identified. The three identities and four gestures mean that there are now 12 classes to be learnt. Table 3 gives the results for these tests. When compared to the group-based results in Table 2(b), it can be seen that overall generalisation is lower, although a significant proportion of the test data is still correctly classified. This indicates that non-facial cues, such as posture and gait, could be used in this form as additional evidence for face recognition applications.

Table 3. Results for identity/gesture TDRBF networks: trained and tested with gesture sequences of all three people, looking both for identity and gesture.

Train/Test Sequences	Initial % Correct	% Discarded	% Correct After Discard
12/36	78	50	94
24/24	96	17	95

4.5   Discussion

Although Berthold [2] used the integration layer to cope with shifts in time, the scale of events was not discussed. In particular, here we have to cope with different speeds of movement and pauses within the overall gesture, as well as the starting frame of the gesture being variable. Such speed variation can be handled by a recurrent network, or via training data which explicitly demonstrated the classes at different speeds (time-warping).

To simplify the results here, an integration layer was not used during the testing stage. The 'pixels-changed' threshold, looking at overall movement within the frame, was effective within this database in identifying start and end points of gestures, but would not be robust in more general situations, especially if the scene contained more than one person. We anticipate that adding an integration layer would improve results, because the extra variation in starting point for the test sequences (through their iterative application on successive frames) would give extra contextual information for identification.

5   Observations

Several points can be seen from the results:

– Simple preprocessing techniques such as frame differencing and thresholding can be effective in extracting useful motion information and segmenting gestures in time.
– Several types of TDRBF network can be trained to distinguish gestures over specific time windows:
  • Person-specific gesture models: trained and tested on one person
  • Group-based gesture models: trained and tested within a known group of individuals
  • Generic gesture models: trained on one person, tested on other people
– The TDRBF network is shown to be able to distinguish between arbitrary gestures, with a high level of performance, even without the benefit of an integration layer. The thresholding in time of the gestures allowed a single time window to be applied to the network, rather than several consecutive positions.
– Some characteristics of an individual's expression of gestures may be sufficiently distinctive to identify that person.

6   Conclusion

In summary, the time-delay RBF networks showed themselves to perform well in our gesture recognition task, creating both person-specific and generic gesture models. This is a promising result for the RBF techniques considering the high degree of potential variability, present even in our highly constrained database, arising out of the different interpretation of our predefined gestures by each individual.

In our new project, we aim to develop and evaluate real-time user behaviour models based on temporal prediction of continuous pose and gesture change [8, 26]. The user would have minimal awareness of the system which will aim to estimate and predict essential body parameters such as head pose, walking, sitting, standing, talking, pointing and waving gestures as well as expression. Such a model will be essentially appearance-based in order to provide real-time behaviour interpretation and prediction. It is important to note that we are not attempting to model the full working of the human body. Rather we will aim to exploit approximate and computationally efficient RBF techniques, which support partial view-invariance, sufficient to recognise people's expressions and gestures in dynamic scenes. Such task-specific representations need to be used to avoid unnecessary computational cost in dynamic scene interpretation [5].

Most existing recurrent network models take a long time to train, but simple time-delay RBF networks provide a fast and effective method of identifying arbitrary behaviours [14]. The main problem with this alternative strategy for learning behavioural models is that it is difficult to classify the same behaviour evolving at different speeds using a single time-window. Solutions to this problem require either a) subdividing the behaviours into fast and slower versions and/or b) merging these in a second stage of behavioural analysis. This flexibility may turn out to be an advantage in practice as the intentional force of a fast pointing action (urgent) may be different from a slower action. We therefore plan to explore the use of full generative RNNs [10] for general behavioural control that can be learnt incrementally using many examples and time-delay RBFs for individual intentional control which needs to be learnt rapidly from a few examples.

Acknowledgements

The authors gratefully acknowledge the invaluable discussion, help and facilities provided by Shaogang Gong and Stephen McKenna during the development and construction of the gesture database.

References

1. S. Ahmad and V. Tresp. Some solutions to the missing feature problem in vision. In S. J. Hanson, J. D. Cowan, and C. L. Giles, editors, *Advances in Neural Information Processing Systems*, volume 5, pages 393–400, San Mateo, CA, 1993. Morgan Kaufmann.

2. M. R. Berthold. A Time Delay radial basis function network for phoneme recognition. In *Proceedings of IEEE International Conference on Neural Networks*, volume 7, pages 4470–4473, Orlando, FL, 1994. IEEE Computer Society Press.

3. C. M. Bishop. *Neural Networks for Pattern Recognition*. Oxford University Press, Oxford, UK, 1995.

4. A. F. Bobick. Computers seeing action. In R. B. Fisher and E. Trucco, editors, *Proceedings of British Machine Vision Conference*, pages 13–22, Edinburgh, 1996. BMVA Press.

5. H. Buxton and S. Gong. Visual surveillance in a dynamic and uncertain world. *Artificial Intelligence*, 78:431–459, 1995.

6. R. Cutler and M. Turk. View-based interpretation of real-time optical flow for gesture recognition. In *Proceedings of IEEE International Conference on Automatic Face & Gesture Recognition*, pages 416–421, Nara, Japan, 1998. IEEE Computer Society Press.

7. J. Elman. Finding structure in time. *Cognitive Science*, 14:179–211, 1990.

8. S. Gong. Visual observation as reactive learning. In *Proceedings of SPIE International Conference on Adaptive & Learning Systems*, pages 265–270, Orlando, FL, 1992.

9. J. A. Hertz, A. Krogh, and R. G. Palmer. *Introduction to the Theory of Neural Computation*. Addison-Wesley, Redwood City CA, 1991.

10. G. E. Hinton and Z. Ghahramani. Generative models for discovering sparse distributed representations. *Philosophical Transactions of Royal Society London, Series B*, 352:1177–1190, 1997.

11. A. J. Howell. *Automatic face recognition using radial basis function networks*. PhD thesis, University of Sussex, 1997.

12. A. J. Howell and H. Buxton. Face recognition using radial basis function neural networks. In R. B. Fisher and E. Trucco, editors, *Proceedings of British Machine Vision Conference*, pages 455–464, Edinburgh, 1996. BMVA Press.

13. A. J. Howell and H. Buxton. Towards unconstrained face recognition from image sequences. In *Proceedings of International Conference on Automatic Face & Gesture Recognition*, pages 224–229, Killington, VT, 1996. IEEE Computer Society Press.

14. A. J. Howell and H. Buxton. Recognising simple behaviours using time-delay RBF networks. *Neural Processing Letters*, 5:97–104, 1997.

15. A. J. Howell and H. Buxton. Towards visually mediated interaction using appearance-based models. In *Proceedings of ECCV'98 Workshop on Perception of Human Action*, Freiburg, Germany, 1998.

16. M. I. Jordan. Serial order: A parallel, distributed processing approach. In J. L. Elman and D. E. Rumelhart, editors, *Advances in Connectionist Theory: Speech*. Lawrence Erlbaum, Hillsdale, NJ, 1989.

17. Y. Le Cun, B. Boser, J. S. Denker, D. Henderson, R. E. Howard, W. Hubbard, and L. D. Jackel. Backpropagation applied to handwritten zip code recognition. *Neural Computation*, 1:541–551, 1989.

18. S. J. McKenna and S. Gong. Tracking faces. In *Proceedings of International Conference on Automatic Face & Gesture Recognition*, pages 271–276, Killington, VT, 1996. IEEE Computer Society Press.

19. S. J. McKenna and S. Gong. Gesture recognition for visually mediated interaction using probabilistic event trajectories. In *Proceedings of British Machine Vision Conference*, Southampton, UK, 1998. BMVA Press.

20. S. J. McKenna, S. Gong, and Y. Raja. Face recognition in dynamic scenes. In A. F. Clark, editor, *Proceedings of British Machine Vision Conference*, pages 140–151, Colchester, UK, 1997. BMVA Press.
21. J. Moody and C. Darken. Learning with localized receptive fields. In D. Touretzky, G. Hinton, and T. Sejnowski, editors, *Proceedings of 1988 Connectionist Models Summer School*, pages 133–143, Pittsburgh, PA, 1988. Morgan Kaufmann.
22. J. Moody and C. Darken. Fast learning in networks of locally-tuned processing units. *Neural Computation*, 1:281–294, 1989.
23. M. C. Mozer. Neural net architectures for temporal sequence processing. In A. S. Weigend and N. A. Gershenfeld, editors, *Time Series Prediction: Predicting the Future and Understanding the Past*, pages 243–264. Addison-Wesley, Redwood City, CA, 1994.
24. A. Pentland. Smart rooms. *Scientific American*, 274(4):68–76, 1996.
25. C. Pinhanez and A. F. Bobick. Approximate world models: Incorporating qualitative and linguistic information into vision systems. In *Proceedings of AAAI'96*, pages 1116–1123, Portland, OR, 1996.
26. A. Psarrou, H. Buxton, and S. Gong. Modelling spatio-temporal trajectories and face signatures on partially recurrent neural networks. In *Proceedings of IEEE International Conference on Neural Networks*, volume 5, pages 2226–2231, Perth, Australia, 1995.
27. Y. Raja, S. J. McKenna, and S. Gong. Tracking and segmenting people in varying lighting conditions using colour. In *Proceedings of IEEE International Conference on Automatic Face & Gesture Recognition*, pages 228–233, Nara, Japan, 1998. IEEE Computer Society Press.
28. M. Turk. Visual interaction with lifelike characters. In *Proceedings of International Conference on Automatic Face & Gesture Recognition*, pages 368–373, Killington, VT, 1996. IEEE Computer Society Press.
29. A. Waibel, T. Hanazawa, G. Hinton, K. Shikano, and K. Lang. Phoneme recognition using time-delay neural networks. *IEEE Transactions on Acoustics, Speech, & Signal Processing*, 37:328–339, 1989.
30. C. R. Wren, A. Azarbayejani, T. Darrell, and A. P. Pentland. Pfinder: Real-time tracking of the human body. In *Proceedings of International Conference on Automatic Face & Gesture Recognition*, pages 51–56, Killington, VT, 1996. IEEE Computer Society Press.
31. C. R. Wren and A. P. Pentland. Dynamic models of human motion. In *Proceedings of IEEE International Conference on Automatic Face & Gesture Recognition*, pages 22–27, Nara, Japan, 1998. IEEE Computer Society Press.

Interpretation of Pointing Gesture: The PoG System

Rachid Gherbi and Annelies Braffort

LIMSI-CNRS, Paris-Sud University
BP 133, 91403 Orsay Cedex - France
{gherbi,braffort}@limsi.fr

Abstract. We present in this paper a system named PoG. Its role is to recognise and interpret natural pointing gestures in the context of a multimodal interaction. The user's hand gestures are tracked by a camera located above a building plan. The user points to a room on the plan with his index finger while using speech to ask for some information from the system. The PoG system is composed of an extraction process, which computes visual primitives, a recognition process, providing the name of the gesture, and a localisation process, which computes the coordinates of the index tip.

1   Introduction

The study presented here has been done in the context of a given application, which is a system providing information about tenants, rooms and routes in a building, and can answer questions like "*Who is in this room?*" or "*Show me the way from here to here?*" in real time.

A 2D plan of the building is placed on a table, and a camera is located above the plan to track the user's gestures. A microphone is located near the mouth of the user. The user can interact with the system by means of speech and pointing gestures.

In this context, a first step of the study was to determine which gestures are spontaneously performed by users [1], while interacting with the system.

Our work focused on the gestures for which the hand shape and the movement represent 82% of the corpus, while keeping in mind that other forms of gestures can be met in normal communication. The chosen gesture vocabulary contains pointing gestures with an *Index* hand shape, and pointing movements. The following pointing movements have been considered: single pointing (**SP**), pointing twice to the same location (**RP**), pointing twice to two different locations (**LP**), and a non-pointing movement (**NP**).

Most of the studies concerning gesture interaction, e.g. [2], [3], [4], [5], do not consider as a whole problem the recognition task, e.g. recognition of a SP gesture, and the interpretation task, e.g. computation of a pointed location (see [1] for more details). The system presented here, named **PoG** (**Po**inting **G**esture), attempts to integrate these two tasks. It tracks, recognises and then interprets the user's pointing gestures.

A. Braffort et al. (Eds.): GW'99, LNAI 1739, pp. 153–157, 1999.
© Springer-Verlag Berlin Heidelberg 1999

2   Functional Architecture of PoG

PoG processes video sequences, where the hand appears, points to one or two chosen locations on a building map, and disappears. It must provide as output two kinds of information: the *name (SP, RP, LP, NP) of the recognised gesture* and the *localisation values (x and y coordinates)*. The global architecture of PoG is composed of three modules (Fig. 1): **extraction** of the *visual primitives* from the video sequence; **recognition** of the gesture type, by comparing with learned examples of the different types of gestures, and **localisation** of the pointed position, by computing the coordinates of the index tips in the appropriate frames of the video sequence.

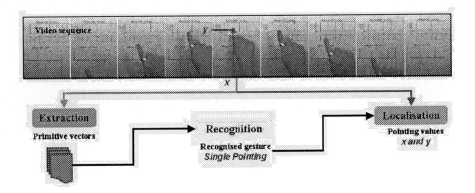

Fig. 1. Functional architecture of PoG

The success of the recognition process depends directly on the appropriateness of the gesture representation, i.e. the choice of the visual primitives.

Some of the primitives must represent dynamic information because gestures are deeply dynamic,. Thus, we use a primitive, named *Movement*, representing the amount of movement of the gestures, computed by edge-image differences of the video sequences. Another dynamic primitive named *Pause* allows us to take into account the number of pauses during the gesture.

In addition, some gestures can have the same dynamics but differ in the shape of the hand. So, we use a shape-based primitive, named *NbFingers*, which computes the number of open fingers.

These three primitives are grouped in a vector, and the output of the extraction module is a sequence of primitive vectors which represents the gesture.

The recognition process transforms these numerical vectors into the appropriate symbolic value: SP, RP, LP or NP. The chosen recognition tool is HTK (Entropic Co). The corpus (total of 120 samples) is composed of 30 samples of each type of gesture. Half of the data files have been used during the training process, and the second half has been used during the evaluation process.

Once the recognition process has provided the name of the recognised gesture, the localisation process is used to complete the interpretation of the gesture. This process is applied zero times (NP), once (SP, RP) or twice (LP), depending on the kind of gesture. It is concerned with the determination of the index tip and the orientation of the index in order to locate the user pointed location on the map of the building.

It takes the appropriate image (determined by means of the Pause primitive) as input and returns the pointing coordinates. First, it proceeds by a coarse-determination of pointing zone (including the index), applied on the edge image of the hand. Second, within this small zone, the tip and the orientation of the index are detected (Fig. 2).

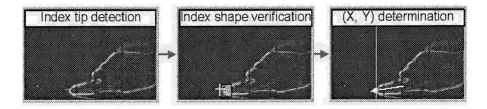

Fig. 2. Index tip detection and verification and (x, y) coordinates determination

3 Evaluation of the System

The recognition process of PoG is evaluated by employing two criteria: on one hand, each visual primitive is used separately to evaluate the recognition capabilities of PoG, in order to highlight which type of gesture (SP, RP, LP, NP) the primitive is suitable for (Table 1); on the other hand, all primitives are combined to evaluate the performance of PoG to recognise each gesture and all gestures together (Table 2).

Table 1. Recognition rates by visual primitives

Gestures	Visual primitives		
	Movement	Transition	Pause
SP	13.33%	33.33%	73.33%
RP	46.67%	00.00%	46.67%
LP	33.33%	46.67%	80.00%
NP	60.00%	93.33%	68.66%

The results in Table 1 show that the Pause primitive performs well in detecting the SP and LP gestures, and the Transition primitive detects the NP gestures efficiently. The Movement primitive seems not to be clearly helpful in detecting any of the given gestures. None of these visual primitives alone seems sufficient for the detection of the RP gestures. The results are presented as a confusion matrix in Table 2 and show that SP and LP gestures are better identified than RP and NP gestures. For the latter two gestures the chosen visual primitives are not sufficient to correctly represent them. With these primitives, it is not possible to differentiate SP and RP gestures. The two last columns of Table 2 show the recognition results when considering the case "SP is different than RP" and the case "SP is semantically the same as RP". If we consider SP and RP as a single gesture (this is possible in the context of this application), we obtain a global recognition rate of around 80%.

Table 2. Recognition evaluation by gesture

Gestures	Results by gesture				Total	Total Recognition Rates	
	SP	RP	LP	NP		SP$\neq$RP	SP = RP
SP	12	3	0	0	15	80.00%	100%
RP	5	7	1	2	15	46.66%	80.00%
LP	1	2	12	0	15	80.00%	80.00%
NP	0	4	10	1	15	66.66%	66.66%
All gestures (SP, RP, LP, NP)					60	68.33%	81.66%

4   Conclusion and Perspectives

We have presented the system PoG, whose aim is to recognise and interpret natural pointing gestures in a multimodal context. Currently, the extraction and localisation processes are implemented, the recognition process has been evaluated and the localisation process is under evaluation. PoG has been integrated in a multimodal plate-form (Chameleon European project #24493) allowing the user to use speech, language and gesture modalities. In the future, other kinds of visual primitives have to be analyzed to enhance the current PoG system. The next step of this study will be to extend the PoG system to analyse *3d pointing interaction with virtual objects* and to recognize *other types of co-verbal gestures*.

References

1. Braffort, A., Gherbi, R.: Video-Tracking and Recognition of Pointing Gestures using Hidden Markov Models. In Proceeding of IEEE Inter. Conf. on Intelligent Engineering Systems, Vienna, Austria, September, 1998.
2. M. Assan, M., Grobel, K.: Video-Based Sign Language Recognition Using Hidden Markov Models. In Gesture and Sign Language in Human- Computer Interaction, I. Wachsmuth & M. Fröhlich (Eds.), Lecture Notes in Artificial Intelligence # 1371, Springer-Verlag, 1998.
3. Nölker, C., Ritter, H.: Detection of Fingertips in Human Hand Movement Sequences. In Gesture and Sign Language in Human-Computer Interaction. I. Wachsmuth & M. Fröhlich (Eds.), Lecture Notes in Artificial Intelligence # 1371, Springer-Verlag, 1998.
4. Latoschik, M. E., I. Wachsmuth, I.: Exploiting Distant Pointing Gestures for Objects Selection in a Virtual Environment. In Gesture and Sign Language in Human-Computer Interaction, I. Wachsmuth & M. Fröhlich (Eds.), Lecture Notes in Artificial Intelligence # 1371, Springer-Verlag, 1998.
5. Kahn, R. E., Swain, M. J.: Understanding people pointing: The Perseus system. In Proceedings of the International Symposium on Computer Vision, November 1995.

Control of In-vehicle Systems by Gestures

Jean-François Kamp[1], Franck Poirier[1], and Philippe Doignon[2]

[1] UBS-VALORIA Laboratory, rue Yves Mainguy, 56000 Vannes, France
{Jean-Francois.Kamp,Franck.Poirier}@univ-ubs.fr
[2] Renault-Technocentre, avenue du golf 1, 78288 Guyancourt Cedex, France
Philippe.Doignon@renault.fr

Abstract. In this paper, we propose a new input interface for interaction with in-vehicle systems (traffic information, car phones etc). The new device is a touchpad of small dimensions designed to record any control-gesture drawn with the finger by the user. An analysis is carried out of the tasks to be achieved by the driver and a method called "brainstorming"is used to generate a set of possible gestures. A neural network approach is applied for the recognition of gestures. The method is tested on a database of 5252 uppercase letters written by 101 different writers. The average error rate is less than 6,5%. The method is also of great interest in terms of speed and memory space.

1 Introduction – Problem

This work is carried out in collaboration with Renault Research Department. In the near future, car manufacturers will put on the market high- technology in-vehicle systems such as car phones, traffic information, route guidance etc. The main problem is that most of these new systems require the user to program or manipulate data, sometimes while driving. These manipulations become a very difficult task since the control devices are often reduced to small switches and push-buttons.

2 Proposed Solution

To solve this problem, we propose a new input interface to control in-vehicle systems. This new device is a touchpad of small dimensions (6 by 6 cm) with the purpose to record any gesture made by the user which is, in the present case, the drawing with the finger of a symbol, character or digit.

The general idea is to recognize the symbol drawn by the driver and to match it with predefined patterns triggering specific actions for on-board systems. For example, if the pattern is a letter or a digit, the action simply consists in writing a new alphanumeric item in the phone book or in searching for a name (street, town) in a list. Furthermore, new gestures can be created to which special actions are associated as for example: «delete the selected item», «ask for help», «zoom-in on the map».

A. Braffort et al. (Eds.): GW'99, LNAI 1739, pp. 159–162, 1999.

The purpose of this paper is, in a first part, to explain the approach followed to generate and select the specific set of gestures which will be used to interact with the in-vehicle systems. In a second part, the gesture recognition method is presented and evaluated.

3   Generation of the Dialogue Gestures

As suggested by several authors [1], before setting up the interactive vocabulary, it is necessary to carry out an analysis of the tasks achieved by the driver. The main tasks achieved by the user are the following:
- access to information: traffic, weather information, train time-table,
- data input: route destination, phone book, storage of a radio station,
- system activation: car phone system, route guidance system, car radio etc.

To accomplish these tasks, the driver goes through tree structured menus displayed on a small graphic screen. The display shows not only textual information (items of a menu, items of a list) but also fields to enter alphanumeric data and graphical maps. Hence, the actions carried out by the user are more precisely: moving a cursor in a list (1), moving a cursor on a map (2), displaying a list of menus (3), activating a system (4), selecting an item in a list (5), writing a new alphanumeric item (6), searching for an alphanumeric item in a list (7), storing a new item (8), deleting an item (9), canceling (10), asking for help (11), going back to the top menu (12). The method chosen to generate the symbols is known as «brainstorming»[2] and consists in convening a group of people in order to discuss the construction of an innovating device, in our case, the tactile system. At the meeting, a series of ideas were discussed to solve the following problem: for each of the twelve actions enumerated above, find a corresponding gesture to activate it when drawn on the touchpad by the user. Among the whole set of proposals, a selection was carried out on the basis of the following criterions:
- minimization of the manipulation times required to trigger a given action,
- selection of discriminating symbols to facilitate the recognition process,
- selection of mnemonic symbols. It is known that people can memorize up to a maximum of 5 to 7 different elements without making mistakes [3].

Table 1 shows some examples of gestures selected for drawing on the touchpad.

Table1. Examples of selected gestures

Actions	Gestures	Remarks
• Moving a cursor in a list • Moving a cursor on a map		Drawing of a line horizontally, vertically, diagonally anywhere on the touchpad
• Writing a new alphanumeric item • Searching for an alphanumeric item		Recognition of the letters/digits which compose the alphanumeric item
Deleting an item		Mnemonic symbol well known in the literature
Asking for help		Mnemonic symbol
Going back to the top menu		Mnemonic symbol

4   The Gesture Recognition Method

The method used to recognize the gestures is a neural network, called Dynamic Vector Quantization (DVQ) presented in [4]. In this paragraph we show that the connectionist classification method DVQ is well adapted to in-vehicle recognition.

4.1   Problem Specification

The gesture recognition system we analyse has the following characteristics:
- the gestures are drawn on a touchpad consisting in a 6 cm square tablet. They are drawn one by one on the entire screen and there is thus no segmentation problem to be solved,
- the gestures drawn are uppercase letters.

Because the system has to be operated by the driver in real traffic conditions, the following constraints are added:
- a symbol is drawn only with the finger, without using any handwriting tool,
- the user does not have any visual feedback of his/her drawing. In particular, there is no background LCD display.

4.2   General Overview of the Method

The neural network in this case has besides input and output a single hidden layer. The DVQ algorithm has multiple advantages: simplicity of architecture and implementation relying on a single parameter (T) and very fast supervised training. To build the neural network it is trained on the first part of a database containing labelled gestures. When this training stage is completed, the network is used in the recognition (test) stage, to classify the samples of the second part of the database. The parameter T controls the training procedure. For low values of T, the training will increase the number of neurons. Conversely, high values of T will lead to a small number of neurons.

4.3   Evaluation of the Method

To evaluate the performances of the DVQ, a series of laboratory experiments has been conducted. The training and the test sets are randomly chosen 10 times among a database which contains 5252 uppercase letters. In this way, we obtain an average recognition rate (on 10 different simulations). The writers of the test set are all different from those of the training set. Parameter T directly affects the total number of neurons (N) in the network. If $T = 0$, this number will be maximum (N=Nmax) and if $T = \infty$, it will be minimum (N=Nmin). The horizontal-axis (Fig. 1) represents the average number of neurons per class: N/Nmin, Nmin=26 for the letters. When N/26 is high (=5, Fig. 1), the network clearly tends to specialize on the training set, resulting in a lower recognition rate. In the case where N/26=1, Fig. 1 shows that the recognition rate remains practically maximum (93,6% on average). This demonstrates that with only one neuron by class (minimum network size) the network discriminates well between the classes.

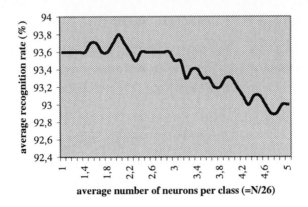

Fig.1. Average curve of recognition rate

5   Conclusion

To interact with in-vehicle systems, the task analysis and the brainstorming method led us to select a set of candidate gestures. Of course, this choice must be confirmed by future experiments carried out in the vehicle.

To recognize the gestures, a connectionist method was used and tested on uppercase letters drawn by 101 writers. The results lead to the following conclusions:

- given the conditions of the experiments (handwriting without visual feedback and only with the finger), the DVQ algorithm gives good results (93,8% on average),
- the unique neuron per class leads to a network of minimal size, reducing the decision time to a minimum in the test stage. Hence, the DVQ method is of great interest in terms of speed and memory space. This point is particularly important for in-vehicle systems.

References

1. Mayhew, D.J.: Principles and guidelines in software user interface design. Prentice Hall, (1992)
2. Byrne, J.G., Barlow, T.: Structured Brainstorming: a Method for Collecting User Requirements. Proceedings of the Human Factors and Ergonomics Society 37th Annual Meeting, Vol. 1 (1993) 427–431
3. Miller, G.A.: The magical number seven plus or minus two: Some limits on our capacity for processing information. Psychological Review, 63, (1956) 81–97
4. Poirier, F., Ferrieux, A.: DVQ: Dynamic Vector Quantization – An incremental LVQ. Proceedings of ICANN91, Helsinki, (1991)

Section 4: Sign Language

French Sign Language: Proposition of a Structural Explanation by Iconicity

Christian Cuxac

Département des Sciences du Langage,
Université Paris VIII,
2 rue de la liberté, F-93 526 Saint-Denis cedex 02, France
Phone: +33-01-49-40-64-18

Introduction

In this article, I shall attempt to demonstrate that sign languages are linguistic objects which provide us with increasingly tangible means of accessing cognitive activity. This is possible by virtue of the existence in language of the visible, iconic manifestation of a dynamic process, which is set in motion by deaf signers to speak of experience outside of the situation of the utterance.

To begin with, I will limit my line of enquiry to so- called 'imagistic iconicity'; this seems to be the most basic and practical definition, that is, when there is a formal resemblance between the sign or signs and what is being referred to in the extra-linguistic world of experience.

1 The Process of Iconisation for Deaf Individuals

Sign languages are equipped with a standard lexicon: this is a grouping of discrete items, which display referential iconicity to varying degrees (thus contained within an iconic continuum).

However, the great originality of sign language ties in the possibility of having recourse to other structures, endowed with great iconic value – but which function more or less independently of this standard lexicon. These structures are quite similar from one sign language to another, right down to the specific forms employed. They are what the deaf from different language communities use in order to communicate, both at programmed conferences and in chance meetings between individuals. The amazing thing about this is that the practice of any one particular sign language enables the signer to communicate efficiently with anyone practising another sign language – thus transcending the specificity of any one particular sign language.

Even more fascinating is the fact that children born deaf (hearing-impaired) in an environment made up exclusively of hearing individuals constitute a unique group who yet manage to communicate: these individuals are placed in a situation where they derive no benefit from (verbal) solicitation by other members of the community, and where – given an average level of intelligence – they are unable to put into place the normal process of language acquisition, insofar as

A. Braffort et al. (Eds.): GW'99, LNAI 1739, pp. 165–184, 1999.

this concerns a first (spoken) language. Without being educated in specialised programs (for the learning of an oral language artificially), and without encountering other deaf persons already practising a sign language (that is, the acquisition of sign language as a first language under the normal conditions of a linguistic environment), we might well wonder how they manage this communication with the surrounding population. And yet, few researchers have directed their efforts to studying this very basic problem. For it is only in the observation of such linguistic data that we can provide a solid foundation for theoretical developments.

This is precisely what one finds in Yau [1], and after him by Dos Santos Souza [2], who collected a considerable body of data on the constitution of gestural languages (and particularly vocabularies) by isolated deaf adults. This research has shown firstly that the attested, ordered strata of signifying forms are indeed very similar, but are influenced at the same time by the cultural environment surrounding them – ereby indicating that, for any of the strata, such extreme hypotheses as "there are certain things which have yet to be named", and "only culturalized forms can be expressed" are in fact overly categorical responses which result from the problem being poorly stated. Secondly, it is clear from this research that as far as the closely related strata of signifying forms are concerned, the attested forms which support this finding are strongly resemblance from one individual signer to another.

The phenomena observed by Yau [1], and after him by Dos Santos Souza [2], are corroborated by what we know about the creation of signs by deaf children growing up in a "hearing" environment [3]. Before coming of school age, these children attempt to communicate with others by means of gestures of their own contrivance. If the family is indisposed towards these gestural creations and refuses to lend them any credence, the child will stop the creative process. If, on the contrary, the family adopts the child's signs, a familial gestural code will be set up. This code is formally similar to the vocabularies observed by Yau [1] in isolated deaf adults.

These lexicalised gestural creations or signs, which provide proof of the human aptitude for categorising, permit us to advance the hypothesis of stabilised pre- linguistic conceptual forms. The latter seem to be based essentially in visual perception or, to avoid over-simplification, in the perceptual-practical universe. The strong resemblance between the gestural forms which are retained for communication indicates that a process of (mental) iconisation of experience has been set up, and furthermore that this process itself is based on the repetition and recognition of salient shapes, the description of the outlines of these shapes and/or the iconic gestural re- introduction of the salient shapes of categorised referents.

This hypothesis merits several remarks. First, the fact that these stabilised conceptual forms take on linguistic meaning by functioning as signs certainly reinforces their stability. Second, these categorisations seem to derive from a semiotic intent involving referential iconisation processes of extra- linguistic reality expressed by means of gestural sequences; the latter have functions which are just as much categorising as they are specifying. The difference between a sign representing a type and a sign representing a specified individual seems to reside in its being marked by the environment in which it occurs – whether in mime, in the gaze or in the context – which accompanies these gestural ensembles. Third, if there seems to be no gestural difference between the type and the manifestation of an individual example extracted from the type, the form of the signs thus created nevertheless exhibits a cognitive differentiation, separating referentially stabilised entities, and the events related to them. We find here a difference similar to that established by Langacker [4] between "things" and "processes". Indeed, the former are rendered by signs which specify a shape or the outline of a shape, or by gestural complexes which associate a description of the outline of a shape and an action frequently associated with this shape; whereas the latter never have recourse to specifications of shape and are rendered exclusively either by personal transfers (cf. below), or by signs in which movements, representing actions, iconically play a major role. This all goes to show that the iconic differentiation between "things" and "processes" argues strongly in favor of the noun/verb opposition as a cognitive, pre- linguistic given.

This in turn leads us to formulate the hypothesis concerning the iconicity of lexical creations., that is, as a process of iconisation conceived not merely as an aid to conceptualisation, but rather as a construction (utilising whatever means the gestural mode of signifying can provide) which simultaneously facilitates the co-construction of meaning by the addressee (for example, children seem to have a knowledge of other people's capacities for understanding very early on).

Along similar lines, but transposed into the framework of communication between adults, we might mention the utilisation of the iconic process in international conferences, where an accumulation of strongly iconic characteristics produces generic forms [5]. Equally well known is the inverse process, whereby the iconicity of standard generic items is re-motivated and is transformed into the specific ("that tree over there, that I'm pointing out"; "this house over here"; "like that", etc.) because the sign is placed in front of the gaze of the person creating it.

Taken together with the quite general value of this process of iconisation representing the perceptual world, the strong, iconic resemblance of the forms which are retained for use bear witness to the fact that deaf individuals in isolation repeat the first phases in the constitution of sign language in their familial microcosm.

We must never lose sight of the fact that – and this is the reason why congenital deafness is such a formidable analytic tool – firstly, all of the sign languages utilised in the world at present take analogous situations of communication as their starting point, although on the somewhat larger scale of the population in question (it is the univocity of the starting point, together with its dating, which constitute fictions); and secondly, the genesis of signs has always taken place more or less according to the same scenario. The serendipitous creation of small communities of deaf people in large cities (which one finds as early as the works of Plato), and later the institutionalised gatherings of deaf children in educational systems from the mid-eighteenth century onwards, did nothing more than extend – all the while accelerating – the process of semio- genesis brought into play by isolated deaf persons growing tip in the midst of the hearing family.

As my point of departure, I will take a primary semiotic intentionality having recourse to a process of iconisation which expresses both the generic and the specific, but which does not differentiate gesturally between the two. I will then try to account for the distinction between "great" iconic structures and the standard signs which today characterise the sign languages both utilised by large populations, and having a long history of institutionalised use.

With this aim in mind, I will advance the hypothesis that this primary iconisation split into two sub- branches, according to whether or not the process of iconisation serves the express aim of representing experience iconically: I shall term this "iconic intent".

2   Iconic Intent and High Iconicity

In the first case, iconicity is produced in a process of iconisation, evolves over time and is perfected, whether one chooses to consider the ontogenetic development of the deaf child living with his peers, or the historical development of the deaf community. For example, this evolution has resulted in increasingly sophisticated specifications and transfers of forms (cf. below) made possible by paradigms of hand configurations, as well as increasingly complex types of movement which enable one to reshape sense experience in the signing space with extreme precision. If we take the most fundamental example – that of a past lived experience – the iconising ambition corresponds to "*so, it happened like this*", and one shows the experience while recounting it; or "*it was in a room like this*", and one shows the room while describing it; or "*where a character like this one*", and one shows the person while imitating them, and so on. This procedure is a bit like what is termed in criminology as the reconstitution of a crime.

All languages enable the speaker to construct such reconstitution of experience, but spoken languages limit one to saying it without actually showing it (except for instances of gestural adjuncts: a fish "*this big*", or the postural imitation of characters or voice imitation in reported speech).

Not so for sign languages, where the demonstrative dimension "*like this*" can be activated at any moment through showing and imitating (as if I were the person of whom I speak, whatever his actions might be).

2.1   The Structural Characteristics of High Iconicity

High iconicity is the term I use to refer to the structural traces -in the realm of discourse- of a process of iconisation which sub-serves the iconic intent; that is, when the demonstrative dimension "*like this*" is conserved.

After considerable reflection, I have chosen to subsume the entirely of these structures under the heading of "transfers". This term seems appropriate in the sense that it is a matter here – beforehand – of transferring real or imaginary experience and slightly reshaping it, projecting it into a three dimensional discursive space we will call the "signing space", which is the space in which messages are made manifest.

As these structures, which are common to different sign languages have been catalogued elsewhere [5], the rapid review which follows should suffice.

2.1.1 Transfers of Size and/or Form

Specification is an operation which is used to designate a size or a form. The corresponding hand configurations are discrete and limited in number, The movement involved refers to the use of the form in space and is part of a continuum. At the start of a signed narrative, specification refers to the places or characters in the story. It marks out the individual from the typical (specific from the general) mid corresponds to what is indicated by *It's a...* in English, or *C'est un(e)...* in French.

2.1.2 Situational Transfer

The most general example of situational transfer is as follows. Within a paradigm of a limited number of hand configurations, the subservient and immobile hand indicates a stable place ("locative") and in relation to which the dominant hand represents a mobile agent, particularised by its special configuration. The form of the immobile locative represents a trans-categorical referential shape (flat and vertical shapes, laterally projecting shapes, round shapes, etc.) known as a "classifier". The movement effected by the dominant hand is contained within a continuum. This structure corresponds to operations which are indicated by *There is a ...which ...* in English, or *Il y a, un(e) ...qui ...* in French.

2.1.3 Personal Transfer

In personal transfer, the.. signer disappears and 'becomes' a protagonist in the narrative; his gestures correspond to the gestures effected by the character he refers to, and whose place he has taken. Here, the hand configurations (limited in number) represent types of action, such as walking, seizing, and so on. Personal transfers usually correspond to those operations which are indicated by *and there s/he is'. (do)-ing (something)...* in English, and by *et, le/la voilà qui...* in French.

These extremely iconic structures do not have temporal-aspectual markers, their use being exactly like that of the English present progressive forms. They can be combined in double transfers, thus linguistically dividing the speaker's body-effecting situational transfers, (with the signer's arm arid subservient hand) and personal transfers (with the speaker's dominant hand, the whole of his/her body, and face, mimicry included, and the gaze).

All of these structures, insofar as movement is concerned, are a relevant part of a dynamic continuum. They are not discrete in the structuralist sense, and their signifying form(s) cannot be transcribed into a written protocol (otherwise, the analogy loses its relevance). Their function is rather to represent the (demonstrative) mode of *"like this"*, showing everything while telling (specification and situational transfers) and the *"like this"* combined with *"as if"*, showing and acting out while telling (personal. transfers and double transfers).

The inclusion of these structures in French Sign Language is necessary. if there is to be mutual translation among the various languages. In fact, using only standard signs without any personal transfers, it is impossible to translate into FSL (i.e., French Sign Language, in French: Langue des Signes Française) such absurd statements as '*the chocolate eats the boy*'. Statements such as these require a personal transfer; the speaker must 'become' the chocolate.

Each of these iconic structures, which slightly reshapes real or imaginary experience through the iconicity of the image, can be classed with the reference types categorised by Desclés [6] and is entirely compatible with the hypothesis of a perceptual (essentially visual) basis for language.

I would like to make one final comment as far as structuralist postulates are concerned. If the medium corresponds indeed to a phenomenon of substance, then the possibilities of iconicity, four- dimensionality, and analogical representations which the visual-gestural medium offers calls into question the (so-called) independence of form and substance.

2.2   The Functional Characteristics of High Iconicity

The structural possibilities of sign language allows extremely detailed and descriptively accurate scripts to be produced using an iconic interleaving both syntagmatically and paradigmatically [7, 8]. These narrative practices, which are difficult to conceive in oral language, are frequently met in sign language and figure even as a truly cultural behaviour. These structures of high iconicity are essentially used during well defined language activities:

- Construction of specific agent reference frames;
- Construction of semantic spatial relations (agent location and changes in position in relation to fixed reference points, relations part/whole, etc).

These structures, up to and including the forms employed, are very similar between different sign languages. These structures are used by the deaf members of different linguistic communities, when communicating with each other. This allows communication to be rapidly established between members, even if each sign language has a specific nature.

Moreover, the mode of communication depends on the capabilities of each person. When signing, the locutor jumps from one mode of communication to the other, passing from highly iconic structures to a standard discourse mode depending on what he/she wishes to express.

The existence and the constant employment of an iconicised discourse in different sign languages opens new opportunities for a more powerful and general semiology on *saying* and *showing*. This semiology is open to application on oral language as well, through the integration of non verbal elements associated with these languages.

The highly iconic character, both through its universal and high figurative aspects, answers questions concerning basic cognitive filtering limited to the iconicised mode. When studying the succession of iconic structures, while telling a story for example, one can extract interesting information on different types of relations such as background/subject, locationing/located, stable/unstable, agent schemas.

3   The Construction of Reference Exclusive of Iconic Intent

The second sub-branch of iconicity mentioned earlier (cf. §2), exclusive of iconic intent, has contributed to a considerable increase in the standard lexicon.

When a sign is input into the lexicon with an iconic intent, doubting the interest of such an input in order to understand cognitive functioning has no sense. This is completely different when iconicity is not intended, like in language activities where standard signs are used. Indeed, the use of standard signs, which are themselves discrete units corresponds rather to a generic intent.

Then two questions may be raised:

- First, how to explain that iconicity, which is present, to a certain level, in standard signs in language activities where iconic intent is not the main aim?
- Secondly, how can we reconcile the presence of iconicity, although it is contradictory to the underlying cognitive mechanisms?

Here I am putting forward the hypothesis that this increase in the standard lexicon must have been concomitant with an evolution toward a formal resolution of signifying forms which was increasingly economical and systematic. However, this systematisation of the lexicon was dependent on a logic of economical conservation with regard to iconicity, which accompanied both the constraints of an optimal adaptation to the reception of messages by the visual system, as well as constraints concerning ease of articulation. Here we find a classic pattern of the economical evolution of language (as advanced by both Frei [9] and Martinet [10]) which is structured around a logic of iconic conservation – which in a sense sets the possible limits for this evolution. This double structure of economy and iconicity is best illustrated at present by the creation of neologisms in the sign languages which pass through similar stages, only much more quickly than those we have seen up to this point. These begin with primary iconisation, branching off towards generic reference with air economical resolution in the limited framework of maintained iconicity.

The development afforded by an economical evolution, coupled with the conservation of iconicity, has given rise to major structural characteristics; these have been analysed in detail elsewhere [11]. If we leave aside the iconic intent for the moment. these characteristics (or structural parameters) can be listed under three headings "or French Sign Language. First, there is the semantically molecular character of the standard signs, which can be broken down into configuration, orientation and movement; second, there is the simultaneity of the gaze, mimicry and signs, as well as other facial and bodily movements; and third, we find a simultaneity within signs which, above and beyond the overall iconicity of the lexicon, iconically specialises each one of these three parameters at the syntactic level.

Finally, the semantic relations between standard items utilises space in an economical and relevant fashion to mark the whole range of locative relationships, including the greater part of relations between agents; the latter are represented as spatialised and animated "mini-scenario".

As a conclusion to this paragraph, I should add that the major structural characteristics having to do with the relationships between signs are to be found in nearly the same form in the various sign languages which have been studied to date.

3.1   The Molecular Character of the Standard Signs

A model which integrates an iconic component only makes sense if the iconicity of standard signs is a phenomenon which influences the lexicon in a important way. In contrast to numerous descriptions of sign languages which have qualified as marginal the iconicity of signs, we show that this phenomenon is underestimated and in fact characterises a large majority of standard signs.

First of all, it is necessary to define the nature of this iconicity: This will be carried out using LSF vocabulary from [12] and [13]. A quick examination shows that the signs can be classified as *globally iconic*, where all the sign formation parameters come together gesturally to illustrate a categorised reference shape, or *partially iconic*, where only one or two parameters are influenced by iconicity.

3.1.1 Standard Sign Globally Iconic

For globally iconic signs:

- The *configuration* of the dominant hand represents a basic reference shape;
- The *movement* shows the contour of this shape (or a part of it) or an action performed by this shape;
- The *location* represents a stable shape, which localises the shape shown by the dominant hand. It is usually a particular location on the body, which can be the non-dominant hand.

These signs do not make up the major part of the lexicon but their number is not negligible.

As examples, we can cite:

- a large proportion of signs representing animals, like [TORTOISE], [FISH], [ZEBRA], [ELEPHANT];
- objects from nature like [TREE], [FIR];
- consumable objects like [LEEK], [EGGPLANT], [ANANAS];
- manufactured objects used in every day living activities [BOWL], [TABLE], [WINDOW], [BOTTLE], [BOOK], etc;
- and numerous anthroponomic words.

Another kind of global iconicity is represented by signs which are derived from the imitation of an action. These signs are formally close to the structures of *personal* or *double* transfer. Here also, they are numerous:

– [TO WASH UP], [TO WASH THE FACE], [TO CATCH], [TO TAKE], etc.

3.1.2 Standard Sign Globally Iconic

For partially iconic signs, from an iconic point of view:

– the *configuration* of one or two hands is related to referent shapes, like in [BRIDGE], [HOUSE],
– the *localisation* on the body is related to a referent localisation, like in [HEART], [EYE],
– and the hand *movement* is related to a referent action when performing the signs [KEY], [SPOON], [PLAYING CARD].

Therefore, the signs related to the action of feeding [TO EAT], [TO DRINK], are located near the mouth, whereas the signs related to intellectual activities [TO THINK], [TO REFLECT], [ERUDITE] are located near the head. The capture and grabbing actions are performed with a closing hand or a thumb-index pinch, while emissions are performed by an opening hand followed by finger extension.

We can add to this list the following signs:

– the signs of of an imitation type which are highly culturalised, as [CRAZY], [FEAR], [GOOD BYE], [NOTHING], [GOOD],
– the signs of second iconic exploitation based on dactylologic traces of the dominant language (the cases of a condensation like in [PARIS] which is a rebus-like sign combining the P letter in dactilology and the location-movement of the sign [CENTER]),
– the sign [LIVER PÂTÉ], where the same P letter is performed near the liver on the body,
– the exploitation of written forms based on specific domains like in [PSYCHOLOGY], [PHILOSOPHY], [ADDITION], [MULTIPLICATION], [EQUAL], [PERCENTAGE], [QUESTION],

In this way we can see that the quasi-totality of a standard vocabulary may be iconically justified, at least for one of the formation parameters.

The point is that there is a logic about iconicity: the sign parameters are iconically compatible with the objects they refer to. This is at least as important as the observation of iconicity to defend the idea of a non equivalence between the significant organisation of sign languages and the phonologies of oral languages.

This constitutes the other indispensable part toward the comprehension of the proposed model, in order to show the significant organisation of signs languages. This model is characterised by the adjunction of a constraint of maintenance or conservation of iconicity, for both articulation and perceptual constraints.

Conservation or maintenance are defined regarding the iconic traces of the iconisation process which is at the origin of the formation of all the sign languages used in the world. This process is continuously used by deaf children during the acquisition phase of the sign language.

3.1.3 Internal Organisation of Standard Signs

The model proposed here renders obsolete exclusively "phonological" analyses applied to sign languages. The explanation will be based on a standard unit, which is maximally iconic in its parametric composition: [TO MEET]. The formation parameters are the following:
- Configurations of the two hands: Vertical forms (index fingers)
- Orientation: The two index facing
- Movement: Linear movement of the two forms
- Location/movement: toward the other

Based on this idea, the signs are considered as a whole (units of molecular type) where each parametric element can convey some meaning, and can give some specific contribution to the global meaning of the unit. The comparison of standard signs with a molecular organisation is a metaphor which can help us to understand the internal organisation of the LSF standard vocabulary: A sign can be considered as a conglomerate of meaning atoms, for which only the grouping into a sign (one molecule) is linguistically attested. If we consider the concept that signs are purely phonological, it is not possible to theoretically justify that distinctive features which are purely *signifiant* have regularly and commonly a *signified* value.

Minimal units which are used in the composition of standard signs are close to morphemic units used in oral language. For example:
- In FSL, the sign [TO MEET], the configuration *straight index* conveys the meaning "thin vertical shape" (in the context, it means "human being").
- In oral French, the morpheme "ier" can be associated with the meaning "tree" (pommier, figuier) or "job" (charcutier, épicier) depending on the context.

3.1.4 Morphemic Values Inventory

We now give an inventory of morphemic values for each parameter. We have kept only the shape- meaning constant that have an indubitable iconic property and are often used.

Concerning the *configuration* parameter, where the morphemic iconic value is the most evident, we can look at the list of high iconicity configurations listed in [11] and [5]. For most of them, their signified values are directly transposable in the scope of standard signs. However, the homology is not complete. For example, the configuration "flexed major and other fingers open and extended" is not included in the inventory of high iconicity, but is productive in the scope of the standard signs. Its signified meaning is "contact, contact relation". This configuration is used in the signs [CONTACT], [TO TOUCH], [TO STING], and, with a metaphoric extension, in [TO HAVE EXPERIENCE] (location at the head level) and in [EMOTIONALLY MOVED] (location near the heart), [TOUCHY, SENSITIVE].

Concerning the *location* parameter, the evident iconic morphemic values often used are the following:

- The mouth, where most of the signs related to ingestion (associated to a movement toward ourselves) or to vocal emission (associated to a movement toward the exterior, often repeated) are located
- The heart, where numerous signs related to emotion are located
- The eyes, for the signs related to visual perception
- The head (particularly at the temple level) for most of the signs related to intellectual activities and idea world.

We can also associate auto-referential values of body parts, like in [NOSE], [NECK], [FOREHEAD], and associated activities, like in [TO SMELL], [COLD], [TO STRANGLE], [TO KILL], [BUTCHER], [BAPTISM], [CATHOLIC], etc., but this necessitates detailed research work which beyond the scope of this paper.

We will also take into account the morphemic value that is inherent from facial mimics which, systematically associated to some signs, gives them an interrogative value [WHO ?], [WHY ?] interro- negative [SURE ?] or negative [NO POINT], [NOT FINISHED] etc.

For the movement parameter, we have carefully dissociated the internal morphemic value, that is correlated to the semantic of the units (notably verbal: catching = closure of the hand, emissions = opening of the hand), and the added aspectual morphemic value (external) which is the object of a syntactic choice (for example: repetition of movement, amplitude, velocity, etc.).

The point of view adopted here is to study the LSF at a semantic level (including the unit relationships) which allows us to consider the verb as a central organiser which distributes the dynamic relationships between agents. The topologic modelling of the internal dynamics that is linked to the verb semantics allows René Thom [14, 15] to present a paradigm of irreducible agent morphologies.

We are surprised by the similarity between graphs of elementary morphologies and the movement form of the signs that are the conceptual equivalents in LSF.

This is particularly true for morphologies which are related to the surviving and the continuation of species. The same thing can be noticed about the morphology of the capture that happens in LSF by the closing of a previously opened configuration of the hand. This can be illustrated by verbs such as [TO TAKE], [TO TEAR OUT], [TO CATCH], [TO UNDERSTAND], [TO LEARN ...a lesson], [TO TAKE PLACE], [TO HEAR ...news]

In the same way, for the morphology of bifurcation (emission) that happens in LSF when there is an opening of a previously closed configuration of the hand, that we find in verbs like [TO EMIT], [TO SHOUT], [TO DIFFUSE], [TO INFORM], [TO PUT THE LIGHT ON] Similarity also between the morphology of:

- "to finish" and [TO GO UP TO THE END]
- "to change" and [TO CHANGE], [TO BECOME]
- "to reject" and [TO REFUSE], [TO REJECT], [TO DISMISS]
- "to shake" and [TO SHAKE], [TO JUMP]

With some extrapolation, we can see in LSF [TO GIVE (from me to you)], [TO GIVE (from you to me)], in context, the (vertical) bodies of protagonists on which figure the parallel horizontals of the graph (the stable agents) and the movement of the hands linking the two bodies such as in the discontinuity of the morphology of *giving*.

3.2   The Simultaneity of Information and the Semantic Specialisation of Signing Parameters

When a message is transmitted by a sign language, several parameters combine simultaneously to construct its meaning: posture, body and facial movements, but especially the signer's gaze and its direction, facial mimicry, and hand gestures. Each of these last three parameters is essential to the elaboration of the meaning that is conveyed by the message. Irrespective of the particular sign language, each parameter appears to have a specialised and very specific semantic function.

3.2.1 Gaze

The signer's gaze governs the interaction and signals changes of discourse genre. In highly expressive iconic structures such as personal transfers or double transfers, the gaze of the signer is that of the character transferred. The end of a personal transfer is signalled by the signer's gaze meeting that of the addressee.

Apart from structures of personal transfer, the signer's gaze, directed at the signs he makes, indicates the referential value of these signs, drawing them into the realm of '*like that*'. Directed towards a point in space, however, the gaze not only signals that the construction of a reference is imminent; it also, (like the mouse attached to a PC), activates this portion of the signing space, creating a sort of secondary deixis belonging to the signed utterance.

3.2.2 Facial Mimicry

Facial mimicry has considerable semantic importance, its values differing according to the context in which it is used. In standard utterances, it indicates the signer's state of mind, and possesses a modal value ('doubtful', 'interrogatory', 'detrimental', etc.). When mimicry accompanies nouns, its value is qualifying (*small, beautiful, spongy*, etc.) or quantifying (*a bit, a lot*, etc.). In personal transfers, it indicates the state of mind of the protagonist in the transferred phrase, or his manner of accomplishing the action.

I should like to add one parenthetical remark concerning facial mimicry. Due to the nature of the medium employed, one might say that sign languages lead us naturally to question the relevance of the generally allowed distinction between the verbal and the non-verbal. All else being equal, according to this distinction, the facial expressions and postures of the signing subject would be classed as non-verbal. The problem is that in personal transfer structures, when the signing subject embodies the character he is telling about, his mimicry which could be assimilated to adverbs of manner, is attributed to the protagonist of the narrative action. This mimicry, however, is the same as that which characterises the signer outside of personal transfer, as the signing subject who participates interactively. It would be absurd to consider it as non-verbal in the latter instance and verbal in the former. Thus the distinction between the verbal and non-verbal blurs, thereby pushing back the frontiers of what is normally considered as 'language'.

3.2.3 Signs

Standard signs have an iconicity that is often metonymic when referring to a class of established referents. As discrete items, easily transcribed with *ad hoc* notational systems, they have four simultaneous parameters: positioning, hand configurations, hand orientation, and actual movement. Each parametric element entering into their composition can be exploited at a semantic- syntactic level (in contrast to their inherent 'atomic' value which we have examined above (§3.1).

Let us summarise with respect to standard verbal items. The modal value of facial expression (or mimicry), the interactive and referential value of the gaze, and the phatic value of head movements (small nods on the signer's part) all are superimposed on the verbal-gestural unit which, depending on its meaning, might include in addition:

- via hand configuration: the agent (verbs of motion), the instrument (e.g. [TO DRINK]), the patient (e.g. [TO EAT]);
- via hand positioning: the corporal locative (e.g. [TO OPERATE], [TO BLEED]) etc.;
- via hand movement : aspects of the action (such as 'repeatedly', 'unaccomplished', 'rapidly') etc.;
- via the orientation-positioning-movement complex: the semantic relationship governing the agents participating in the discourse process ('agent', 'patient', 'beneficiary').

3.3   The Spatialisation of Semantic Relations

Since by definition not everything can be said at the same time, the relationships between items are indicated essentially by introducing spatial relationships between these items in a relevant manner. We shall consider the case of non-specific references which involve spatial and temporal relationships as well as agent relationships.

3.3.1 Spatial Reference

Whatever the discourse genre to be represented, the general tendency is to use first-order iconic structures to express spatial relationships between (signed) items. Thus, even a sentence communicated by standard signs such as 'each evening after eating he watches television' is usually ended by the repetition of [TELEVISION] as a classifier 'flat- surfaced rectangular object', then by the standard sign [TO SEE] in semi-personal transfer posture with the associated mimicry of the transferred character directed (with passage toward a double transfer) toward the classifier (rectangular object...) both sign are effected by the dominant hand. In fact, this sentence in standard signs is followed by '*and it happened like this...*'.

For non-specific spatial relationships, standard signs are (wherever possible) spatialised directly, without recourse to first-order iconic structures. Let us take as at example [*coming home from work*]. [HOME/'house'] is first signed to the signer's right and [TO WORK] to his left. [COMING HOME] is then signed by using the place where [TO WORK] was signed as a starting point, and that of [HOME/'house'] as the end point of the movement.

When standard signs cannot be moved (e.g. where there is contact with the body) the gaze-pointing combination comes into play. Thus, in order to speak of a person who has left for the United States to go on a training course as the sign [UNITED STATES] is made; the signer's gaze is directed up and to his left at the same time, activating that portion of space. The anaphoric use of pointing then relates [UNITED STATES] to the space activated by the signer's gaze. After this, the signs [TO WORK], [TO TRAVEL AROUND], [TO INVESTIGATE], [FOR A YEAR], are effected in the relevant portion of space.

As far as spatial relationships between nouns are concerned, the unmarked order localizer/localised, fixed/mobile, container/contained, ground/figure is compulsory; no recourse to isolated linguistic elements with the relational function of prepositions is necessary. Whenever possible (for example, with the standard signs [HOUSE] and [WINDOW]), signs which are the focus of the signer's gaze are placed in the signing space according to the spatial relationships each entertains with the other. Should this not be an option (when, for example, standard signs necessitate contact with the body), signs are reintroduced by a classifying hand configuration ('flat form', 'round form', 'form with lateral projections', etc.). The relationship is achieved via the classifying hand configuration of the localizer (subservient hand) and another classifier or specifier of form representing the most movable object (dominant hand). A case in point is the part/whole relationship. The semantic specification of interrelated elements is effected via standard signs, then the relationship between them is conveyed via first-order iconic structures (specifying or classifying hand configurations which re-introduce standard signs and place them in relevant positions).

3.3.2 Temporal Reference

Temporal relationships between items are also spatialised. The moment of the interaction and tense within the utterance are signalled in relation to the body of the locutor: forwards for future and backwards for past, with the distance from the body graduated accordingly.

When temporal relationships are independent of the moment of the interaction, a horizontal time-line is used whose direction (right-to-left or left-to-right) is not pertinent in an absolute sense, but becomes relevant depending on the circumstances. This time- line is always perpendicular to the movements marking tense within the utterance.

Thus, to take an example from data I myself have collected, a referential mark is constructed. First the standard sign is given [1978], followed by the signer's gaze activating a portion of space. Then there is the anaphoric re-introduction by the specific hand configuration, that is to say, a vertical referential marker (index finger of the subservient hand raised) effected at this same point in the signing space, nod of the head to indicate co- reference, and pointing of the dominant hand toward the classifying configuration of the subservient hand. Then the time-line is constructed. (In this example, 'before' is to the left of the mark, with 'after' and up until [NOW] being to the right).

Afterwards, a second referential mark [1970] win be established to the left in the same manner. These spatialisations, imbued with temporal value, will be exploited continually thereafter. Thus the standard sign [THE DEAF] (dominant hand) simultaneously taken up anaphorically by the subservient hand to relate [THE DEAF] to the indicated space [1970], means *the deaf of/at that time*. Then [GOING AROUND TOGETHER] in the same position of space completes the utterance.

3.3.3 Reference to Agents

In referential constructions, the gaze-pointing combination distributes the standard signs spatially, functioning in the same way as for spatial or temporal relationships.

The signer's gaze and pointing interact in the overall signing space, combining the enunciative space (i.e., the gaze) and the space of the utterance itself (i.e., pointing).

The gaze is employed before pointing. As the spatial dimension of FSL makes it possible to construct a three-dimensional situation which more or less reshapes reality, one could say that the use of the gaze constitutes a kind of paradoxical deictic process, to the extent that the situation or the reference always remains to be constructed.

Even where there is no express intention to reproduce experience spatially, there still can be a series of mini-scenarios in which agents and verbal notions are put into play together. The agents are signed into spatial relationships either directly or by pointing (in this case they are re-introduced anaphorically and assigned to a portion of space); the verbal items on the other hand distribute semantic roles, by virtue of their orientation and movement. One might therefore be justified in speaking of schematic iconicity (I prefer this term to that of diagrammatic iconicity, which is commonly used), which is not subject to an iconic intent, and which is constructed in the signing space according to circumstance.

3.3.4 A Review of Referential Pointing to Selected Portions of Space

First of all, I would like to make an additional remark concerning pointing gestures, which are very frequently utilised. In a one-hour corpus of data I assembled, I was able to count more than 1200 occurrences (excluding self-reference), of which approximately 950 were instances of referential pointing, and which we shall discuss here.

I will recall the fact that pointing is not an element which directly activates the pertinent portions of the signing space. It re-introduces or "re-activates" elements which have been previously assigned a spatial dimension and which are activated by the simple fact of the signer's gaze being directed at them; it is this last factor which plays an essential role in signing.

Since pointing does not actually create meaning, its true worth is dependent on its relation to the gaze (however, this is not the case with the simple re-introduction of agents by pointing at them). Its main function is rather to ensure discursive cohesiveness and coherence in a dialogic, referential space which is constructed through the focusing of the signer's s gaze.

Then again, there can be instances of complex pointing, linking the agent to a temporal or locative referent. If such a temporal or locative construction has not yet been put into place, it would seem that a double pointing gesture (evidently preceded by the gaze) should be the usual way to go about it. If in fact a temporal or locative construction has already been put into place, a pointing gesture with one hand suffices (i.e. the reintroduction of the agent by pointing, assuring the temporal or locative link to a portion of space previously activated). The signer's gaze can be directed at these pointing gestures, although this does not seem strictly necessary.

There can also be instances of simple pointing at agents, that is, configurations corresponding to pronominal forms (*him/her, he/she* and so on). The gaze is not normally directed at these pointing gestures. However, the gaze must necessarily be directed at these gestures if the anticipated reference is of a spatial order (for example, if the agent is to participate in an action involving movement); and the gaze can, to a lesser extent, be directed at these pointing gestures if the relation to the agent to be constructed ("agent, patient, action") necessitates a relevant spatial orientation for the verb in the signing space.

Generally speaking, simple pointing is a form of anaphor, since the semantic specification contained in standard signs has previously been made manifest; nevertheless, examples of cataphoric forms do exist. At times, when this specification has already been made, it is possible for a pointing gesture to intervene before the standard sign is reintroduced a second time. In such instances semantic specification can be compared to a form of insistence.

The complex functioning of pointing underscores our line of reasoning; pointing can extend. from the simple re-introduction of a sign to a function linking two elements in the same portion of signing space, combining them semantically.

3.3.5 The Creation of Standard Signs Having a Nominal Function

I maintain, following Langacker [16], that signs having a nominal function are part of an operation, of instantiation. To put it another way, they are part of referential anchoring constructions, which make it possible to differentiate between the specific, instantiated individual and the type. There are concurrently two ways of instantiating in FSL, each competing with the other. The first is always subservient to an iconic intent, the second is not. In the latter case, we have pointing gestures with the various related functions mentioned above (pointing preceded by the gaze, undefined by the gaze, unaccompanied by the gaze; simple, double or repeated pointing; cataphoric, simultaneous or anaphoric pointing in relation to the standard item). In the former case, the utterance shifts into the demonstrative mode "like this" through the re- introduction of the standard sign, which moreover always has an anaphoric value: this is accomplished by means of a hand configuration of high iconicity.

In general these two means of instantiating standard signs, determined by an express intention, are compatible with the following relations of equivalence: whatever is not dependent on an express intention to represent experience iconically, or iconic intent, and therefore not a case of high iconicity tends toward genetic referential value (genericity); on the other hand, whatever is dependent on an express intention to represent experience iconically, and which includes structures of high iconicity tends toward specific referential value. This equivalence is statistical, but by no means systematic in overtly generic utterances For example, an utterance such as: "Cats are animals that love to sleep in armchairs", can shift effortlessly (at the termination of signing into the "like this" mode of the iconic intent.

4   Iconicity and Language as Systems of Differentiation

The inclusion of sign languages among the world's languages affects not only linguistic epistemology: there is also an impact on commonly accepted notions concerning language acquisition, such as the concept of a critical age. I personally know several congenitally deaf people who, educated among the hearing and for whom oral French could not be a first language, acquired FSL late (after ten years of age). Nevertheless, their practice of this language is completely similar to that of native signers. On the other hand, even if those deaf children to whom signing is forbidden suffer cruelly from a lack of linguistic communication (I speak of those, and they are numerous, who never really master an oral language), their behaviour – although disturbed – cannot be considered outrageous. Despite their lack of a first language, they nonetheless manifest coherent and adequate behavioural patterns in their relationships to the. world and to others.

Along the same lines, isolated deaf people spontaneously create signs (specification of size and form, personal transfers, standard signs) in order to communicate with the hearing population around them [1]. I was present, and became extremely moved, when a deaf French adult was introduced to a young deaf Moroccan man who, for the first time in his life, was able to communicate with another deaf person. The dialogue took place via signs which the young man used with his hearing family, and which he had been inventing himself since his childhood.

All these observations lead one to consider that proto-linguistic conceptual stabilisation's do in fact exist; they are categorisations of a perceptual- practical origin which are forerunners of linguistic grounding [6, 17].

My observation of the creation of signs by isolated deaf people leads me to postulate the existence of a fundamental type of cognitive differentiation from which both nouns (referentially stable, mid distinguished by their perceptual shapes) and verbs (recurrent, meaningful, discontinuous processes of daily experience) might originate. Some of these became central in man's specific development as man. I refer the reader to R. Thom [14, 15] and to that set of what he calls 'elementary morphologies'. (Whilst on this topic, it is impossible not to mention the marked similarity which exists between the graphs of these elementary morphologies on the one hand, and on the other, the movement of those signs in FSL which correspond to them semantically.)

One might be critical about limiting the object 'language' to the referential function. Where then would one fit in pragmatics or, more especially, the concept of language as a system of signs, the identity of each being that which the others are not? In short, is not iconicity, because it is associated with reference, a problem for the essential Saussurian concept of arbitrariness?

I believe that this criticism stems from a fundamental misreading of structural linguistics. In fact, two distinct meanings of the word 'arbitrary' are confused, based on this mistaken premise: the functioning of oral language units as parts of a system based on differences has been deduced from their non-iconicity.

I think that what is so characteristic of language, and differentiates it so specifically from other systems, derives from a capacity much more fundamental to human nature. This capacity simply adapts itself to language, as it does to non-linguistic behaviour. It is the very same capacity which causes a child to replace the lid on a pot of jam from which he has eaten, despite having been told not to; the same capacity causes a human to remove all trace of his footprints; the same which leads humans to creates false tracks; the same which affirms the truth of what is known to be false etc. This capacity consists in the application of two concomitant processes to a particular element in a behavioural sequence, the first being a process which cuts the term off from its referent, and the second being a process of de- contextualisation. The element is thus raised for others to the conceptual level of a sign, and can be made to signify perhaps even the opposite of its referential meaning. it is this 'meta-capacity' which opens up language, like any other set of signs, to a paradigmatic dimension (de-contextualised elements seen from the angle of their mutual differences).

This capacity sweeps across referential items of different categories, and at the semantic level (and irrespective of the particular language) permits the derivation of a verb from any noun (that is, of any item which refers to a class of stable referents). The fact that it is – or is not – attested in a given language depends on the 'ritualised' syntactic properties of that particular language.

In a world where language exists as a system of differences, whether items are iconic or not is, in fact, immaterial I shall illustrate this point with a few examples taken from FSL.

 - [TO OPEN a door] might mean, depending on the context: *begin, to be the starting point*, but also *open* (a quality of a person's character).
 - A good example of the fact that iconicity does not necessarily entail a one-to-one relationship with the referent comes from schools (e.g. Metz) which

have no finger spelling tradition (the possibility of spelling words from an oral language with a finger alphabet). The signs for the days of the week, for instance, are based on significant events of the day in question : thus, *Thursday, Friday,* and *Saturday* are expressed respectively by the signs [SHOWER] (the day for a compulsory shower), [FISH], [GYMNASIUM].

– Lexical creations function in a similar manner. [HEARING] signed near the forehead (a neologism) describes a deaf person who thinks and acts like a hearing one. And the same principle is used vita specialised signs for games or jokes. One of my friends, a professor, specialises in electric cabling. His profession is signed [PROFESSOR + ELECTRICITY]; this latter sign is made by moving the two index fingers side by side (its origin being the representation of the two ends of an electric arc). When the professor became over-excited during a meeting, a deaf person calmed things down by signing '*It's OK, he is* (PROFESSOR + ELECTRICITY)', whilst moving his index fingers on each side of his head: ("It's not surprising; he's got electricity on the brain").

5 Sign Languages as Cognitive Languages

The theoretical principles outlined above constitute, I believe, a starting point for an exhaustive description of French Sign Language. The verb is the distributor of agent roles; its spatial orientation manifests the semantic roles of the agents, depending on the specific position assigned to them in space. In short, I have disregarded syntactic notions and definitions such as the verb as a class of commutable units specialised in the predicate function, the syntactic subject and object, etc.

Might not syntax be due to that very slow diachronic ritualisation, phylogenesis, of which R. Thom speaks? In other words, it represents the economic resolution, at a formal level, of earlier problems connected with the construction of meaning. The fact that this ritualisation has been pushed to extremes in oral languages would be a consequence of the medium itself, whose constraints allow few iconic resolutions (or none at all, i.e., imagistic iconicity). Similarly, these constraints render impossible the use of space in a pertinent manner, and strongly limit the possibilities of reshaping ('anamorphising') practical and perceptual experience. Syntax could be considered as having the same function among semantic units as phonology has among phonological units. A level of organisation within individual units does indeed exist in sign languages; however, this cannot be assimilated to phonology, because the diverse parameters which enter into the formation of signs are themselves frequently meaningful. To account for this 'organisational' level, Stokoe has recently proposed the notion of 'semantic phonology' [18].

The title of this final section should be understood thus: the fact that sign languages are cognitive languages is banal in the sense that all languages are cognitive objects and all uses of a language have to do with cognitive processes. This statement is less banal, however, if it refers to the linguistic traces of cognitive operations in languages where the synthetic levels of syntax and phonology are absent and where formal, less constrained resolutions might constitute examples of a more direct contact with cognition (according to Langacker's conception of his term [4]).

Thus, if one accepts as legitimate the linguist's choice of certain syntactic problems as points of departure for analysing the language he works with, sign languages lead us to question the validity of models which postulate, as much from phylogenetic as ontogenetic points of view, the autonomy of a syntactic level vis-à-vis the more all-inclusive problem of the construction of meaning.

References

1. Yau, S.-C.: *Création de langues gestuelles chez des sourds Isolés.* Doctorat d'Etat Thesis (post PhD), Paris VII University, 1988.
2. Dos Santos Souza, I.: *Quand les gestes deviennent une proto-langue.* DEA report (post graduate), Science du Langage department, Paris VIII University, 1999.
3. Goldin-Meadow, S. and C. Mylander: *Spontaneous sign systems created by deaf children in* two cultures. In Nature 391(6664):279–281, 1998.
4. Langacker, R.: *Foundations of cognitive grammar, Vol. 1.* Stanford University Press, 1987.
5. Cuxac, C.: *La Langue des Signes Française.* Faits de Langues, Ophrys, (in press).
6. Desclés, J.P.: *La prédication opérée par les langues (ou à propos de l'interaction entre langage et perception).* In Langages, 103:83–96, 1991.
7. Sallandre, M.-A.: *Les procès en Langue des Signes française; une approche dans le récit, en fonction des degrés d'iconicité,* Maîtrise report (master), Paris X, Nanterre, 1998.
8. Sallandre, M.-A.: *La dynamique des transferts de personne en Langue des Signes Française,* DEA report (post graduate), Science du Langage department, Paris VIII, Saint-Denis, 1999.
9. Frei, H.: *La grammaire des fautes.* Slaktine Reprints, Genève-Paris, 1982.
10. Martinet, A.: *Economie des changements phonétiques.* Francke S.A., Berne, 1955.
11. Cuxac, C.: *Fonctions et structures de l'iconicité dans les langues des signes; analyse descriptive d'un idiolecte parisien de la Langue des Signes Française.* Thèse de Doctorat d'Etat (post PhD), Paris V University, 1996.
12. Moody, B.: *La langue des signes. Dictionnaire bilingue élémentaire. Vol 2.* IVT, Paris, 1986.
13. Moody, B.: .: *La langue des signes. Dictionnaire bilingue élémentaire. Vol 3.* IVT, Paris 1990.
14. Thom, R.: *Stabilité structurelle et morphogenèse.* Ediscience, Paris, 1972.
15. Thom, R.: *Modèles mathématiques de la morphogenèse,* Christian Bourgoisn, Paris, 1980.
16. Langacker, R.: *Foundations of cognitive grammar, Vol. 2.* Stanford University Press, 1991.
17. Petitot, J.: *Syntaxe topologique et grammaire cognitive.* In Langages, 103:97–128, 1991.
18. Stokoe, WC.: *Semantic phonology.* In Sign language Studies, 20(71):107–114, 1991.

HMM-Based Continuous Sign Language Recognition Using Stochastic Grammars

Hermann Hienz, Britta Bauer, and Karl–Friedrich Kraiss

Department of Technical Computer Science
Aachen University of Technology (RWTH), Germany
Phone: +49-241-8026105   Fax: +49-241-8888308
Ahornstrasse 55, D-52074 Aachen
hienz@techinfo.rwth-aachen.de
http://www.techinfo.rwth-aachen.de

Abstract. This paper describes the development of a video-based continuous sign language recognition system using Hidden Markov Models (HMM). The system aims for automatic signer dependent recognition of sign language sentences, based on a lexicon of 52 signs of German Sign Language. A single colour video camera is used for image recording. The recognition is based on Hidden Markov Models concentrating on manual sign parameters. As an additional component, a stochastic language model is utilised, which considers uni- and bigram probabilities of single and successive signs. The system achieves an accuracy of 95% using a bigram language model.

1 Introduction

Sign languages, although different in form, serve the same functions as a spoken language. They are natural languages which are used by many deaf people all over the world, e.g., GSL (German Sign Language) in Germany or ASL (American Sign Language) in the United States. Hearing people have difficulties to learn sign language and simultaneously the majority of those people who were born deaf or who became deaf early in live, have only a limited vocabulary of the accordant spoken language of the community in which they live. As a consequence the development of a system for translating sign language into spoken language would be of great help for deaf as well as hearing people.

This paper outlines a system design and implementation of a video-based continuous sign language recognition system as a first and important step towards a translation system (sign-to-text). Furthermore, an automatic recognition system for sign language could be used for developing gestural human-machine interfaces.

Sign languages are visual languages and they can be characterised by manual (handshape, handorientation, location, motion) and non-manual (trunk, head,

A. Braffort et al. (Eds.): GW'99, LNAI 1739, pp. 185–196, 1999.

gaze, facial expression, mouth) parameters [2]. One-handed and two-handed signs are used. For one-handed signs only the so called dominant hand performs the sign. For two-handed signs both hands of the signer make the sign (symmetrical/non-symmetrical); the second hand is called non-dominant hand . The 3D space in which both hands act for signing represents the signing space. If two signs only differ in one parameter they are called a minimal pair.[10]

The developed system uses a single colour video camera in order to minimise the necessary hardware components and resulting adjustments. Recognising signs by means of a video-based system basically leads to different problems. Problems may be connected to the recording as well as to the signing person himself. It is neccessary to solve the following problems:

- While signing, some fingers or even a whole hand can be occluded.
- The system must be able to detect sign boundaries automatically.
- A sign is affected by the preceding and the subsequent sign (co-articulation).
- Movements of the signer, like shifting in one direction or rotating around the signer's body axis, must be considered.
- Each sign varies in time and space. Even if the same person tries to perform the same sign twice, small changes of speed and position of the hands will occur.
- Using a single colour video camera, the projection of the 3D scene on a 2D plane results in loss of depth information. The reconstruction of the 3D-trajectory of the hand in space is sometimes not possible.
- The processing of a large amount of image data is time consuming, so real-time recognition is difficult.

The property of HMMs to compensate time and amplitude variances of signals has been proven for speech and character recognition [7]. Due to these characteristics HMMs appear as an ideal approach to sign language recognition. Like speech, sign language can be considered a non-deterministic time signal. Instead of words or phonemes we here have a sequence of signs. However, different from speech recognition where the smallest unit is the phoneme, linguistics have not yet agreed on subunits for signs. Thus each sign is modelled with one HMM.

Aiming for signer dependent recognition, the same person trains and tests the system. The presented recognition system concentrates on manual sign parameters. Non-manual sign parameters are not used for this task. Properties, such as incorporation and indication of sign language will be ignored at the moment. The training- and test corpus consists of GSL–sentences which are meaningful and grammatically well-formed. All sentences are built according to the grammar of GSL. Furthermore, there are no constraints regarding a specific sentence structure. Continuous sign language recognition in this context means that signs within a sentence are not separated by a pause. In order to improve recognition accuracy a language model is introduced.

2   Related Work in the Field of Automatic Continuous Sign Language Recognition

The aim of this section is to briefly discuss systems which are concerned with the recognition of continuous sign language.

Braffort [3] presented a recognition system for french sign sentences based on a dataglove. Signs are divided into conventional signs, non-conventional signs and variable signs. The recognition system is based on HMMs. Two modules are used for recognition. One for classifying conventional signs and another one for recognising the remaining two classes. The system achieves a recognition rate of 96% and 92% for the two modules on a lexicon of 44 sign sentences (vocabulary of 7 signs).

Liang et al. [6] used linear ten-states HMMs for the recognition of continuous taiwanese sign language. Data acquisition is carried out by using a dataglove. The system is designed to classify 250 signs. A recognition rate of 80.4% is reached.

Starner and Pentland [9] presented a video-based system for the recognition of short sentences of ASL, with a vocabulary of 40 signs. Signs are modelled with four-states HMM. A single camera is used for image recording. The recognition rate is 75% and 99%, allowing only simplest syntactical structures.

In 1997, Vogler and Metaxas [11] described a HMM-based system for continuous ASL recognition with a vocabulary of 53-signs. Three video cameras are used interchangeably with an electromagnetic tracking system for obtaining 3D movement parameters of the signer's arm and hand. The sentence structure is unconstrained and the number of signs within a sentence is variable. Vogler et al. performed two experiments, both with 97 test sentences: One, without grammar and another with incorporated bigram probabilities. Recognition accuracy ranges from 92.1% up to 95.8% depending on the grammar used.

3   Theory of Hidden Markov Models

This section briefly discusses the theory of HMMs. A more detailed description of this topic can be found in [7, 8].

Given a set of N states s_i we can describe the transitions from one state to another at each time step t as a stochastic process. Assuming that the state-transition probability a_{ij} from state s_i to state s_j only depends on preceding states, we call this process a Markov chain. The further assumption, that the actual transition only depends on the very preceding state leads to a first order Markov chain. We can now define a second stochastic process that produces at each time step t symbol vectors x. The output probability of a vector x only depends on the actual state, but not on the way the state was reached. The output probability density $b_i(x)$ for vector x at state s_i can either be discrete or continuous.

This double stochastic process is called a Hidden Markov Model (HMM) λ which is defined by its parameters $\lambda = (\Pi, A, B)$. Π stands for the vector of the initial state-transition probabilities π_i, the $N \times N$ matrix A represents the state-transition probabilities a_{ij} from state s_i to state s_j, and B denotes the matrix of the output densities $b_i(x)$ of each state s_i.

Given the definition of HMMs, there are three basic problems to be solved [7]:

- The evaluation problem: Given the observation sequence $O = O_1, O_2, \ldots, O_T$, and the model $\lambda = (\Pi, A, B)$, the problem is how to compute $P(O \mid \lambda)$, the probability that this observed sequence was produced by the model. This problem can be solved with the Forward-Backward algorithm.
- The estimation problem: This problem covers the estimation of the model parameters $\lambda = (\Pi, A, B)$, given one or more observation sequences O. No analytical calculation method is known to date, the Viterbi training represents a solution, that iteratively adjusts the parameters Π, A and B. In every iteration, the most likely path through an HMM is calculated. This path gives the new assignment of observation vectors O_t to the states s_j.
- The decoding problem: Given the observation sequence O, what is the most likely sequence of states $S = s_1, s_2, \ldots, s_T$ according to some optimality criterion. A formal technique for finding this best state sequence is called the Viterbi algorithm.

4   HMM-Based Approach to Continuous Sign Language Recognition

In the previous section, the basic theory of HMMs has been introduced. This section details our approach of an HMM-based recognition system for continuous sign language. Figure 1 shows the components of the system.

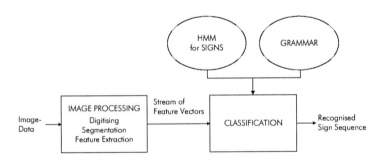

Fig. 1. Components of the video-based continuous sign language recognition system

After recording, the sequence of input images is digitised and segmented. In the next processing step features regarding size, shape and position of the fingers, hands and body of the signer are calculated. Using this information a feature vector is built that reflects the manual sign parameters (Sec. 4.1). Classification is performed by using HMMs (Sec. 4.2). For both, training and recognition, feature vectors must be extracted from each video frame and input into the HMM (Sec. 4.3 and 4.4). Incorporated grammars provides additional constraints on the data and simplifies the recognition process (Sec. 5).

4.1   Feature Extraction

Since HMMs require feature vectors, an important task covers the determination and extraction of features. In our approach the signer wears simple coloured cotton gloves (see figure 2), in order to enable real-time data acquisition and to retrieve easily information about the performed handshape.

Fig. 2. Coloured markers at the dominant and non-dominant hand of the signer (The coloured markers at the wrist and elbow are not relevant for this task)

Taking into account the different amount of information represented by the handshape of the dominant and non-dominant hand and the fact that many signs can be discriminated only by looking at the dominant hand, different gloves have been chosen: one with seven colours - marking each finger, the palm, and the back of the dominant hand - and a second glove in a eighth colour for the non-dominant hand.

A threshold algorithm generates Input/Output-code for the colours of the gloves, skin, body and background. In the next processing step the size and the centre of gravity (COG) of the coloured areas are calculated and a rule-based classifier estimates the position of the shoulders and the central vertical axis of the body silhouette [4]. Using this information we build a feature vector that reflects the manual parameters of sign language, without explicitly modelling them.

Table 1 shows how the manual parameters of sign language are represented by the feature vector.

Table 1. Feature vector for coding manual sign parameters

Manual parameter	Feature
Location	x-coordinate, relative to central body axis y-coordinate, relative to height of the right shoulder Distance of the COGs of the dominant and non-dominant hand
Handshape	Distances of all COGs of the coloured markers of the hand to each other (dominant hand only)
Handshape/ Orientation	Size of coloured areas
Orientation	Angles of the fingers relative to the $x - axis$ (dominant hand only)

4.2   Hidden Markov Modelling

Having discussed the determination of the feature vector, the aim of this section is modelling sign language with HMMs. In our approach each sign is modelled with one HMM. Figure 3 illustrates the modelling of a sequence of continuous signs with one HMM for each sign.

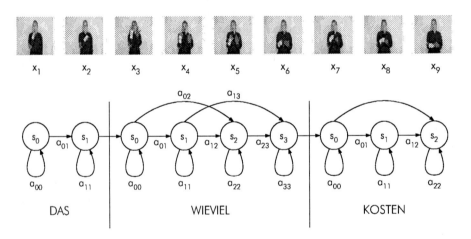

Fig. 3. Image sequence of the sentence DAS WIEVIEL KOSTEN (' How much does that cost?'). Modelling each sign of the sentence with one Bakis-HMM

The first row of the figure shows two images of the sign DAS, four images of the sign WIEVIEL and three images of the sign KOSTEN as recorded by the video camera. For each image a feature vector X is calculated. The sequence of feature vectors represents the observation sequence O. The order of visited states forms the state sequence. In case that for the training procedure several sequences composed of the same number of states (for each sign) would be recorded, the assignment of the feature vectors to the states would be obvious. However, when dropping the assumption of a constant image number, the assignment of the vectors to the states is no longer clear, the state sequence is hidden. With Bakis topology for each HMM, the system is able to compensate different speed of signing. An initial state of a sign can only be reached from the last state of a previous model.

4.3   Training HMMs on Continuous Sign Language

Training HMMs on continuous sign language is very similar to training isolated signs. One of the advantages for hidden Markov modelling is that it can absorb a range of boundary information of models automatically for continuous sign language recognition. Given a specific number of observation (training) sequences O, the result of the training are the model parameters $\lambda = (\Pi, A, B)$. These parameters are later used for the recognition procedure.

Since the entire sentence HMM is trained on the entire observation sequence for the corresponding sentence, sign boundaries are considered automatically. With this kind of training, variations caused by preceding and subsequent signs are incorporated into the model parameters. The model parameters of the single signs must be reconstructed from this data afterwards.

Figure 4 illustrates how the training on continuous sign language is carried out.

The overall training is partitioned into the following components: the estimation of the model parameters for the complete sentence, the detection of the sign bounderies and the estimation of the model parameters for single signs. For both, the training of the model parameters for the entire sentence as well as for single signs, the Viterbi training is employed. After performing the training step on sentences, an assignment of feature vectors to single signs is clearly possible and with that the detection of sign boundaries.

The Viterbi training of HMMs for isolated signs is depicted in figure 4.

The first step is the determination of the number of states of the HMM. This is only carried out for single signs. The total number of states for a sentence is equal to the sum of states of the signs within the sentence. A fixed number of states for all signs is not suitable, because the database contains very short signs with around four frames and different, longer signs with about 30 frames. Even the length of one sign can vary considerably. Therefore the number of vectors in the shortest training sequence is chosen as the initial number of states for the HMM of the corresponding sign. Next, the system assigns the vectors of each sequence evenly to the states and initialises the matrix A, i.e., all transitions are set equally probable. Using the initial assignment the mean and deviation values of all components of the emission distributions of each state can be calculated. After viterbi alignment the transition probabilities a_{ij} are re-calculated and the split criterion is examined. With a sufficient convergence the parameters of an HMM λ_i are available, otherwise the next iteration is requested.

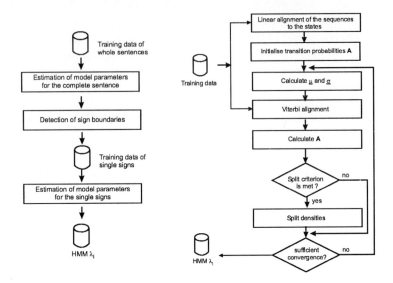

Fig. 4. Block diagram of estimating HMM model parameters for continuous sign language recognition (left); Viterbi training for a single HMM λ_i (right)

4.4   Recognition of Continuous Sign Language

In continuous sign language recognition, a sign may begin or end anywhere in a given observation sequence. As the sign boundaries connot be detected accurately, all possible beginning and end points have to be accounted for. Furthermore, the number of signs within a sentence are unknown at this time.

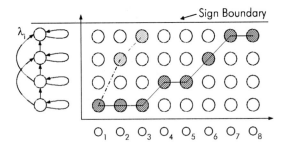

Fig. 5. Two possible paths to reach the boundary of a sign

There exists different paths to reach the boundary of a sign (see figure 5). One possible path needs the first three observation signals to get to the sign boundary, while within another assignment all observation vectors are used for modelling HMM λ_i.

This converts the linear search, as neccessary for isolated sign recognition, to a tree search. Obviously, an optimal full search is not feasible because of its computational complexity for continuous sign recognition. Instead of searching all paths, a threshold is used to consider only a group of likely candidates. These candidates are selected in relation to the state with the highest probability. Depending on that value and a variable B_0 a threshold for each timestep is defined [8]. Every state with a calculated probability below this threshold will be discarded from further considerations. The variable B_0 influences the recognition time. Having many likely candidates, i. e., a low threshold is used, recognition needs more time than considering less candidates. B_0 must be determined by experiments.

5 Stochastic Language Modelling

In our approach continuous sign language recognition is based on two knowledge sources: the visual model and the language model. Visual modelling is carried out by using HMMs as described in the previous section. Language modelling is discussed in this section. It should be noted that the development of language modelling technology has already been done by the speech recognition community [5].

The task of language modelling is to capture the inherent linguistic constraints in sign language in order to improve recognition accuracy. Different level of language knowledge such as syntax, semantic and pragmatic are valuable for the recognition process.

In our approach a stochastic grammar, known as unigram and bigram probabilities has been implemented. In a bigram model, the probability of a sign depends on the preceding sign. Such a modelling technique contains both, syntactic and semantic information. Within a foregoing step the probabilities must be trained from all signs $|V|$ of a large training corpus. Unfortunately, we only have a small training corpus available. The Jeffrey method is well suited and therefore used for this task [8].

The relative frequency of two successive signs $\hat{p}(f_i \mid f_{i-1})$ is then defined as

$$\hat{p}(f_i \mid f_{i-1}) = \frac{\#(f_i, f_{i-1}) + 1}{\#(f_{i-1}) + |V|}, \tag{1}$$

if a bigram model is assumed. The function $\#$ counts how often the number of the signpair $(f_i \mid f_{i-1})$ in its argument appears in the given training corpus.

These probabilities guide finally the recognition process and leads to different transition probabilities at the sign boundaries.

Generally, the Jeffrey method makes each sign succession, which in the bigram case is any possible combination of two signs of the vocabulary, occured at least once. This leads to an over-estimation of seldom sign successions.

6   Evaluation of the System

During evaluation of the system the recognition performance is identified.

On the input side a colour video camera is used. A Pentium-II 300 PC with an integrated image processing system allows the calculation of the feature vectors at a processing rate of 13 frames per second. In order to ensure correct segmentation, there are few restrictions regarding the clothing of the signer. The background must have a uniform colour.

6.1   Training- and Testdata

The vocabulary of the sign database consists of 52 signs representing seven different word types, such as nouns, verbs, adjectives, etc. The signs were chosen from the domain *Shopping at the Supermarket*. Since a critical issue in HMM-based language recognition systems is training data, we collected 3.5 hours of training and 0.5 hours of test data on a video tape. The system is trained and tested by one person. The native language of the signing person is german. The person is working as an interpreter for GSL and therefore did not learn the signs explicitly for this task.

Preparing the training set, we focused on the construction of sign sentences with different sign order. It is important to mention that the independent test set includes sign successions which are not part of the training set. No intentional pauses are placed between signs within a sentence, but the sentences themselves are separated. Constraints regarding a specific sentence structure are not allowed. The avoidance of minimal pairs is not an aim. All sentences of the sign database are meaningful and grammatically well-formed. Each sentence ranges from two to nine signs in length. [1]

6.2   Experiments

The experiments carried out are based on signer-dependent recognition. The sign recognition results are illustrated in table 2.

Table 2. Sign accuracy (B_0 - Threshold for beam search algorithm)

Language model	B_0	Accuracy
No model	1.05	92.2 %
	1.20	94.0 %
Unigram	1.05	94.2 %
Bigram	1.05	95.0 %

As can be seen from table 2, without incorporated language model, sign accuracy is ranging from 92.2% to 94% depending on the beam search threshold

B_0. Different values of B_0 are correlated with different restrictions of the search space. Given unigram probabilities and a B_0 of 1.05, 94.2% sign accuracy is achieved. A recognition rate of 95.0% is reached when using a bigram language model.

6.3   Analysis and Discussion

Analysing the results, it can be stated that the system is able to recognise continuous sign language. Considering a lexicon of 52 signs the system achieves an accuracy of 95.0% using a bigram language model.

Looking closer at the results it is obvious that the system discriminates most of the minimal pairs. Figure 6 depicts eight one-handed signs, where the location, movement and orientation of the dominant hand are very similar. Another

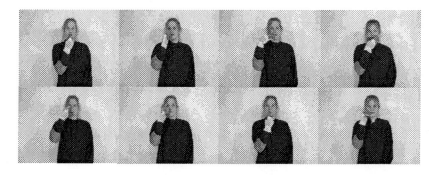

Fig. 6. Example of minimal pairs

important aspect is the fact that the unseen sign transitions in the test set are recognised in a good manner. Furthermore, the achieved recognition performance indicates that the system is able to handle the free order of signs within a sentence. Thus, the system can be used for all aspects of sign language.

An interesting problem is that the system produces a large number of deletion errors. Presumably, the reason for that is the bad estimation of the number of states for each sign (see Sec. 4.3). Performing a sign in the context of a sentence, the duration of the same sign varies depending on the preceding and successive sign. Therefore, increasing the number of states will not neccessarily lead to better results. Examining the sign accuracy when a language model is used, the performance increases by 2.0% for the unigram case and by 2.8% for the bigram case. The main cause for that is the fact that the training corpus which was used for estimating of uni- and bigram probabilities is far from being large enough. Finally, shorter lasting signs cause more errors than longer lasting signs. This is because shorter signs are more influenced by surrounding signs. Comparing one- and two-handed signs one can state that two-handed signs are better recognised. This can be explained by the fact that less minimal pairs exist for two-handed signs in the vocabulary.

7   Summary

In this paper we introduced an HMM-based continuous sign language recognition system. The system is equipped with a single colour video camera for image recording. Real-time image segmentation and feature extraction are achieved by using simple coloured cotton gloves. The extracted sequence of feature vector reflects the manual sign parameters. In our approach two knowledge sources are utilised for sign language recognition: the visual model and the language model. Visual modelling is carried out using HMMs, where each sign is modelled by a single HMM. A stochastic language model is introduced, with considered uni- and bigram probabilities of single and successive signs. Heading for user-dependent recognition, the system achieves a sign accuracy of 95%, based on a lexicon of 52 signs of German Sign Language.

References

1. Bauer, B.: *Videobasierte Erkennung kontinuierlicher Gebärdensprache mit Hidden Markov Modellen.* Diploma Thesis, Aachen University of Technology (RWTH), Department of Technical Computer Science, 1998.
2. Boyes Braem, P.: *Einführung in die Gebärdensprache und ihre Erforschung.* Signum Press, Hamburg, 1995.
3. Braffort, A.: *ARGo: An Architecture for Sign Language Recognition and Interpretation.* In P. Harling and A. Edwards (Editors): Progress in Gestural Interaction, pp. 17–30, Springer, 1996.
4. Hienz, H. and K. Grobel: *Automatic Estimation of Body Regions from Video Images.* In Wachsmuth, I. and M. Fröhlich (Editors): Gesture and Sign Language in Human Computer Interaction, International Gesture Workshop Bielefeld 1997, pp. 135–145, Bielefeld (Germany), Springer, 1998.
5. Jelinek, F.: *Self-organized Language Modeling for Speech Recognition.* In A. Waibel and K.-F. Lee (Editors): Readings in Speech Recognition, pp.450–506, Morgan Kaufmann Publishers, Inc., 1990.
6. Liang, R.H. and M. Ouhyoung: *A Real-Time Continuous Gesture Recognition System for Sign Languages.* In Proceedings of the Third International Conference on Automatic Face and Gesture Recognition, Nara (Japan), pp. 558–565 1998.
7. Rabiner, L.R. and B.H. Juang: *An Introduction to Hidden Markov Models.* In IEEE ASSP Magazin, pp. 4–16, 1989.
8. Schukat-Talamazzini, E.G: *Automatische Spracherkennung.* Vieweg Verlag, 1995.
9. Starner, T., J. Weaver and A. Pentland: *Real-Time American Sign Language Recognition using Desk- and Wearable Computer-Based Video.* In IEEE Transactions on Pattern Analysis and Machine Intelligence, 20(12):1371–1375, 1998.
10. Stokoe, W., D. Armstrong and S. Wilcox: *Gesture and the Nature of Language.* Cambridge University Press, Cambridge (UK), 1995.
11. Vogler, C. and D. Metaxas: *Adapting Hidden Markov Models for ASL Recognition by using Three-Dimensional Computer Vision Methods.* In Proceedings of IEEE International Conference and Systems, Man, and Cybernetics, pp. 156–161, Orlando (USA), 1997.

A Method for Analyzing Spatial Relationships Between Words in Sign Language Recognition

Hirohiko Sagawa and Masaru Takeuchi

Multi-modal Functions Hitachi Laboratory, RWCP,
1-280 Higashi-koigakubo, Kokubunji-shi, Tokyo 185-8601, Japan
{h-sagawa,mtakeuch}@crl.hitachi.co.jp

Abstract. There are expressions using spatial relationships in sign language that are called directional verbs. To understand a sign-language sentence that includes a directional verb, it is necessary to analyze the spatial relationship between the recognized sign-language words and to find the proper combination of a directional verb and the sign-language words related to it. In this paper, we propose an analysis method for evaluating the spatial relationship between a directional verb and other sign-language words according to the distribution of the parameters representing the spatial relationship.

1 Introduction

Sign language is the usual method of communication for hearing- impaired people, but it is not commonly understood by others. Accordingly, a system for automatically translating sing language is necessary to support communication between hearing-impaired people and others.

A sign-language sentence is represented as a sequence of several sign language words. To translate sign language into spoken language, it is necessary to recognize each sign-language word represented in the sign language sentence.

Some previous work on sign language recognition focuses on isolated sign recognition [1–6]. This work uses multi-layered neural network [1], recurrent neural network [2], instance-based learning (IBL) [3], dynamic programming (DP) matching [4] or rule-based matching (RBM) [5,6]. There is also previous work focused on continuous sign language recognition [7–11]. In this work, continuous DP (CDP) matching [7], RBM [8] or Hidden Markov Models (HMMs) [9,11] was used to recognize sign language words from the inputted gesture of the sign language sentence. The methods in [7] and [8] could only recognize each sign-language word from the inputted sign-language sentence. On the other hand, the methods based on HMMs involved rule-based grammar [9] or statistical grammar [10,11] to generate a sequence of the recognized sign language words.

In the previous work using the rule-based grammar and statistical grammar, the temporal relationship between the words in a sign- language sentence was considered. However, the spatial relationship between them was not considered. In a sign-language translation system, it is also necessary to analyze the

A. Braffort et al. (Eds.): GW'99, LNAI 1739, pp. 197–209, 1999.

grammatical and semantic relationship between the sign-language words. One grammatical expression in sign language is the expression based on the spatial relationship between the sign-language words. Such an expression is called a directional verb [12]. The direction of motion of the directional verb or the position where the directional verb is represented is related to the position where the subject or the object of the directional verb is represented. Therefore, the sign-language words related to the directional verb can be found by analyzing the spatial relationship between the directional verb and other sign language words. In [13], importance of the spatial relationship between the sign-language words was discussed, however, the method for analyzing the spatial relationship was not developed.

In this paper, we will propose a method for analyzing the spatial relationship between the sign-language words and for determining which sign-language words are related to the directional verb.

2   Sign Language Recognition System

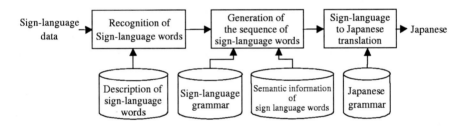

Fig. 1. Structure of the sign-language recognition system

The structure of the sign-language recognition system we are developing is shown in Fig.1. In the recognition of sign- language words, each sign-language word represented in the inputted data of a sign-language sentence is recognized. In the generation of the sequence of sign-language words, the possible sequences of sign-language words are generated. In the sign language to Japanese translation, the sequences of sign-language words are translated into Japanese sentences using the Japanese rules of grammar.

In the recognition process, gesture components, such as the figure of hand, the direction of palm, linear motion and circular motion, are recognized from the inputted sign-language data, then the sign- language words are recognized by integrating the recognized gesture components according to the time and spatial relationship between them [8]. The gestures of sign-language words are described by combining the gesture components in accordance with the gesture model shown in Fig.2. In Fig.2, the G-state, C-element and S-element are defined as follows.

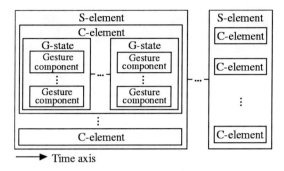

Fig. 2. Model of a sign-language gesture

G-state (state of gesture component):
The G-state consists of gesture components that are all of the same type, but which have different attributes.
C-element (concurrent element):
The C-element represents a sequence of G-states.
S-element (sequential element): The S-element consists of several C-elements that are represented simultaneously, and forms a simple gesture.

Each gesture component is represented as a set that consists of the kind of gesture component, the part of hand that represents the gesture component, and the attributes. The attributes can be represented as either constant values or as the variables. The attributes specified as variables are extracted from the sign-language data and outputted with the recognized sign-language words.

In the generation of the sequence of sign-language words, the sequence of sign-language words is generated by analyzing the relationship between the recognized sign language words using the outputted attributes of gesture components, the sign-language grammar, and the semantic information of the sign-language words.

3   Directional Verb

The grammatical expression in sign language that is based on the spatial relationship between sign-language words is called a directional verb because it corresponds to a verb in spoken language [12]. The direction of motion of the directional verb or the position where the directional verb is represented is related to the position where the sign-language words corresponding to the subject or the object of the directional verb is represented. An example of a sign-language sentence that includes a directional verb is shown in Fig.3. In Fig. 3 (a), the word {he} is represented on the right side of the signer and the word {she} is represented on the left side. Here, {} denotes the sign-language word. The directional verb {speak} is represented from the position of {he} then moves to the position of {she}. In this case, the start position of the motion indicates

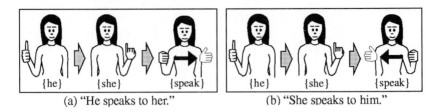

(a) "He speaks to her."   (b) "She speaks to him."

Fig. 3. Example of a directional verb

the subject and the end position indicates the object. Therefore, in Fig. 3 (a), the subject is {he} and the object {she}, and the meaning of the sign-language sentence is «he speaks to her». On the other hand, in Fig. 3 (b), the direction of motion is reversed. In this case, the subject becomes {she} and the object {he}, and the meaning of the sign-language sentence is «she speaks to him».

Because the spatial relationship between the directional verb and other sign-language words represents the grammatical and semantic relationship between them, we believe that such a spatial relationship can be used to analyze the grammatical and semantic relationship between sign-language words. To confirm this, we extracted parameters that represented the spatial relationship between sign-language words from our sign-language data, and analyzed the difference between the direction of motion of the directional verb and the positions where the sign-language words related to it were represented [14]. As the result, we found that the parameters were distributed within a certain range, but the spatial relationship was not precisely represented in actual sign-language sentences. Therefore, it is necessary to analyze the relationship between the sign language words according to the spatial relationship used in the actual sign-language expressions.

The method we describe in this paper finds the sign-language words related to the directional verb by extracting the distributions of parameters that represent the spatial relationship between the directional verb and the sign-language words related to it from actual sign-language data and by analyzing the spatial relationship between the directional verb and other sign-language words according to the extracted distributions.

4   Method for Analyzing Spatial Relationship

The parameters representing the spatial relationship must be defined to analyze the spatial relationship between sign-language words. We call such parameters «spatial parameters». The correspondence between the spatial parameters and the semantic information has to be described as grammatical information because the spatial relationship between the directional verb and the sign-language words related to it specifies not only the grammatical relationship but also the semantic relationship between them. The analysis of the spatial relationship is performed based on the spatial parameters, the grammatical information, and the semantic information.

In the following section, the spatial parameters, the grammatical information, the semantic information and an algorithm used to analyze the relationships between sign-language words are discussed.

4.1 Spatial Parameters

The directional verb's direction of motion and the position where the directional verb is represented correspond to fixed positions that are determined by the situation of the conversation in advance when the subject or the object of the directional verb is the first person or the second person. On the other hand, they are determined relative to the positions where the sign-language words corresponding to the third person are represented when the directional verb is related to a third person [14]. Therefore, the following parameters are used to represent the spatial relationship between the directional verb and the sign-language words related to it.

For the first and second person:

Parameter 1: the start and end position of the directional verb.

Parameter 2: the angle between the direction vector of the directional verb and the forward vector for the signer.

For the third person:

Parameter 3: the angle between the direction vector of the directional verb and the vector from the start or end position of the directional verb to the position where the sign-language word is represented (Fig.4). Which position of the directional verb is used depends on the meaning of the start and end positions of the directional verb.

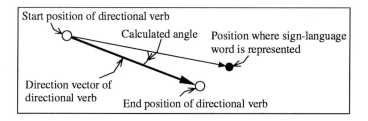

Fig. 4. Definition of parameter 3

Parameter 4: the ratio of the distance between the position of the sign-language word mapped on the direction vector of the directional verb and the start or end position of the directional verb to the distance between the start and end positions of the directional verb (Fig.5). Which position of the directional verb is used depends on the meaning of the start and end positions of the directional verb.

Parameter 5: the ratio of the distance between the positions of the two sign-language words mapped on the direction vector of the directional verb to the

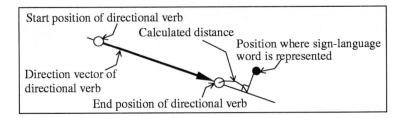

Fig. 5. Definition of parameter 4

distance between the start and end positions of the directional verb (Fig.6). This parameter is used when two sign-language words are related to the directional verb.

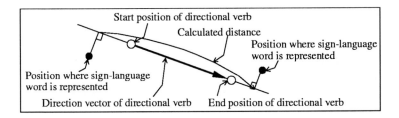

Fig. 6. Definition of parameter 5

4.2   Semantic Information

There are several methods to describe the semantic information, for example, the case frame and the semantic network. The analysis method discussed here does not depend on the methods to describe the semantic information if only the contents in the semantic information associated with the spatial parameters can be specified. Therefore, we do not discuss the details of the semantic information and use a simple case frame as shown in Fig.7.

```
<CONCEPT  NAME=speak>
    <CASE  KIND=agent>  human  animal  </CASE>
    <CASE  KIND=goal>  human  </CASE>
    <CASE  KIND=object>  matter  </CASE>
  <CLASS>  action  </CLASS>
  </CONCEPT>
```

Fig. 7. Case-frame example

A case frame includes the name of the concept, the kinds of cases, and the classification of the concept. In Fig.7, these elements are described using the tags – <CONCEPT>, <CASE>, and <CLASS>, and only the basic cases such as agent, object, and goal are considered [15].

4.3   Grammatical Information

The grammatical information includes the correspondence of the spatial parameter and the case in the semantic information as shown in Fig.8. In Fig.8, the list of concepts corresponding to the sign-language word is described between the tags <SIGN_WORD> and </SIGN_WORD>. The KIND in the tag <CASE> specifies the kind of case, and the FILLER specifies the kind of spatial parameter. The spatial parameters mentioned above are classified into two types – the parameter based on the start position of the directional verb and the parameter based on the end position. Therefore, start_direction or end_direction can be specified as the FILLER.

The example shown in Fig.8 means that the start position of the sign-language word {speak} corresponds to the agent of the concept «speak»and the end position corresponds to the goal.

```
<SIGN_WORD   NAME=speak>
   <CONCEPT   NAME =speak>
      <CAES   KIND=agent   FILLER=start_direction>
      <CASE   KIND=goal   FILLER=end_direction>
   </CONCEPT>
</SIGN_WORD>
```

Fig. 8. Example of the grammatical information

4.4   Algorithm to Analyze the Spatial Relationship

In this method, the spatial parameters used to evaluate the first and second person are different from these used for the third person. Therefore, the relationship between the directional verb and other sign-language words is analyzed according to the flowchart shown in Fig.9. In this algorithm, it is assumed that recognition of the sign-language words has been finished.

The evaluated value for the spatial relationship between the directional verb and the selected sign-language words is calculated based on the distributions of the spatial parameters that are assumed to be normal distributions. The evaluated value E_r is calculated by Eq. (1).

$$E_r = \left(\prod_{i=1}^{n} e^{-\frac{(X_i - A_i)^2}{2\sigma_i^2}} \bullet \sim E_w \right)^{\frac{1}{n+1}} \tag{1}$$

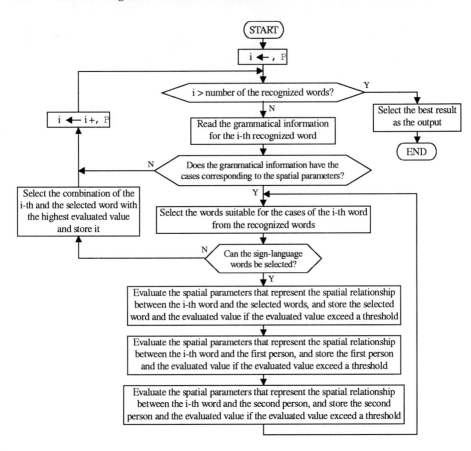

Fig. 9. Flowchart to analyze the relationship between the directional verb and other words

Here,

X_i: spatial parameter
A_i: average of X_i
σ_i^2:   variance of X_i
n: number of spatial parameters
E_w: evaluated value of the selected word

5   Experiment

The proposed method was implemented on a Pentium II 266MHz PC. And we carried out an experiment to find the sign-language words related to the directional verb from the recognized sign-language words by using the developed system. In this experiment, we selected two typical directional verbs – {speak} (Fig.10(a)) and {look} (Fig.10 (b)). Usually, the directional verb relates to two sign language words, and the above directional verbs are in this type. There

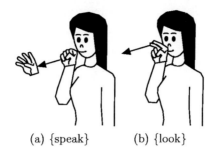

(a) {speak}   (b) {look}

Fig. 10. Directional verbs for the experiment

Table 1. Sign language sentences used in the experiment

Sentence	Sign language words
I speak to him.	{I}* {he} {speak}
He speaks to me.	{he} {I}* {speak}
He speaks to her.	{he} {she} {speak}
I look at him	{I}* {he} {look}
He looks at me.	{he} {I}* {look}
He looks at her.	{he} {she} {look}

*sometimes omitted

is the directional verb relating to only one sign-language word. We can easily apply the proposed method to such directional verb by removing the parameter 5 when the spatial relationship is evaluated. We also collected 158 samples of six sign-language sentences (Table 1) from two signers and 100 of those samples were used to calculate the distributions of the spatial parameters. The values of the spatial parameters used in this experiment were shown in Table 2.

The templates used in the recognition of sign-language words were created from the samples for each sign-language word shown in Table 1. The sign-language words were recognized from the sentence samples by using the created templates, and the sign- language words related to the directional verb were found from the recognized sign-language words.

We defined the following detection rates to evaluate the results of our experiment.

First detection rate: the ratio of the number of correct sign-language words that are detected as first candidates to the total number of sign-language words related to the directional verb.

First-to-fifth detection rate: the ratio of the number of correct sign-language words that are detected as first to fifth candidates to the total number of sign- language words related to the directional verb.

Table 2. Values of the spatial parameters used in the experiment

Spatial parameter	Average	Variance
Parameter 1 for the first person	(0.0, 38.7)	(82.7, 225.0)
Parameter 1 for the second person	(0.0, 22.1)	(82.7, 225.0)
Parameter 2 for the first person	0.0	0.327
Parameter 2 for the second person	0.0	0.327
Parameter 3 for the subject	0.0	0.637
Parameter 3 for the object	0.0	0.055
Parameter 4 for the subject	-0.230	0.327
Parameter 4 for the object	0.535	0.236
Parameter 5	1.20	0.327

Table 3. Detection rates for the sign-language words

Signer	First detection rate	First-to-fifth detection rate
A	93.1%	95.1%
B	93.8%	100.0%
Average	93.4%	97.0%

The time range for each sign-language word represented in the sentence sample was labeled. Detected sign-language words were considered correct candidates when they were labeled sign- language words and were related to the labeled directional verb. The detection rates are shown in Table 3. The reasons why the correct sign-language words were not detected as first candidates are shown in Table 4.

Table 4. Reasons why the correct words were not detected as first candidates

Reason of error	Error rate
The third person was mistaken for the first or second person.	4.8%
A candidate not represented in the sign-language sentence was detected.	1.8%

We also tested whether the correct combination of the directional verb and the sign-language words related to it could be detected as the recognition result of the sign-language sentence. To do this, the evaluated value for each detected combination of the directional verb and the sign-language words related to it was defined and the first detection rate and the first-to-fifth detection rate for the correct combinations were calculated. The evaluated value for the combination is defined as the sum of the evaluated value of the recognized directional verb, the evaluated value of the spatial parameters, and the evaluated value of the sign-language word related to the directional verb. The detection rates are shown in Table 5.

Table 5. Detection rates for the combinations

Signer	First Detection rate	First-to-fifth detection rate
A	75.5%	90.8%
B	90.0%	98.3%
Average	81.0%	93.7%

6   Discussion

The first detection rate for the sign-language words related to the directional verb was 93.4% and the first-to-fifth detection rate was 97.0%. This shows that it is not sufficient to determine the sign- language words related to the directional verb according to the spatial relationship, but this process is a useful way to narrow down the candidates.

The main reason why the correct sign-language words were not detected as first candidates is that the first or second person was detected instead of the sign-language word corresponding to the third person. Fig.11 shows an example of the spatial relationship between the directional verb and the third person in such a case. The third person is usually represented on the right or left side of the signer (e.g., position A in Fig.11). Then the sign-language word represented at position A is detected as the word related to the directional verb even if the direction of motion of the directional verb slightly differs from the direction to

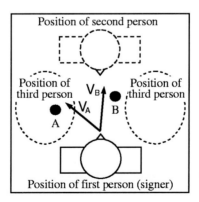

Fig. 11. Example of the relationship between the directional verb and a third person

position A (e.g., vector V_A). However, the third person is sometimes represented in front of the signer (e.g., position B in Fig.11). In this case, the possibility that the second person is detected is increased when the direction of motion of the directional verb follows vector V_B. This problem can be solved by giving the first and second person a lower priority than that of the third person when the third person is represented in a sign- language sentence. Another problem is that surplus candidates of sign-language words that are not represented in the sign-language sentence are often detected as the recognition result. Therefore, the third person cannot be simply selected even when included in the recognition result of the sign-language words.

The surplus candidates cause detection errors (Table 4), and both the surplus candidates of sign-language words related to the directional verb and the surplus candidates for the directional verb are a problem. Our proposed method can also be applied to the surplus candidates for the directional verb. As a result, a high evaluated value is often given to a combination consisting of a surplus candidate for the directional verb and the sign-language words related to it. As shown in Table 5, the first detection rate for a combination of the directional verb and the related sign language words is 81.0% and the first-to-fifth detection rate is 93.7%. These results show that many evaluated values for the wrong combinations are higher than the evaluated values for the correct combinations. Clearly, surplus candidates for the directional verb are serious problems and the number of these candidates must be reduced to improve the recognition accuracy for a sign-language sentence when using an analysis based on the directional verb. The grammatical expressions used to complement the directional verb, such as pauses, finger pointing, facial expressions, and nodding can be used to reduce the number of surplus candidates. To apply these expressions in the recognition of sign-language sentences, we are planning to analyze a large amount of sign-language sentence data because the functions of these expressions are not particularly clear in Japanese sign language.

7   Conclusions

The method we proposed for analyzing the spatial relationship between the directional verb and the sign-language words related to it is based on the distributions of the parameters representing the spatial relationship. We found experimentally that the detection rate for the sign-language words related to the directional verb was 93.4%, and this confirmed that the proposed method was useful. However, the number of recognized sign-language words that were not actually represented in the sign-language sentence must be reduced to improve the recognition accuracy for a sign-language sentence when using the proposed method. To achieve this, we are planning to develop an analysis method based also on the grammatical expressions that complement the directional verb.

References

1. Waldron, M. B., Kim, S.: Isolated ASL Sign Recognition System for Deaf Persons. IEEE Transactions on Rehabilitation Engineering, Vol. 3, No. 3 (1995) 261-271
2. Murakami, K., Taguchi, H.: Gesture Recognition Using Recurrent Neural Networks. Proceedings of the CHI'91 (1991) 237-242
3. Kadous, M.W.: Machine Recognition of Auslan Signs Using PowerGloves: Towards Large-Lexicon Recognition of Sign Language. Proceedings of the Workshop on the Integration of Gesture in Language and Speech (1996) 165-174
4. Fujii, M., Iwanami, T., Kamei, S., Nagashima, Y.: Recognition of Global Articulator of Signs Based on the Spatio- Temporal Image. Proceedings of the Eleventh Symposium on Human Interface (1995) 179-184 [in Japanese]
5. Teshima, T., Matsuo, H., Takata, Y. Hirakawa, M.: Virtual Recognition of Hand Gestures in Consideration of Distinguishing Right and Left Hands and Occlusion. Human Interface News and Report, Vol.10, No.4 (1995) 467-464 [in Japanese].
6. Matsuo, H., Igi, S., Lu, S., Nagashima, Y., Takata, Y., Teshima, T.: The Recognition Algorithm With Non- Contact For Japanese Sign Language Using Morphological Analysis. Gesture and Sign-Language in Human-Computer Interaction (1998)
7. Ohki, M.: The Sign Language Telephone. 7th World Telecommunication Forum, Vol.1 (1995) 391-395
8. Sagawa, H., Takeuchi, M., Ohki, M.: Methods to Describe and Recognize Sign Language Based on Gesture Components Represented by Symbols and Numerical Values. Knowledge-Based Systems, Vol.10, No.5 (1998) 287-294
9. Starner, T., Weaver, J., Pentland, A.: Real-Time American Sign Language Recognition Using Desk and Wearable Computer Based Video. IEEE Transaction on Pattern Analysis and Machine Intelligence, Vol. 20, No. 12 (1998) 1371-1375
10. Vogler, C., Metaxas, D.: ASL Recognition Based on a Coupling Between HMMS and 3D Motion Analysis. Proceedings of the International Conference on Computer Vision (1998) 363-369
11. Liang, R.-H., Ouhyoung, M.: A Real-time Continuous Gesture Recognition System for the Taiwanese Sign Language. Proceedings of The Third IEEE International Conference on Automatic Face and Gesture Recognition (1998) 558-565
12. Kanda, K.: Lecture on Sign Language Study. Fukumura Publisher (1994) [in Japanese]
13. Braffort, A.: ARGo: An Architecture for Sign Language Recognition and Interpretation. Progress in Gestural Interaction (1997) 17-30
14. Sagawa, H., Takeuchi, M.: A Study on Spatial Information for Sign Language Recognition. Proceedings of the 13th Symposium on Human Interface (1997) 231-236 [in Japanese]
15. Tanaka, H., Tsujii, J.: Natural Language Understanding. Ohmsha, Ltd. (1988) [in Japanese]

Toward Scalability in ASL Recognition: Breaking Down Signs into Phonemes

Christian Vogler and Dimitris Metaxas

VAST Laboratory
Department of Computer and Information Science
University of Pennsylvania
200 S. 33rd Street, Philadelphia, PA 19104-6389
U.S.A.
cvogler@gradient.cis.upenn.edu, dnm@central.cis.upenn.edu

Abstract. In this paper we present a novel approach to continuous, whole-sentence ASL recognition that uses phonemes instead of whole signs as the basic units. Our approach is based on a sequential phonological model of ASL. According to this model the ASL signs can be broken into movements and holds, which are both considered phonemes.

This model does away with the distinction between whole signs and epenthesis movements that we made in previous work [17]. Instead, epenthesis movements are just like the other movements that constitute the signs.

We subsequently train Hidden Markov Models (HMMs) to recognize the phonemes, instead of whole signs and epenthesis movements that we recognized previously [17]. Because the number of phonemes is limited, HMM-based training and recognition of the ASL signal becomes computationally more tractable and has the potential to lead to the recognition of large-scale vocabularies.

We experimented with a 22 word vocabulary, and we achieved similar recognition rates with phoneme-and word-based approaches. This result is very promising for scaling the task in the future.

1 Introduction

Gestures are destined to play an increasingly important role in human-computer interaction in the future. Humans use gestures in their everyday communication with other humans, not only to reinforce the meanings that they convey through speech, but also to convey meaning that would be difficult or impossible to convey through speech alone. Surely, to make human-computer interaction truly natural, computers must be able to recognize gestures in addition to speech. Furthermore, gesture recognition is an important part of virtual reality environments, where the user must be able to manipulate the environment with his hands.

Closely related to the field of gesture recognition is the field of sign language recognition. Because sign languages are the primary mode of communication

A. Braffort et al. (Eds.): GW'99, LNAI 1739, pp. 211–224, 1999.

for many deaf people, and because they are full-fledged languages in their own rights, they offer a much more structured and constrained research environment than general gestures. Thanks to linguistic research since the early 1960s, the properties of sign languages, especially of American Sign Language (ASL), have become well-understood. For these reasons, sign language recognition offers an appealing test bed for researching the more general problems of gesture recognition. Last but not least, working sign language recognition systems would also make the interaction of deaf people with their surroundings easier.

Possibly the most significant property of sign languages is that signs do not consist of unanalyzable wholes. They can be broken down into parts in a systematic manner, much like words in spoken languages can be broken down. Such a breakdown is an essential prerequisite for building truly scalable systems with large vocabularies (or gesture sets).

Yet, to date, research on systematically breaking down signs into their constituent parts for recognition purposes has been sketchy. If such research addressed the problem at all, it followed the early transcription system of ASL by Stokoe [15]. This system has several shortcomings, the most serious of them being that it treats all aspects of signs as occurring in parallel. More recent research in the late 1980s and early 1990s has shown that sequentiality is a very important feature of sign languages, and that it should in fact be the base for a good phonological model of ASL [10, 3].

In this paper we explore the possibilities of basing continuous, whole-sentence ASL recognition on a sequential phonological model. Our focus is strictly on phonology. We do away with the distinction between whole signs and epenthesis movements that we made in previous work [17], and unify them in a single phonological framework. Epenthesis movements are just like the movements that constitute signs. Although morphology, syntax, and semantics are important aspects of sign language recognition, they are beyond the scope of this paper. For simplicity, we do not address handshapes and nonmanual features, such as facial expressions, in this paper either. However, this is not a limitation, because they can be expressed in terms of phonemes as well.

We begin with an overview of related work, then proceed to a discussion of ASL phonology, and show how Hidden Markov Models (HMMS) can be used to capture statistical variations in sign movements. We then provide preliminary experiments with a 22 sign vocabulary to validate our assumptions about phonological modeling of ASL. Finally, we provide a discussion of open research questions.

2 Related Work

Much previous work has focused on isolated sign language recognition with clear pauses after each sign. These pauses make it a much easier problem than continuous recognition without pauses between the individual signs, because explicit segmentation of a continuous input stream into the individual signs is very difficult. For this reason, work on isolated recognition often does not generalize easily to continuous recognition.

M. B. Waldron and S. Kim use neural networks to recognize a small set of isolated signs [19]. They use Stokoe's transcription system [15] to separate the handshape, orientation, and movement aspects of the signs. M. W. Kadous uses Power Gloves to recognize a set of 95 isolated Auslan signs with 80% accuracy, with an emphasis on computationally inexpensive methods [8]. R. Erensthteyn and colleagues use neural networks to recognize fingerspelling [4].

K. Grobel and M. Assam use HMMs to recognize isolated signs with 91.3% accuracy out of a 262-sign vocabulary. They extract the features from video recordings of signers wearing colored gloves [6].

A. Braffort describes ARGo, an architecture for recognizing French Sign Language. It attempts to integrate the normally disparate fields of sign language recognition and understanding [1]. Toward this goal, S. Gibet and colleagues also describe a corpus of 3D gestural and sign language movement primitives [5].

Most work on continuous sign language recognition is based on HMMs, which offer the advantage of being able to segment a data stream into its constituent signs implicitly, thus bypassing the difficult problem of segmentation.

T. Starner and A. Pentland use a view-based approach with a single camera to extract two-dimensional features as input to HMMs with a 40-word vocabulary and a strongly constrained sentence structure [14]. They assume that the smallest unit in sign language is the whole sign. H. Hienz and colleagues use HMMs to recognize a corpus of German Sign Language [7].

Y. Nam and K. Y. Wohn [11] use three-dimensional data as input to HMMs for continuous recognition of a very small set of gestures. They introduce the concept of movement primes, which make up sequences of more complex movements.

R. H. Liang and M. Ouhyoung use HMMs for continuous recognition of Taiwanese Sign Language with a vocabulary between 71 and 250 signs. [9] They work with Stokoe's model [15] to detect the handshape, position, orientation, and movement aspects of the running signs. Unlike other work in this area, they do not use the HMMs to segment the input stream implicitly. Instead, they perform explicit segmentation based on discontinuities in the movements. They perform the integration of the handshape, position, orientation, and movement aspects at a higher level than the HMMs. The sequential aspects of sign language also manifest themselves only at that higher level.

We used HMMs for continuous ASL recognition with a vocabulary of 53 signs and a completely unconstrained sentence structure in [17, 18]. In [18] we used whole-word context-dependent modeling for the HMMs, which segment the input stream implicitly. We coupled this approach with a purely computer-vision based analysis that segments the input stream explicitly and extracts its geometric properties to back up the HMM modeling. In [17], we dropped whole-word context-dependent modeling in favor of modeling transitions between signs explicitly. These transitions are known as **movement epenthesis** (cf. Sec. 3.3) and are an integral part of ASL phonology. However, we still used whole signs as the smallest units of ASL.

In this paper we extend the work in [17]. Our goal is to abandon the notion of whole signs as the smallest units of ASL and replace them with phonemes. We strive to treat the aspects of ASL phonology at the HMM level as comprehensively as possible, including the sequential aspects. We now summarize the relevant linguistic research in ASL.

3 American Sign Language Phonology

A **phoneme** is defined to be the smallest contrastive unit in a language; that is, a unit that distinguishes one word from another. In ASL, an example of such a phoneme would be the movement toward the head in the sign for "father" (see Fig. 3, left picture). Note that there is still considerable controversy among linguists whether such units in ASL can justifiably be called "phonemes." Some researchers prefer to call them "cheremes," so as to make the manual aspects of sign languages explicit.

In this paper we do not attempt to argue for or against the use of the term "phoneme." In the following, whenever we use this term, we mean the smallest identifiable subunits of ASL that we believe to constitute the fundamental building blocks of this language.[1] We generally follow the established terminology of spoken language linguistics, because many of its concepts have equivalents in sign language linguistics.

Phonemes are especially interesting for recognition purposes, because their number is limited in any language, as opposed to an unlimited number of words that can be built from the phonemes. In the case of the Movement-Hold model described in the next section, the total number of phonemes is around 150–200. This limited set of phonemes helps keeping speech recognition tractable. We attempt to show that they can also help keep ASL recognition tractable.

We now review some of the research on ASL phonology. This review is by no means exhaustive. For other approaches to ASL phonology see, for example, [13], [2].

3.1 Stokoe's System

W. Stokoe realized that signs can indeed be broken down into smaller parts [15]. He used this observation for devising a transcription system. This transcription system assumes that signs can be broken down into three parameters, which consist of the location of the sign (**tabula** or **tab**), the handshape (**designator** or **dez**), and the movement (**signation** or **sig**).

A fundamental assumption of this system is that the tab, dez, and sig contrast only simultaneously. That is, variations in the sequence of these parameters within a sign are considered not to be significant.

---

[1] That is, we call the units of the Movement-Hold model [10] "phonemes." See Sec. 3.2.

3.2   Segmental Models

S. Liddell and R. Johnson argued convincingly against Stokoe's assumption that there was no sequential contrast in ASL. They went even further and made sequential contrast the basis of ASL phonology [10]; that is, instead of emphasizing the simultaneous occurrence of phonemes in ASL, they emphasized sequences of phonemes. Such models are called **segmental models.**

S. Liddell and R. Johnson describe two major classes of segments in their Movement-Hold model in [10], which they call **movements** and **holds.** Movements are defined as those segments during which some aspect of the signer's configuration changes, such as a change in handshape, a hand movement, or a change in hand orientation. Holds are defined as those segments during which all aspects of the signer's configuration remain stationary; that is, the hands remain stationary for a brief period of time.

Signs are made up of sequences of movements and holds. Some common sequences are *HMH* (a hold followed by a movement followed by another hold, such as "good"), *MH* (a movement followed by a hold, such as "sit"), and *MMMH* (three movements followed by a hold, such as "father"). Attached to each segment is a **bundle of articulatory features** that describe the hand configuration, orientation, and location. In addition, movement segments have features that describe the type of movement (straight, round, sharply angled), as well as the plane and intensity of movement. See Fig. 1 for a schematic example.

Although the Movement-Hold model has some shortcomings, such as the absence of nonmanual features and the presence of redundancy, its basic sequential structure has been accepted [3]. There are other segmental models, such as Wendy Sandler's Hand-Tier model [13] and Diane Brentari's syllable-based model [2]. These models differ primarily in what constitutes a segment. Describing them in detail is beyond the scope of this paper.

The Movement-Hold model (or a modification of it) looks like a natural fit for HMM-based recognition, because there can be a one-to-one correspondence between the major segments of a sign and individual HMMs (cf. Sec. 4.1). Whether

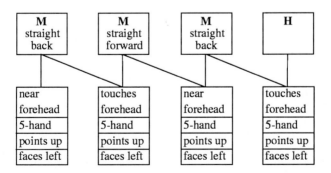

Fig. 1. Schematic description of the sign for "FATHER" in the Movement-Hold model. It consists of three movements, followed by a hold.

Table 1. Partial list of movements. Note that the description of the movements deviates from the approach used by the Movement-Hold model.

Movement	Transcriptions used
straight	str_{Away}, str_{Toward}, str_{Down}, str_{Up}, str_{Left}, str_{Right}, $str_{DownAway}$, $str_{DownRightAway}$
short straight	$str_{ShortUp}$, $str_{ShortDown}$
circle in vertical plane	rnd_{vP}
wrist rotation	rot_{Away}, rot_{Toward}, rot_{Up}, rot_{Down}

this model is truly the best choice among the segmental models is an open question that should be resolved in future research.

In this paper, we focus only on the movement types and the locational features of the Movement-Hold model. We have to make modifications to it, because in this model wrist rotations are described in the articulatory bundles attached to hold segments. Thus, there is a distinction between wrist rotations and normal movements. This distinction is difficult to map to HMMs, so we model wrist rotations as movement segments instead.

In Table 1 and Fig. 2 we give a partial overview of the different descriptions of movements and locations that we used. In addition, the locations can be modified with the distance from the body, and with the vertical and horizontal distance from the basic location.

If a location does not touch the body, it can be prefixed with one of these distance markers: p (proximal), m (medial), d (distal), or e (extended), in order of distance to the body. If a location is centered in front of the body, the distance marker is suffixed with a 0. If the location is at the side of the chest, the distance marker is suffixed with a 1, and if the location is to the right (or left) of the shoulder, the distance marker is suffixed with a 2. For example, d-1-TR means a location a comfortable arm's length away from the right side of the trunk (torso). Further markers describe the vertical offset to the basic location and whether the location is on the same side or opposite side of the body as the hand. These are described in detail in [10].

3.3   Phonological Processes

S. Liddell and R. Johnson also describe several phonological processes in ASL [10]. A phonological process changes the appearance of an utterance through well-defined rules in phonology, but does not change the meaning of the utterance. In order to achieve robustness, a recognition system must be able to cope with such processes.

The most basic, and at the same time also most important phonological process is called **movement epenthesis**. It consists of the insertion of extra movements between two adjacent signs, and it is caused by the physical characteristics of sign languages. For example, in the sequence "father read," the sign

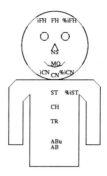

Fig. 2. Partial list of body locations used in the Movement-Hold Model

for "father" is performed at the forehead, and the sign for "read" is performed in front of the trunk. Thus, an extra movement from the forehead to the trunk is inserted that does not exist in either of the two signs' lexical forms (Fig. 3).

Movement epenthesis poses a problem for ASL recognizers, because the appearance of the movement depends on which two signs appear in sequence. We handle this problem by modeling such movements explicitly. Ideally, these movements should be captured by the same phonemes as we use for the movements within signs. Unfortunately, epenthesis movements are not as well-defined and researched as the movements that constitute the actual signs. Therefore, we choose to model each epenthesis movement as a separate unit for the time being. We do not yet model any other phonological processes in ASL, such as hold deletion and metathesis (which allows for swapping of the order of segments under certain circumstances).

We now cover briefly how to model ASL phonemes with HMMs.

Fig. 3. Movement epenthesis. The arrow in the middle picture indicates an extra movement between the signs for "FATHER" and "READ" that is not present in their lexical forms.

4   Hidden Markov Models

There are always statistical variations in the way that humans perform movements, even if they perform two identical signs successively. A recognition system must be able to handle these variations. HMMs are a state-based statistical model especially suitable for modeling a signal over time. They have been used successfully in speech, gesture, and sign language recognition.

The underlying idea is to have a distinct HMM for each phoneme. These HMMs are trained to yield the maximum probability for the signal representing their respective phonemes. For the recognition task, compute the probabilities that parts of the input signal could have been generated by the HMMs and pick the most probable HMM as the recognized phoneme. For a thorough discussion of HMM theory see [12], and for a thorough discussion of using HMMs for sign language recognition, see [18, 17].

4.1   Phoneme Modeling with HMMs

Training HMMs that represent movement and hold phonemes is a straightforward process. However, from looking at the phonetic transcriptions of ASL signs, it becomes clear that many signs start with a movement phoneme (that is, they follow the *MH, MMMH,* or *MHMH* pattern). Since we classify movement phonemes only by their type and direction of movement, which can take place anywhere in the signing space, we do not get a good estimate of a sign's location until we encounter the first hold segment. Particularly for the *MMMH* pattern, this can lead to unnecessary classification errors for the sign's location.

This problem can be alleviated by adding HMMs that do not have a phonetic equivalent in the Movement-Hold model. We call these special HMMs "**X**." Their sole purpose is to obtain an estimate of the location at the beginning of signs that begin with a movement segment. They are different from hold models in that they do not require the hand to remain stationary for any length of time.[2]

Thus, modeling a particular sign now consists of chaining together the appropriate X, M, and H models. Figure 4 shows the models constituting the sign for "father."

Fig. 4. Chained HMMs forming the sign for "FATHER". The X model describes a location near the forehead, the M models describe straight movements, and the H model describes a hold touching the forehead.

---

[2] The role of these special HMMs seems to be very similar to the X segments in the latest, as of yet unpublished, version of the Movement-Hold model.

Training the HMMs representing the epenthesis phonemes is more complicated than training the movement and hold HMMs. The reason is that there are many more epenthesis movements than models of any other kind of phonemes. In the worst case, there must be an epenthesis model from every location in the signing space to every other location in the signing space. Just for the 20 major body locations defined by the Movement-Hold model, this would yield $20^2 = 400$ models, as opposed to the approximately 150–200 phonemes constituting a sign in the Movement-Hold model.

Fortunately, we can reduce the number of epenthesis models by taking advantage of the similarities between many of the epenthesis phonemes. For example, there is no appreciable difference between a movement from the side of the forehead to the chest, and the center of the forehead to the chest (*iFH* to *CH*, and *FH* to *CH*, respectively). Thus, these two movements can be covered by a single model. Applying such optimizations allowed us to cut the number of epenthesis models in half. Future work should express epenthesis models completely in terms of the movements that already exist in ASL, so as to alleviate this problem even more.

The single greatest advantage to breaking down the signs into the individual phonemes is that it limits the number of HMMs that need to be trained. There is only a finite number of distinct phonemes, whereas the number of possibilities to combine them into words is practically unlimited. Although there is no real benefit in modeling phonemes as opposed to whole signs for small-scale applications, it is the only way to make large-scale applications possible. The benefits become particularly obvious when context-dependent HMMs are used. Using a HMM for every possible sequence of two phonemes is tractable, because of the limited number of phonemes that can occur in sequence. Using a HMM for every possible sequence of two signs is not, because the number of required models is the square of the vocabulary size.

4.2   Local Features and Global Features

Recognition performance depends significantly on the features that are extracted from the input signal. Some features that we use are extremely localized; that is they characterize the signal only in the immediate vicinity of a specific point in time. Both the position of the hands in the signing space and the velocities of the hands are examples of local features. They do not reveal anything about the behavior of the signal even a hundred milliseconds from the time at which they are sampled.

In contrast, ASL movement phonemes describe geometric properties of the signal on a more global level, such as movements along a straight line, or along an arc. Thus, it is desirable to have a quantitative measure of some of the signal's global properties. An example of such a measure is how well the signal fits a line or a plane within a specific time interval.

This measure can be easily computed by estimating the covariance matrix over the points in the time interval and taking its eigenvalues. If the largest eigenvalue is significantly larger than the other two eigenvalues, the signal fits a line well. If the two largest eigenvalues are nearly equally large, and significantly larger than the smallest eigenvalue, the signal fits a plane well. These relationships can be quantified with two numbers by taking the square roots of the two largest eigenvalues, and normalizing them such that the sum of the square roots of all three eigenvalues is 1.

5   Experiments

We designed several experiments to verify that breaking down signs into phonemes is a viable approach in ASL recognition. Our vocabulary consisted of 22 signs with the phonetic transcriptions listed in Appendix A. The total number of X, M, and H phonemes in this vocabulary was 43, and the number of epenthesis models was 46.

We collected 499 sentences of different length, with 1604 signs overall, with an Ascension Technologies MotionStar^{TM} magnetic tracking system. This system gave us three-dimensional positions and orientations of the hands and other body parts at 60 frames per second. We split the 499 sentences into 400 training examples with 1292 signs and 99 test examples with 312 signs. We conducted three different types of experiments, one of which was a control experiment that measured the performance of word-level HMMs along with movement epenthesis modeling. This control experiment was similar to the one conducted in [17]. The other two experiments tested the performance of the phoneme-level HMMs, one without global features, and one with global features.

To keep the experiments simple, we looked only at features extracted from the right hand. In all cases, the local features were the right hand's position in space, relative to the signer's base of the spine, and the right hand's velocities. The global features consisted of the two largest normalized eigenvalues, as described in Sec. 4.2. The results are given in Table 2. We use word accuracy as our evaluation criterion. It is computed by subtracting the number of insertion errors from the number of correctly spotted signs.

Table 2. Results of recognition experiments. H denotes the number of correct signs, D the number of deletion errors, S the number of substitution errors, I the number of insertion errors, and N the total number of signs in the test set.

Type of experiment	Word acc.	Details
word-level	92.95%	H=296, D=6, S=13, I=3 N=312
phoneme-level, local features	90.06%	H=286, D=8, S=18, I=5, N=312
phoneme-level, global features	93.27%	H=294, D=3, S=12, I=3, N=312

The results indicate that the phoneme-level HMMs did not perform significantly worse than the word-level HMMs. They also indicate that global features are a valuable characterization of the signal. Both the breakdown of signs into movement and hold phonemes, and the research on global features look promising.

6   Summary and Future Outlook

We showed that it is possible for phoneme-level HMMs to achieve ASL recognition performance comparable to word-level HMMs. Even though more work needs to be done to establish the validity of the results, they are already very important. The entire question of whether it is possible to scale ASL recognition to large vocabularies hinges on this result. We also showed that analyzing the input stream for global features has the potential to make a large impact on recognition performance.

However, breaking down the signs into phonemes is only the first step toward scalability. So far, we have looked only at the right hand of the signer, but it is also necessary to capture the parallel aspects of sign languages; for example using both the left and the right hands, using hand configuration, and using facial expressions.

Future work needs to verify that the phoneme breakdown generalizes. It also needs to find a way to integrate the parallel aspects of sign language without getting bogged down in the large number of combinations of phonemes that can occur in parallel. Preliminary extensions to our framework seem to show that the phoneme modeling works just as well with the left hand as it did with the right hand, and that the answer to modeling the parallel aspects of ASL lies in using several HMMs in parallel [16].

Future research should also look at ways to express the epenthesis phonemes in terms of phonemes that occur during regular signs, so as to cut down further the number of distinct phonemes. Finally, training biphone or triphone context-dependent HMMs, analogous to speech recognition, might be a way to improve recognition performance even further.

Acknowledgments

This work was supported in part by a NSF Career Award NSF-9624604, ONR Young Investigator Proposal, NSF IRI-97-01803, AFOSR F49620-98-1-0434, and NSF EIA-98-09209.

A   Phonetic Transcriptions

This table shows the phonetic transcriptions of the 22 sign vocabulary. The phonemes beginning with "M" denote movements, the phonemes beginning with "M" denote holds, and the phonemes beginning with "X" denote the special HMMs designed to estimate locations at the beginning of a sign.

Sign	Transcription
I	$X\text{-}\{p\text{-}0\text{-}CH\}$ $M\text{-}\{str_{Toward}\}$ $H\text{-}\{CH\}$
man	$H\text{-}\{FH\}$ $M\text{-}\{str_{Down}\}$ $M\text{-}\{str_{Toward}\}$ $H\text{-}\{CH\}$
woman	$H\text{-}\{CN\}$ $M\text{-}\{str_{Down}\}$ $M\text{-}\{str_{Toward}\}$ $H\text{-}\{CH\}$
father	$X\text{-}\{p\text{-}0\text{-}FH\}$ $M\text{-}\{str_{Toward}\}$ $M\text{-}\{str_{Away}\}$ $M\text{-}\{str_{Toward}\}$ $H\text{-}\{FH\}$
mother	$X\text{-}\{p\text{-}0\text{-}CN\}$ $M\text{-}\{str_{Toward}\}$ $M\text{-}\{str_{Away}\}$ $M\text{-}\{str_{Toward}\}$ $H\text{-}\{CN\}$
interpreter	$X\text{-}\{m\text{-}1\text{-}CH\}$ $M\text{-}\{rot_{Down}\}$ $M\text{-}\{rot_{Up}\}$ $M\text{-}\{rot_{Down}\}$ $X\text{-}\{m\text{-}1\text{-}CH\}$ $M\text{-}\{str_{Down}\}$ $H\text{-}\{m\text{-}1\text{-}TR\}$
teacher	$X\text{-}\{m\text{-}1\text{-}CH\}$ $M\text{-}\{rot_{Away}\}$ $M\text{-}\{rot_{Toward}\}$ $M\text{-}\{rot_{Away}\}$ $X\text{-}\{m\text{-}1\text{-}CH\}$ $M\text{-}\{str_{Down}\}$ $H\text{-}\{m\text{-}1\text{-}TR\}$
chair	$X\text{-}\{m\text{-}1\text{-}TR\}$ $M\text{-}\{str_{ShortDown}\}$ $M\text{-}\{str_{ShortUp}\}$ $M\text{-}\{str_{ShortDown}\}$ $H\text{-}\{m\text{-}1\text{-}TR\}$
try	$X\text{-}\{p\text{-}1\text{-}TR\}$ $M\text{-}\{str_{DownRightAway}\}$ $H\text{-}\{d\text{-}2\text{-}AB\}$
inform	$H\text{-}\{iFH\}$ $M\text{-}\{str_{DownRightAway}\}$ $H\text{-}\{d\text{-}2\text{-}TR\}$
sit	$X\text{-}\{m\text{-}1\text{-}TR\}$ $M\text{-}\{str_{ShortDown}\}$ $H\text{-}\{m\text{-}1\text{-}TR\}$
teach	$X\text{-}\{m\text{-}1\text{-}CH\}$ $M\text{-}\{rot_{Away}\}$ $M\text{-}\{rot_{Toward}\}$ $M\text{-}\{rot_{Away}\}$ $H\text{-}\{m\text{-}1\text{-}CH\}$
interpret	$X\text{-}\{m\text{-}1\text{-}CH\}$ $M\text{-}\{rot_{Down}\}$ $M\text{-}\{rot_{Up}\}$ $M\text{-}\{rot_{Down}\}$ $H\text{-}\{m\text{-}1\text{-}CH\}$
get	$X\text{-}\{d\text{-}0\text{-}CH\}$ $M\text{-}\{str_{Toward}\}$ $H\text{-}\{p\text{-}0\text{-}CH\}$
lie	$X\text{-}\{iCN\}$ $M\text{-}\{str_{Left}\}$ $H\text{-}\{\%iCN\}$
relate	$X\text{-}\{m\text{-}1\text{-}TR\}$ $M\text{-}\{str_{Left}\}$ $H\text{-}\{m\text{-}0\text{-}TR\}$
dont-mind	$H\text{-}\{NS\}$ $M\text{-}\{str_{DownRightAway}\}$ $H\text{-}\{m\text{-}1\text{-}TR\}$
good	$H\text{-}\{MO\}$ $M\text{-}\{str_{DownAway}\}$ $H\text{-}\{m\text{-}0\text{-}CH\}$
gross	$X\text{-}\{ABu\}$ $M\text{-}\{rnd_{VP}\}$ $M\text{-}\{rnd_{VP}\}$ $H\text{-}\{ABu\}$
sorry	$X\text{-}\{\%iSTu\}$ $M\text{-}\{rnd_{VP}\}$ $M\text{-}\{rnd_{VP}\}$ $H\text{-}\{\%iSTu\}$
stupid	$X\text{-}\{p\text{-}0\text{-}FH\}$ $M\text{-}\{str_{Toward}\}$ $H\text{-}\{FH\}$
beautiful	$X\text{-}\{p\text{-}0\text{-}FH\}$ $M\text{-}\{rnd_{VP}\}$ $H\text{-}\{p\text{-}0\text{-}iFH\}$

References

1. A. Braffort. ARGo: An architecture for sign language recognition and interpretation. In A. D. N. Edwards P. A. Harling, editor, *Progress in gestural interaction. Proceedings of Gesture Workshop '96*, pages 17–30, Berlin, New York, 1997. Springer.
2. D. Brentari. Sign language phonology: ASL. In J. A. Goldsmith, editor, *The Handbook of Phonological Theory*, Blackwell Handbooks in Linguistics, pages 615–639. Blackwell, Oxford, 1995.
3. G. R. Coulter, editor. *Current Issues in ASL Phonology*, volume 3 of *Phonetics and Phonology*. Academic Press, Inc., San Diego, CA, 1993.
4. R. Erenshteyn and P. Laskov. A multi-stage approach to fingerspelling and gesture recognition. Proceedings of the Workshop on the Integration of Gesture in Language and Speech, Wilmington, DE, USA, 1996.
5. S. Gibet, J. Richardson, T. Lebourque, and A. Braffort. Corpus of 3d natural movements and sign language primitives of movement. In I. Wachsmuth and M. Fröhlich, editors, *Gesture and Sign Language in Human-Computer Interaction. Proceedings of Gesture Workshop '97*, Berlin, New York, 1998. Springer.
6. K. Grobel and M. Assam. Isolated sign language recognition using hidden Markov models. SMC, pages 162–167, Orlando, FL, 1997.
7. H. Hienz, K.-F. Kraiss, and B. Bauer. Continuous sign language recognition using hidden Markov models. In Y. Tang, editor, *ICMI'99*, pages IV10–IV15, Hong Kong, 1999.
8. M. W. Kadous. Machine recognition of Auslan signs using PowerGloves: Towards large-lexicon recognition of sign language. In *Proceedings of the Workshop on the Integration of Gesture in Language and Speech*, pages 165–174, Wilmington, DE, USA, 1996.
9. R.-H. Liang and M. Ouhyoung. A real-time continuous gesture recognition system for sign language. In *Proceedings of the Third International Conference on Automatic Face and Gesture Recognition*, pages 558–565, Nara, Japan, 1998.
10. S. K. Liddell and R. E. Johnson. American Sign Language: The phonological base. *Sign Language Studies*, 64:195–277, 1989.
11. Y. Nam and K. Y. Wohn. Recognition of space-time hand-gestures using hidden Markov model. ACM Symposium on Virtual Reality Software and Technology, 1996.
12. L. R. Rabiner. A tutorial on Hidden Markov Models and selected applications in speech recognition. *Proceedings of the IEEE*, 77(2):257–286, 1989.
13. W. Sandler. *Phonological Representation of the Sign: Linearity and Nonlinearity in American Sign Language*. Number 32 in Publications in Language Sciences. Foris Publications, Dordrecht, 1989.
14. T. Starner and A. Pentland. Visual recognition of American Sign Language using Hidden Markov Models. *International Workshop on Automatic Face and Gesture Recognition*, pages 189–194, Zürich, Switzerland, 1995.
15. W. C. Stokoe. *Sign Language Structure: An Outline of the Visual Communication System of the American Deaf*. Studies in Linguistics: Occasional Papers 8. Linstok Press, Silver Spring, MD, 1960. Revised 1978.
16. C. Vogler and D. Metaxas. Parallel hidden Markov models for American Sign Language recognition. ICCV, Kerkyra, Greece, 1999.
17. C. Vogler and D. Metaxas. Adapting hidden Markov models for ASL recognition by using three-dimensional computer vision methods. SMC, pages 156–161, Orlando, FL, 1997.

18. C. Vogler and D. Metaxas. ASL recognition based on a coupling between HMMs and 3D motion analysis. ICCV, pages 363–369, Mumbai, India, 1998.
19. M. B. Waldron and S. Kim. Isolated ASL sign recognition system for deaf persons. *IEEE Transactions on Rehabilitation Engineering*, 3(3):261–71, September 1995.

Section 5: Gesture Synthesis and Animation

A Complete System for the Specification and the Generation of Sign Language Gestures

T. Lebourque and S. Gibet

LIMSI-CNRS, BP 133, Université Paris-Sud, 91403 Orsay, France
{lebourqu,gibet}@limsi.fr

Abstract. This paper describes a system called *GeSsyCa* which is able to produce synthetic sign language gestures from a high level specification. This specification is made with a language based both on a discrete description of space, and on a movement decomposition inspired from sign language gestures. Communication gestures are represented through symbolic commands which can be described by qualitative data, and traduced in terms of spatio-temporal targets driving a generation system. Such an approach is possible for the class of generation models controlled through key-points information. The generation model used in our approach is composed of a set of sensori-motor servo-loops. Each of these models resolves in real time the inversion of the servo-loop, from the direct specification of location targets, while satisfying psycho-motor laws of biological movement. The whole control system is applied to the synthesis of communication and sign language gestures, and a validation of the synthesized movements is presented.

1 Introduction

The integration of communication gestures and sign language gestures has proved to be relevant in many computer applications. This integration implies the study of both gestures recognition and synthesis. The objective of the research described here is to develop a software system which allows to interactively design, create and compose sign language or communication gestures. The idea is to avoid the specification of tedious sequences of joints movements, or to use systematically pre-recorded gestures. The long-term goal of such research is to provide a high level specification of gestures, and to automatically generate in real-time complex and realistic hand-arm motion. Such a system should provide a way of exploring and producing a large variety of communication gestures, and, in particular, sign language gestures. The generated gestures should be natural from a perceptive point of view, and according to biomechanical or psychomotor laws characterising movement.

2 Related Works

The specification, control and animation of human gesture lead to multidisciplinary work. This work involves both the animation and control of multi-joint

A. Braffort et al. (Eds.): GW'99, LNAI 1739, pp. 227–238, 1999.

figures for movement generation and higher level movement specification. Until a recent past, researches focus on the animation and control of human figures. Movements specification was, most of the time, dedicated to the computer animation domain. These specifications were made fo general body movements, such as walking or grasping, and were not actually useables to describe complex communication gestures.

Most of the human animation systems try to make a virtual human move and act like a real human. But they do not take into account the ability of gestural communication. At the moment, most of the systems that include communication gestures treat co-verbal gestures. They are often limited to a set of pre-recorded movements which correspond to a particular state of mind [1] or which are associated to a verbal expression [2]. However gestural communication involves richer body movements than a set of pre-established signs, and an animation system that includes human communication gestures has to be able to produce a great variety of these gestures.

Studies on gestures' specification remain relatively rare. Most of the works deal with very low level movements [3], more general specifications of body movements [4,5] or specification of complex tasks [6]. Other studies, aiming at writing sign language, adress the problem of signs notation. Two main systems have been developped: Hamnosys [7] and Signwriter [8]. The first one is very accurate and tries to describe all the parameters of the different signs involved in a sentence, and the way they are arranged. Because of its accurarcy and its completeness, it is relatively hard to use. In Signwriter, much simpler and more iconic, only salient characteristics of the signs are written. It makes this system easier to use, but requires a good knowledge of the sign language.

3   Qualitative Communication Gestures Specification: The Qualgest System

In this section we will give a description of the qualitative gestural command: the QualGest system. From a detailed analysis of French Sign Language gestures, we propose a space representation around the signer (the agent producing the signs), and define a set of movement primitives, hand configuration and hand orientation which are combined to describe a gesture.

3.1   Study of the French Sign Language

Our study has consisted in analysing the French SL dictionary [?], and extracting its main significant features and their number of occurrence. 1359 signs have been observed and the resulting data were stored in a database. This database has been started for the purpose of a sign language's recognition system designed during a previous work in the laboratory [9], and we have completed it to include information useful for sign language description and generation.

The database includes five cooccurring parameters used in French SL:

- The *configuration* that is the hand shape;
- The *orientation* that gives the directions pointed by the palm and the metacarpus;
- The *movement* which corresponds to the arm's movement, and, more precisely, to hand's kinematics;
- The *location* which is the position where the sign occurs. A same sign may be indeed realised in different parts of space, depending of its meaning;
- The *facial expression* which has a complementary role in the sentence by giving the mode, for example. We did not really study this parameter as we do not treat it for the moment.

Configuration is, in 80% of the signs, static, which means that the fingers do not move while the other parameters may vary. Furthermore, the observation of the signs emphasises the possible configuration's parameterisation. A large number of configuration may indeed be described from a small set of basic configuration. For example, a pointing hand shape may be constructed from a basic fist hand shape with an outstretched index finger.

Movement have been classified in five main primitives:

- *Static*: The arm is motionless during the gesture. About 17% of the signs are concerned with this primitive;
- *Line*: the hand's trajectory in space is a straight line. This primitive appears in about 43% of the signs.
- *Arc*: the hand follow an arc in space. It represents about 26% of the primitives.
- *Circle*: the hand's trajectory is an ellipse (about 11% of the signs);
- *Complex*: the trajectory is more complex than in the other primitives, or is composed of several primitives (movements in zig-zag, sinusoid, etc.) and appears in about 3% of the signs.

The proportions above highlight the small number of primitives required to describe signs: complex signs can be specified as a combination of several basic primitives.

The observation of the *orientation* showed that two kinds of orientation are used in sign language. The first kind, which is the most used in FSL, is called *relative orientation* because the hand's orientation remains unchanged in the wrist referential. It is the most used orientation in French Sign Language. The other kind is called *absolute orientation*. This orientation remains constant in the absolute referential (the center of mass's referential).

In addition to these observations, we have noticed that, most of the time, orientation is static during the sign, that is explicit movements of the wrist are rather rare.

We did not study the location of the signs, as we consider it is included in the movement parameter.

This study gave us important information about the kind and the number of primitives necessary to specify French Sign Language gestures. In addition, a discrete representation of the space surrounding the signer had to be defined, according to the spatial nature of gestures.

3.2   Space Representation

The description of hand-arm movements requires the use of a space representation. This representation does not need to be very accurate, but necessitates
the definition of a finite number of key locations or key areas in the reachable
workspace.

Existing approaches use the notions of orientation and topology to represent the relative positions of objects. We can refer to the survey proposed by
Hernàndez about qualitative spatial representations [10].

We propose a representation which is based on a discretization of the space
around the signer's body. The representation is centered on the signer: the
signer's center of gravity is the center of the representation. A position in space
is described by the combination of a discrete direction and a discrete distance.
The direction defines a half line, and the distance gives a position on this half
line. The space is cut into six main directions that belong to the sagittal, frontal
and horizontal planes: left, forward, right, backward, up and down (Fig. 1). In
addition, there are three possible distances: near, intermediate and far. The first
distance is at about 10 cm from the body, the far distance corresponds to the
zone reached by the arm in quasi-extension, and the intermediate distance is at
a median position between these two distances.

Additional directions can be given by combining the main directions. For
example, if we use the up and forward directions, we create an intermediate
forward-up direction making 45° angle with the horizontal plane (Fig. 1). With
this system, 16 valid directions can be described. If we exclude the backward
direction for the location descriptions (since positions in the back of the body
are not reachable), 12 directions can be specified.

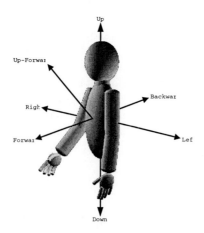

Fig. 1. The main directions. New directions can be created by combining the main
ones.

In addition to this method, we have defined 33 corporal references like *ear* (that may be the left or the right one) or *nose* which can be used with a contact or proximity notion.

A position in space is specified by one of these expression:

> *Point*(**direction**, [**distance**])

or   *Point*(*near*, **corporal reference**)

or   *Point*(*contact*, **corporal reference**)

Where **direction**, **distance** and **corporal reference** are elements of the sets previously defined. *Point*, *near* and *contact* are key words of the description language. The [] around distance mean that this parameter is optional. If the distance is not specified, the intermediate distance is used by default.

With this qualitative spatial description, we are able to describe positions in the near environment of the signer.

3.3 Movement Primitives

Elementary movements are represented by primitives which can be assembled to obtain the desired result. The primitives are based on the French Sign Language analysis presented in the first section.

Five movements classes have been determined:

- *Pointing movements* that are the result of a position in space reached by the hand,
- *straight line movements* for which the hand's trajectory follows a straight line in space,
- *curved movements* for which the hand's trajectory follows a curved path,
- *circle movements* that draw an ellipse in space,
- *wave movements* that are more complex and represent movements for which the hand follows a sinusoid.

In the language description, key words are noted in italic, variables in boldface. "**Spatial position**" or "**SP**" denotes a location described with the qualitative description of space defined in the previous section (table 1).

Table 1. The main primitives' description

One end-point	*Pointing*(**spatial position**)	⊗
Two extremity points	*Line*(**SP**, **SP**)	⊗———⊗
Two extremity points plus one intermediate	*Curve*(**SP**, **SP**, **SP**)	⊗ ⊗
Four points included in the circle	*Circle*(**SP**, **SP**, **SP**, **SP**)	⊗ ⊗
Two points and a real	*Wave*(**SP**, **SP**, *real*)	(see Fig. 2)

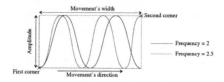

Fig. 2. Wave movement primitive representation.

3.4 Hand Configuration

To describe a configuration, it is necessary to define a set of basic configurations and to identify the fingers. In our description, fingers are identified by their noun: *thumb, index, middle, ring* and *little*.

The basic configurations are those of the French Sign Language. They are listed in Fig. 3.

Fig. 3. Basic hand configurations: angle, hook, spread, fist, straight.

A set of modifiers have been added to make possible the creation of new hand shapes from the basic ones by modifying the fingers' shape individually. These modifiers are:

- *Spread, clenched* to change the space between fingers,
- *Angle, hook* or *round* to specify respectively a straight finger perpendicular to the palm, a "tensed" finger, and a rounded shape finger.
- *Contact* that indicates a contact between the extremity of fingers (essentially between the thumb and other fingers).
- *Crossing* for the fingers that cross each others (crossing the index and middle finger, for example).

A configuration is described by the following sequence:
Configuration(**basic configuration, list of modifiers**)
with:
basic configuration = *Spread, Fist, Angle, Hook, Straight*
and:

list of modifiers =	**modifier(finger)**
or	*contact*(**list of fingers**)
or	*crossing*(**list of fingers**)

For example, the configuration where the hand is closed and only the index finger is tensed is described by: *Configuration(fist, straight(finger))*

With such a method, we can specify all the valid configurations used in French SL.

3.5   Hand Orientation

The hand orientation is described by two directions that indicates where the palm and metacarpus are pointing.

We have introduced in Section 3.1 the two possible orientations used in sign language: relative and absolute orientations. We have introduced these notions in our specification language. An orientation is then described by: *Orientation*(**direction, direction**[, *absolute*]), where **direction** denotes one of the directions of the qualitative spatial description, and the optional keyword *absolute* indicates the orientation type which is relative by default.

At this point we are able to compose all these gesture elements to specify a complete gesture.

3.6   Gesture Specification

A gesture is composed of elements that occur either in sequence or in parallel. At a low level, the different parameters of a sign (orientation, configuration, movement, and location) are combined in parallel. In addition, a lot of signs are composed of several sub-gestures that occur sequentially. Furthermore, we generally need to prepare a gesture. It means that a given gesture begins with a certain configuration of the hand and the arm. This preparation phase and the gesture itself occur sequentially.

We propose an imperative language to describe in a hierarchical way the composition of gestures (Fig. 4).

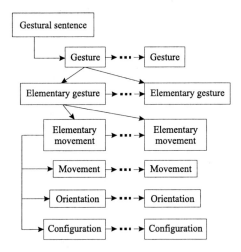

Fig. 4. Hierarchical description of gestures.

First of all, movement, configuration and orientation primitives are assembled in sequence to form elementary movements. These elementary movements are combined in parallel to form an elementary gesture. These elementary gestures are composed in sequence or in parallel to create a gesture. At last a gestural sentence can be specified as a succession of gestures (Fig. 4).

Elementary movements enable the creation of the gesture's part that involves only one complete arm (with the hand). Elementary gestures introduce the second arm to create gestures that belong to a sentence. When elements occur in parallel, they begin simultaneously.

3.7   Synchronisation

In the gesture description language, we have introduced several ways to synchronize the movement of corporal segments according to other corporal segments. For instance, we may desire to open the hand when the arm reaches its middle point course, or trigger the movement of one arm according to the other arm.

Three kinds of synchronisation have been introduced:

- Relative time synchronisation when a gesture element's starting time is given relative to another;
- Absolute time synchronisation, when the exact occurrence date is given;
- Synchronisation by an external event which allows an element to start when a given event arises.

In conclusion, we propose a qualitative system of gestural command specification which is as independent as possible from the gesture generation system. QualGest is based on a qualitative spatial specification dedicated to communication gestures. Gestures are specified by the way of an imperative language. This specification can then be translated into set of low-level instructions that will be provided to the animation engine.

4   Control of Virtual Humans: The GeSSyCa System

4.1   The Movement Generation Model: The SIAM Model

The model that is used in this work, the SIAM model, has been presented in [11] and in [12]. This model is an inversion model of sensori-motor loops. It resolves the following inverse problem: the state parameters are computed according to the sensory features extracted from the simulated motion.

In order to control a complex hand-arm system, the above model has been extended and adapted. The arm is modelled by an articulated chain with seven degrees of freedom and is controlled by targets in the cartesian space. Each finger of the hand is modelled by a similar closed-loop system, and is controlled by targets expressed in the angular space (configuration targets).

A very intersting feature of this model is its ability to produce natural arm movements in real time from a simple goals specification. Indeed, the movement is described by a list of discrete targets in the cartesian space or in the angular configuration space.

Another interesting feature of such a model is its capability to anticipate movements according to the context, and to concatenate small movements with smooth transitions. This allows us to build gestures from a small number of primitives that can be easily concatenated. Moreoever, it eases the linkage of the model with a QualGest's specification.

4.2   Architecture of the GeSSyCa System

The arm is decomposed in several articulated chains: the arm itself (from the shoulder to the wrist), the wrist and the hand, which is composed of five articulated chains. Each chain is controlled by a SIAM model. So, there are 7 control loops running in parallel to control one arm. The command for the whole system is made of a sequence of spatial and configuration targets, either targets, destined to one of the articulated chains of the arm.

Prior to the set of SIAM models piloting the complete arm, a controller is in charge of receiving all the targets resulting from a given specification. It has to schedule them to the appropriate loops at the right time. This controller is cadenced by an external clock that gives a reference necessary to coordinate the whole system. The controller also verifies that the movement is correctly performed, and that there is no problem in the execution.

5   Results and Validation

The GeSSyCa system has been programmed and has been validated in two ways. First we have verified the perceptive quality of the generated gestures during a qualitative validation process. The aim of this work was to verify that the synthetic gestures looked natural from a perceptive point of view.

In addition, we performed a quantitative validation by confronting the data coming from the animation engine to real gestures data. This confrontation has been performed by direct comparison between natural and artificial data, and also by using psychomotor laws such as Fitt's law or "power 2/3" law.

The animation system has been implemented on a SGI O2 with Open GL. The software works in real time with a rate of 8 frames per second.

Fig. 5. An example of GesSyCa output: a pointing gesture: hand and arm are simultaneously controlled

Two kinds of validation have been performed: a validation by comparison with real gestures and a validation based on invariant laws characterizing human movements.

In order to compare synthetic an real gestures, we had to constitute a corpus of gestures. The corpus is based on movements recorded using a Flock Of Birds sensor system from Ascension Technology. It contains recordings of each primitives we have defined in *QualGest*, performed two times with three amplitudes, by two different subjects. We have recorded some additional gestures to validate the coarticulation capabilities of our animation engine.

Comparison between synthetic data coming from the animation engine and real data has been mainly performed via speed profiles. Only some examples of the results are presented below. Other results can be found in [12]

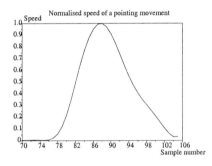 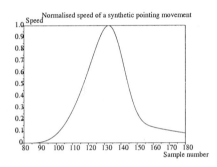

Fig. 6. Human pointing gestures are characterised by a bell curved speed profile (left curve). The animation engine reproduce this feature (right curve). For each curve, time is represented horizontally and normalized speed is on vertical axis.

For curved movements, we have compared both speed profiles and the ratio $\frac{V}{R^{\frac{1}{3}}}$, where V is the tangential velocity and R the radius of curvature. This ratio has been computed from normalized data and is showed on Fig. 7.

In addition, we have studied the SIAM model's ability to link gestures to each others. We have verified that the animation engine can automatically append a gesture to another without visible transition. In order to illustrate this feature, we have concatenated three movement primitives: a curved forward movement, followed by a backward line movement, followed by forward curved movement. Velocity profiles of each primitive taken separately are regrouped in Fig. 8.

The velocity profile of the three primitives concatenation if showed in Fig. 9.

Therefore, the comparison with real gestures (direct or by the way of movement's laws) have showed the validity of the SIAM model to produce natural human gestures. In addition, we have produced signs and small sentences in French Sign Language. The specification of these signs and sentences have been made with the QualGest language. This description system has simplified the

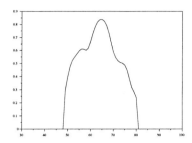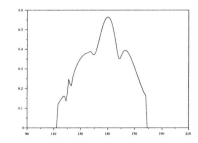

Fig. 7. $\frac{V}{R^{\frac{1}{3}}}$ for curved movements. Synthetic data is on the right. For each curve, time is represented horizontally.

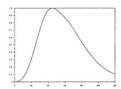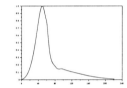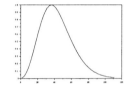

Fig. 8. Velocity profiles of, respectively from left to right, a curved movement, a line movement and a curved movement

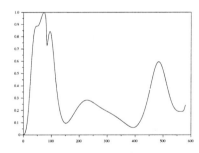

Fig. 9. Velocity profile of the concatenation of three different movement

specification task. Furthermore, the description files are very compact (about 60 lines of description for a 4 signs sentence).

6 Conclusion and Perspectives

A specification and control model is presented in this paper, which is applied to the animation of complex articulated chains representing two hand-arm systems. A qualitative description of the gestural command is proposed, through an imperative language of gesture specification. In addition, a formalism for the discretization of space around the signer has been defined, because of the spatial nature of gestures.

The specification and control system is coupled to a generation system. This one is composed of a set of sensory-motor loops respectively associated to each articulated chain representing the arms or the fingers of the hand. The generated movements keep the main invariant of human movement.

Using such a system, it is then possible to connect a semantic level to the produced gestures. With the introduction of semantic, we can consider the translation from written language to sign language. Moreover, we can also consider the production of co-verbal gestures or of non verbal communication gestures. Indeed, it is possible to establish a link between a mood, a situation and the gestures to produce.

References

1. Pascal Béchairaz and Daniel Thalmann. A model of nonverbal communication and interpersonal relationship between virtual actors. In *Proceedings of Computer Animation'96*, pages 58–67. IEEE Computer Society Press, June 1996.
2. Justin Cassel, C. Pelachaud, Norman I. Badler, M. Steedman, B. Achorn, T. Becket, B. Douville, S. Prevost, and M. Stone. Animated conversation: Rule-based generation of facial expression, gesture & spoken intonation for multiple conversational agents. In *Proceedings of SIGGRAPH'94*, 1994.
3. Moon-Ryul Jung, Norman Badler, and Noma Tsukasa. Animated human agents with motion planning capability for 3d-space postural goals. *The Journal of Visualization and Computer Animation*, 5:225–246, 1994.
4. Thomas J. Smith, Jianping Shi, John P. Granieri, and Norman I. Badler. Jackmoo, an integration of jack and lambdamoo. In *Pacific Graphics'97*, 1997.
5. Norman I. Badler. Virtual humans for animation, ergonomics and simulation. In *IEEE Workshop on non-rigid and articulated motion*, June 1997.
6. Norman I. Badler, Bonnie Webber, Jugal Kalita, and Jeffrey Esakov. *Animation from Instructions*, chapter 3, pages 51–93. Morgan Kaufmann Publishers, 1991.
7. Sigmund Prillwitz, Regina Leven, Heiko Zienert, Thomas Hanke, and Jan et al. Henning. *HamNoSys, version 2.0, Hamburg Notation System for Sign Languages - An introductory guide*. Signum Press, 1989.
8. Valerie Sutton. The signwriting literacy project. In *Impact of Deafness On Cognition AERA Conference*, San Diego California, April 1998.
9. Annelies Braffort. *Reconnaissance et compréhension de gestes, application à la langue des signes*. PhD thesis, Université Paris-XI Orsay, June 1996.
10. Daniel Hernández. *Qualitative representation of spatial knowledge*, volume 80 of *Lecture Notes in Artificial Intelligence*. Springer-Verlag, 1994.
11. Sylvie Gibet and Pierre François Marteau. A self-organized model for the control, planning and learning of non-linear multi-dimensional system using a sensory feedback. *Journal of Applied Intelligence*, 4:337–349, 1994.
12. Thierry Lebourque. *Spécification et génération de gestes naturels. Application à la Langue des Signes Française*. PhD thesis, Université Paris XI - Orsay, December 1998.

Sign Specification and Synthesis

Olivier Losson and Jean-Marc Vannobel

Laboratoire I3D (CEP) – IRRH,
Bâtiment P2, Cité Scientifique,
59655 Villeneuve d'Ascq (France)
Tel. (33) 3 20 43 48 76, Fax. (33) 3 20 43 65 67
{lo,jmv}@cal.univ-lille1.fr

Abstract. A description in terms of elementary primitives is proposed, in the view of sign language synthesis. Gradual combination leads to global sign specification. Grammatical inflexions are also taken into account in the sign hierarchic description built. Particular attention is focused on hand configurations synthesis from fingers primitives and hand properties, and on location and orientation computation issues. From sign features edition to virtual animation, here are laid the foundations of a new interface intended for deaf people.

1 Introduction

Signs used within the deaf community have been enriched throughout the centuries. They are now extremely evolved forms of communicative gestures. But sign language is not mere gestures, as recent linguistic studies have shown. For it is grounded on strong formationnal and grammatical rules, and is able to convey as subtle meanings as oral languages. The abundant linguistic research sign language has given rise to also gives evidence for its membership among actual living languages.

But it has suffered from severe repression until recent past in many countries. As a result, deaf people still have to struggle against subeducation in their community. About half of them encounter difficulties in reading which, besides a yearn for reading one's own mother tongue, appeals to sign language synthesis. In comparison with video, synthetic signs offer many advantages, among which easiness of creation (with the availability of the virtual signer and exemption of constraining signing conditions), transmission and generation of whole sentences from isolated signs.

From the first 3D sign synthesis [1], the computing power of computers has increased so much that it is henceforward possible to obtain synthetic signs in nearly real-time from a high-level specification. But surprisingly enough, few attempts have been made to achieve such a goal. Our project precisely intends to generate a signed sentence from its textual description, made of written preordered lexical items (stemming from forward grammatical and semantic analyses).

A. Braffort et al. (Eds.): GW'99, LNAI 1739, pp. 239–251, 1999.

2   Specifying Signs Features

One of the basic underlying principles in our specification process is the identification of primitive features shared by the widest range of signs, and their successive grouping into more and more global elements. Such a gradual combination requires careful description of the component parts leading to sign specification as a whole.

Linguistically salient basic features have been first identified by Stokoe [2] under the minimal pair substitution criterion: two signs may differ in only one of the following gestural phonemes:

- the tabular (TAB), that is the location of the hand(s) in space;
- the designator (DEZ), that is the hand(s) shape(s), relatively to the TAB;
- the signation (SIG), which is the action of the DEZ in the dynamic phase of the sign.

Battison [3] added the hand(s) orientation to this set of *gestemes* and several pertinent values have been defined for each of those classes [4]. Other studies (among which [5]) have proved besides that the latter were both valid and psycholinguistically salient.

This section presents the sign grammar that has been built to specify the manual part of signs. It is grounded on the results of those linguistic studies, and endowed with extra features like symmetry, repetition or dynamic. Taking care for clarity, a hierarchic form is here preferred to the equivalent set of rewriting rules.

2.1   Shift primitives

Most of the time, complex trajectories correspond to iconic shapes (as in *Christmas_tree*) or movements of real objects (like the falling leaves in *autumn*). But they are scarce in sign languages [6] and thus are treated here as combinations of basic movements called *shift primitives*. This feature consists of a change of the wrist position according to either a straight line, an arc-shaped or a circular trajectory.

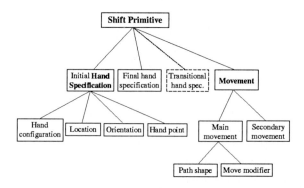

Fig. 1. Hierarchy of a *Shift primitive* (lower levels of the sign structure)

Figure 1 above details the corresponding structure: the initial and final postures (named *specifications*) of the hand are bundled with the movement itself, together with an optional specification of transition. Considerations of synthesis-specific needs have lead to define several additional elements with regards to the gestural phonemes:

- When the hand comes in contact with a body part (torso, face or other arm), it is more convenient to specify this precise point than the wrist position. The location feature should then concern a specific hand point, like the thumb tip in *proud* (Fig. 2).
- Speed and dynamic of the movement may be inflected through the *move modifier*. Such modulations are used to represent the tense of a sign. Sudden acceleration and deceleration at the beginning and the end of the movement satisfyingly reflect such a kinetic stress marking signs intensification. Together with an appropriate concomitant facial expression, such processes are useful to distinguish some pairs of signs like *run* and *hurry-up*.
- A *secondary movement* is sometimes superimposed on the main movement. several kinds of such small repeated motions of the fingers or wrist have been defined, like twisting the forearm, rubbing or wiggling the fingers (see Fig. 2).

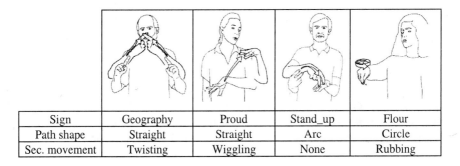

Sign	Geography	Proud	Stand_up	Flour
Path shape	Straight	Straight	Arc	Circle
Sec. movement	Twisting	Wiggling	None	Rubbing

Fig. 2. Examples of different path shapes and secondary movements [1]

2.2 Sign Specification

A *shift* is defined according to the implication of the hands in a sign (see Fig. 3). Its description may either be composed of a single shift primitive reflecting the presence and activity of the sole strong hand, or include the weak hand specification if the latter is present but static, or at last require shifts primitives for both articulators. It has been shown [7] that there is a strong tendency to symmetry in two-handed signs forming and evolution. Our study of a 300 French signs corpus has given confirmation of it, and we have tried to characterize this property.

---

[1] Signs are reproduced with kind permission of IVT, Ch[au] de Vincennes, F-94300 Vincennes.

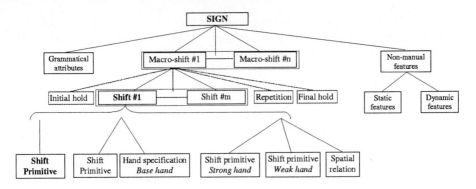

Fig. 3. Upper levels of the sign structure

We have encountered only two-handed signs with identical hand configurations and symmetrical orientations, but symmetry may also involve location and/or movement. Full symmetry about the sagittal plane is by far the most common, whereas a radial plane is sometimes concerned instead. Sign *sandwich* (Fig. 4) represents another group of signs, in which all parameters but location are symmetrical. A third important class is composed by anti-symmetrical signs, where initial and final hands specifications are exchanged alternately.

It occasionally happens that both arms do not start and stop moving at the same time. But such cases are very limited (about 15 in 1300 signs); that is why, rather than adding an extra synchronization feature, those occurrences will be spatially decomposed into different shifts by the user.

Given that we assumed before that movement was of simple type, complex moves are regarded here as combinations of such straight or arc-shaped paths. Sign *chimney* below for instance is composed of two shifts having straight displacement. In such series called *macro-shifts*, initial hand specification of a given shift is inherited from the previous one. A repetition feature has been added at the present level in order to describe complex paths (as zigzags) easily.

Sign	Milk	Sandwich	Shelves	Buttons	Chimney
Repetition feature	Simply repeat	Simply repeat	Repeat from displaced point	Repeat from current point	None
Symmetry feature	Anti-symmetry	Constant gap about the sagittal plane	Symmetry about the sagittal plane		

Fig. 4. Examples of the differents values for the *Repetition* and *Symmetry* features

Above all, repetition plays some important linguistic role. It may be purely lexical or result from grammatical inflexions. Many studies have proved that it was used to express definite and indefinite plurals [8], emphasis [9], as well as aspectual modulations on adjectival predicates [5]. Simple lexical repetition is common in sign languages, but other forms can be used to specify repeated movements to be synthesized (see Fig. 4).

A few signs include very numerous movements or complex interaction between the articulators. Especially, compounds for superordinate categories (such as *musical_instrument* or *fruit*) are composed of two or three basic representative signs (respectively *clarinet-piano-guitar* or *apple- pear-peach* for instance). Lexical items are described in those cases as collections of macro- shifts. Table 1 shows however that even multiple shifts are marginal, and that one single shift is often sufficient to describe a sign.

Table 1. Occurrence statistics of the various features in a French signs corpus

		Single shift			Multiple shifts		
		Strong hand moving	Both hands moving		Strong hand moving	2 hands moving	Total
			Full sym.	Other sym.			
No sec.	No repet.	84	43	11	8	13	52%
mvt.	Rep mvt	71	26	13	3	4	39%
Sec. mvt.		17	9	0	0	0	9%
Total		57%	26%	8%	4%	5%	100%

The paralinguistic role played by non-manual features is of the same kind as in oral languages. But they also carry grammatical information in sign language. Facial expressions are implied in topicalization, conditional clauses, questions, negation, and so on. The signer leans forward in order to stress imperative rather than unmarked declarative sentences, while shoulders position (just as head direction) is implied too when establishing or designating locations on the signer's scene. Such features have been therefore included in our description.

3   Hand Configurations

Hand configurations have not been further detailed above, but the first step in the synthesis process was to set up a method aimed at being able to generate as many different hand shapes as possible. Our system can describe the hand configurations identified by several inventories on American [10] and French [11] Sign Languages. It is strictly synthesis-oriented and thus does not take thin linguistic features into account as HamNoSys does [12]. It has been split into three levels: finger shape primitives, hand global properties and constraints on joints.

Table 2. Fingers and thumb configuration primitives

	Name	Description	Ex.*	Name	Description	Ex.*
Fingers primitives	C	Mid-flexed finger at all joints		O	Like in 'C' but with lighter flexions	
	Bent	Flexed finger at all joints		NearFlat	Like 'Flat' but with less flexion at the MCP joint	
	Flat	Right-angled finger relatively to the palm		Hook	Extended finger at MCP joint, flexed at interphalangeal ones	
	E	Finger like in the 'E' of the manual alphabet		Stiff	Flexed finger except at distal interphalangeal (DIP) joint; pad contacts the lower part of the palm	
	Extended	Extended finger (in palm plane)		*Examples here illustrate the various primitives for index finger*		
Thumb primitives	Bent	Bent thumb folded in the hollow of the hand		Flat	Thumb in the palm plane, contacting the second index finger metacarpal	
	E	Thumb like in the 'E' of the manual alphabet		Hook	Hooked thumb, flexed at interphalangeal (IP) joint	
	Extended	Extended thumb (in palm plane)				

3.1 Configuration Primitives of Fingers

Hand digits can be divided into two groups according to their behaviour. Fingers on the one hand flex in the same way with slight differences in angles limits and in mutual interaction at the metacarpophalangeal (MCP) joint. Thumb on the other hand has a larger reachable workspace due to ampler movements of abduction and to the axial rotation occurring at the carpometacarpal (CMC) joint. Nevertheless, the latter may be approximated to a fixed value, and a finger shape primitive be therefore defined as a set of three flexion angles and one abduction-adduction (see Fig. 5).

Nine finger shape primitives and five ones for the thumb were found sufficient to describe (together with hand properties) the main configurations in use in sign languages. Marginal ones with particular diacritics may however still require an explicit angles specification. But some others (like 'Flat', 'Hook' or 'Bent' in Table 2) require only five fingers configuration primitives with additional abduction if necessary. Notice that no fingers contact involvement is considered in the 'E' configuration; this one has been therefore included as a primitive at the present level.

3.2   Hand Global Properties

Hand properties are defined as features implying several digits, as in the thumb opposition with fingers. Several types of such relations occur in hand configurations:

- Flat opposition with (resp. without) contact between *pads* of thumb and of another finger having 'Flat' (resp. 'NearFlat') configuration;
- Round opposition with (resp. without) contact between *tips* of thumb and of another finger having 'O' (resp. 'C') configuration;
- Thumb tip contacts the *ventral* part (middle phalanx) of a finger (having 'Hook' configuration in most cases);
- Thumb covers a flexed finger on the back of its middle phalanx;
- Thumb stands between two fingers, especially index and middle fingers.

Abduction-adduction has also been included in hand properties – for it generally concerns two up to the four fingers (as in a spread hand) –, as well as crossing of index and middle fingers.

Table 3. Hand global properties (finger 1=thumb, 2=index, 3=middle, 4=ring, 5=little)

Name	Parameters		Assigned	Description	Examples	
	Name	Values	Finger(s)		Param.	FSL
Tip	i	2 .. 5	1	Tip contact between thumb and finger i	2	
Pad	i	2 .. 5	1	Flat contact between thumb and finger i	2	
Abducted Abduct	none i, j	$i=2..4, j=i+1$	2 .. 5 $i, i+1$	Abduction of whole hand Abduction of fingers i and j *Both exist for adduction too*	2, 3	
Cross or Crossed	i, j	2, 3	2, 3	Forefinger and middle finger crossing	2, 3	
Covered	i	2 .. 5	1, i	Thumb covering of one or more fingers	2,3,4	
Ventral	i	2 .. 5	1	Ventral contact between thumb and finger i	2	
Thumb Between	i, j	$i=2..4, j=i+1$	1	Intercalation of thumb between fingers i and j.	2, 3	

The different types of hand global properties are recorded in Table 3 with illustrative examples. Notice that some of them do set fingers shapes, while configuration primitives are maintained in others. This strategy is intended to describe easily cases in which thumb is opposed to a finger without contact. In manual letters *C* and *O* for instance, thumb has the same configuration, whereas pad contact is present in *O* but not in *C*.

One could think that other properties could be included in our description, such as radial contact between thumb and a finger phalanx (but this one seems marginal), or thumb pad coming in touch with a finger nail. We have merged the latter with dorsal contact, from which it does not seem significantly distinct.

Some constraints on MCP joints have also been considered, in order to avoid generating unnatural hand shapes. Fingers are assumed not to flex freely on that joint but rather to be constrained by the flexion of the neighbour fingers. Inequalities given in [13] have been applied as dynamic angle limits, together with an artificial MCP abduction reflecting fingers convergence towards the scaphoid point when the hand closes to a fist.

3.3   Hand Configurations Synthesis

The upper human body has been modeled by connected polygonal segments. Points are given in the local coordinate system attached to the proximal joint of each segment such that x is the main skeleton axis about which roll ψ takes place. Flexion-extension φ is moreover defined about the z axis and abduction-adduction θ about the y axis (Fig. 5).

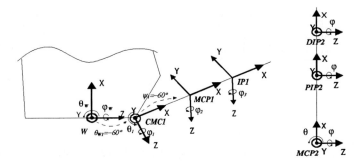

Fig. 5. Thumb and finger kinematic models

Thumb postures must be computed in hand properties, such that the fingertip x_T reaches a given hand point. This is no trivial inverse kinematics issue, on account of a great articulatory complexity. Such a goal has been achieved adapting a positioning method [14] of robots manipulator arms, and preliminary simplification of the model assuming fixed CMC axial rotation and MCP flexion.

Expressing the distance from x_T to the target location x as a function of a single unknown α_i (successively θ_1, φ_1 and φ_3):

$$x_T = a_\alpha \sin \alpha_i + b_\alpha \cos \alpha_i + d_\alpha, \tag{1}$$

the minimum of distance $|x - x_T|$ is obtained for the following values:

$$\alpha_i^* = \text{Arctan}\left(\frac{{}^t a_\alpha(d_\alpha - x)}{{}^t b_\alpha(d_\alpha - x)}\right) \quad \text{and} \quad {}^t(a_\alpha \sin \alpha_i^* + b_\alpha \cos \alpha_i^*)(d_\alpha - x) > 0. \tag{2}$$

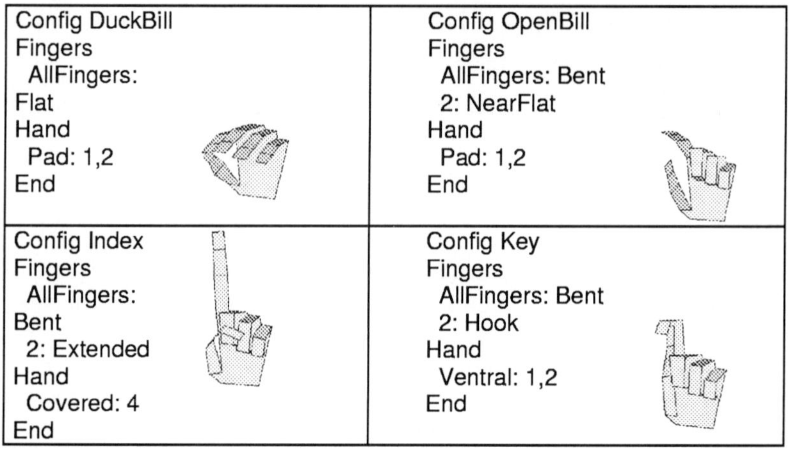

Config DuckBill
Fingers
  AllFingers:
Flat
Hand
  Pad: 1,2
End
	Config OpenBill
	Fingers
	  AllFingers: Bent
	  2: NearFlat
	Hand
	  Pad: 1,2
	End

Config Index
Fingers
  AllFingers:
Bent
  2: Extended
Hand
  Covered: 4
End
	Config Key
	Fingers
	  AllFingers: Bent
	  2: Hook
	Hand
	  Ventral: 1,2
	End

Fig. 6. Synthesis of hand configurations from their textual description

This method provides realistic thumb shapes and hand configurations, as shows Fig. 6.

4 Sign and Signed Sentences Syntheses

4.1 Location

In a visuo-gestural language as sign language, location is very much on the fore. Spatial mechanisms are used to express all kinds of notions such as size, shape, absolute or relative position, but also time reference (thanks to the time line) and pronominalization (through localization and indexic references). Some signs may vary in terms of location under temporal, pronominal or spatial inflexions. But location is first of all phonetically significant and requires therefore special attention.

In a synthesis view like ours, body points (including those on the face, weak hand and arm) can be expressed as spatial coordinates. The first step was thus to be able to determine arm angles for each point in space. Redundancy of the arm structure have induced us to:

1. select for each key point in space one quadruplet of arm (shoulder and elbow) angles among a set given by iterations on θ_s in the following equations:

$$s\varphi_s = \frac{BC \pm A\sqrt{A^2 + B^2 - C^2}}{A^2 + B^2},$$

with $A = 2l_1 x c\theta_s - 2l_1 z s\theta_s, B = 2l_1 y, C = l_1{}^2 - l_2{}^2 + x^2 + y^2 + z^2 nn$

$$l_2 c\varphi_e = x c\theta_s c\varphi_s + y s\varphi_s - z s\theta_s c\varphi_s - l_1 \tag{3}$$

$$l_2 s\psi_s s\varphi_e = x s\theta_s + z c\theta_s,$$

where c means *cosine*, s *sine*, and l_1, l_2 are the upper arm and forearm lengths.

2. average for any spatial point the quadruplets of the neighbouring key points, according to the distance to each of them.

The arm configurations generated by this method are natural in the whole reachable workspace of the wrist.

4.2 Orientation

Orientation is the third main parameter of sign. It consists in the determination of three angles (pronation-supination ψ_e, wrist abduction θ_w and flexion φ_w). Several possibilities have been considered, depending on whether a hand point is to be located at the given position instead of the wrist (see Sect. 2.1).

Absolute orientation of the palm $^{R_0}A_{R''_w} = (\sigma\,\nu\,\alpha)$ given by vectors n (normal to the palm) and i (according to the virutally extended index finger) can be successfully computed in both cases. If a hand point M is given in the wrist local coordinate system R''_w, the absolute wrist location must be preliminary determined as:

$$\overrightarrow{OW}_{R_0} = \overrightarrow{OM}_{R_0} - {}^{R_0}A_{R''_w}\overrightarrow{WM}_{R''_w} \tag{4}$$

This defines the arm angles as well as the current orientation $^{R_0}A_{R'_e} = (s\,n\,a)$ at the elbow. Wrist angles can then be found as:

$$\psi_e = -\text{Arctan}\left(\frac{{}^t n\alpha}{{}^t a\alpha}\right), \ \theta_w = \text{Arctan}\left(\frac{{}^t s\alpha.c\psi}{{}^t a\alpha}\right), \ \varphi_w = -\text{Arctan}\left(\frac{{}^t s\nu}{{}^t s\sigma}\right). \tag{5}$$

Relative orientation (explicit definition of wrist angles) may however only be used when no hand point has been specified.

4.3 Movement Generation

In their work about the synthesis of hand-arm gestures, T. Lebourque and S. Gibet [15] use a sensori-motor model in which the command is a series of target locations or angle configurations. The control system uses a minimal effort criterion to determine the joint angles state coordinates.

For the first development steps of our prototype, a simpler method has been implemented. Being henceforth able to compute the angles of the arm- hand system for any posture in space, we use simple interpolation between the initial and final ones. The latter is nevertheless non-linear for straight and arc- shaped paths. Extra studies on motion tracking have proved indeed that their speed profiles could be approximated by gaussian curves, with a maximum value roughly proportional to the total course. Circular moves on the contrary exhibit quasi-constant speed after a very short transitory period.

Those speed profiles are used to compute the points corresponding to the different frames to be generated. Moreover, special operators may affect those standard curves in order to reflect particular dynamics and kinetic stress.

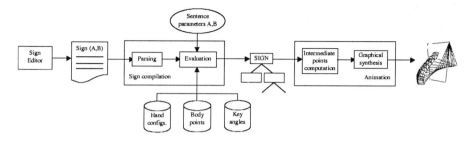

Fig. 7. Synopsis of sign synthesis

4.4   From Edition to Synthesis

Two edition levels have been set up in order to distinguish the sentence own parameters from sign description. Sentences are streams of lexical items and escape characters undertaking grammatical information (clause descriptor, localization, ...) Most of those discourse parameters affect signs by superimposing non-manual features (facial expression, shoulders position, etc.) but also by passing them arguments. Special verbs in sign language agree indeed with their subject and/or object (like *give* in Fig. 8) while others may incorporate a size-and-shape specifier, manner or direction of movement.

Whether sign language should exist in a written form is a major debate and several sets of symbols have been proposed. For signs and sentences encoding, we have opted for a textual readable form for legibility and easiness of transmission purposes. The sign description is parsed and then evaluated (considering arguments) if its syntax is correct (see Fig. 7). The result of this evaluation is a sign tree specification similar to the ones presented in Sect. 2.

The underlying model of the animation module is a complete hierarchic tree of the upper body in which segments are grouped together into high-level structures accepting global messages. Face for instance may be assigned specific expressions such as questioning, surprise or anger. The graphical three-dimensional synthesis is achieved thanks to connected polygons having angle-dependent col-

Fig. 8. Textual description and frames of sign *give*

ors and hidden surfaces removed. This results from a compromise between computation speed and representation sharpness, and provides synthetic signs in quasi real-time.

Figure 8 above shows an example of sign synthesis accepting sentence parameters. Sign *give* has here subject *I* (left) and in turn object *you* (middle) and *him* (right frame). But locations can be used instead so as to reference pre-settled characters in a story. Notice that the first two images exhibit neutral expression for the face, whereas the third one has undergone flexion of the imperative mode within a signed sentence, and therefore shows protruding eyes and shoulders.

5   Conclusion and Future Work

The sign synthesis system presented is now well set up with high-level specification of hand configurations, location and orientation. Automatic coarticulation and the determination of pauses between signs must still be improved. But the underlying structure of sign description seems generic enough to provide ability to generate not only most of the signs we have encountered but take also specific grammatical processes into account.

An exhaustive validation of the synthetic signs by native deaf signers will be of course one of the most important works to be fulfilled. If the virtual signer already exhibits interesting and significant results, the development of the most complex signs should be accompanied by close examination of their expressive potential. A connection is to be made at last with previous works about written French grammatical and semantic analyses, in order to make a new step towards sign language interfaces.

References

1. Shantz, M., Poizner, H.: A Computer Program to Synthesize American Sign Language. Behavior Research Methods and Instrumentation, 14, 5, (1982) 467–474
2. Stokoe, W.C., Casterline, D.C., Croneberg, C.D.: A Dictionary of American Sign Language. Linstok Press, Silver Spring (1976)
3. Battison, R.: Phonological Deletion in American Sign Language. Sign Language Studies, 5 (1974) 1–19
4. Liddell, S.K., Johnson, R.E.: American Sign Language: The Phonological Base. Sign Language Studies, 64 (1989) 195–277
5. Klima, E., Bellugi, U.: The Signs of Language. Harvard University Press, Cambridge London (1979)
6. Gibet, S., Richardson, J., Lebourque, T., Braffort, A.: Corpus of 3D Natural Movements and Sign Language Primitives of Movement. In: Wachsmuth, I., Fröhlich, M. (eds): Lecture Notes in Artificial Intelligence – Proc. Gesture Workshop'97. Springer-Verlag, Berlin (1998) 111–121
7. Wilbur, R.B.: Description Linguistique de la Langue des Signes. Langages, 13, 56 (1979) 13–34
8. Fischer, S., Gough, B.: Verbs in American Sign Language. Sign Language Studies, 18 (1978) 17–48

9. Rondal, J., Henrot, F., Charlier, M.: La Langue des Signes. Pierre Mardaga ed., Bruxelles (1986)

10. McIntire, M., Newkirk, D., Hutchins, S., Poizner, H.: Hands and Faces: A Preliminary Inventory for Written ASL. Sign Language Studies, 56 (1987) 197–241

11. Moody, B.: La Langue des Signes – Tome 1: Histoire et Grammaire. International Visual Theatre (I.V.T.). Ellipses, Paris (1983)

12. Prillwitz, S., Zienert, H.: Hamburg Notation System for Sign Language: Development of a Sign Writing with Computer Application. In: Prillwitz, S., Vollhaber, T. (eds):Current Trends in European Sign Language Research – Proc. 3rd European Congress on Sign Language Research. Signum, Hamburg (1990) 355–380

13. Lee, J., Kunii, T.L.: Constraint-based Hand Animation. In: Magnenat-Thalmann, N., Thalmann, D. (eds): Models and Techniques in Computer Animation World. Springer-Verlag, Berlin (1993) 110–127

14. Kobrinski, A.A., Kobrinski, A.E.: Bras Manipulateurs des Robots – Architecture et Théorie. Mir eds., Moscow (1989)

15. Lebourque, T., Gibet, S.: Synthesis of Hand-arm Gestures. In: Harling, P.A., Edwards, A.D.N. (eds): Progress in Gestural Interaction – Proc. Gesture Workshop '96. Springer, Berlin (1997) 217–225

Active Character: Dynamic Reaction to the User

Shan Lu and Seiji Igi

Communications Research Laboratory
4-2-1 Nukui-Kitamachi, Koganei, Tokyo 184-8795, Japan
{lu,igi}@crl.go.jp

Abstract. This paper describes a computer-character system intended to create a natural interaction between the computer and the user. Using predefined control rules, it generates the movements of the computer character's head, body, hands, and gaze-lines according to changes in the user's position and gaze-lines. This system acquires the user's information about the user's position, facial region, and gaze-lines by using a vision subsystem and an eye-tracker unit. The vision subsystem detects the presence of a person, estimates the three-dimensional position of the person by using information acquired by a stationary camera, and determines the locations of the face and hands. The reactive motions of the computer character are generated according to a set of predefined if-then rules. Furthermore, a motion-description file is designed to define simple and complex kinds of gestures.

1 Introduction

The computer is entering our daily lives and playing an increasingly important role in our life and work. Although advanced computer systems often provide a graphical user interface (GUI), it is not always easy for a novice to use it. An easy-to-use user interface is becoming one of the most important features of computers designed for the general public.

Since there is a great demand for computers that can interact more naturally with the user, a new kind of interface, called the computer character interface (CCI), is being developed in a wide range of areas [1]. This kind of interface has many more features than today's GUI, and the most important is that it uses a natural dialogue style in order to complete the interaction between the user and computer. The participants in a human-human conversation exchange messages by using verbal and nonverbal information at the same time. The nonverbal information — such as facial expressions, gestures, and gaze-lines — is a necessary part of conversations between people and should also play an important role in conversations between people and computers.

If we want the computer character in the CCI to maintain a natural conversation, we need to consider how and when nonverbal information should be presented. Many computer characters show users the visual presentations of facial expressions or gestures from only one viewpoint [2, 3]. However, since these presentations do not consider user feedback, they cannot offer effective information. In Ref.[4], a face-to-face communicational virtual character was reported.

A. Braffort et al. (Eds.): GW'99, LNAI 1739, pp. 253–264, 1999.

However, this system uses the wired body-suit to acquire the user's information, and these units affect the use's behaviors in conversation with the computer character. Here we describe a character system that can generate nonverbal information — including gaze lines, facial expressions, and gestures — that correspond to changes of the user's gaze-line and position. We call it the active character, and this paper describes its basic configuration of the active character and the technology it uses to monitor the user's gaze line and to generate the computer character's gaze line and movement.

2   Overviews of the Active Character

2.1   Nonverbal Communication

People use both verbal and nonverbal information when they converse, and nonverbal information plays as important role as verbal information. Nonverbal information has basically two functions: transferring specific meaning, and adjusting conversation. Prominent kinds of nonverbal information are interpersonal distance, direction of the gaze, body contact, body gradient, body direction, facial expression, posture, gesture, and hand movement [5].

Except for body contact all of these items can be used in a conversation between a person and a computer character. Appropriate nonverbal information can be used to adjust the conversation and make the interaction smoother. For example, if the computer system takes into account the distance between the user and the character (the distance between the user and the screen), it can adjust details of the character's movements so that character's gestures are created comprehensibly. And, the system can infer the interests of the user and establish eye contact by catching the direction of the user's gaze.

Many computer conversation characters (some with and some without a human appearance) have been developed, and most of these characters are designed for unidirectional information: from the computer to the user. Such a character depends on the explicit indications of the computer system or the user and cannot act autonomously. Our goal is to develop a conversational character that can observe the user situation and react to the user.

2.2   Basic Elements

There are three fundamental function components for the active character. The first component acquires the verbal and nonverbal information of the user, and the second component generates the nonverbal information of the character. The third component plays a control role for determining what kind of reaction the character should make.

Figure 1 shows a picture of an active character. The component of the user's information collection obtains the user's situation such as facial expressions, gestures, gaze lines, and positions. The component of motion generation creates the movements and presents them to the user according to the indication from the motion control component. The motion control component makes the decision to correspond to the change in the user's situation based on predefined rules. The current implementation of the active character uses following nonverbal information.

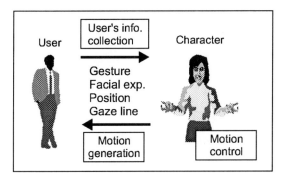

Fig. 1. Nonverbal information exchanged between the user and the computer character.

The gaze line: Eye contact is a very important factor in conversation. The presence meeting system emphasizes the coincidence of the gaze line to enhance the presence effect [6]. In our active character system, the user's gaze lines are monitored and used to adjust the character's gaze line.

The position: The characteristics of the physical environment affect conversations between people. For example, people tend to speak informally at a close distance, and to speak more formally at a longer distances [7]. The active character resizes itself according to changes in the user's position and adjusts it's gaze line to keep it directed toward the user .

Gestures and facial expressions: Gestures and facial expressions are both linguistic and nonlinguistic signals. Nodding, for example, is a linguistic signal representing agreement. Here we handle gestures and the facial expressions only as nonlinguistic signals.

3   Implementation of the Active Character

The conceptualistic structure of this active character system is shown in Fig. 2. The user-position-monitoring module tracks the position of the user and the position of the user's facial region. The gaze-line-monitoring module uses an eye-tracker to track the user's gaze line. The motion-control module uses predefined rules and the information from the monitoring modules to determine what kind of behavior should be generated. The gaze-lines and movements of the character are generated and presented on the screen by the gesture-generation and gaze-line-generation modules.

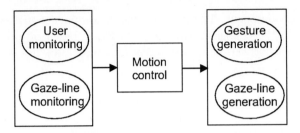

Fig. 2. System structure.

3.1   Monitoring the User

The following user information is monitored by using a vision subsystem.

The presence of the user: The appearance of the user is used as a trigger starting the conversation,

The position of the user: The system tracks the user and when the user's position changes, it accordingly resizes and reorients the character displayed on the screen.

The facial region of the user: Information about the location of the user's face is necessary for controlling the gaze lines of the character and for implementing the recognition of facial expressions.

The following three conditions are assumed, and these conditions are easily satisfied in a typical laboratory or office.

Condition 1: The background of conversational environment does not suddenly change.

Condition 2: The lighting is constant. This condition is easily satisfied by cutting off outside light.

Condition 3: The video camera is stationary, and the lens is fixed.

Figure 3 shows the main steps and components for detecting the user's presence, position, and facial region from acquiring the 2-D image to estimating the 3-D location of the user.

Person detection Since the background is constant (according to Conditions 1, 2, and 3), a subtraction image between the current and background image can be used to judge the presence of user. The background image is created by averaging three continuous images in which no person is presence. Then, a subtraction image S between the current image I and the background image B is calculated and is used to make a judgement. If the summation of pixel's lightness in the subtraction image S is larger than a threshold, the system can judge that a person is presence. In our system, the threshold is determined automatically by use of the Otsu's method [8]. If none of person is detected, the background image is renewed by the current image I.

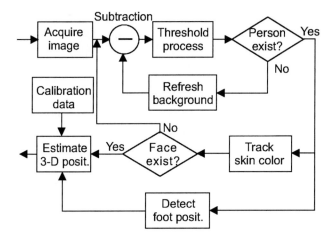

Fig. 3. Main steps and components for detecting the user's presence, position, and facial region.

The facial region detection Once the presence of a person is detected, a skin-color-tracking process is started in order to find the face within the person area. This tracking process is based on color histogram matching [9]. Firstly, a small color area is interactively selected in a pre-acquired image as the initial model image. Then the image to be processed is divided into some small image areas (called patch image), and the similarity of color between the patch images and the model image is calculated. The following steps describe the detection processing.

1. Convert the color model of image from RGB to HSV [10]. The process aims at obtaining constant color representation and absorbing the intensity variations.
2. Divide the input image into patch images, and calculate the color histogram $H_I(i,j)$ of the H, S component.
3. Select a model image and calculate its color histogram $H_C(i,j)$.
4. Select a patch image, and calculate its matching rate M as equation (1).

$$M = \frac{\sum min(H_C(i,j), H_I(i,j))}{\sum H_C(i,j)} \tag{1}$$

5. When the matching rate M is larger than a pre-determined threshold, the current patch image belongs to the skin-color area. If M is less than the threshold, the current patch image is no skin-color.
6. If the current patch image is the skin-color area, the model image is replaced by this patch image. Then return to 4. The purpose of renewing the model image is for selecting color area as close to the model as possible.

If no patch image belonging to the skin-color area is found, the process finishes. Some isolated patch images remain probably after the color-tracking process, and they affect the identification of the face and hands. A iterative process of erosion and dilation is used to remove them. Finally, the k-means algorithm [11] is used to identify the face area and the hand area. The centroid of each area is output as the position of that area.

Figure 4 shows the results of the person-detection and the facial-region-detection process. The top-left image is the background image, the top-right image is the input image, the bottom-left image show the detected person area, and the bottom-right image shows the detected face and hands area. The original images are RGB color ones with the spatial resolution 320×240. The skin areas including the facial region and the hand regions are extracted by the color-detection process with 5×5-pixel patch. The results in Fig. 4 show that this method is effective for detecting the location of skin-color regions, but that facial features and expressions are not easily recognized at this resolution.

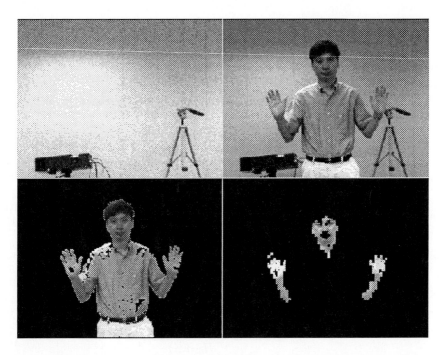

Fig. 4. Images of original background (top-left), input (top-right), person (bottom-left), and skin-color (bottom-right) region extracted by person-detection process.

3-D position estimation Since the environment and camera are fixed (Conditions 1 and 3), a 3-D position can be estimated from a 2-D position in an image [12]. The environment and camera are calibrated in advance as shown in Fig. 5.

The area in which the user moves is divided into meshes, and the relationship of the position in 2-D image and 3-D position in of each mesh area is measured and recorded. According to this relationship, 3-D position can be estimated by using the 2-D coordinate (x, y) of the pixel. Here the user location is defined as a point which's y-coordinate has the minimum value within the detected person region.

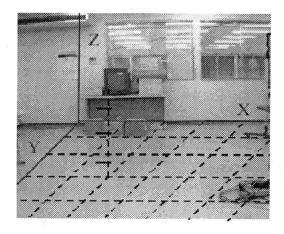

Fig. 5. Calibration of the environment and camera.

The same way can be used to estimate the x- and y- coordinates in the 3-D coordinate system from the centroid of the detected face area. Also, since the stature of the person is invariant, this height is converted into the z-coordinate of the face area.

3.2   Monitoring Gaze Lines

sect:gazeline A remote-style eye-tracker unit (made by ASL) is used to track the user's gaze-lines. This unit illuminates the eye of the user with near-infrared light, and tracks the movement of the eyeball by using an eye camera. It estimates the angle of the gaze line by extracting the pupil center and the position of the corneal reflex based on the tracked eyeball image [13]. The detected gaze-line data is transferred to the host computer via a serial line (RS232C). Since few bytes are needed to specify gaze-lines, a 19200-bps line can satisfy the requirement for a real-time processing.

Once the gaze lines data are known, the user's point of interest can be estimated by the following process. First we define the user's point of interest as gaze point that satisfies two conditions. The first condition is that the gaze lines stay in a specific area (threshold window A) continuously, and the second condition is that the time the user's gaze stays in that specific area is greated than a threshold time T. The point of interest is estimated by an iterative process. Let P_i be the position of the gaze point, and define an $a{\times}b$ window area (A) at the start point P_0. When all P_i $(0 \le i < T)$ are located inside the area A, P_t is defined as the point of interest. If one gaze point P_k is out of the area A, let P_k be the next start point, and repeat the above process.

3.3   Motion Control and Generation

Motion control The motion-control module generates signals needed to generate and adjust the character's gaze-lines and movements according to the position and gaze-lines of the user. Figure 6 illustrates the basic structure of the motion control and generation.

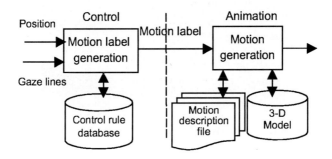

Fig. 6. Motion control and generation.

A motion-label-generation module determines what kind of movements should be created and sends the result to the motion-generation module. The control-rules define the reaction corresponding to the user information. The rules are predefined in the *if-then* style. The following are two examples of control rules.

Example 1:

If the user appears in the view of the character

Then make a bow (greeting)

Example 2:

If the user gazes at the face of the character

Then gaze at the user's face

The condition of "*if*" describes the user information by using the following statement.

$$[Target = Behavior] \langle\ Operator\ \rangle\ [Target = Behavior]$$

Where, *Target* defines the monitoring targets of the active character such as "*Gazeline*" or "*Person*", and *Behavior* defines the user's behaviors. And *Operator* is a logical operator including "*AND*" and "*OR*". An *AND* operator represents that two behaviors occur at the same time. For example, in order to describe such a condition as the user appears in the conversation area and gazes at the face of character, the following statement is used.

Person = ViewIn And Gazeline = Face

At the *"Then"* statement, the character's movements are defined. These movements include the gaze-lines and gestures. According this statement, the motion-label-generation module generates and sends a corresponding motion-label to the motion-generation module to generate the gesture. If this statement indicates the gaze-line animation, the target position (such as face, hands, body) is given.

Table 1 shows examples of the user's behavior and the corresponding character's reactions this system can process. Clearly, these rules is not enough to simulate a real human-human conversation.

Table 1. The user's behavior and the active character's reaction.

User's behavior	Character's reactions
walk into the conversation space	gaze at user and make a greeting gesture
walk out the conversation space	make a goodbye gesture
walk around the conversation space	follow and gaze at the facial region
wave the hands	gaze at the hands
gaze at the character's face and body	gaze at the face

Motion generation The motion-generation module in Fig. 6 synthesizes the movements of the character based on the motion label from the motion-label-generation module. A motion label is used to define a specific gesture, and is related with a motion description file. A motion description file defines the movements of joints as a motion unit in a gesture. All movements of the character are combinations of these motion units. The movements of any motion unit are defined in a motion description file with one of the following types:

1. The frame data description: The rotation angles of moving joints are designated on each of the frames in a motion unit. The motion data obtained from the motion-capture system can be used typically in this type.
2. The complement description: Only the key frames in a motion unit are defined. In these frames the rotation angle of joints generating the character movements is defined. The entire animation sequences are created using the forward kinematics by parametric interpolation for the joint angle.
3. The serial compositive description: Define a complicated movement by serializing several motion labels defined in 1 and 2. Each motion unit is started serially.
4. The parallel compositive description: Define a complicated movement by generating several motion units as defined in 1 and 2 in parallel.

Figure 7 shows two snapshots of generated movements. On the left is the motion "making a bow" and on the right is the gesture "considering something."

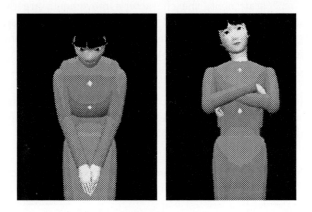

Fig. 7. Snapshot of generated gestures.

The animation of eyeball movements generates the gaze line. The eyeball is modeled as a partial sphere [14], and the surface of the lens (pupil is located at the same position) is modeled using a partial sphere with a different diameter. Rotating the eyeball model creates the animation of eyeball movement.

4   Hardware System and Performance

Figure 8 shows the hardware structure of our active character system. The workstation 1 (SUN Ultra1) equipped a 3-CCD video camera and image grabber (Snapper) acquires and processes color images. It runs the procedures for detecting person and facial region. The workstation 2 (SGI Indigo2) plays a role of the motion control and generation. The eye tracker detects the user's gaze-lines and sends the results to the workstation 2 through RS232C. A shared memory area is built to store the data transferred from the workstation 1 and the eye tracker. The motion-control module implemented on the workstation 2 reads the data from this shared memory area at a 30-Hz rate, and responds in real-time to the changes of the gaze-lines and the user's position.

The image-processing required for determining the position of the user and the location of the user's facial region is a time-consuming procedure. Table 2 is an experimental result that shows the average process times of the four main steps in the person-detection process. The results in the table show that the step detecting the face and hands by skin-color consumes the half of all process time. This is mainly because the RGB-to-HSV conversion is a time-consuming computing. An alternative color model could decrease the computing time [15]. The

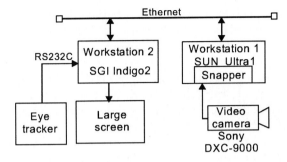

Fig. 8. Structure of the hardware system.

results in Tab. 2 show the system can work at high frame rate (approximatively 23 frames per second.) and satisfy the requirement for a real-time process.

Table 2. The average process time of the main four steps in the user-detection process. The numbers of right column are the average values by running the process 120 times on the 160×120 video image.

Process steps	Process time(second)
1. Image capturing	0.004605
2. Detection of people	0.007717
3. Tracking face and hands region	0.022497
4. Clustering and 3-D measurement	0.008322
Total	0.043141

5   Conclusions

In this paper we described a novel computer-character system that can react to the changes in a user's gaze-line and position. The reactions of the character include such nonverbal responses as gestures and the adjustment of gaze-lines. Methods for determining the user's 3-D position and for finding the user's face have also been described. This system uses an eye-tracker to monitor the user's gaze-lines, and the system generates the character's gestures and adjusts the character's gaze-lines by using a predefined rule database. So one can easily change the character's reaction to the user by changing those rules. We used a motion-description file to define the motion unit, and complex gestures can be produced by combining these motion units. Furthermore, the motion-description file provides two basic method to describe the character's movements. One is define the movements of joints only in the key frames, and it is appropriate to the simple motion. Another basic method uses the rotation data of all joints for all of frames. This kind of rotation data can be acquired by using motion-capture system, it is appropriate to the complex motion.

As showed in 3.3, some infantile nonverbal conversation is accomplished by monitoring the user's behaviors and generating the character's reaction. Although the capacity for detecting the user information restricts the free conversation between the user and the character, the control-rules provide a flexible method to generate the character's movements. It is clear that more control-rules and more powerful user-detection unit are needed to achieve the real natural conversation between the user and computer character. Another point that is needed to be taken into account is the facial expressions. Although there are some researches intended to synthesize and recognize them, the real natural interaction including the facial expressions between the user and the computer character is still challenge.

References

1. Bradshaw, J.M. (Ed.): Software Agents. AAAI/MIT Press (1996).
2. Takeuchi, A., and Nagao, K.: Communicative facial displays as a new conversational modality. Human Factors in Computing Systems: INTERCH'93 Conference Proceedings, ACM (1993).
3. Cassell, J., et al.: Animated conversation: rule-based generation of facial expression, gesture and spoken intonation for multiple conversational agents. In Proc. of SIGGRAPH '94 (1994).
4. Thorisson, K.R.: A mind model for multimodal communicative creatures and humanoids. International Journal of Applied Artificial Intelligence, Vol. 13, No. 4 (1999) 449–486.
5. Raffler-Engel, W.: Aspects of Nonverbal Communication. Swets and Zeitlinger B. V (1980).
6. Sellen, A.J.: Speech patterns in video-mediated conversation. In Proc. of CHI'92 (1992) 49–59.
7. Patterson, M.L.: Nonverbal Behavior: a Functional Perspective. Springer-Verlag (1983).
8. Otsu, N.: Discriminant and least-squares threshold selection. In Proc. of 4th Inter. Joint Conf. on Pattern Recognition (1978) 592–596.
9. Swain, M.J., and Ballard, D.H.: Color indexing. International Journal of Computer Vision, Vol. 7, No. 1 (1991) 11–32.
10. Saxe, D. and Foulds, R.: Toward robust skin identification in video images. In Proc. of Inter. Conf. on Automatic Face and Gesture Recognition (1996) 379–384.
11. Gose, E., et al.: Pattern Recognition and Image Analysis. Prentice Hall PTR (1996) 213–217.
12. Wren, C.R., et al.: Pfinder: real-time tracking of the human body. IEEE Trans. on Pattern Analysis and Machine Intelligence, Vol. 19, No. 7 (1997) 780–785.
13. Hutchinson, T.E., et al.: Human-computer interaction using eye-gaze input. IEEE Trans. Systems, Man & Cybernetics, Vol. 19, No. 6 (1989) 1527–1543.
14. Parke, F.I. and Waters, K.: Computer Facial Animation. A K Perters, Ltd. (1996) 198-206.
15. Ahmad, S.: A usable real-time 3D hand tracker. Conference Record of the Asilomar Conference on Signals, System and Computers (1994) 1257–1261.

Reactiva'Motion Project: Motion Synthesis Based on a Reactive Representation

Frédéric Julliard and Sylvie Gibet

LIMSI-CNRS, BP 133, Université Paris-Sud, 91403 Orsay, France
{julliard,gibet}@limsi.fr
http://www.limsi.fr/Individu/julliard

Abstract. This work is part of the SAGA (SYNTHESIS AND ANALYSIS OF GESTURES FOR ANIMATION) project which aim is to develop a real time animation system for articulated human bodies. The purpose of the REACTIVA'MOTION project is to propose new methods for designing and synthesizing skilled motions requiring coordination features and reacting to external events, such as walking or juggling. Motions are specified by the way of a reactive representation ; the reactivity results from the execution which takes into account sensory data provided by the environment.

1 Introduction

Human locomotion and juggling activity can be both represented by a repetitive structured pattern. Nevertheless, our everyday experience shows us that these kinds of motions cannot be explained only by stereotype behaviors. Stepping over an obstacle, changing direction or accelerating gait, for instance, depend on motor programs guided by orders coming from the central nervous system.

In this paper, we propose a model to control in real-time the animation of virtual characters. We expect the motion synthesis to be sufficiently believable and to be produced adaptatively to the environmental context. The approach presented below realizes a good compromise between realism and real-time. It considers gait as the result of controlled motor skills or tasks where events representing sensory information may influence the motion execution. We describe here a methodology, called *reactive representation*, which specifies how to combine in space and time these motor skills.

2 Approach

Different approaches have been proposed to coordinate and to synchronize elementary motions provided by the generation model : as stated by Zeltzer, task-level animation systems schedule the execution of motor programs to control animated characters [1]. Finite state machines provide common execution models used in robotics and in animation fields [2]. Other approaches use fuzzy and temporal logic representations, or integrate different motion control techniques

A. Braffort et al. (Eds.): GW'99, LNAI 1739, pp. 265–268, 1999.

to combine several motion units executed by a set of articulated chains [3]. Our approach aims to provide :

- **Reactivity** which allows a real time motion execution, by taking into account without delay, the environment configuration.
- **Significant high level parameters** which could be modified during the execution.
- **Deterministic executions**, to ensure the temporal pattern of the motion combination.
- **Expressivity** : we would like to specify, without ambiguity, a particular execution model which expresses which action should be activated according to the synchronization constraints.
- **Behavioral or temporal property validation** on the execution model which results from the specification language.

The motion production line is shown in Figure 1. The designer specifies his motion by using a high level description language. The movement is built from elementary motion units. Then, this description is translated into a formal specification by the way of a reactive language.

This specification formally expresses the behavior of the corresponding motor program from a set of events, collisions for instance or higher level visual information. This approach allows deterministic executions and the verification of temporal or behavioral program properties. It is also based on a modular design concept : a parameterized specification can be stored and then re-used for the design of more complex motions.

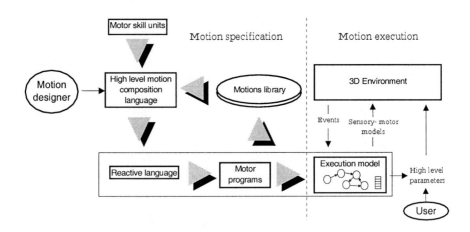

Fig. 1. The motion production line

The specification clarifies on the one hand the intrinsic structure of the motion coordination and on the other hand its relations with the environment. It is expressed into motor programs and translated into finite state automata which control the motion generators. Each of these sensory-motor models consists in a closed loop system which uses a visual feedback to automatically update the control parameters of the articulated body. Besides, the instruction associated to each servo-loop system is reduced t o key-positions called targets which express a kind of intention previous to the performed movement. The generation model thus associates a discrete command with an auto-organized system driving continuous signals. It ensures realism in the synthesized motion and facilitates the control task which consists in specifying a limited number of key-positions.

This generative model integrates constraints linked to psycho-motor laws. We proved in previous work that it is well adapted to synthesize arm movements [4]. A sign language generation system based on this model has been developed [5] [6] [7] [8]. We also proved that these sensory-motor models can be assembled to control the movement of the whole human body [9]. Elements of coordination and synchronization have been expressed through th e reactive language ELECTRE.

3   Example: Avoidance of Obstacles During Gait

When we encounter a pavement, we often adapt our step length in order to avoid stumbling against the kerb. This application highlights how the nearness of a pavement can be taken into account by the walker.

In this simple example, reactivity is treated at particular instants. At these instants, the pavement proximity is evaluated. If a threshold is reached, the modification of gait parameters is triggered (step length and swing phase elevation). The motion is specified by the way of a finite state automata which describes a temporal pattern of the walking cycle. This pattern corresponds to a parallel combination of swing and stance phases defined from motor units and expressed as a set of targets. Therefore, significant high level parameters, like step length, allow changes in gait during motion execution.

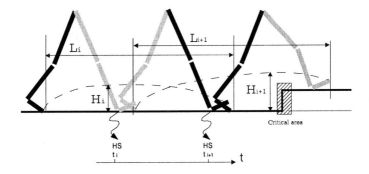

Fig. 2. The pavement encounter

This mechanism is illustrated in Figure 2 and can be formalized as follows :

$$\{L_{i+1}, H_{i+1}\} = \mathcal{F}(\xi_i) \tag{1}$$

where suffixes i and $i+1$ denote the states of variables, respectively before and after an occurence of a heel strike (HS) event. L and H are high level gait parameters, respectively the step length and the required elevation to avoid the collision. $\mathcal{F}$ is a function which updates L and H according to the environmental context ξ ($\xi_i = \{L_i, H_i, \text{PAVEMENT PROXIMITY}, \ldots\}$). This implementation implies that the duration of $\mathcal{F}$ is negligible and atomic that is to say that it cannot be interrupted by another update process.

4   Conclusion and Perspectives

A real-time control system and a motion design approach have been described for the animation of characters. The application presented here proposes one particular reactive strategy. Our approach has to be improved by treating other reactivity forms. The formal aspect of the design process defines exactly how the system reacts to its environment. Therefore, it is possible to validate some behavioral (qualitative) or temporal (quantitative) properties by analyzing the execution model.

Finally, the modularity which characterizes this approach opens new perspectives for designing movements. From libraries of pre-built elementary movements, the designer will be able to compose macroscopically complex movements, for example gymnastic figures.

References

1. Zeltzer, D.: Motor control techniques for figure animation. IEEE Computer Graphics and Applications (1982) 2(9):53–59
2. Zeltzer, D., Gaffron, S.: Task level interaction with virtual environments and virtual actors. International Journal of Human-Computer Interaction (1996) 8(1):73–94
3. Badler, N.I., Phillips, C.B., Webber, B.L: Simulating Humans. Oxford University Press (1993)
4. Gibet, S., Marteau, P.F.: A self-organized model for the control, planning and learning of nonlinear multi-dimensional systems using a sensory feedback. Journal of Applied Intelligence 4 (1994), 337–349
5. Lebourque, T.: Spécification et génération de gestes naturels, Application à la langue des signes française. PhD Thesis, University of Paris XI, Orsay (November 1998)
6. Lebourque, T., Gibet, S.: High level specification and control of communication Gestures: the GESSYCA system . Computer Animation'99, Geneve, Switzerland (May 1999)
7. Lebourque, T., Gibet, S.: In proceedings of Gesture Workshop'99, Gif sur Yvette, France (March 1999)
8. Gibet, S., Julliard, F., Lebourque, T., Marteau, P.F.: Simulation of human motions using a sensory motor approach. 3rd IMACS/IEEE International Multiconference on Circuits, Systems, Communications and Computers, Athens, Greece (June 1999) 125–130
9. Julliard, F., Gibet, S.: De l'utilisation de languages réactifs vers l'animation adaptative de personnages articulés. Journées de l'Association Française d'Informatique Graphique, Dunkerque, France (December 1998) 195–202

The Emotional Avatar: Non-verbal Communication Between Inhabitants of Collaborative Virtual Environments

Marc Fabri, David J. Moore, and Dave J. Hobbs

Virtual Learning Environments Research Group
Faculty of Information and Engineering Systems, School of Computing
Leeds Metropolitan University
Leeds LS6 3QS, United Kingdom
M.Fabri,D.Moore,D.Hobbs}@lmu.ac.uk

Abstract. Collaborative Virtual Environments (CVEs) are distributed virtual reality systems with multi-user access. Each inhabitant is represented by a humanoid embodiment, an avatar, making them virtually present in the artificial world. This paper investigates how inhabitants of these CVEs can communicate with each other through channels other than speech, and it is primarily concerned with the visualization and perception of facial expressions and body postures in CVEs. We outline our experimental work and discuss ways of expressing the emotional state of CVE inhabitants through their avatars.

1 Introduction

Natural human communication is based on speech, facial expressions, body posture and gestures. While speech is an obvious instrument for mediating our thoughts and ideas, social intercourse also depends heavily on the actions, postures, movements and expressions of the talking body [1]. Social psychologists argue that more than 65% of the information exchanged during a person-to-person conversation is carried on the nonverbal band [2, 3]. Therefore, it is expected to be beneficial to provide such communication channels in CVEs in some way.

Potential applications for such CVE systems are all areas where people cannot come together physically, but wish to discuss, collaborate on, or even dispute certain matters. The Virtual Learning Environments (VLE) research group at Leeds Metropolitan University is primarily concerned with the use of CVE technology in Distance Learning systems. Nonverbal means of expression are important for the facilitation of interaction between tutor and learner, as well as between fellow learners [2]. Acceptance and understanding of ideas and feelings, encouraging and criticizing, silence and questioning – all involve nonverbal elements of interaction and it can be argued that computer-based educational technologies ought to emulate this. For a detailed discussion of the relevance of interaction for learning and potential benefits of using CVE technology the reader is referred to [4].

A. Braffort et al. (Eds.): GW'99, LNAI 1739, pp. 269–273, 1999.

2   User Representation in Collaborative Virtual Environments

In CVEs, inhabitants are usually represented by humanoid embodiments, generally referred to as *avatars*. Since each avatar is both part of the perceived environment and represents the user that is doing the perceiving [5], inhabitants potentially develop a strong sense of mutual awareness. Furthermore, and this is of particular importance for systems which support communication between inhabitants, the avatar can provide direct feedback about one particular user's actions, direction and degree of attention and interactive abilities, to the other inhabitants.

However, this does not necessarily imply that a *good* avatar has to be a realistic and accurate representation of the real world physiology. There is evidence that approaches aiming to reproduce the human physics in detail may in fact be wasteful [6]. A more abstract approach, reflecting representation issues in simple or unusual ways, may be more appropriate and supportive to perception and cognition [7].

We are therefore investigating the use of simple but distinctive visual clues to mediate the emotional state of a CVE user and to assign a personality to their avatar. We focus particularly on mediating emotions and attitudes as these factors are essential to human social interaction [3]. It is held that, where communication of changing moods and emotional states is concerned, nonverbal information is far more important than verbal information [1].

There are three approaches to the problem of capturing and displaying nonverbal means of expression of CVE users through their avatars [8]:

1. *Directly controlled:* Face and body movements are captured and the avatar is modified directly, ideally in real-time, via virtual 'strings' like a marionette, cf. [9].
2. *User-guided:* The user defines tasks and movements to perform and the virtual 'strings' are controlled via a secondary device, e.g. mouse or keyboard, cf. [4, 8].
3. *Autonomous:* The virtual human is assumed to have an internal state that depends on its goals and sensor information from the environment. The controlling user modifies this state, e.g. re-defines goals and starts tasks, cf. [10, 11].

Our work is concerned with a control mechanism that lies somewhere between the user-guided and the autonomous approach. This enables us to use high-level visualization metaphors and provide an intuitive interface, while at the same time taking into account the potential and richness of nonverbal communication.

For example, instead of faithfully visualizing limb and face movements of an angry user, anger could be visualized by a red-faced avatar with distinctive, possibly exaggerated facial features. Likewise, an avatar jumping up and down whilst waving its arms would signal excitement – without actually requiring the user to perform this act as would be necessary with a directly controlled avatar.

3   The Expression of Emotion

There are various channels for nonverbal communication, such as the face, gaze, gesture, or body posture, all of which could be mediated in CVEs to some degree. The most immediate indicator for the emotional state of a person is the face. It reflects interpersonal attitudes, provides feedback on the comments of others, and is regarded as the primary source of information next to human speech [2]. For these reasons, humans naturally pay a great deal of attention to the messages they receive from the faces of others. Considerable research has shown that there are six universal emotions, which can be accurately communicated by facial expressions [12]: *surprise, fear, disgust, anger, happiness*, and *sadness* (see Fig. ref245f1). It is held that these six emotions have an innate physiological basis and a clear meaning across cultures [3].

Another strong indicator for emotion, and particularly attitude, is body posture. By taking on certain postures, people can send clear signals regarding their current willingness and ability to engage in social interaction [3]. Such attitude postures are often combined with hand and arm gestures. There is evidence that, similar to facial expressions, certain postures also have a clear meaning across cultures [3], among others *welcoming, rejection, incomprehension*, and *attention* (see Fig. ref245f1).

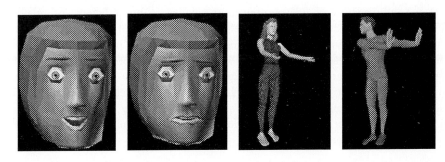

Fig. 1. Surprise and sadness face, welcoming and rejection posture. (Copyright virtual head geometry and processes Geometrek, www.geometrek.com. Copyright postures VLE group)

The potential of using nonverbal communication means in CVEs is clearly not exhausted with this limited set of facial expressions and postures. However, because of their universality, we consider them particularly suitable for investigating the effects the introduction of emotion has on interaction in virtual environments.

4   Experiments on Perception and Cognition of Emotion

Cognitive psychology research suggests that there are internal, probably innate, physiognomic schemata that support the perception of members of our own species, and enable emotion recognition [13]. This process of recognizing emotion works even with very simple or very few distinctive visual clues, and it is seen as an important function of interpersonal interaction [14].

This evolutionary developed skill to *read* emotions from signals of the body is considered as being highly beneficial to communication in CVEs. We argue that an emotionally expressive user embodiment can aid the communication process and provide information that would otherwise be difficult to mediate.

We are currently undertaking controlled experiments to support this argument, and are comparing different approaches to the visualization of inhabitants' emotional states in collaborative virtual environments. Virtual Reality Modeling Language (VRML) is used to build differing environments for the purposes of the experiments. The aim is to establish when it is beneficial to model real world human interaction directly, and when the use of visual metaphors would be preferable.

Preliminary findings in this ongoing research suggest that the psychological basis for recognizing emotions can quite reasonably be applied to avatar-based interaction in CVEs. The virtual interlocutor, depicting merely a few distinctive facial or physical clues, potentially takes on a personal and social role in the virtual space. It becomes a true representation of the underlying individual, not only visually, but also in a social and emotional manner.

Should this prove to be borne out by the experimental studies, it will allow systems falling short of full photographic quality to be sufficient for relaying across networks, with consequent benefits for the quality of service where bandwidth and connectivity breakdowns may otherwise cause problems. Dependent on the results of these studies, further work may then go on to investigate other aspects of the human communication process with a view to designing avatars that can most effectively exploit the channels and parameters that prove most influential. In the long term, we would see this as informing design of a new style of Human Computer Interaction, modeled more closely on our natural human-to-human mode of interaction.

References

1. Morris, D., Collett, P., Marsh, P., O'Shaughnessy, M.: Gestures, their Origin and Distribution. Jonathan Cape Ltd., London (1979)
2. Knapp, M.L.: Nonverbal Communication in Human Interaction. 2nd edn. Holt, Rinehart and Winston Inc., New York, (1978)
3. Argyle, M.: Bodily Communication. 2nd edn. Methuen & Co. Inc., New York (1988)
4. Fabri, M., Hobbs, D.J.: What you see is what I mean: Virtual Encounters in Distance Learning Systems. In Proc. 4th Int. Conf. Network Entities. Leeds, UK (1998) 25–30
5. Slater, M., Wilbur S.: Speculations on the Role of Presence in Virtual Environments. Int. J. Presence. 6 (6). MIT Press (1997) 603–616
6. Benford, S.D., Bowers, J., Fahlén, L.E., Greenhalgh, C.M., Snowdon, D.: User Embodiment in Collaborative Virtual Environments. In Proc. Human Factors in Computing Systems (CHI'95). ACM Press (1995)

7. Godenschweger, F., Strothotte, T., Wagener, H.: Rendering Gestures as Line Drawings. Lecture Notes in AI, Vol. 1371. Springer Verlag, Berlin Heidelberg New York (1997)
8. Capin, T.K., Pandzic, I.S., Thalmann, N.M., Thalmann, D.: Realistic Avatars and Autonomous Virtual Humans in VLNET Networked Virtual Environments. In Earnshaw, R.A., Vince, J. (eds.): Virtual Worlds in the Internet. IEEE Computer Society Press (1998)
9. Pandzic, I.S., Kalra, P., Magnenat- Thalmann N., Thalmann D. (1994) Real-Time Facial Interaction. In Int. J. *Displays*, 15 (3)
10. Gerhard, M., Fabri, M., Moore, D.J., Hobbs, D.J.: Agents for Networked Virtual Learning Environments. In Proc. 5th Int. Conf. Network Entities. Krems, Austria (1999) (in press)
11. Johnson, W.L., Rickel, J., Stiles, R., & Munro, A.: Integrating Pedagogical Agents into Virtual Environments. In Int. J. Presence, 7(6). MIT Press (1998)
12. Ekman, P., Friesen, W.F.: Facial Action Coding System. Consulting Psych. Press (1978)
13. Fabri, M., Gerhard, M., Moore, D.J., Hobbs, D.J.: Cognitive Processes in Collaborative Virtual Environments. In Proc. Eurographics-UK. April 1999, Cambridge, UK (1999)
14. Dittrich, W.H., Troscianko, T., Lea, S.E.G., Morgan, D.: Perception of emotion from dynamic point-light displays presented in dance. In Perception (25). (1996) 727–738

Section 6: Multimodality

Communicative Rhythm in Gesture and Speech

Ipke Wachsmuth

Faculty of Technology, University of Bielefeld
D-33594 Bielefeld, Germany
ipke@techfak.uni-bielefeld.de

Abstract. Led by the fundamental role that rhythms apparently play in speech and gestural communication among humans, this study was undertaken to substantiate a biologically motivated model for synchronizing speech and gesture input in human computer interaction. Our approach presents a novel method which conceptualizes a multimodal user interface on the basis of timed agent systems. We use multiple agents for the purpose of polling presemantic information from different sensory channels (speech and hand gestures) and integrating them to multimodal data structures that can be processed by an application system which is again based on agent systems. This article motivates and presents technical work which exploits rhythmic patterns in the development of biologically and cognitively motivated mediator systems between humans and machines.

1 Introduction

Gesture and speech are the corner stones in natural human communication. Not surprisingly, they are each paid considerable attention in human-machine communication. It is apparent that advanced multimedia applications could greatly benefit from multimodal user interfaces integrating gesture and speech. Nevertheless, their realization faces obstacles for which research solutions to date have barely been proposed. The multimodal utterings of a user have to be registered via separate channels, as concurrent speech and gesture percepts. These channels have different time delays, that is, information from signal preprocessing is distributed in time. In order to process gesture and speech in their semantic connection, their temporal correspondence must first be reconstructed.

Observations in diverse research areas suggest that human communicational behavior is significantly rhythmic[1] in nature, for instance, in the way how spoken syllables and words are grouped together in time (speech rhythm) or how they are accompanied by body movements, i.e. gestures[2]. In theoretic and practical

---

[1] **Rhythm:** Following Martin [12] we define "rhythm" to mean relative timing between adjacent and nonadjacent elements in a behavior sequence, i.e., the locus of each element along the time line is determined relative to the locus of all other elements in the sequence.

[2] **Gesture:** For the purpose of this paper it is sufficient to understand "gestures" as body movements which convey information that is in some way meaningful to a recipient.

A. Braffort et al. (Eds.): GW'99, LNAI 1739, pp. 277–289, 1999.

approaches attempting to mimic natural communication patterns in human-computer interaction, rhythmic organization has so far played a non-existent role. This paper takes a stance that rhythmic patterns[3] provide a useful mechanism in the establishment of intra-individual and inter-individual coordination of multimodal utterances. Based on a notion of timed agent systems, an operational model is proposed which is stimulated by findings from empirical research and which was explored in multimodal perception and integration of concurrent modalities, in particular, speech and hand gestures.

In the next section, we discuss representative findings from empirical research that substantiate the function and role of rhythm as it pertains to human communication. We then argue, in Sect. 3, that the idea of rhythmic organization should be a good starting point to deal with some problems of multimodal interfaces for accepting open input. The original contribution of the article lies in conceptualizing an agent-based model, described in Part 4, that accounts for some of the empirical findings and makes them available for technical solutions. A multimodal input agency is described which builds on rhythmic patterns and which served as a framework for conceptualizing a human-computer interface. Results and further prospects are discussed in Part 5. In the age of information society, rhythms might also be a more general paradigm for human machine communication, and we conclude with a brief vision of this aspect.

2   Rhythm in Human-Human Communication

Various findings from psychological and phonetics research have revealed forms of rhythmic synchronization in human communicational behavior, with respect to both the production and the perception of utterances. Like the coordination of rhythmic limb movement (for a review, cf. [21]), speech production and gesturing requires the coordination of a huge number of disparate biological components. When a person speaks, her arms, fingers, and head move in a structured temporal organization (self-synchrony), which was found to be synchronized across multiple levels [4]. The so-called gesture stroke is often marked by a sudden stop which is closely coupled to spoken words. Particularly for stress-timed languages[4], when spoken fluently, temporal regularities are observed between stressed syllables and

---

[3] **Rhythmic patterns** are event sequences in which some elements are marked from others (accented); the accents recur with some regularity, regardless of tempo (fast, slow) or tempo changes (accelerate, retard) within the pattern. Since rhythmic patterns have a time trajectory that can be tracked without continuous monitoring, perception of initial elements in a pattern allows later elements to be anticipated in real time; cf. [12], [13].

[4] **Stress-timed language**: In general phonetics, it is assumed that "stress-timed" languages like English, German, and Danish tend to have a relatively constant duration of stress groups, independent of the actual number of phones or syllables involved in these groups. Thus, the time duration between the capitalized syllables in e.g. (a) "the BUS to GIF" and (b) "the BUSes to VerSAILLES" may be expected to be approximately the same when spoken by the same speaker under the same external conditions; cf. [3].

accompanying gesture strokes. They are more clear for pointing gestures/deictics [17], whereas gestural beats and verbal stress are not synchronized in a strict rhythmic sense [16]. Furthermore, it was found that the rhythm in a speaker's utterances is readily picked up by the hearer (interactional synchrony), in that the body of a listener, within short latency following sound onset, entrains to the articulatory structure of a speaker's speech [4]; there may even be interpersonal gestural rhythm [16].

Under constrained conditions, Cummins and Port [6] found a metrical 'foot' to be a salient unit in the production of speech for native English speakers. Quasi-rhythmical timing phenomena in unconstrained speech production (text reading, mostly Swedish) are reported by Fant and Kruckenberg [7]: An average of interstress intervals[5] of the order of 500 ms (milliseconds) appears to function as a basic metrical reference quantum for the timing of speaking pause duration, and quantal rhythmic sub-units of the metrical foot are suggested by average durations of stressed syllables, unstressed syllables and phoneme segments of the order of 250 ms, 125 ms and 62.5 ms. The tempo and coherence of rhythmic patterns is speaker-specific; and average segment durations within a phrase are influenced by the density of content words and thus are not entirely "on foot". Similarly, Broensted and Madsen [3] have found intra-speaker variabilities in speech rates of English and Danish speakers due to time equalization of stress groups and utterances.

As for perception, Martin [12]; [13] observed that rhythmic and segmental aspects of speech are not perceived independently in that segmentation is guided by rhythmic expectancy. Temporal phenomena were identified by Pöppel [20] on two significant time scales. Indication was found for a high-frequency processing system that generates discrete time quanta of 30 ms duration, and a low-frequency processing system that sets up functional states of ~ 3 s. Evidence for the high-frequency processing systems comes, in part, from studies on temporal order thresholds: Independent of sensory modality, distinct events require a minimum of 30 ms to be perceived as sucessive. The low-frequency mechanism binds successive events of up to 3 s into perceptual units. Support for such a binding operation comes from studies on the temporal reproduction of stimuli with different duration; temporal integration for intervals up to 2–3 s has also been observed with movement control and with the temporal segmentation of spontaneous speech. This integration is viewed to be automatic and presemantic in that the temporal limit is not determined by what is being processed.

Explanations found by the above-mentioned researchers agree in the observation that communicative rhythm may be seen as a coordinative strategy which enhances the effectiveness of speaker-listener entrainment. By expectable periodicities, rhythm seems to provide anticipations which help listeners perform segmentation of the acoustic signal and synchronize parts of speech with accompanying gesture. That is, the listener is apparently able to impose a temporal,

---

[5] **Interstress interval**: the time measured from the onset of the vowel in a stressed syllable to the onset of a vowel in the next stressed syllable, excluding those interrupted by a syntactic boundary.

'time window'-like structure in the perception of utterances which aids in the grouping and integration of the information transmitted. A specific universal integration mechanism is suggested by the Pöppel [20] studies: Intervals of up to 3s can be mentally preserved, or grasped as a unit. This is particularly true for cross-connections among the different sensory modalities, and this temporal integration is viewed as a general principle of the neuro-cognitive machinery.

3   Rhythm in Human-Machine Communication

As was argued above, there is evidence that communication among humans is strikingly rhythmic in nature. When this is true, then this observation should also be relevant in human-machine communication. For instance, Martin [13] has suggested that computational models of speech perception by humans should incorporate a *rhythmic expectancy component* which, starting from utterance onset, extrapolates ahead within the constraints supplied by the current information. In human-machine communication such approaches to mimic biological communication patterns have yet to be attempted.

At the same time the call for multimodal user interfaces, like interfaces that combine the input modalities of speech and gesture in a computer application, requires a more explicit understanding of how these modalities are perceived and integrated. Multimodal input facilities are crucial for a more natural and effective human-computer interaction where information of one modality can serve to disambiguate information conveyed by another modality [14]. Building multimodal input systems requires, on the one hand, the processing of single modalities and, on the other hand, the integration of multiple modalities [5]. To enable a technical system to coordinate and integrate perceived speech and gestures in their natural flow, two problems have to be solved [23]:

The segmentation problem: Given that the system is to process open input, how is the right chunk of information determined that the system takes in for processing at a time? How are consecutive chunks linked together?

The correspondence problem: Given that the system is to integrate information from multiple modalities, how does it determine cross-references, i.e., which information from one modality complements information from another modality?

To date, research solutions have barely been proposed how to reconstruct a user's multimodal utterings, which are registered on separate channels and distributed in time, in their natural temporal connection. Early attempts to realize a multimodal input system are the PUT-THAT-THERE system [1] and CUBRICON [18]. These systems are restricted to analyze speech and gestural input sequentially, and they do not allow gestural input in a natural form but, rather, as static pointing direction. More recent systems, e.g. [9]; [2]; [19], allow the parallel processing of two or more modalities. Nevertheless these approaches do not support what is called open input, i.e. instructing a system without defining where an instruction starts or ends, as well as the resolution of redundancies or inconsistencies between pieces of information of different modalities.

The observations in the previous section suggest that the analysis of communicative rhythm could be used to improve technical mediator systems between humans and machines. By exploiting segmentation cues, such as gesture stroke and stress beat in speech, the communicative rhythm could be reproduced, and possibly anticipated on, by the system. It could help to impose time windows for signal segmentation and determine correspondence of temporally distributed speech and gesture percepts which precede semantic analysis of multimodal information.

4   A Multimodal Interface Based on Timed Agents

In a first technical approach we have employed the idea of communicative rhythm to determine how spoken words and hand pointing gestures belong together. For a preview, the multimodal input stream is segmented in time windows of equal duration, starting from utterance onset in one modality. Input data from multiple modalities registered within one time cycle are considered as belonging to the same instruction segment, and cross-references are resolved by establishing correspondence between gesture percepts and linguistic units registered within a time cycle. As this will not always work, time-cycle-overspanning integration needs also be considered. These ideas are in the first place motivated by the above-mentioned findings on temporal perception in humans [20] and earlier ideas about rhythmic expectancy in speech perception [13].

4.1   Materials and Methods

The setting of our work is communicating with virtual environments, i.e., computer-graphics-based three-dimensional scenes which can be changed interactively by user interventions. The study reported here was carried out in the VIENA project [24] where the prototypical application example is the design of a virtual office environment. The VIENA system can process instructions from a user to execute alterations of the scene by means of an agent-based interface. Instructions can be transmitted by spoken natural language and by pointing gestures which are issued via a simple Nintendo data glove. In this study we have used a Dragon Dictate Version 1.2b speech recognizer which processes (speaker-dependent) isolated words. An instruction is spoken as a sequence of words:

put | <gesture> this | computer | on | <gesture> that | table

where the sound onsets of consecutive words follow each other by approx. 600 ms. Pointing gestures are issued, at about the time of the spoken "this" or "that", by glove-pointing at one of the displayed objects. A glimpse of the environment that was used in this study can be obtained from Fig. 1.

As the principal method to register and process information perceived from different sensory channels, we use a processing model that realizes distributed functionalities by the interplay of multiple software agents. The single agent is an autonomous computational process that communicates and cooperates with

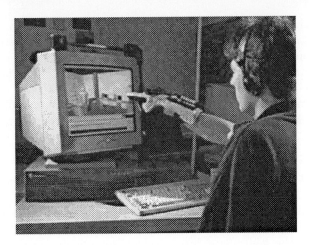

Fig. 1. Instructing the VIENA system by combined speech and gesture input

other agents based on a variant of the contract-net protocol [25]. A system of such agents, termed "agency", realizes a decentral processing of information. The core of the VIENA agency (cf. Fig. 2) consists of a number of agents that take part in mediating a user's instruction to change the scene in color and spatial layout. Typically, the functionality of each single agent is achieved in a sense-compute-act cycle, i.e., **sense** input message data, **compute** function, **act** by sending resulting messages to other agents, or to effectors like the graphics system.

The basic model of agent performance is event-driven, that is, there are no temporal constraints as to when a cycle is completed. However, in the context of integrating modalities from different sensors, temporal processing patterns become also relevant and especially so when taking into account a close coupling of speech and gesture input. Led by this observation, we have extended the basic agent model to be *timed*. To this end, we have provided for a temporal buffer for sensed information and, besides event-driven control, temporal constraints by way of time-cycle-driven patterns of processing, supporting a low-frequency "rhythmic" segmentation procedure.

In our first approach, time cycles spanning a **sense-buffer-compute-act** sequence executed by the single agents have a fixed duration which can be varied for experiments. The multimodal input agency described below is comprised by a number of agents dedicated to (1) sensory and linguistic input analysis and (2) the coordination and processing of multimodal input information.

4.2   Multimodal Input Agency

To address the aspects of open input and correspondence in multimodal instructions, we have developed a multimodal input agency, as shown in the right part of Fig. 2. It is comprised by a set of timed listener agents which record, analyze,

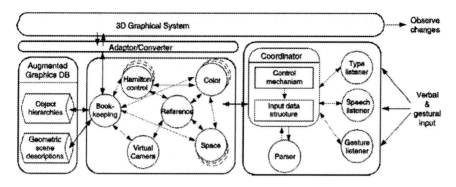

Fig. 2. VIENA agent interface with mediators (left) and multimodal input agency (right)

and elaborate input information from different sensory channels, and a coordinator mechanism, also realized as a timed agent system, which integrates analyzed sensory information. This information is then passed on to the application system (mediating agency) shown in the left part of Fig. 2.

The input agency consists of a set of modality-specific input listeners, a parser for linguistic analysis, and a coordinator. Three listener agents, i.e., a speech listener, a type listener, and a gesture listener, track and analyze sensor data from the microphone, the keyboard, and the data glove, respectively. Assisted by the parser, the coordinator analyzes and integrates the inputs received from the listeners and generates an internal task description that is posted to mediator agents. The mediating agency determines the according changes in the virtual environment and updates the scene visualization. Multimodal instructions are issued by speaking to the microphone and using the glove for pointing. Typewritten input can be used in unimodal (verbal) instructions.

The input agency performs a time- and event-driven routine to integrate multiple (speech and gesture) modalities. Whereas input agents are "listening" for input events in short polling cycles of 100 ms, the coordinator agent processes information in fixed time cycles of a longer periodicity of 2 s. The actual values were found by experiments with the VIENA system which have shown that time cycles with durations of 100 ms and 2 s, resp., work best for the single-word recognition system and glove-based gesture recognizer used in the study. The 100 ms rhythm was determined by the fact that the glove sends a maximum of 10 data packets per second; thus a higher-frequency polling would cause unnecessary communication overhead.

The 2 s integration rhythm was determined in experiments probing the overall computational cost of the VIENA system, as measured from the onset of a speech instruction to the output of a new scene visualization while varying the length of the integration cycle time by 1-s increments. In these experiments we used instructions of different lengths, i.e. a 4-word, a 7-word, and a 10-word instruction. The sound onsets of consecutive words were computer-controlled to follow each other by 600 ms, independent of whether one-, two-, or four-syllable words were spoken in. That is, speech input for the 4, 7, 10-word sentences took a bit more than 1800, 3600, and 5400 ms, respectively. The following, unimodal, spoken instructions were used ("saturn" and "andromeda" are names that refer to the two computers shown on the screen in Fig. 1):

move | the | chair | left
put | the | palmtree | between | saturn | and | andromeda
put | the | palmtree | between | the | back | desk | and | the | bowl

The integration process realized in the input agency is a combination of time and event-driven computations. In the following sections we explain in more detail how the segmentation and the correspondence problem (cf. Sect. 3) are treated in the VIENA multimodal input agency. In full detail the method is described in [11].

4.3   Open Input Segmentation: The Tri-state Rhythm Model

The basic approach to segment the multimodal input stream is to register input events from the different modalities in time cycles imposed by the coordinator agent, resulting in a tri-state rhythm model which is illustrated in Fig. 3. As input data within one time cycle is considered as belonging to the same instruction segment, the coordinator agent, accordingly, buffers information received from the speech and gesture listeners, to integrate them when a cycle is completed (cf. Sect. 4.4).

The first time cycle (z1) starts at signal onset when the user inputs a (verbal or gestural) instruction, resulting in a first input event (e1 at time te1). This causes the coordinator to reach a state "swing" which continues as long as signals are received on one of the listener channels, modeling a rhythmic expectancy. The coordinator subsides swinging when no further input event occurs within a

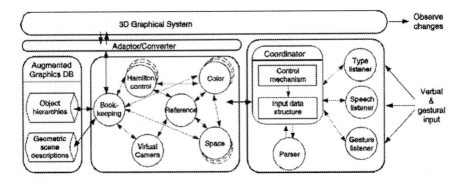

Fig. 3. Tri-state rhythm model (swing-subside-wait); each cycle in state "swing" or "subside" timed equally

full cycle. The "subside" state changes to "wait" once that k, e.g. 2, event-free cycles are recognized or, when triggered by a new event, returns to "swing". The "wait" state is of indefinite time; it will change to the "swing" state again upon receiving a new input event.

The time- and event-driven integration method is interwoven with the segmentation process. It consists of a cyclical four-step process comprised by functions `sense`, `buffer`, `compute`, and `act`. Whereas `sense` and `buffer` are continued until the current time cycle is completed, `compute` and `act` are executed at the end of each time cycle. The function `sense` allows that input events sent by the listeners are received as messages, whereas the function `buffer` extracts relevant message information and collects them in an input data structure which is organized in time cycles. The coordinator agent performs these two steps as long as the current time cycle has not elapsed. At the end of a time cycle, the function `compute` interprets the multimodal information stored in the input data structure. Afterwards, the function `act` determines appropriate agents in the mediator agency and posts the corresponding tasks to them.

4.4   Correspondence in Multimodal Integration

The interpretation function `compute` resolves cross-references between verbal and gestural information in the input data structure and produces an overall task description that corresponds to the multimodal input of the user. Two cases are distinguished: (1) in the *time-cycle-internal interpretation*, information of just the most recent time cycle is used; (2) in the *time-cycle-overspanning interpretation*, data of the last n time cycles is used. Having determined what kind of interpretation has to be performed, the coordinator analyzes the speech and gesture modality separately and merges information of the different modalities in a multi-step evaluation procedure that considers both temporal and linguistic features to compute the most appropriate cross-references. Then it disambiguates all kinds of references with the help of specific agents in the mediator agency, and checks whether or not the resulting instruction is complete with respect to domain-dependent requirements. If incomplete, the coordinator waits for information that expectedly would occur within the next time cycles or, when cycling has subsided, it presents the user with his/her incomplete instruction for editing.

The actual integration in the `compute` phase is done by establishing correspondence between gesture percepts and so-called gesture places within integration intervals. *Gesture places* are time-stamped information slots, determined in spoken-language analysis, which formalize expectations about events that provide missing object or direction specifications from the gesture channel. Potential gesture places are specifications of reference objects or locations derived from speech input. The valuation of gesture places is calculated by the heuristics "the more ambiguous a reference described in the verbal instruction, the higher the valuation of a gesture place." If there are two gesture places for only one gesture percept, resolution of correspondence between cross-modal events is led by their closeness in time and by comparing ambiguity values associated with speech sections; e.g., "the chair" is less ambiguous (with respect to reference) than the deictical "there" in the sentence "put the chair there." An example where closeness in time is relevant is the instruction "put this computer on that table" if only one gesture percept is available (presupposing that one indexical is clear from previous context). In this case closeness in time would be indicative in that one of the pairs "¡gesture¿ this" or "¡gesture¿ that" would have higher weight. Further examples for possible combinations of speech and gesture inputs to disambiguate objects and locations are following:

> put | <gesture> this | computer | on | the | blue | table
> move | <gesture> that | to | the |left
> make | <gesture> this | chair |green
> put | <gesture> this | thing | <gesture¿ there
> put | the | bowl | between | <gesture> this | and | <gesture> that | computer

Segmentation of multimodal input streams is thus realized in a way that open input is possible where the start and end of instructions need not be defined. Augmented by a multi-step fusion mechanism, redundancies and inconsistencies in the input stream can be handled comfortably to establish correspondence in multimodal integration.

5   Discussion and Further Prospects

This exploratory study was carried out in the context of research toward advanced human-computer interfaces and with the rationale to establish more natural forms of multimodal human machine communication. In detail we have desribed a method that is based on processing patterns which coordinate different input modalities in rhythmic time cycles. Based on the novel notion of timed agents realizing rhythmic mechanisms in temporal perception, we were able to

- develop a theoretical model of temporal integration of multiple input modalities
- implement the model in a prototype application and show that it is operational
- gain further insights into advantages of the 'right' rhythm by exploring the running model in experiments

In our first experiments we have used data-glove pointing and a simple word-by-word speech recognizer, allowing only very crude speech rhythm. Nevertheless, the very fact that the production as well as the technical perception of multimodal user utterings was rhythmically constrained in time was decisive for the comparably simple solution of multimodal integration. Realizing rhythmic expectancy, the tri-state segmentation model sustains equal temporal constraints beyond the current portion of signal transmitted and aids in the processing of a steady input stream. Even when our method is still far from mimicking communicative rhythm more succintly, we feel that some progress was made with respect to open input segmentation and the correspondence problem. There is reason to believe that these ideas carry further even when more obstacles have to be overcome.

The realization of a more elaborated system prototype, reaching from recognition of complex gestures over (continuous) speech-and-gesture integration to linkage with a target application of virtual prototyping, is now the goal of the SGIM project (Speech and Gesture Interfaces for Multimedia) in Bielefeld. We have taken steps to refine our basic approach to the demands of a more natural multimodal interaction. The illustrations in Fig. 4, taken from the SGIM interaction scenario, convey that work is underway to realize more fluent speaking and gesturing in multimodal input. Segmentation cues are available from speech as well as gestural rhythm; we were able to make use of some of them in first instances. Work is underway to further build on these ideas [22]. We have also begun to research the issue of natural timing of generative gesture by making an articulated figure able to produce it in real time [10].

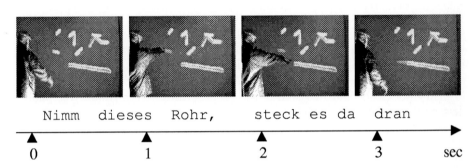

Nimm   dieses   Rohr,   steck es da   dran

0   1   2   3   sec

Fig. 4. Natural speech and gesture input in a virtual construction scenario ("Take this pipe, mount it there-to")

An issue for future work is how the system could be enabled to entrain to the communicative rhythm exhibited by the individual user. We have successfully completed first experiments which support the idea that adaptive oscillators [15] could provide a method to adjust the so far equal-sized integration time windows in reasonably short latency, i.e., within about 1–2 s. This adjustment might allow to mimic a stretching or shrinking of segmentation time windows (like musical ritardando or accelerando, resp.) by responding to the tempo of user utterances while preserving the hierarchical temporal structure of integration intervals. Of further interest in our research will be the .5 s beat that seems to mark a grid on which accented elements (e.g., stressed syllables) are likely to occur [8]. We hope to get insights as to how a low frequency segmentation mechanism, as used in the VIENA study, goes together with rhythm patterns on a finer-grained time scale.

Finally, I would like to take the chance to express my vision of an idea that I feel could be beneficial for future information society, namely, "rhythmic" systems. Whereas computer scientists and engineers have been mainly concerned with making throughput cycles of interactive applications faster, little thought was given to the question if speed is the only or most important issue. Given a choice of awaiting a system response as fast as possible, but at indeterminate time, or at *anticipatory* time, many users might prefer the second over the first option. Thus it seems worthy to conceive systems that are 'rhythmic' in the sense that they produce their response to a user's query in expectable time, so the user is not as much 'soaked' in waiting for a system output. Needless to say, such a conception would require a still more profound understanding of the communicative rhythm that is natural and comfortable to a human. It does not seem totally off hand to pursue technical solutions achieving steady throughput cycles which neither stress patience nor impose uncomfortable haste on users, by meeting rhythmic expectancy as experienced natural by humans.

Acknowledgements

This work profits greatly from contributions of the members of the AI Group at the University of Bielefeld. In particular, Sect. 4 builds on the dissertation by Britta Lenzmann. Her assistance, as that of my research assistants and doctoral students Timo Sowa, Martin Fröhlich, Marc Latoschik, and Ulrich Nerlich are gratefully acknowledged. The VIENA project was in part supported by the Ministry of Science and Research of the Federal State North-Rhine-Westphalia under grant no. IVA3-107 007 93.

References

1. R.A. Bolt. "Put-That-There": Voice and gesture at the graphics interface. *Computer Graphics, 14*(3): 262–270, 1980.
2. E. Bos, C. Huls, & W. Claasen. EDWARD: Full integration of language and action in a multimodal user interface. *Int. Journal Human-Computer Studies, 40:* 473–495, 1994.
3. T. Broendsted & J.P. Madsen. Analysis of speaking rate variations in stress-timed languages. *Proceedings 5th European Conference on Speech Communication and Technology (EuroSpeech)*, pages 481–484, Rhodes 1997.
4. W.S. Condon, Communication: Rhythm and structure. In J. Evans & M. Clynes (Eds.): *Rhythm in Psychological, Linguistic and Musical Processes (pp. 55–77)*. Springfield, Ill.: Thomas, 1986.
5. J. Coutaz, L. Nigay, & D. Salber. Multimodality from the user and systems perspectives. In *Proceedings of the ERCIM-95 Workshop on Multimedia Multimodal User Interfaces*, 1995.
6. F. Cummins & R.F. Port. Rhythmic constraints on stress timing in English. *Journal of Phonetics 26:* 145–171, 1998.
7. G. Fant. & A. Kruckenberg. On the quantal nature of speech timing. *Proc. ICSLP 1996*, pp. 2044–2047, 1996.
8. J. Kien & A. Kemp. Is speech temporally segmented? Comparison with temporal segmentation in behavior. *Brain and Language 46:* 662–682, 1994.
9. D.B. Koons, C.J. Sparrell, & K.R. Thorisson. Integrating simultaneous input from speech, gaze, and hand gestures. In M.T. Maybury (Ed.): *Intelligent Multimedia Interfaces (pp. 257–276)*. AAAI Press/The MIT Press, Menlo Park, 1993.

10. S. Kopp & I. Wachsmuth. Natural timing in coverbal gesture of an articulated figure, Working notes, Workshop "Communicative Agents" at Autonomous Agents 1999, Seattle.

11. B. Lenzmann: *Benutzeradaptive und multimodale Interface-Agenten.* Dissertationen der Künstlichen Intelligenz, Bd. 184. Sankt Augustin: Infix, 1998.

12. J.G. Martin. Rhythmic (hierarchical) versus serial structure in speech and other behavior. *Psychological Review 79*(6): 487–509, 1972.

13. J.G. Martin. Rhythmic and segmental perception. *J. Acoust. Soc. Am. 65*(5): 1286–1297, 1979.

14. M.T. Maybury. Research in multimedia and multimodal parsing and generation. *Artificial Intelligence Review 9*(2–3): 103–127, 1995.

15. D. McAuley. Time as phase: A dynamical model of time perception. In *Proceedings of the Sixteenth Annual Meeting of the Cognitive Science Society,* pages 607–612, Hillsdale NJ: Lawrence Erlbaum Associates, 1994.

16. E. McClave. Gestural beats: The rhythm hypothesis. *Journal of Psycholinguistic Research 23*(1), 45–66, 1994.

17. D. McNeill. *Hand and Mind: What Gestures Reveal About Thought.* Chicago: University of Chicago Press, 1992.

18. J.G. Neal & S.C. Shapiro. Intelligent multi-media interface technology. In J.W. Sullivan and S.W. Tyler, editors, *Intelligent User Interfaces, pages 11–43.* ACM Press, New York, 1991.

19. L. Nigay & J. Coutaz. A generic platform for addressing the multimodal challenge. In *Proceedings of the Conference on Human Factors in Computing Systems (CHI-95),* pages 98–105, Reading: Addison-Wesley, 1995.

20. E. Pöppel. A hierarchical model of temporal perception. *Trends in Cognitive Science 1*(2), 56–61, 1997.

21. G. Schöner & J.A.S. Kelso. Dynamic pattern generation in behavioral and neural systems. *Science, 239:* 1513–1520, 1988.

22. T. Sowa, M. Fröhlich, & M.E. Latoschik, Temporal symbolic integration applied to a multimodal system using gestures and speech, *this volume.*

23. R.K. Srihari. Computational models for integrating linguistic and visual information: a survey. *Artificial Intelligence Review 8:* 349–369, 1995.

24. I. Wachsmuth & Y. Cao: Interactive graphics design with situated agents. In W. Strasser & F. Wahl (eds.): *Graphics and Robotics (pp. 73–85),* Springer, 1995.

25. M. Wooldridge & N.R. Jennings. Intelligent agents: Theory and practice. *Knowledge Engineering Review, 10*(2): 115–152, 1995.

Temporal Symbolic Integration Applied to a Multimodal System Using Gestures and Speech

Timo Sowa, Martin Fröhlich*, and Marc Erich Latoschik**

AG Wissensbasierte Systeme
Technische Fakultät, Universität Bielefeld
Postfach 100 131, D-33501 Bielefeld, Germany
{tsowa,martinf,marcl}@TechFak.Uni-Bielefeld.DE

Abstract. This paper presents a technical approach for temporal symbol integration aimed to be generally applicable in unimodal and multimodal user interfaces. It draws its strength from symbolic data representation and an underlying rule-based system, and is embedded in a multiagent system. The core method for temporal integration is motivated by findings from cognitive science research. We discuss its application for a gesture recognition task and speech-gesture integration in a Virtual Construction scenario. Finally an outlook of an empirical evaluation is given.

1 Introduction

Today's computer system users demand for interfaces which are easy to use and easy to learn. To cope with that demand, research in intelligent human-machine interfaces has become more important in the last few years. Therefore our group works to bridge the gap between the user and the machine through a mediating system which translates the user's input into commands for the machine and vice versa.

We focus on problems where command languages or WIMP (Windows, Icons, Mouse, and Pointing device) interfaces show their limitations most drastically, i.e. in interactive 3D computer graphics or Virtual Reality. It is desirable here to address a system in a natural manner, for example by allowing natural language and gestural utterances as input, because command languages are far too difficult to learn and to use. WIMP interfaces tend to overload the user with thousands of functions hidden in hierarchical menu structures. In contrast, it is a comparatively simple task for human beings to describe a 3D scene and to reference objects within that scene using gestures and speech.

While human utterances naturally consist of different modalities which are gathered by various sensor systems, we have to integrate the information from

* Scholarship granted by "Graduiertenkolleg Aufgabenorientierte Kommunikation" of the Deutsche Forschungsgemeinschaft (DFG)
** Supported by the Ministry of Science and Research (MWF) of the Federal State North Rhine-Westfalia in the framework of the collaborative effort "Virtual Knowledge Factory"

A. Braffort et al. (Eds.): GW'99, LNAI 1739, pp. 291–302, 1999.

those channels into one single utterance to interpret what the user does and what he says. To fulfill the integration task we propose a generic, easily adaptable approach, based on a hierarchical, symbolic data representation as introduced in [4]. In the processing stages from descriptive to semantic representation, background and context knowledge has to be used. In addition to that, based on cognitive findings (e.g. Pöppel [14], Ballard [1]), we propose a data model which is visualised as an extruded triangle as shown in Fig. 1.

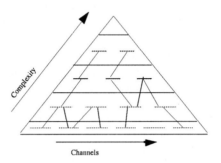

Fig. 1. Integration Hierarchy (further explanation see text), taken from [4]

Input data and model internal data can reach much vaster dimensions than in traditional interface techniques, hence it is a computational time consuming task. Therefore we use a distributed multi-agent system, in which agents are assigned to individual data sources to immediately analyze the incoming information.

This paper concentrates on the integration framework and its application. In Sec. 2, we describe the theoretical foundations of the integration framework and its implementation. In Sec. 3, we present an example implementation of a gesture recognizing multi-agent system based on the framework. In Sec. 4, we describe its general application in a complex system for Virtual Construction and assembly. Finally an outlook of an empirical evaluation is given in Sec. 5.

2   Integration Framework

2.1   Existing Approaches

Although there is no standardized mechanism for multimodal integration, most existing approaches are built on temporal coincidence. Following this basic principle, all fragments of utterance from different modalities are time-stamped and considered for integration if they are close enough in time. Nigay and Coutaz [13], for example, implemented a generic framework for multimodal temporal integration. They distinguish between three fusion steps in a data structure called *melting pot*, where the first two levels are based on temporal neighbourhood. Mircotemporal fusion combines data with nearly the "same" timestamp, macrotemporal fusion is used in case of temporal proximity, whereas contextual fusion is time-independent and merges data according to semantic constraints. The melting pot itself is a data structure which consists of entries that make up the instruction for the application system. Johnston et al. [7] evaluate temporal proximity with a time window of 3 to 4 seconds. Their system combines pen-gestures and speech input for a map-based application. Besides the introduction of a time window they also consider the precedence of gesture over speech, which was ascertained in an empirical study. They use this knowledge to refine the integration mechanism.

A system for the recognition and integration of coverbal depictive gestures with speech (ICONIC) is presented by Sparrell et al. [16]. In their approach the gesture representation is based on features, computed from the raw data of the cyber-glove and position tracker operating in 3D-space. In this system integration is speech-driven: If a word or phrase can be augmented by a gesture, the interpreter searches for suitable segments in the gesture stream. A segment matches if its stroke phase (the expressive part of a gesture) is temporally close to the word or phrase under consideration.

All proposals and systems have in common that integration of multimodal data is performed on the top-level within a fixed temporal window [2]. Since integration steps can be found on many levels of the integration triangle (Fig. 1), we developed a method that is applicable to many tasks. We use a common representation scheme for the different types of data and a rule-based integration mechanism. Our method is implemented in a program that we call *Integrator Agent*.

2.2 Symbolic Representation and Symbol Hierarchies

In our approach a symbolic data representation is used to apply common processes of integration in all levels of the hierarchy.

The symbols are organized in a conceptual hierarchy according to the superordinate relations between them. This allows an efficient and short notation, because we can use superconcepts for the expression of generally applicable knowledge. Since we deal with time-critical and often uncertain input, each symbol is augmented by a time interval, which represents the lapse of time of the symbol's validity, and a confidence value, which can be used to model vague concepts and uncertainty. Any kind of symbol shares these properties, so we created a common superconcept, called *Hypothesis*. Specialized subconcepts of *Hypothesis* may be, for example, hypotheses about the speech input, hypotheses about gestures and their features, or hypotheses about fixations of an object recorded with an eye-tracker.

2.3 Rule-Based Integration

Background knowledge about the relationship of different symbols is used in the step of integration which is henceforth called *integration knowledge*. To provide a flexible framework for integration tasks, we have chosen a rule-based approach to express integration knowledge. Following we give a simple natural language example for such a rule:

> *If the index finger is stretched, and if all other fingers are rolled (pointing handshape) and if the hand simultaneously is far away from the body, then we have a pointing gesture.*

Production systems are an appropriate means to cope with such kinds of rules. Their core component consists of an inference engine, that matches preconditions of a rule-set against the knowledge that is currently present in memory and executes the consequences (the rule "fires"). The rule in our example will fire if two symbols for "pointing handshape" and "far away from body" are present in memory and their temporal relation (i.e. cooccurrence) is fulfilled. After execution, a new symbol for "pointing gesture" is present in the memory. It may be used as a command for an application or as a basis for further integration steps, if "pointing gesture" is one of the preconditions for another rule.

Using a rule-based system supports modularity since every rule is an encapsulated piece of knowledge and it shortens develop-and-test cycles. This enables the system designer to experience with different rules and to think about the system design on the task-level rather than on the implementation level. A drawback is the complexity in the execution stage. Since many of the symbols satisfy rule preconditions, the number of rule executions increases with the number of symbols. This leads to an exponential complexity for the execution cycle, usually seen as a drawback per se. What we have done to alleviate this effect will be discussed in the next part.

2.4   Alleviating Complexity by Using Time Windows

Experimental results from cognitive psychology and linguistics suggest that temporal integration in the human brain obeys limitations as a matter of principle. Pöppel [14] emphasizes, for example, that a fusion of successive states of consciousness is possible up to a threshold of about three seconds. This period of time characterizes the subjective presence. McNeill [12] proposes the concept of "growth points" that represent the semantic content of an utterance from which gestures and speech develop in close relation. He suggests a temporal displacement of approximately one or two seconds between two successive semantical units. Similarly, Ballard [1] presents an organization of human computation into temporal bands of 10 seconds for complex tasks, 2 seconds for simple tasks, 300 ms for physical acts, etc. Different tasks and acts – like moving the eyes or saying a sentence – show a tightly constrained execution time.

Based on these results, we can conclude that there is no need to keep each symbol forever. Obviously the importance of a symbol decreases with time and the system can remove the symbol if the timespan from assertion time until "now" exceeds a certain threshold. For the analysis of the current input, it makes no difference if the user has stretched his index finger five seconds ago. The timespan of memorizing symbols depends on their degree of *semantic content*. More complex symbols have a larger temporal scope. Therefore the system enables the designer to adjust the size of the integration window and to build a hierarchy of Integrator Agents with different temporal windows. Fig. 2 shows the general structure of an Integrator Agent. The introduction of a limited temporal

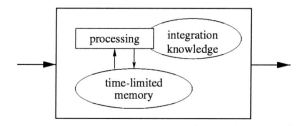

Fig. 2. Integrator Agent: general structure

integration helps to alleviate the effects of the exponential complexity during the execution cycle. Since nonrelevant symbols are removed from memory, they are not considered for pattern-matching anymore. Additionally, the symbols with high semantic content tend to be sparse compared with low-level symbols. This compensates the larger temporal window of a high-level Integrator.

2.5 Implementation

The implementation of the Integrator Agency is based on *CLIPS (C Language Integrated Production System)*, which is an expert system tool developed by the Technology Branch of the NASA/Lyndon B. Johnson Space Center since 1986. The core component of CLIPS is a production system that directly supports knowledge representation with independent rules, and pattern-matching of the rule preconditions with the RETE algorithm. In addition, conceptual hierarchies can be modeled within the CLIPS language, since it contains an object-oriented part, called *COOL (CLIPS Object Oriented Language)*. COOL-classes are used to represent the concepts, whereas the concrete symbols are represented with instances of COOL-classes. The representation of the user, for example, stretching his index finger may be an instance of the class `IndexStretched`. Its CLIPS-notation may look like this:

```
(ins42 of IndexStretched (begin-timestamp 764538752 909821234)
                         (end-timestamp 764538753 870426876)
                         (confidence 0.7))
```

In this case, `IndexStreched` is a subclass of `Hypothesis`, and `ins42` is one concrete instance of this class. The components `begin-timestamp`, `end-timestamp` and `confidence` are inherited from `Hypothesis`. Of course a class may be augmented with additional components.

We embedded the CLIPS functionality in a C++ class `Integrator` and added the temporal limitation of the integration window. Furthermore we provided methods to cope with rhythmical information like beats, that originate from independent sources. These can be used as a basis for future developements. As a prototypical example we implemented a gesture segmentation cue based on hand tension [5] to get a first impression of the beat/rhythm guided integration.

The Integrator itself was embedded in a further C++ class `IntegratorAgent` which enables the program to communicate with other distributed agents. These agents may be specialized recognizers that process input data from physical devices, they may be other Integrator Agents with another time window, or, finally, the application itself.

3   Gesture Recognition Using HamNoSys

The framework described above can be used for integrating atomic-gesture symbols to complex-gesture symbols (unimodal integration), or for integrating symbols from different data sources, i.e. complex-gesture symbols and symbols delivered by a speech sub-system (multimodal integration). In this section we present an example of unimodal integration for gesture recognition.

To recognize gestures of the upper limbs we use a system [4] that encodes sensor features taken from 6 degree of freedom position sensors and data gloves into symbols. The set of symbols is a formalized subset (HNS') of the Hamburg Notation System (HamNoSys) [15] which encodes the *form*, not the meaning of a gesture. The features used in this HNS' notation are the same features used in the recognition process.

In this section we will not deal with the interpretation of a gesture, that is left to higher levels of the integration hierarchy.

Both HamNoSys and HNS' represent postures and motions of the upper limbs by a special set of characters. For example the diver's "all clear" gesture (also interpretable as a very rude one in different context) is encoded "∂rₒ⊽" and a "push away" or "stop here" gesture is encoded "ᙏₐₒ±", as shown in Fig. 3.

Fig. 3. Gesture and its HamNoSys encoding: ᙏₐₒ±

Each noteworthy feature of the represented gesture is encoded in a subset of semantically and therefore syntactically disjunct symbols. Groups – which can be seen as words – of such symbols, each taken from a different set, then encode a whole gesture.

If our recognizing agent [4] detects a feature set, it submits this HNS' represented hypothesis to the distributed Integrator Agency and an Integrator Agent will receive that message. After that, the integration process takes place as introduced above, with the additional knowledge of HNS"s syntax and semantic. The semantic of HNS' is defined by its semantic function, mapping HNS' words to their meaning, which is a subclass of class **Hypothesis** of the Integrator.

Besides a number of symmetry and grouping operators the feature focused here is the transition from one state (posture) to another one: $z_{pre}, z_{post} \in L :$ $z_{pre} \mapsto z_{post}$. This introduces a notation of concurrence (concatenation of symbols) and posteriority ($\mapsto$ operator). These temporal constrains are enforced by the temporal integration functions SEQUENCE and PARALLEL which operate inside the integration window only.

3.1   From Atomic-Gesture Symbols to Complex-Gesture Symbols

Every hypothesis used by an Integrator Agent is an instance of the **Hypothesis** class. The pattern-matching for the preconditions of the CLIPS rules checks if instances of certain classes are currently present in memory. The definition of the classes from a specific domain belongs to the integration knowledge, which is stored in a domain specific knowledge base.

For HNS' we derived the class **HNSHypothesis** from **Hypothesis** as the new base class of all subsequent classes. **HNSHypothesis** is augmented by a slot called **hand**, which indicates whether the dominant (usually right) or the subordinate hand is meant. The higher level symbols (hypotheses) are defined by a rule constructor using implementations of the PARALLEL and SEQUENCE operators (here using CLIPS Object Oriented Language, COOL), such as:

```
expression = method superclass {"(" expression ")"} | class
method     = <COOL method; yields instance of type "superclass">
superclass = <COOL class>
class      = <COOL class>

i.e.: Wave = PARALLEL Hypothesis LocStretched
             (SEQUENCE Hypothesis LocLeft LocRight)
```

Analyzing this structure, it is easy to see that this scheme can be cascaded to construct symbols of increasing levels of complexity. To limit the memory size and the message flow, we use a runtime task oriented top down symbol definition structure. That is, every agent located higher in the hierarchy informs its inferiors which symbols it can handle, and only those symbols are taken into account by the inferior agent and are reported back to it's superior. The evaluation of the gesture recognition system is currently in progress. We plan to use data from a series of experiments (see Sec. 5) to test the performance and recognition rates on a set of manually defined gestures.

4   Applications of the Integration Framework

In the previous sections we introduced a formal method to merge symbolic information, i.e. HNS' hypotheses about gesture events, resulting in combined and hence more complex gesture symbols and therefore gaining a higher level of abstraction.

As we pointed out, specific rules could be defined to implement relation tests between temporal properties of hypotheses. The described framework itself is not limited to only these tests, fundamentally any kind of integrative work could be done after defining the required relation tests and the resulting event(s). To use the already defined rules, it is favourable to adopt the system to areas that comprise a hierarchy of symbols and sub-symbols with a basic structure ordered according to the symbols' temporal appearance.

4.1   Exploring New Interaction Techniques

One primary goal of our work was to establish a system for a gesture detection task and to use it for the integration of gestures and speech. Considering a stand-alone gesture detection that could be used for an automatic sign-language recognizer, the usefulness seems obvious, for instance: to support disabled people or to operate systems in noisy industry environments. In order to further emphasize the importance of these new interface techniques we also have to take a look at areas where such interaction seems advantageous [19]. Dealing with this manner, one of our specific goals is the exploration of advanced human-computer interfaces in real operable systems.

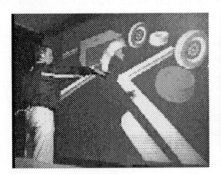

Fig. 4. A user – located in front of a large screen display – performs a selection and a rotation task of an object while interacting with the Virtual Construction application.

In the SGIM project (Speech an Gesture Interfaces for Multimedia) we investigate the benefits of multimodal input during the process of Virtual Construction [8]. Once a user is not bound to Cathode Ray Tube -centered workplaces, either using large screen displays – like we utilize in our specific setup – using Head Mounted Displays or when operating systems that lack any visual feedback, for example embedded systems in the household, interacting with the system becomes a burden when it is still based on common user interface devices: keyboard and mouse and their 3-D equivalents.

4.2   Gesture Detection in Virtual Construction

When the user is immersed in the virtual scene and surrounded by visualized objects, there is in fact a limited and well defined set of interaction elements that are required during this type of instructor/constructor setup [9]. To communicate changes of the actual scene, a primary step is to identify objects and locations in the virtual space. Deictic gestures, by means of pointing to objects [10], is a natural way how humans can refer to spatially arranged items around them.

The evaluation of a pointing gesture is separated into two single tasks. First of all, the qualitative analysis triggers the gesture event, meaning its temporal occurrence. In case the major concern is just the detection of a gesture, in other words to determine just the time of occurrence and the type of a gesture, nothing else is to be done. Contrary to that, our goal is the evaluation of deictic and mimetic gestures to manipulate a virtual scene, hence utilizing the quantitative aspects of gestures.

This is achieved in a following processing step. In the case of a pointing gesture detection, the system follows an imaginary beam rooted at the users' limb pointing. If an object lies in the beam path, an object-reference hypothesis containing this object and the describing information, like its color, is generated. Selecting objects is just the first step in interacting with the system. Further manipulations of objects, in terms of rotating or moving them, must be possible. Current work enhances the gesture detection modules in SGIM with quantitative methods for identifying these geometric transformations.

4.3   Multimodality: Combining Gestures and Speech

In SGIM the gesture interpretation is combined with a speech input and recognition system. Deictic gestures, for instance, are supported using verbal object descriptions. For the basic groundwork of this task we use a commercial (Dragon Dictate) as well as a non-commercial tool that is developed by the "Applied Computer Science" group of our department. Whereas the first one detects only single words, forcing the user to concentrate on a proper pronunciation and slow speech generation, the second one is capable of continuous, user-independent speech recognition [3], a vital requisite for an intuitive interface. Both tools deliver just plain text as output, which now is processed and further analyzed.

To achieve a satisfying and fast respond of our system, and in contrast to a full semantic language understanding approach, every detected word is classified to its affiliation as soon as it is recognized. In addition to name objects or to describe the types they belong to, objects attributes like color and position serve as a major source of referential information. Examples of typical speech fragments during this *selection task* encompass phrases like: *"take the upper red wheel"*, *"connect this thing with"* or *"put this front cover over there"*. The word-spotter module performs a word-match test with its internal database. In this pool all the different object- and typenames and their relations, as well as attributes and words for location references are stored. If a word matches e.g. the color *red*, we carry out two actions:

1. Search if the last word generated is an object-reference hypothesis; if so, further specialize it, and enrich it with the new content (color *red*).
2. If there is no pending object-reference hypothesis then generate a new one.

4.4   Using the Basic Framework During Temporal Integration

The resulting hypotheses generated from both, gesture and speech input streams, have the same level of abstraction and hence the same format. At this integration level, the source of the information only plays a minor role, namely to check if both modalities have produced at least one hypothesis to form a system command. Now both streams are equally taken into account and support their semantic interpretation with new potential: on the one hand, precarious information from one source, e.g. missing or wrong words during the speech recognition process, can be compensated for by the other source and vice versa. On the other hand, redundant information as well can be used to amplify the probability of a specific hypothesis. To achieve this, we are working on the application of our standard framework for this task.

The described method is obviously underspecified for a complete automatic integration pass. Therefore our current research focuses on the estimation and designation of adequate time intervals we have to take into account during the integration. Where are the start- and endpoints, and how long does it take the user for a complete coherent interaction? As described in section 2.3 and in [11], first attempts used fixed temporal frames with a certain length based on cognitive findings. Furthermore there are two other interesting temporal aspects of multimodal utterance.

The first one is to exploit segmentation cues like the measured hand-tension [5] during gesticulation; this parameter changes significantly between different gestures and, therefore, could be used as a hint to determine the beginning and end of an utterance. The evaluation of the hand-tension cue in a corpus of experimental data (see Sec. 5) shows first promising results. The second aspect does not assume a fixed temporal interval predetermined by the system designer but is based on a different pattern. It is noteworthy that in particular, human gesture and speech production seems to be linked closely together in a rhythmic fashion. Gesture strokes and speech timing as well as accentuation are closely correlated. Thus it seems to be another promising way to exploit rhythmic coherence for its usefulness in gesture and speech integration [18]. If we succeed in extracting the basic rhythmic pattern from user input, we are going to add adequate rules to the integration system. The basic framework developed so far is already capable of handling this type of information.

5   Experimental Evaluation

To evaluate our approach of solving the correspondence problem of multimodal integration (i.e. which gesture or feature belongs to which word or phrase) and to test our implementation, experimental data is needed. Although some insights from psychology and linguistics can be applied, experimental results in these fields mostly refer to narrative discourse. Additionally, experiments yielding quantitative results, for example about the timing of pointing gestures and corresponding words, are not appropriate for our 3D VR scenario. Hence, we collected empirical data about speech and gestures using a similar setting as used in our virtual construction application. In a first stage 37 subjects (26 male, 11 female, age 21-49 years) were told to name simple virtual objects on a wall-size display and to point at them. In a second stage the subjects had to describe more complex virtual objects. Handshape and hand/body positions were registered using data-gloves and 6DOF-trackers, speech was digitally recorded and the subjects were videotaped.

The evaluation of the data is currently in progress. Results concerning timing issues of speech and gesture will be used to refine the rules for integration. Results about the different shapes of gestures used will be utilized to improve the gesture recognition.

6   Conclusion

In this paper we presented a framework for unimodal and multimodal integration of time based symbolic information and gave some supplying examples. We showed how insights taken from cognitive science led us to a symbolic data representation and a rule-based system which we embedded in a multi-agent system. Furthermore we described how we applied our integration framework on the wider context of the SGIM project to illustrate its usability. In the future we will experiment with different time windows, add various segmentation cues, and try to exploit rhythmic coherence for the benefit of the integration task.

References

1. Dana H. Ballard. *An Introduction to Natural Computation*. MIT Press, Cambridge, MA, USA, 1997.
2. C. Benoit, J. C. Martin, C. Pelachaud, L. Schomaker and B. Suhm. Audio-Visual and Multimodal Speech Systems. In D. Gibbon (Ed.) *Handbook of Standards and Resources for Spoken Language Systems - Supplement Volume*, to appear.
3. G.A. Fink, C. Schillo, F. Kummert, and G. Sagerer. Incremental Speech Recognition for Multimodal Interfaces. In *IECON'98 - Proceedings of the 24th Annual Conference of the IEEE Industrial Electronics Society* [6], pages 2012–2017.
4. Martin Fröhlich and Ipke Wachsmuth. Gesture recognition of the upper limbs: From signal to symbol. In Wachsmuth and Fröhlich [17], pages 173–184.

5. Philip A. Harling and Alistair D. N. Edwards. Hand tension as a gesture segmentation cue. In Philip A. Harling and Alistair D. N. Edwards, editors, *Progress in Gestural Interaction: Proceedings of Gesture Workshop '96*, pages 75–87, Berlin Heidelberg New York, 1997. Dep. of Computer Science, University of York, Springer-Verlag.

6. IEEE. *IECON'98 - Proceedings of the 24th Annual Conference of the IEEE Industrial Electronics Society*, volume 4, Aachen, September 1998.

7. M. Johnston, P. R. Cohen, D. McGee, S. L. Oviatt, J. A. Pittman and I. Smith. Unification-based Multimodal Integration. *35th Annual Meeting of the Association for Computational Linguistics, Conference Proceedings*, pages 281–288, Madrid, 1997.

8. Bernhard Jung, Marc Erich Latoschik, and Ipke Wachsmuth. Knowledge based assembly simulation for virtual prototype modelling. In *IECON'98 - Proceedings of the 24th Annual Conference of the IEEE Industrial Electronics Society* [6], pages 2152–2157.

9. Marc Erich Latoschik, Martin Fröhlich, Bernhard Jung, and Ipke Wachsmuth. Utilize speech and gestures to realize natural interaction in a virtual environment. In *IECON'98 - Proceedings of the 24th Annual Conference of the IEEE Industrial Electronics Society* [6], pages 2028–2033.

10. Marc Erich Latoschik and Ipke Wachsmuth. Exploiting distant pointing gestures for object selection in a virtual environment. In Wachsmuth and Fröhlich [17], pages 185–196.

11. Britta Lenzmann. *Benutzeradaptive und multimodale Interface-Agenten*, volume 184 of *Dissertationen zur Künstlichen Intelligenz*. Dissertation, Technische Fakultät der Universität Bielefeld, Infix Verlag, Sankt Augustin, March 1998.

12. D. McNeill. *Hand and Mind: What Gestures Reveal about Thought*. University of Chicago Press, Chicago, 1992.

13. L. Nigay and J. Coutaz. A generic Platform for Addressing the Multimodal Challenge. *Human Factors in Computing Systems: CHI '95 Conference Proceedings*, pages 98–105, ACM Press, New York, 1995.

14. Ernst Pöppel. A hierarchical model of temporal perception. *Trends in Cognitive Sciences*, 1(2):56–61, May 1997.

15. Siegmund Prillwitz, Regina Leven, Heiko Zienert, Thomas Hanke, and Jan Henning. *HamNoSys Version 2.0: Hamburg Notation System for Sign Languages: An Introductory Guide*, volume 5 of *International Studies on Sign Language and Communication of the Deaf*, Signum Press, Hamburg, Germany, 1989.

16. C. J. Sparrel and D. B. Koons. Interpretation of Coverbal Depictive Gestures. *AAAI Spring Symposium Series*, pages 8–12. Stanford University, March 1994.

17. Ipke Wachsmuth and Martin Fröhlich, editors. *Gesture and Sign-Language in Human-Computer Interaction: Proceedings of Bielefeld Gesture Workshop 1997*, number 1371 in Lecture Notes in Artificial Intelligence, Berlin Heidelberg New York, Springer-Verlag, 1998.

18. Ipke Wachsmuth. Communicative Rhythm in Gesture and Speech. This volume.

19. Alan Daniel Wexelblat. Research challenges in gesture: Open issues and unsolved problems. In Wachsmuth and Fröhlich [17], pages 1–12.

A Multimodal Interface Framework
for Using Hand Gestures and Speech
in Virtual Environment Applications

Joseph J. LaViola Jr.

Brown University Site of the NSF Science and Technology Center
for Computer Graphics and Scientific Visualization
PO Box 1910, Providence, RI 02912 USA
jjl@cs.brown.edu
http://www.cs.brown.edu/people/jjl

Abstract. Recent approaches to providing users with a more natural
method of interacting with virtual environment applications have shown
that more than one mode of input can be both beneficial and intuitive as
a communication medium between humans and computer applications.
Hand gestures and speech appear to be two of the most logical since
users will typically be in environments that will have them immersed
in a virtual world with limited access to traditional input devices such
as the keyboard or the mouse. In this paper, we describe an ongoing
research project to develop multimodal interfaces that incorporate 3D
hand gestures and speech in virtual environments.

1 Introduction

Multimodal interaction provides many benefits over traditional unimodal metaphors such as WIMP (Windows, Icons, Menus, Point and Click) interfaces [16].
By providing more than one mode of input, human computer interaction is
augmented in two ways. First, users can interact more naturally and intuitively
with multiple modes of input since, in many cases, human to human interaction
occurs in this way. Second, a UI can achieve a better understanding of what
operation it needs to perform by providing it with multiple input streams. This
second point is especially important when dealing with input modes that do not
have perfect recognition accuracy such as speech and hand gesture recognition.

There are a number of different types of input mode combinations used in
multimodal interaction such as a stylus and puck [19], pen-based gestures and
voice [8], and eye tracking, lip reading, handwriting recognition, and face recognition [17]. The common thread between all of these systems is that the user's
hands interact with the application using 2D input. This is inappropriate for
virtual environment applications where the user is immersed in a 3D world and
must interact with 3D objects. Therefore, a more natural way to interact in a
virtual environment is to allow the user's hand to move freely in three dimensions
to perform the various tasks that the application requires. Adding speech to the

A. Braffort et al. (Eds.): GW'99, LNAI 1739, pp. 303–314, 1999.

interface lets the user interact with the virtual environment in a similar manner to the way humans communicate with other humans. Incorporating speech into the interface also provides the user with the benefits of multimodal interaction.

This paper describes an ongoing research project to develop multimodal interfaces using 3D hand gestures and speech for virtual environment applications. It describes our initial interface framework and two preliminary applications currently being developed. It addresses the previous work in developing multimodal frameworks with specific interest in the mode integration schemes used. It then provides a discussion of the hardware configuration and software architecture for our framework. Early stages of a scientific visualization and 3D interior design layout application are described followed by a discussion of future plans for the project and a conclusion.

2   Previous Work

The use of a multimodal interface that integrates hand gesture and voice can be traced back to Bolt's "Put That There" system [3]. This system used a pointing hand posture and voice commands to create, manipulate, and edit simple 2D primitives such as squares and circles in a Cave-like [9] environment. Bolt improved his earlier work in 1992 with a multimodal interface that used hand gestures along with speech for manipulating 3D objects [4]. Another system to incorporate speech and hand gestures for creating B-Spline based 3D models was developed by Weimer and Ganapathy [18]. However, their system was menu driven and did not take advantage of whole hand input. Other multimodal work that uses both hand gestures and speech can be found in [1] [2] [12].

An important aspect of multimodal interaction is the integration of the different modes of input used. A number of different integration strategies have been developed for a variety of different input modes. Johnston developed a unification-based integration scheme [11] based on research conducted by Oviatt [14] [15] into people's integration patterns when using more than one mode of input. This scheme uses typed feature structures [6] to represent the semantic contributions of the different modes which allows for the individual modalities to compensate for each other's errors.

Expert systems have also been used to integrate multiple modes of input as shown in Billinghurst's work [2]. In his system, a set of if-then production rules, which encode domain knowledge, are used to integrate speech and hand gesture. These rules map high level semantic information from the inputs to generate a somewhat intelligent response. Another approach to input integration is to use frames [17]. In this case, frames consist of slots that hold information from a single input mode. The command interpreter takes these frames and determines the appropriate action to take. An advantage of this approach is its flexibility for incorporating more than two modes of input. Note that other strategies such as agent-based approaches [7] and guided propagation networks [13] have also been developed for integrating multiple modes of input.

3   Hardware Configuration for the Framework

The hardware configuration we use for our virtual environment applications has many parts as shown in Fig. 1.

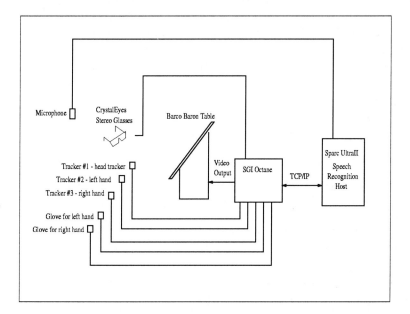

Fig. 1. The various components that make up the hardware configuration for our multimodal interface framework.

The framework uses a SGI Octane graphics workstation as its primary computer. The Octane drives a Barco Baron Table, a four foot by five foot rear projection display device. The table has two StereoGraphics CrystalEyes emmiters placed on either side of it. These emmiters (not shown in the figure) transmit an infrared signal to a pair of shutter glasses the user wears to achieve a stereoscopic view. An Ascension Flock of Birds™ unit with an extended range transmitter is connected to the Octane through a serial interface. The flock has three trackers, one that is attached to the CrystalEyes for head tracked stereo viewing, and the other two are attached to glove-based input devices for position and orientation measurements. A Nissho Electronics SuperGlove™ is worn on the left hand and contains a total of ten bend sensors. On the right hand, the user wears a Virtual Technologies CyberGlove™ which has a total of 18 bend sensors. Both gloves are attached to separate serial ports on the Octane[1].

---

[1] We also have a pair of Fakespace Pinch™ gloves which detect electrical contact at each of the finger tips. The Pinch gloves are used with the scientific visualization application.

A second workstation, a Sun Microsystems Sparc UltraII, is used as the speech recognition server. We use the Hark Speech Recognition system, a commercially available product from BBN Corporation. This Sun workstation is physically located in close proximity to the Barco Baron, and as a result, the microphone is connected to this workstation. This configuration is advantageous since no audio signals are sent from the Octane to the UltraII though a network connection. The only data sent across the network are speech tokens from the recognizer. The other advantage of this configuration is the speech recognizer has its own CPU instead of having to share the Octane's CPU which is used for graphics and processing input device records.

4   Software Architecture

The software architecture for our multimodal interface framework is based on an interface library called Jot [10]. Jot acts as a lower level infrastructure by supplying device drivers, math routines, network communication, stereoscopic capabilities, and an OpenGL abstraction. The interface framework itself is made up of a number of low level components and an integration component (see Fig 2). Each of the low level components perform either posture, gesture or speech recognition and send tokens to the integration component which uses this data to issue commands through callbacks in the application.

4.1   SuperGlove Posture Recognizer

The main function of the SuperGlove posture recognizing component is to process the raw data records from the SuperGlove input device and find recognizable postures which are defined in a template file[2]. The recognizer then sends a token corresponding to the recognized posture to the integration component. The recognition method used is a sum of squares statistic (i.e. similarity statistic) to find the current data record that is most similar to a given templated data record. Postures are recognized in three stages. First a similarity statistic for each possible posture is found using the following formula:

$$ss_i = \sum_{j=1}^{n}(x_{cj} - x_{tj_i})^2 \tag{1}$$

where ss_i equals the ith similarity statistic, x_{cj} equals the jth bend angle of the current posture record, x_{tj_i} equals the jth bend angle of the ith templated posture record, and n represents the number of bend angles measured, in this case ten. Once a similarity statistic is found for each posture[3] in the posture set, the second stage is to find the minimum value which is represented as

---

[2] A templated data record is created in a calibration file before using the application. The user makes a given posture n times (usually about 5) and an average of each data value is taken to get one record.

[3] By finding a similarity statistic for each posture in the posture set, we can sort these values and use a n-best recognition approach. The n-best approach would pass a list

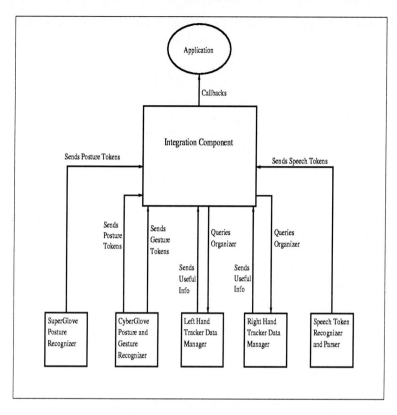

Fig. 2. The components that make up our multimodal interface framework. Arrow indicate direction of data flow.

$$Y = \min(ss_1, ss_2, ...ss_i) \qquad (2)$$

$$P = \begin{cases} Token & : & Y < \epsilon \\ Null & : & Y >= \epsilon \end{cases} \qquad (3)$$

where Y equals the minimum similarity statistic value. The corresponding posture token P is then found from Y only if it is less then a threshold value ϵ otherwise no posture is recognized. Once a value for P has been determined, the third stage is to insert P into a queue which holds the last n posture tokens. The number of elements in the queue is based on informal measurements of the accuracy of the SuperGlove. In this case, we found a twenty element queue to be satisfactory for the applications we are currently developing, but this number could change for other applications. The queue is used to help alleviate false

of posture tokens to the integration component with each token having an associated probability. These probabilities would aid in the determination of the overall task the user wanted to perform.

positives during recognition, and if the majority of the elements in the queue are a given posture token, then that token is sent to the integration component.

4.2 CyberGlove Posture and Gesture Recognizer

The CyberGlove posture and gesture recognizer has similar functionality to the SuperGlove posture recognizer except for additional gesture recognition functionality and small modifications to the posture recognition algorithm.

Posture recognition in this recognizer follows equations 1 thru 3 in the previous subsection but instead of using ten bend angles for the similarity statistic, it uses sixteen. Although the CyberGlove we use has eighteen bend sensors, posture recognition excludes the last two bend sensors which measures wrist pitch and yaw. Exclusion of wrist pitch and yaw in the recognition of postures gives the user more freedom in making them. The second modification to the algorithm is in the number of elements in the posture token queue. Based on our informal tests, the CyberGlove is more accurate than the SuperGlove and, as a result, needs a smaller queue. The number of elements in the token queue has been reduced to ten for this recognizer which makes posture to command response time somewhat faster.

Due to the CyberGlove's improved performance over the SuperGlove, we have also included a simple gesture recognizing element to this component. The gesture recognizer looks for interesting patterns in the glove's angle measurements over time which would be difficult with the SuperGlove because it has less bend sensors. For example, we have a wrist flick gesture which can be used to delete objects in the virtual environment or change the states of the application. The wrist flick gesture is recognized if a change in the wrist yaw angle data has changed rapidly. Because both posture and gesture recognition occur in the same component, there could be a conflict with mistaking postures as part of a recognizable gesture. The posture token element queue helps to resolve this conflict by making sure that a random posture token, which may be a part of a gesture, is not sent to the integration component. As more gestures are added to the framework, we may need to modify the number of elements in the posture token queue specifically to handle posture and gesture conflicts.

4.3 Left and Right Hand Tracker Data Managers

The purpose of these two components is to organize the position and orientation data from the magnetic trackers so that answers to queries made by the integration component are sent back as fast as possible. Both managers have a common structure but do contain different functionality. In a similar manner to the posture recognizers described in sections 4.1 and 4.2, the tracker data managers hold a queue of the last n position and orientation records which provides them with a history of the motion of the hands[4]. Both managers use this information to communicate with the integration component.

---

[4] Currently we use store the last twenty position and orientation records, but this is subject to change based on the amount of motion history we need.

Communication between the tracker data managers and the integration component takes place in two forms. The first form of communication allows the integration component to query the data managers for information that is useful to determine what action to take given what it already knows. Examples of the type of information requested is the current roll of the hand or whether one hand is closer to the display surface than the other. The second form of communication lets the tracker data managers send useful information to the integration component. The managers look for patterns in the motion history of the hand by analyzing the position and orientation data.

The left and right tracker data managers are distinguishable by the types of information processing they do. A common action in virtual environment applications is pointing to or grabbing objects and manipulating them. Therefore, one of the tracker data managers is designed to provide information about what object has been selected for manipulation. This information is obtained by casting rays from the tracker's position into the scene and checking if any objects have been intersected. Once an object has been selected, constrained or unconstrained relative movement information can be obtained from the manager as well. The majority of the other tracker data manager's time is spent determining hand orientation which is used in conjunction with posture recognition. By knowing what orientation the hand is in, a small number of additional postures can be added to the posture set. For example, a fist posture can be turned into 3 distinct postures when the hand's orientation is at 0, 90 and 180 degrees about the Z axis. Currently the left hand tracker data manager handles object selection and manipulation information while the right hand tracker data manager handles orientation information, but this configuration can be changed to accommodate user comfort.

4.4   Speech Token Recognizer and Parser

The speech token recognizer and parser component has two essential parts. The first part is the speech recognition engine itself which runs on a Sun Sparc UltraII and acts as a server. Speech is recognized using the BBN Hark Speech Recognizer. The recognizer is a speaker independent system based on a phonetic dictionary. Speaker independency is both an advantage and a disadvantage in that it requires no training to use but can pick words from other areas in the environment which can cause false positive recognition. Recognizable words and phrases are placed in a grammar file that is loaded into the recognizer upon start up. The recognizer has both continuous word spotting and push-to-talk recognition modes. Currently, we use continuous phrase spotting but plan to incorporate push-to-talk recognition into the framework by having the user depress a foot pedal when speaking to the computer. An advantage of the Hark system is that it allows important recognition parameters to be changed through a parameter file such as speech detection sensitivity, rejection sensitivity, and speed of the recognizer.

Once the Hark system recognizes a word, phrase or a non-recognizable entity, the server sends a string across the network to the application. At this point, the second part of the speech token recognizer and parser takes the string, parses it and sends a one word token to the integration component. Note that one of the important goals of our project is to allow the user to speak to the computer with as much flexibility as possible. As a result, we want the user to have many different possibilities for issuing a voice command. This goal makes the parsing tedious since there are usually many possible combinations of words and phrases that can make up a single command.

4.5   Integration Component

The integration component combines the output from the lower level components[5]. Whenever a speech command, gesture, or posture is sent to the integration component it interprets the available data and sends an appropriate command by callback to the application. The integration component stores the current and previous posture, gesture and speech tokens so it always has a copy of the last token received from each component which is important for determining when one series of posture tokens begin and another series ends. This component also has an individual function that gets called when a particular recognizer sends a token. This separation provides for a cleaner interface.

The integration component is only one instantiated object and each of the recognizer components has a pointer to it. When a recognizer sends a token to the integration component, the specific function for that token class gets called. This function then invokes the action that the application has mapped to this token. The callback action can also check the state of the application and look at other tokens received from other components to either further refine or to reject the action.

An important part of our framework was to allow the user to issue the same command in many different ways using different modes. For example, we want the user to be able to create an object with a voice command, a hand posture, or a hand gesture and use any of these mechanisms at any time. The user may prefer a certain method of interacting with the application, but if that method fails, the user should be able to quickly and easily jump to another method for that particular command. In order to facilitate this type of interface, the integration component prints out what operation it thinks the user wants to perform. It also prints out messages when it does not understand what the user is trying to do. These messages provide the user with feedback which enables them to try the interaction again or proceed to another mode of input. An example of this type of interaction will be discussed in the next section.

---

[5] Note that we are still in the initial stages of implementation of the integration component. As a result, we currently have no general support for handling multiple modes of input simultaneously. Instead, applications can effect their own multimodal integration by querying the integration component about the status of other input streams. The integration component does allow for multiple modes of input to complement each other and this is described in section 5.

5   Applications Using the Framework

We are currently developing two virtual environment applications that use the multimodal interface framework. The first one (shown in Fig 3) is a scientific visualization application for visualizing the flow field around a dataset. The second application is an interior design layout program which will allow users to show and tell the application how they want a room or set of rooms furnished.

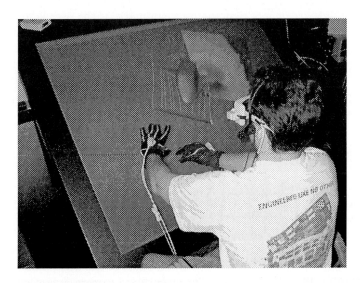

Fig. 3. A user interacting with a dataset for visualizing a flow field around a space shuttle. The user simultaneously manipulates the streamlines with his left hand and the shuttle with his right hand while viewing the data in stereo.

5.1   Multimodal Scientific Visualization

The goal for this application is to provide the user with a more natural and intuitive way of interacting and understanding scientific data and is based on the Virtual Windtunnel project by Bryson [5]. Instead of using bend sensing gloves, this application uses Pinch gloves which allow the user to make pinching gestures by simply touching the fingertips together. Since the Pinch gloves are based on electrical contact, posture recognition algorithms are not needed. As a result, the CyberGlove and SuperGlove recognizers are not used with this application. They are replaced with additional components to the framework that use finite state machines (FSM), which transition from one pinching event to another. These transitions are represented as the arcs in the FSM while the states in the FSM are used for sending tokens to the integration component.

The application allows users to create, modify, drop, pick up, and delete tools that aid in visualizing the flow field data. For example, if a users want to create a rake, they extend their hand toward the display device and ask the application for a rake. The tool then appears in the users hand. Other operations on tools are performed in a similar manner. A user also can manipulate the dataset by grabbing it with either hand and changing its position and orientation in the virtual world.

In many cases, a user will have both hands occupied interacting with the dataset but may still need to issue commands. A multimodal interface provides an excellent way to do this. For example, the application has recording and playback of video segments that the user can make. If the user is manipulating a tool in one hand and the dataset in the other and wishes to record a video segment s/he would have to free one hand and make a gesture to start recording if speech was not available. In our application, the user can keep using both hands for interacting in the virtual world and still issue relevant commands to the application using speech such as starting the recorder, stopping it, and playing back the video.

5.2   Multimodal Interior Design and Layout

The goal of this project it to allow users to show and tell the application how they want the interior of a room or house to be designed. The system is in its early stages of development but does make use of all the components available in our framework. With the current functionality, the user can translate, scale, and rotate the camera about the scene. A fist posture enables the user to perform all three operations depending on the initial angle of the user's hand about the Z axis. If the application does not recognize that a camera operation should be made, it will tell the user and ask for the correct operation. Users can then tell the application what kind of transformation they want to perform. This type of interaction also works in the opposite direction.

The user can also manipulate objects in the virtual world by creating a virtual laser pointer in their left hand by making a gun posture. Once an object is intersected by the laser pointer, it can be picked up and manipulated using a clutching posture or telling the application that the intersected object is the one to manipulate. With the other hand the user can constrain the movement of the object in the left hand. Translation constraints along the three principle axes and the XY, YZ, and XZ planes are currently supported by having the user point in the direction that they want to constraint the object. Speech commands are also available and can be used interchangeably with the hand postures.

At this stage, the creation of objects such as furniture, kitchen appliances, and wall decorations is still under development. We plan to have the user speak and gesture simultaneously to query a database of smart primitives to instantiate objects. For example, the user will say 'chair' and make a gesture which approximates the geometry of the particular chair they want. The application will then go into the database and find the appropriate chair. Of course, if the user knows the exact name of the chair then they do not need to make the gesture but only use speech to create it.

6   Future Work and Conclusions

The multimodal interface framework we are building is still in its early stage of development and, as a result, there is a number of areas in the project that require future work. One of the most important areas deals with the integration component. The integration component needs to be able to handle simultaneous input streams such that redundancy can be used to help resolve errors in the recognition of individual modalities. In order to use this complementary information, we also need to add the n-best approach to our glove posture recognizers which provides a list of possible recognized postures sorted by highest probability. The n-best approach is extremely important for integrating simultaneous modes of input. Another area for future work is finishing the hand tracker data managers by including the routines that will look for interesting features in the tracker data to send to the integration component.

One of the problems with our hardware configuration, which can be seen in Fig 3, is that this user must wear a number of devices and is connected by wires to the computers. An unencumbered solution would be beneficial and as a longer term goal we plan to use computer vision to track the user's head and hands and use an area microphone for speech recognition instead of a headset. As we develop the framework we will also continue to add functionality to the two applications described in section 5 and to develop new ones.

This paper has presented an ongoing research project to create natural and intuitive multimodal interfaces using hand gestures and speech for virtual environment applications. The use of hand gestures and speech as our input modalities allows the user to interact with a computer in a manner that is similar to the way humans communicate with each other. By creating a multimodal interface framework, we hope to develop a variety of useful applications that let the user interact in a virtual environment in an efficient, natural, and enjoyable manner.

Acknowledgments

This work is supported in part by the NSF Graphics and Visualization Center, Advanced Networks and Services, Alias/Wavefront, Autodesk, Microsoft, Sun Microsystems, IBM, GTE, and TACO.

References

1. H. Ando, Y. Kitahara, and N. Hataoka. Evaluation of Multimodal Interface using Spoken Language and Pointing Gesture on Interior Design System. *International Conference on Spoken Language Processing*, 1994, 567-570.
2. M. Billinghurst, J. Savage, P. Oppenheimer, and C. Edmond. The Expert Surgical Assistant: An Intelligent Virtual Environment with Multimodal Input. *Proceedings of Medicine Meets Virtual Reality IV*, 1995, 590-607.
3. R. A. Bolt. Put that there: Voice and Gesture at the Graphics Interface. *Proceedings of Siggraph'80*, 1980, 262-270.

4. R. A. Bolt and E. Herranz. Two-Handed Gesture in Multi-Modal Natural Dialog. *Proceedings of the Fifth Annual ACM Symposium on User Interface Software and Technology*, 1992, 7-14.

5. S. Bryson, S. Johan, and L. Schlecht. An Extensible Interactive Visualization Framework for the Virtual Windtunnel. *Proceedings of the Virtual Reality Annual International Symposium*, 1997, 106-113.

6. R. Carpenter. *The Logic of Typed Feature Structures*, Cambridge University Press, Cambridge, England, 1992.

7. A. Cheyer and L. Julia. Multimodal Maps: An Agent-based Approach. *Lecture Notes in Artificial Intelligence 1374: Multimodal Human-Computer Communication*, (eds.) H. Bunt, R. J. Beun, and T. Borghuis, 1998, 111-121.

8. P. R. Cohen, et al. QuickSet:Multimodal Interaction for Distributed Applications. *Proceedings of the Fifth Annual International Multimodal Conference*, 1997, 31-40.

9. C. Cruz-Neira, D. J. Sandin, T. A. Defanti. Surround-Screen Projection-Based Virtual Reality: The Design and Implementation of the CAVE. *Proceedings of Siggraph'93*, 1993, 135-142.

10. A. S. Forsberg, J. J. LaViola, L. Markosian, R. C. Zeleznik. Seamless Interaction in Virtual Reality *IEEE Computer Graphics and Applications*, 17(6), 1997, 6-9.

11. M. Johnston, P. R. Cohen, D. McGee, S. L. Oviatt, J. A. Pittman, and I. Smith. Unification-based Multimodal Integration. *Proceedings of the 35th Annual Meeting of the Association for Computational Linguistics*, 1997.

12. D. B. Koons, C. J. Sparrell, and K. R. Thorisson. Integrating Simultaneous Input from Speech, Gaze, and Hand Gestures. *Intelligent Multimedia Interfaces*, (ed.) Mark T. Maybury, 1993, 257-279.

13. J. C. Martin, R. Veldman, and D. Beroule. Developing Multimodal Interfaces: A Theoretical Framework and Guided Propagation Networks. *Lecture Notes in Artificial Intelligence 1374: Multimodal Human-Computer Communication*, (eds.) H. Bunt, R. J. Beun, and T. Borghuis, 1998, 158-187.

14. S. Oviatt and E. Olsen. Integration Themes in Multimodal Human-Computer Interaction. *Proceedings of the 1994 International Conference on Spoken Language Processing*, 1994, 551-554.

15. S. Oviatt, A. DeAngeli, and K. Kuhn. Integration and Synchronization of Input Modes during Multimodal Human-Computer Interaction. *Proceedings of CHI'97 Human Factors in Computing Systems*, 1997, 415-422.

16. A. van Dam. Post-WIMP User Interfaces. *Communications of the ACM*, 40(2), 1997, 63-67.

17. A. Waibel, M. T. Vo, P. Duchnowski, and S. Manke. Multimodal Interfaces. *Artificial Intelligence Review*, Special Volume on Integration of Natural Language and Vision Processing, Mc Kevitt, P. (Ed.), 1995, 299-319.

18. D. Weimer and S. K. Ganapathy. Interaction Techniques Using Hand Tracking and Speech Recognition. *Multimedia Interface Design*, (eds.) Meera M. Blattner and Roger B. Dannenberg, New York: Addison-Wesley Publishing Company, 1992, 109-126.

19. R. C. Zeleznik, A. S. Forsberg, and P. S. Strauss. Two Pointer Input For 3D Interaction. *Proceedings of the Symposium on Interactive 3D Graphics*, 1997, 115-120.

Round Table

Stimulating Research into Gestural Human Machine Interaction

Marilyn Panayi[1], David Roy[1], and James Richardson[2]

[1] Natural Interactive Systems Laboratory
University of Southern Denmark, Denmark
{panayi,roy}@nis.sdu.dk
[2] Laboratoire de Physiologie et Biomécanique du Mouvement
Université Paris Sud, France
james.richardson@lpm.u-psud.fr

Abstract. This is the summary report of the roundtable session held at the end of Gesture Workshop '99. This first roundtable aimed to act as a forum of discussion for issues and concerns relating to the achievements, future development, and potential of the field of gestural and sign-language based human computer interaction.

1   Introduction

The concept for this roundtable session arose from discussions at the last Gesture Workshop in Bielefeld in 1998 [1]. Members of the community felt the need to create a forum for discussion of common issues and concerns. This was the first year that we had held a roundtable at the Gesture Workshop and it was attended by many of the workshop participants.

The session started with four short 'facilitating' presentations that represented a range of perspectives, challenges and potential opportunities for gestural HCI research from Europe and the United States. These included research perspectives from the EU and the USA, European Union research funding opportunities, and industry technology transfer programmes in France. The invited contributors were: David Roy, Natural Interactive Systems Laboratory, University of Southern Denmark, Denmark, Michael Underwood, European Commission, Belgium, Thomas Huang, Beckman Institute, University of Illinois, USA and Jean Pierre Gex, CRITT-CCST, Gif-sur-Yvette, France.

In the report that follows, we set out to document some of the contributions in 'reportage style', summarizing the key points made by the invited contributors and the members of the roundtable. It was not the aim of the roundtable to attempt to answer all the questions raised, but rather to use them as a starting point to focus on issues that this community of researchers is trying to grapple with. It can be seen as an attempt to sow the seeds for ongoing discussion at both future events and through our electronic networks[1]. Where possible, contributions have been attributed to their maker. It is not possible to acknowledge

---

[1] Details of the discussion list for gestural HCI can be found at
http://www.mailbase.ac.uk/lists/gesture-sign-lang- tech/

A. Braffort et al. (Eds.): GW'99, LNAI 1739, pp. 317–331, 1999.

all contributions to the workshop session, so contributors are asked to forgive us for any inevitable omissions and errors. Edited written summary contributions received since the roundtable have been incorporated from Matthew Turk, Microsoft, USA, Dimitri Metaxas and Christian Vogler, University of Pennsylvania, USA, Thomas Huang, Beckman Institute, USA and Ipke Wachsmuth, University of Bielefeld, Germany, and David Roy.

2 Short Presentations

European Research Perspective – David Roy

David Roy gave a brief statement and raised questions and issues relating to the evolution of the field. He has been involved in this area of research since the early 1990's and has attended all three of the Gesture Workshop events. His comments at the meeting integrated with further reflections follow:

In the early 1990s, literature in the area of gesture and sign language recognition comprised only a handful of papers. Nine years later, it is encouraging to see that there is now a substantial body of literature. There has been steady progress in gesture recognition, although there are many issues yet to be solved. At the same time, research into the nature of gesture has seen something of a renaissance leading to a rapid increase of interest and research activity. In fact, it is probably fair to say that the realisation of the importance of gesture and multimodality is increasing more or less simultaneously across many domains that deal with human communication, spanning philosophical, scientific and technological areas of inquiry. In light of this, it seems timely to find ways to foster interdisciplinary collaboration. The Gesture Workshop is increasingly instrumental in this process, but also there needs to be strategic resources and funding directed at bringing people together to do research in the multidisciplinary teams required for this area. The European funding framework is clearly a potential source for this[2].

Gesture is an integral part of human communication, and gestural human computer interaction can be considered closely connected to the inherently interdisciplinary domain of human language technology. There seems to be an increasing number of meetings that include a significant gesture component, while gestural HCI or human language technology is not their focus. Although valuable in there own right, they do little to create an interdisciplinary gestural HCI research community, and there is even a danger that they may have a tendency to fragment the growing community. In contrast, the Gesture Workshop series have not been biased towards any particular technological arena, and hence can provide a suitable forum for bringing communities together for discussion of the

---

[2] A joint initiative between the USA and EU is due to start in 2000: International Standards in Language Engineering (ISLE) will contain a Natural Interaction and Multimodality Working Group. This will address issues relating to standardisation that can support research and exploitation in the area of gesture and multimodal language technologies.

common issues and problems, of which there are many. Hopefully, a point will be reached in the development of the field where language technologies will be treated much more holistically in terms of the human and engineering sciences. Only in this way, can we take full account of the richness and complexity of human communication. In this respect, the research approach has often been to narrow. He highlighted the advantages of taking a people focused approach to research from both scientific and usability perspectives:

- It helps place constraints on the problem and helps establish priorities and a road- map for technological research and development.
- Gestures are part of language. The relationship between gestures and spoken language is complex and many gestures of interest for HCI are linked at the level of meaning. Thus, gestural HCI systems have to be based either implicitly or explicitly upon some sort of model, based on linguistic theory, that at minimum, links gestures to context. The pragmatics of language is another area where gesture and speech are strongly integrated – pragmatic models are going to be important for natural and intuitive interaction that can compete with other forms of HCI.

To stimulate discussion, he re-iterated Alan Wexelblat's question put to the community at last year's workshop: What has been achieved in gestural human computer interaction since the work of Schmandt, Hulteen and Bolt at MIT [2], in the 1980's with the 'Put that There' demonstration, almost twenty years ago?

By way of an answer, he suggested that there have been significant advances in gesture recognition, although progress has been at a relatively modest pace in line with an extremely modest level of research funding. Only recently has there been anything approaching a critical mass of research in the area of gestural HCI.

Although, the nature of gesture in communication is beginning to be better understood, still relatively little is known about the usability of gesture and application context for gesture as an interaction modality. This situation needs to be addressed so that we can create a scientific roadmap for effective technological development ensuring rapid progress towards usable, robust and convincing systems that work in the real world. This is the best way to convince industry and funding agencies of the potential of the technology.

Within the gesture recognition community there are a number of contrasting approaches, e.g. computer vision vs. body instrumentation, probabilistic vs. rule-base approaches. What are the common challenges? How are the research agendas similar and how are they different? One suggestion could be that issues begin to converge once we start looking at gesture as part of natural language, although there are also fairly low-level common technological issues.

From his own perspective, he felt that although we can now do more in terms of vision recognition, there was still a need for both machine-vision and body-instrumentation based gesture recognition from both a scientific and application rationale. Body instrumentation overcomes the basic problems of computer vision, such as sensitivity to lighting condition, occlusion, and orientation. Obviously, body instrumentation is no good for the face, and there are acceptance and convenience factors against wearing gloves. What are the main agendas for each area, are they in direct competition with each other, or are the efforts complementary?

Examples of the advantages of each include:

- Body instrumentation:
  Application context: Useful for supplying wearable technology with gestural and postural data, applications where vision techniques are impossible, e.g. confined spaces, applications where there is glove-based haptic feedback.
  Scientific context: More high fidelity parameter extraction leading to better recognition rates for a much larger gesture corpus, therefore more suitable, at least in the short-term for exploring and making use of multimodal language models involving the integration of speech and gesture. Easier to use for gesture synthesis, so data resources have dual use.
- Machine vision based approaches:
  Application context: Unencumbered, so attractive to many sponsoring industry applications such as communication terminals. Area is given impetus by the push to develop automatic human- activity recognition technology for security applications and for automatic search and retrieval of video/multimedia content.
  Scientific context: Enables the exploration of view-based methods, closer to the way that the gestures are perceived so enables application of visual perceptual theory.

The above suggests the complementary rather that competing nature of the two technologies. Thus, it is reasonable to conclude that it would be unwise to focus on one approach in favour of the other.

In terms of the Gesture Workshop series, it has been interesting to see the effects of an increase in the range of backgrounds represented at the meeting. The meeting discussions have clearly benefited from this wider perspective, and hopefully productive collaborations will result. The gestural human- machine interaction community comprises a surprisingly broad range of traditional disciplines and specialist areas spanning science, engineering and the humanities. Looking at the GW attendance list reveals this diversity: computer science, artificial intelligence, pattern recognition, signal processing, computer vision, computer graphics, cognitive science, psycholinguistics, sign linguistics, anthropology, cognitive psychology, neuro-motor control, connectionism, human-factors, usability, human-computer interaction, industrial design, electronic music etc.

Given this diversity, how much do we and should be work interdisciplinary at the project or research level? How can we best benefit from our different expertise? How could our community address this? Is there a mechanism for achieving this cross- disciplinary fertilisation? As may be typical of a young, but expanding field, much of the work in this area seems to be undertaken by Ph.d. students working in relative isolation (Philip Harling and Alistair Edwards organised the first Gesture Workshop to address this issue [3]). It has to be said, that the traditional university educational background poorly equips the researcher for the background knowledge needed to work in our domain. The situation is made worse by the lack of a journal focusing on gestural HCI which has meant that published work is widely dispersed increasing the chance of missing important previous work. Fortunately, the picture is changing. Increasingly, small research groups are emerging, but it remains to be seen how strong these groups will be in terms of encompassing the full range of expertise desirable for gestural HCI research. If we are to arrive at the "killer applications" that motivate users to leave their keyboards and mice behind, we need to create and put effort into interfaces that are convincing in all respects rather than just novel. This will require an interdisciplinary and visionary approach. Looking at the composition of the GW, the prospects for achieving this aim seem encouraging.

European Funding Opportunities: Michael Underwood[3]

Michael Underwood is currently an expert with the European Commission working within DG13. He has an academic background in speech recognition and kindly accepted our invitation to highlight funding opportunities available through the European Commissions' research funding programme. He explained that a new programme was due to start 1999, the 5th Framework Programme. He emphasised the fact that the programme was still evolving and people should consult the most current electronic information available on the internet and encouraged researchers to contact the assigned officers to discuss their ideas. Several changes have occurred between the previous 4th and new 5th Framework programmes and details could be found on http://www.cordis.lu. An online proposal preparation tool is available. A key consideration should be to clarify research objective in relation to the policy objectives.

In terms of resources, 15 billion Euro is available over next 4 years, the new 5th Framework call was actually launched on the same day, as our workshop. There will be further calls for 2000 and 2001. Michael Underwood drew our attentions to key features of the programme these included: two participants from two European countries, some changes to contract condition including changes that make it easier for small companies. The programme is arranged around four thematic programmes, the IST programme being the one of most interest to our research community. The IST programme brings together the previous programmes of ACTS, ESPRIT and TELEMATICS; we are encouraged to register by email to get update of changes to the programme.

The IST programme consists of four key actions: Systems and services for citizen, Multimedia content and tools with a strong emphasis on education, New methods of working and e-commerce, Essential Technologies. Future and Emerging Technologies (FET) and opportunities for Research Networking. There may also opportunities for gesture research in the context of cross-programme initiatives such as 'Design for All'. Michael Underwood encouraged those interested to investigate how their research objectives would fit the programme goals.

---

[3] European Commission, Telematics Application Programme, DGXIII, Brussels, Belgium

A final comment made in the discussion was that funding proposals were evaluated by expert evaluators, and members of the roundtable were encouraged to submit their names to the expert evaluator list as a way of getting to understand the other side of the process and to ensure adequate representation.

A Perspective from the USA: Thomas Huang[4]

Thomas Huang gave a US research perspective in terms of the kind of work being carried out and the infrastructure for its funding. He pointed out that the major source of research funding came from government agencies and for gesture recognition this lay in the brief of the National Science Foundation, specifically the NSF-CIIS/IIS, Human Computer Interaction Programme [4].

Previously some support had come from the DARPA – DOD. In the past, significant resources had been allocated to speech and language and there had been no formalised funding for computer vision research, for example. Now there is greater interest in surveillance applications using machine vision. In terms of industry support of research this was still limited and in the US there was no comparable system to the European initiatives that encouraged industry and small enterprise to participate in research. There are a few exceptions, notably, MIT in Boston and few other individual universities with sponsor arrangements. Typically any grants from industry, where they existed, were small and in the main driven by industry interest in one particular aspect of the research work. Thomas Huang gave a brief insight into the trends in the US that were impacting on research funding, specifically recommendations coming from the Presidential Advisory Committee on Technology. A recent announcement included the recommendation of 360 million dollars for IT, where the NSF would be getting 146 million dollars and a significant increase in its funding with the prospect of starting a number of collaborative initiatives. The driving force for a number of research programmes included: the impact of the internet on information system globalisation - an area that holds particular potential for international collaboration; the motivation of the promise of applications that can harness gesture, gesture analysis in the context of human computer interaction; and the issue of Universal Access – access for anybody, anywhere.

Professor Huang highlighted conferences and workshops that had elements of gesture research. These included: the Automatic Face and Gesture Workshop that was being held in Grenoble in March 2000, an event that up to now had focused predominantly on face recognition; the Workshop on Perceptual User Interfaces that started in 1997 and last year was held in San Francisco, supported by Microsoft. Examples of other events mentioned included the Human Movement Coding Workshop, City University, London, UK, May 1996, the WIGLS workshop, Delaware, October 1996. Reference was made to the fact that over the years ACM-CHI has contained some gestural HCI related components. Naturally, there were the series of International Gesture Workshops held in Europe, that began at York, UK in 1996 of which GW99 is the latest. Members of the

---

[4] Beckman Institute, University of Illinois, USA

roundtable also contributed information about the recent ORAGE'98 meeting in Besançon, France where there were many contributions on speech, gesture and multimodality in interaction including a few technology focused presentations. Also mentioned were a number of workshops for 1999 including: the 7th European Summer School on Language and Speech Communication – Multimodality in Language and Speech Systems (MiLaSS) held in Stockholm, Sweden, July 1999; ESCA Tutorial and Research Workshop on Interactive Dialogue in Multi-modal Sytems, Kloster Irsee, Germany, June 1999; and Physicality and Tangibility in Interaction Workshop in conjunction with the i3 annual conference, Siena, Italy, October 1999.

Gesture research work in the USA was still restricted to a few laboratories and some recent funding initiatives that have gained support through the NSF programme. Examples of some of the laboratories that included work on gesture synthesis and recognition were given. The work focussed predominately on hand gestures and interest in human computer interaction for simple control. These included work at: Applied Science and Engineering Labs at Delaware working with American Sign Language and early work with dynamic arm gesture recognition for HCI for people with physical impairments, more recently Media Lab – Justine Cassell and conversational agents, work at Oregon, Illinois/Penn State, Lucent/Bell and IBM. At Microsoft there was an interest in gesture from the vision analysis perspective and this summer a student of Thomas Huang would be working at Microsoft on gesture analysis, at the Cambridge Research Laboratory, Jim Ray was working on gesture analysis, and there was interest in gesture at Phillips, USA. There is of course, a large body of research on narrative gesture from a psychological perspective in Chicago with the work of David McNeill and his students, and a significant body of work on the face.

Thomas Huang went on to highlight a number of research issues that the community could address, these included: the need for common databases although he envisioned that these would be somewhat application dependent. He mentioned that it was very tedious to create multi-modal databases and there should be access not only to common databases but also a need for common resources in terms of common algorithms, a need for context as this would force us to look at metrics.

Many research groups around the world have been working on hand/arm gesture recognition, with applications to display command, sign language recognition, etc. However, it is fair to say that no one has yet has a firm grip on the following issues:

- In applications where the set of gestures is fairly small and rigid (i.e., the variation of each gesture over time and people is small), then the recognition problem is not very hard. These applications include display control and even sign language recognition. The true difficulty lies in interpreting conversational gestures and incidental gestures. Unfortunately, in display control, sign languages, etc., people cannot avoid to mix in incidental and conversational gestures. Thus, we cannot separate the recognition of conversational/incidental gestures and the more rigid kind of gestures.

- In order to interpret the intention, and the emotional/cognitive state of a person, one needs to take a holistic approach. It is not enough just to track the hand/arm; we need to track the whole body and facial movement. Furthermore, we should also analyse the speech and other sounds made by the person. How to best combine (fuse) the various cues is a most interesting problem.

- As information systems become more and more global, we need to take account of cultural differences in designing such systems. It is truly amazing to see the cultural differences in gesturing. A well-meaning hand gesture in one country may be an obscene one in another. Shaking one's head means "no" in most western countries but agreement in India. Latin people love to wave their arms and hands, while Asian people seldom do. Etc. Thus, we need to be very sensitive in developing gesture interpretation systems on a global level.

Finally, he asked the roundtable to address the issue of motivating applications. He saw his work extending hand gestures to full recognition and gesture in multi-modal context and use.

National funding perspective: Jean- Pierre Gex[5]

Jean Pierre Gex encouraged French research laboratories to submit proposals to CRITT. They had the function of acting as a brokerage service for research institutions and small companies, giving 50% of the funding. For example, last year 200 technology transfers were supported to a maximum of 350k francs. The programme is region specific, Ile de France, with a budget of 300 million francs per year. The small company has to be within Ile de France. The research areas are also specific areas – e.g. computing, telecommunications – software and gesture research would fall into these areas. Other CRITT sections in the programme have the responsibility to deal with other research areas.

3   Roundtable Discussion

The meeting was then opened to the members of the roundtable. The contributions have once again been summarised in 'reportage style' and attributed to the speaker where possible. *Dimitris Metaxas*[6] was invited to give a brief description of the newly set up National Centre for Sign Language and Gesture Research supported by the NSF. The centre was launched September 1998, and is co-ordinated by Dimitris Metaxas at University of Pennsylvania and Carol Neidle at the University of Boston. Within its brief, the centre aims to become a world-wide repository for sign language research resources including both raw and annotated data. They hope to build a link with the European community

---

[5] CRITT-CCST, Gif-sur-Yvette, France
[6] National Centre for Sign Language and Gesture Research, University of Pennsylvania, Philadelphia, USA

perhaps through the 5th Framework programme. Dimitris Metaxas also made the point that we need to include linguists in our future discussions and development of systems.

Members from the roundtable raised the questions of issues that surround data and standardisation and reference was made to earlier attempts at University of Essex to create a data repository for gesture data.

Within the discussion, the issue of how to keep researchers in the field was raised. Even within the short life span the International Gesture Workshop series, colleagues have left the field unable to continue research often started as Masters or Ph.D. projects. It important not to loose expertise in the field through lack of opportunity and this should be a question that we as a community find ways to address.

Thomas Huang mentioned that there was the possibility of bilateral grants travel money from the NSF, and that partly because of globalisation there was a stronger interest in the US in collaboration with European colleagues. Professor Huang also mentioned a recent on-line report containing recommendations for a possible International Science Foundation. There was planned a joint workshop EC/NSF on Virtual Environments and Human-Centred Computing at the end of May/June in Toulouse co-ordinated in Europe by Professor Rae Earnshaw. In addition, information about the forthcoming NSF/EU collaboration initiatives could be found at the NSF web site http://www.nsf.gov.

Michael Underwood mentioned that working with other countries outside of Europe typically means that the funding for that other country came from the appropriate national organisation e.g. NSF. Once again information could be access through the EC web pages.

Matthew Turk[7] gave a brief overview of research at Microsoft. The particular perspective at Microsoft is that they were certainly interested in ideas that were, for example, ten years down the road before reaching product, as opposed to some industries that could only afford to look five years ahead. Around 370 research staff are based at Microsoft in the USA and an additional 40 based at Cambridge in the UK plus an office in Beijing. He felt that many outcomes from gesture and facial expression research could successfully be developed to product e.g. in the areas of graphics and virtual reality. There was also a general interest at Microsoft in how we could be interacting with technology in the future, the future being in the context of the next ten years. In terms of Microsoft funding research, there were a number of funding arrangements with universities.

Fernando Martins[8] mentioned the importance of user issues in research and product development and issues around 'non-tethered' computing. Intel was a company that had the brief of looking ahead in terms of what we would be buying five years down the road.

Matthew Turk stated that the industry perception is that our research community is very small. The questions being asked of us is: How can this technology affect the world at large?

---

[7] Microsoft Research, Washington, USA
[8] Intel Architecture Labs, Intel Corporation, Oregon, USA

Fernando Martins re-framed this question on terms of: How many people are using or could use these type of technologies sustainably? Taking up the challenge made by David Roy at the start of the roundtable he suggested that addressing this issue was a key to stimulating research.

Members of the roundtable challenged the group to think about how if there is no screen and no mouse as was being proposed, how could we use this technology for more creative purposes? The work of artists who are using gesture related technologies was mentioned as making a significant contribution to the exploration of new interaction paradigms involving gesture.

Ipke Wachsmuth[9]: Even though there have been many local successes (such as the improvement in hand gesture recognition), it is at least as important to conceptualize methods for integrated systems that link gesture recognition and interpretation to applications, if the goal of more intuitive human- computer interaction is to be realised.

He expressed the sentiment that the series of Gesture Workshops has shown much more apt approaches to such a goal than, for instance the International Computing and Pattern Recognition (ICPR) and other conferences with are more focussed on technical results for 'enabling technology.' The community which has been formed by way of the three workshops, York, Bielefeld and Gif-sur-Yvette is pursuing themes which compliment progress achieved in other scientific communities interested in gesture. Multimodality is another focus that deserves, and has found, greater attention in the workshops.

He made the point that with gesture recognition there are many difficult problems and we can not always use visual input due to the significant occlusion problems. His laboratory had an interest in natural interaction, where we can already start to recognise gestures. In terms of the use of data gloves, in certain settings it is more convenient such as in industrial settings e.g. future interaction with cars. Some contact has been made through the laboratory with the automotive industry in Germany.

He suggested that the hand should not restrict us as to point of input. Research at Duisburg is using 3 cameras to extend the input area. For full body input, they are using the body model of an American male. Questions were raised in terms of system functionality particularly if you always need to calibrate to the user. The laboratory was interested in applications that were realisable, a combination of simple human action, e.g. fist on which the system is calibrated and then interaction with an agent.

Finally, *Ipke Wachsmuth* emphasised that the content of research rather than exploitation and funding should be our focus. Context and database issues needed more development, if we were interested in applications. He pointed to the mix of disciplines represented by the delegates of the gesture workshops being comprehensive enough, including researchers from both computer and engineering sciences and the humanities who should be able to shed light on the many issues involved in the betterment of gesture based communication in HCI. He suggested that although the community was still not yet advanced with solv-

[9] AG Wissensbasierte Systeme, Technische Facultät, Universität Bielefeld, Germany

ing the problems he wanted to raise two questions: How do we advance our research positions? Should we reduce the aims so that we can move forward?

Martin Fröhlich[9] returned to the questions of the use of data-glove versus machine-vision and made the point that although glove data is relatively clean there still exists unresolved issues.

Both *Thomas Huang* and *Matthew Turk* suggested that there was not a polarity between computer vision and body instrumentation approaches but they were part of the situation and many deeper issues needed to be addressed.

Caroline Hummels[10], responding to the issue of user in the picture of our research. Where was the community vision relating to the human aspects as opposed to the technological aspects? This issue needed to be discussed and debated further.

In the same vein, the question from the floor was put in terms of: How do we use this technology? It was felt that the gap was getting smaller between the possible technologies, acceptance and usability. Substantial investment was needed to fund research that tackled these problems. What we are proposing as a community was the creation of completely new environments for interaction.

4   Post Workshop Reflections

Christian Vogler and Dimitris Metaxas

Christian Vogler and Dimitris Metaxas give a brief summary of previous research and identify a series of questions they felt provided a structure for future research in sign language in the context of HCI:

Previous research as exemplified by Vogler 1998 [5], Erenshteyn et al., 1996 [6], Starner 1995 [7], has focused on the engineering of prototype recognition systems. This research was valuable, because it showed that sign language recognition was a feasible undertaking. On the other hand, it did not touch on the psychological, linguistic, and sociological aspects of sign languages and their users.

We now know that sign language recognition is technically feasible. The current state-of-the-art consists exclusively of signer-dependent recognition; that is, the recognition systems need to be specifically trained for one person. Research has so far fallen into several broad categories. These include computer vision, the phonological aspects of sign languages as shown by the work of Liang 1998 [8], Vogler 1999 [9], the syntactical and higher-level aspects of Sign Languages have been attempted by Hienz 1999 [10] and Vogler 1997 [11], and research into the use of space investigated by Sagawa 1999 [12] and Braffort 1996 [13]. Questions being raised specifically in sign language include how do sign language phonology and syntax interact? Is it possible to take advantage of these interactions to build a more robust and more accurate recogniser? Is it possible to model the use of space in terms of sign language phonology? How it is possible to incorporate

---

[10] Faculty of Industrial Design Engineering, Delft University of Technology, The Netherlands

facial expressions, into a recogniser? Is it possible to use semantic constraints to disambiguate the output of a recogniser? The role of discourse and issues of co-ordinated effort in standardisation of data corpora were also mentioned.

Key technological challenges include: facial parameters in sign language; tracking a detailed handshape in 3D still seems to be an open problem; distinguishing between the syntactical use of space, and the use of space to describe real-world locations. The potentials for future systems were touched upon in terms of full-featured human computer interfaces and the potential of sign language for animation.

In conclusion two further issues were raised: how can we structure our work to ensure that we can have closer and more collaborative links with the deaf community of researchers and users particularly to identify system requirements by user communities? What are the issues relating to computer mediation between deaf and hearing people?

Matthew Turk[11]

It was exciting to bring together a diverse group of researchers who share the intuition that the area of gestural communication is important and potentially very useful in human-machine communication. Like the blind men describing the proverbial elephant, we bring diverse points of view that are not always in harmony, but we benefit from each other's perspective. Yet despite the flood of interest in gesture-related research and technologies in recent years, we (as a loosely-defined community) don't really know what we're doing yet. We don't have an accepted taxonomy or even definition of gesture, we don't understand the potential needs and uses of gesture-based systems, we don't have any compelling market-driving applications, and we're primarily technology-centred (or inquiry-centred, for the social scientists). We are, by and large, developing hammers and hoping to find appropriate nails to hit.

But I don't mean this as criticism – it's a good thing! We are a young and energetic community, and I have no doubt that we will eventually more fully understand the problems and identify the important issues that will lead to useful, usable and more universal interactive systems. How can we continue to make progress toward this goal? My view is that we have to focus equally on people, technology, and the market. Here are some (surely biased) opinions on these issues.

People (a.k.a. "users")
We don't really understand very well how people use gesture. Kendon, McNeill, Cassell, and others who study human behaviour have learned a great deal about gesture in certain contexts (e.g., spontaneous gestures used with speech), and those who study sign language generation and comprehension are adding to our understanding of certain uses of gesture. But much of this understanding

---

[11] Microsoft Research, Washington, USA

is descriptive, not prescriptive. Our understanding of what how people would actually benefit from the use of gesture with computer systems (more generally, any computer- embedded technology) is minimal. We need more thorough, systematic studies of the use of gesture (both ethnography and usability) in human-centred systems. We also must be aware of the social and ergonomic effects of new interaction techniques.

Technology

This is the easy one for most of us, delving into the details of HMMs or support vector machine learning or real-time tracking. I think the key is deciding specifically what problem to tackle. We may come up with elegant solutions, but if the problem is too far abstracted from reality it doesn't really contribute to progress. We need to clearly articulate the problem and the assumptions that we make before jumping into the technical details, and we need to be more thorough in our testing and evaluation. Additionally, we need to keep aware of new technologies that may solve the problem more efficiently (or less expensively) than our current favourite.

The Market

For long-term viability, the research community needs to address problems that will solve real needs, at least eventually, and to explain in some detail how we may get there. The days of unlimited funding for one-paragraph vague proposals are over. We will be more relevant if we understand where the computer industry is headed, and how we can add value to current and expected trends. Like it or not, the companies serving the mass market dominate the technology landscape, and Moore's Law sets a fast pace for them. We must acknowledge that our ability to impact the world is largely constrained by these market forces.

With these comments in mind, here are a few random thoughts:

- What are the driving/motivating applications for this field? Can we point to a few applications of gestural communications that are compelling to convince government and industry to fund this work, and that can serve as common foci in our community?
- Perhaps we should invest the effort to provide common data sets that are large enough and rich enough to enable fair comparisons.
- We are all aware that desktop computing is not the only computing environment to consider (and may well be the minority computing environment before long). When does gesture make sense, and not make sense, in other scenarios?
- Does "gesture" cover everything from static pose to deictic gesture to activity over a period of time – or do we mean something more specific?
- Accounting for co-articulation is vital for most gesture analysis or synthesis systems; we should expect researchers to take this into account.

- Sign language recognition or translation is a very interesting and worthwhile problem. However, it is unlikely to drive a significant market, at least relative to mass-market applications. We should at least be thinking about alternative applications of technology developed for sign language systems.
- Most user interface systems – and especially gesture-based system, from "Put That There" onward – are focused on *foreground* interaction. That is, the interaction is limited to explicit control (selecting, moving, deleting, etc.). We should be exploring more possibilities for *background* interaction (or system awareness), that can make systems more natural and intuitive.

Finally, some comments about tracking technologies and computer vision in particular. I think it is a mistake to consider vision-based tracking as a replacement for data gloves or body suits or other tracking technologies. Each technology is different and has its strengths and weaknesses. For example, even with a strong hand and body model, vision will not be able to determine the specific configurations of the fingers when they are behind the user's back or otherwise visually occluded, while that is no problem for a data glove. Similarly, the data glove cannot easily determine whether or not a hand gesture is visible to the intended audience. Also, the constraints of wearing a tethered device significantly change the user's interaction possibilities and overall experience. Vision is potentially a very general and pervasive technology – like most technologies, it is appropriate in some contexts, but not all.

As with most technologies, we in the field tend to overestimate the short-term potential and underestimate the long-term potential of gesture in human-machine communication. It will be fun someday to tell our grandchildren about the days when computers were these boxes that sat in your office and we used a keyboard and a mouse for all our interaction. (Note that I don't expect to have grandchildren for many years!).

References

1. Wachsmuth, I. and M. Frohlich (eds.): Gesture and Sign Language in Human Computer Interaction, International Gesture Workshop proceedings, Bielefeld, Germany, LNCS/LNAI 1371, 1998.
2. Schmandt, C. et al.: Put That There. SIGGRAPH Video Review 13, New York, ACM., 1984.
3. Harling, P.A. and A.D.N. Edwards (eds.): Progress in gestural interaction. Proceedings of Gesture Workshop '96, pp. 17–30. Springer, Berlin, New York 1997.
4. Web site for National Science Foundation Programme that covers research of interest to the Gesture Workshop community, CISE. 26.10.99 http://www.nsf.gov/home/cise/start.htm
5. Vogler, C. and D. Metaxas: ASL recognition based on a coupling between HMMs and 3D motion analysis. In Proceedings of the IEEE International Conference on Computer Vision, pp. 363–369, Mumbai, India, 1998.
6. Erenshteyn, R. and P. Laskov.: A multi- stage approach to fingerspelling and gesture recognition. Proceedings of the Workshop on the Integration of Gesture in Language and Speech, Wilmington, DE, USA, 1996.

7. Starner, T. and A. Pentland: Visual recognition of American Sign Language using Hidden Markov Models. In International Workshop on Automatic Face and Gesture Recognition, pp. 189–194, Zurich, Switzerland, 1995.
8. Liang, H.R. and M. Ouhyoung: A real- time continuous gesture recognition system for sign language. In Proceedings of the Third International Conference on Automatic Face and Gesture Recognition, pp. 558–565, Nara, Japan, 1998.
9. Vogler, C. and D. Metaxas.: Toward scalability in ASL recognition: Breaking down signs into phonemes. Gesture Workshop presentation, Gif- sur-Yvette, France, 1999.
10. Vogler,.C. and D. Metaxas: Parallel Hidden Markov Models for American Sign Language Recognition. To appear in the IEEE International Conference on Computer Vision, Kerkyra, Greece, 1999.
11. Vogler, C. and D. Metaxas: Adapting hidden Markov models for ASL recognition by using three-dimensional computer vision methods. In Proceedings of the IEEE International Conference on Systems, Man and Cybernetics, pages 156–161, Orlando, FL, 1997.
12. Sagawa, H. and M. Takeuchi: A Method for Analyzing Spatial Relationships Between Words in Sign Language Recognition. In this book, 1999.
13. Braffort, A: ARGo: An architecture for sign language recognition and interpretation. In P.A. Harling and A.D.N. Edwards (eds.), Progress in gestural interaction. Proceedings of Gesture Workshop '96, pp. 17–30. Springer, Berlin, New York 1997.

Author Index

Lecture Notes in Artificial Intelligence (LNAI)

Lecture Notes in Computer Science